Henri
Black migration

c.5

Black Migration:

MOVEMENT NORTH, 1900–1920

Could such a metamorphosis have taken place as suddenly as it has appeared to? The answer is no, not because the New Negro is not here, but because the Old Negro had long become more of a myth than a man. . . . So for generations in the mind of America, the Negro has been more of a formula than a human being—something to be argued about, condemned or defended, to be "kept down," or "in his place," or "helped up," to be worried with or worried over, harassed or patronized, a social bogey or a social burden. . . . When the racial leaders of twenty years ago spoke of developing race pride and stimulating race-consciousness, and of the desirability of race solidarity, they could not in any accurate degree have anticipated the abrupt feeling that has surged up and now pervades the awakened centers. . . . It is a social disservice to blunt the fact that the Negro of the Northern centers has reached a stage where tutelage, even of the most interested and well-intentioned sort, must give place to new relationships, where positive self-direction must be reckoned with in ever increasing measure. The American mind must reckon with a fundamentally changed Negro.

Alain Locke, The New Negro, 1925

Black Migration:

MOVEMENT NORTH

1900–1920

Florette Henri

ANCHOR PRESS/DOUBLEDAY

GARDEN CITY, NEW YORK

1975

For Raymond
Semper Fi

Library of Congress Cataloging in Publication Data

Henri, Florette.
   Black Migration: Movement North, 1900–1920.
   Bibliography: p. 395
   Includes index.
      1. United States—Race question. 2. Negroes—
Social conditions—To 1964. 3. Negroes—Employment.
4. Rural-urban migration—United States. I. Title.
E185.61.H489   301.45′19′6073
ISBN 0-385-04030-X
Library of Congress Catalog Card Number 74-9453

Contents

Preface   vii

CHAPTER 1
Threshold of a New Century   1

CHAPTER 2
The Great Migration   49

CHAPTER 3
City Within a City   81

CHAPTER 4
Life and Death in the Inner City   93

CHAPTER 5
Pushing Ahead in the Economy   132

CHAPTER 6
Paths to a Place in the Society   174

CHAPTER 7
Counterattack: Racist Thought   208

CHAPTER 8
Prejudice in Action   237

CHAPTER 9
In the Great War for Democracy   269

vi   *Contents*

CHAPTER 10
Home to White America   306

CHAPTER 11
Heading Home to Blackness   332

NOTES   344

BIBLIOGRAPHY   395

INDEX   409

Preface

This study attempts to chart the paths of change—demographic, geographic, economic, political, social, psychological, even semantic—along which the black people of America traveled between the beginning of the twentieth century and the end of World War I. In a time of change for all Americans, the changes for black Americans were particularly dramatic in every aspect of their lives. In 1900, black people were practically invisible on the American scene; by 1920 they were visible, audible presences everywhere in the national life. How and why did it happen?

The changes affected, directly or indirectly, a very large number of people. It is impossible to say exactly how many, because census counts of blacks have always been unreliable, and must have been particularly so at a time when the states had different definitions of Negro: in Oregon and Nebraska, for example, a person was legally a Negro if he had at least one grandparent of African ancestry; in Florida, Georgia, South Carolina, Indiana, and Missouri, if he had one African great-grandparent; and in Alabama, if he had one African great-great-great-grandparent. However inaccurately, the 1900 census reported roughly 8,834,-000 black people in the total United States population of 76,-094,000, or 11.5 per cent. By 1920 blacks had increased to 10,463,000 but had dropped proportionately to less than 10 per cent because the total population had grown to 106,466,000. At both the beginning and end of the period, most blacks lived in the South (7,923,000 in 1900; 8,912,200 in 1920). But what is significant is that the *rate* of increase was only about 12.5 per cent in the South, compared to northeastern states, where the black population nearly doubled, and north-central and western states, where it increased by 60 per cent.

Those were decades when black people moved not only out of the South but away from the farm. Urbanization had been in progress for many years before 1900, but at first the flow was from rural South to urban South, then from both rural and urban South to urban North. With the start of the Great War in Europe, industrial employment opportunities boomed, and blacks went North in sharply increasing numbers. By 1917–18 they were pouring into northern cities, especially those with heavy industries, so that Detroit's black population in 1920 was eight times as great as in 1910; Cleveland's was four times as great, and Chicago's was two and one-half times as great.

Many of them found jobs, and earned more money in a month than they had ever seen at one time before. Yet there were heartaches. Black migrants of the war period had heard from northern friends of a freer life and full manhood status once a man got out of the South. But as great numbers of blacks crowded into and overflowed the ghettos of northern cities, they found they had brought Jim Crow and the "Negro problem" right along with them. Now, the premigration blacks in the North were the same race as the southern migrants, yet they had no acute sense of being a "problem" until their southern brothers joined them. Suddenly there were too many Negroes, whites felt, too many in the neighborhood, at the plant, in the classroom. How many makes too many is a question yet to be answered; recent studies of integrated neighborhoods indicate a pressure point at about 10 to 15 per cent. Somewhere along the line, what had been an acceptable black population became too many blacks living too close to whites, and racial violence erupted. Still, in spite of troubles with white neighbors and white labor unions, black men and women continued to work their way into industry, business, and the professions in the North, and their children went to schools perhaps not good but far better than in the South.

Paralleling black advances, racist ideas multiplied and flourished in those twenty years at every level from the university president to the cop on the beat. Scientists busied themselves with curious studies of the races and stocks of mankind, adducing

Darwinian theory to support their conviction that blacks were low in the evolutionary line. Nordics (or Teutons or Anglo-Saxons) were hailed as the highest group, followed by Alpines and then by Mediterraneans in descending order of excellence, and finally people of color; the higher the Nordics were hoisted, the lower fell their counterweighting black and brown brothers. Politicians welcomed these theories as justifying the exploitation of the darker races in the imperialist rush for colonies. The general public, white, was titillated by easy-to-read racist books such as *The Passing of the Great Race,* a record-breaking best seller, and by that obscene masterpiece in the new medium of film, *The Birth of a Nation.* The United States Army could quote the opinion of one of its medics that the black man was "bestial by nature" and "superstitious, treacherous, mendacious, and unreliable" as reason enough to make him the workhorse of the service.

For most black people, the painful progress of the past twenty years ended with the end of the war. They skidded downward in the economy as soon as war production ended and white workers stepped out of uniform, and the Depression struck before the blacks had gained back any considerable ground. By the end of the 1920s, the black man was worse off in almost every material way in northern ghettos than he had been in 1900 in the South plowing a white man's fields. But if the content of life for a black man was not enriched, its style had undergone a vastly promising change, and he was a different kind of man. He had more respect for himself and less for whites. He had higher goals and the startling insight that whatever he was going to gain he would gain only by fighting for it. The younger generation, proudly calling themselves "New Negroes" or "black men" instead of the timid appellation "colored" of twenty years earlier, had learned that equality could not be negotiated; it must be won.

The facts of this twenty-year struggle make up the story that follows, a dynamic and significant narrative. But behind the facts lies a still more significant theme, a meaning, and the more one learns about these twenty years of black history the more that theme clamors for recognition: black Americans in the early decades of the century had far more of a hand in shaping their future than historians of the period tend to perceive, or at least to convey. These black men and women are too often viewed, sometimes even by themselves and by the most judicious white commentators, as passive reactors instead of active forces; as objects, not subjects, of events. But to this investigator it became very clear that they were not merely products, but often major causes of change. They were choosers, makers, and doers. Nobody drove the black man out of the South; he himself made the decision to leave familiar scenes and faces, to make a frightening journey to an unknown place with a strange, perhaps hostile, way of life. Nobody forced him to exchange rural southern poverty, where one was at least not likely to starve if one could put on a convincing act of subservience and devotion, for the far rougher, uglier, filthier, more menacing poverty of a northern ghetto. Nobody insisted that the black man of means and education take insults, abuse, and mistreatment to serve as an Army officer. No one made black parents work themselves sick to provide clothes so their children could go to school, and to escape, if they possibly could, from the vicious ghetto. Yet many blacks did these things, changing themselves, their world, their children's future.

To all those who raised questions and helped me find answers I am delighted here to express my thanks. Scholars with whom I communicated were uniformly generous in sharing their ideas and enthusiasm, and I want to acknowledge my gratitude to them all, especially Elsa E. Robinson, Edward M. Coffman, Herbert J. Seligmann, William F. Fleming, Rayford Logan, and the late Ulysses G. Lee. The staffs of the Morland Room at Howard University, of the Manuscript Division of the Library of Congress, of the Old Military Records section of the National Archives, were always eager to place their knowledge and skills at my service. For much of the World War I story I wish to thank Arthur E. Barbeau, my collaborator in an earlier book on that subject, who gave me unreserved permission to lean on that work for my chapter in this book concerning the black war experience. Among unexpected sources of help I must mention John McLeod, librarian of the Association of American Railroads, to whom I owe many of the vivid details of the northward migration. With affectionate gratitude I must particularly mention my own Harborfields Public Library, where the directors, reference librarians Melvon L. Ankeny and Elizabeth L. Iber, with Helen Field and all the staff, seemed actually to enjoy satisfying the heavy demands I made on their time and skills. My critic-in-residence was a poet, and there is no more discerning eye for the soft spots than a poet's, no tongue more merciless in pointing them out; now, for those chapter-by-chapter sessions I would so happily have skipped, but which made me dig a little deeper, think a little harder, and write a little more incisively, I gratefully salute my husband.

CHAPTER 1

Threshold of a New Century

> Desperate men easily seize upon some
> scapegoat to sacrifice to their unhap-
> piness; it is a kind of magic by which
> they feel for the moment that they
> have laid the misery that has been tor-
> menting them. In this they are ac-
> tively encouraged by their rulers and
> exploiters, who like to see them occu-
> pied with this violence, and fear that
> if it were denied them they might de-
> mand something more difficult.
>
> Ruth Benedict,
> *Race: Science and Politics*

The 1890s sounded several loud warnings of the collapse of black prospects in America. The three shrillest were Booker T. Washington's abnegation of black equality in his Atlanta Exposition speech of 1895; the U. S. Supreme Court's blessing on Jim Crow in its Plessy *v.* Ferguson decision of 1896; and the total eclipse by 1898 of the Populist movement with the resurgence of the solid Democratic South. If indeed American blacks had been, before the Populist era, "a host of dusky children untimely put out of school,"[1] as Woodrow Wilson put it, they were mature graduates by the end of it, because the Populist experience was a cram course in politics and economics for the isolated small farmer, black and white, of the South and Middle West.

The agrarian revolt out of which Populism emerged was basically a protest of farmers (not all of them poor) against falling produce prices that put them in debt, manipulation of land values and of the currency in favor of their creditors, and monopolistic practices that made it virtually impossible for farmers to break even after paying for the storage and transportation of their corn, wheat, and cotton. In the South, cotton prices declined steadily from $.30 per pound just after the Civil War to $.09 in 1886 and then to $.06 in 1893. In 1898, of 271 farmers in a Georgia district, 3 had gone bankrupt and sold out, 162 were in debt, and 53 cleared nothing; the other 53 came out ahead that year, but of those only 5—less than 2 per cent of the total—realized a profit of $100 or more. Things were not much better for the "Exodusters," black southern farmers who from 1879, after the end of Reconstruction, had trekked North and West, settling chiefly in Kansas and Nebraska, although life was freer and more secure in states that had no history of slavery. After record crops in 1882 and 1884, which encouraged farmers to buy more and more land, prices dropped sharply; then came almost a full decade of drought. Poor crops should have driven prices up, but unfortunately for the western farmers there was enough grain being produced east of the Mississippi to keep prices depressed. By 1890, 90 per cent of the farmland in Kansas, Nebraska, and the Dakota Territory was mortgaged at rates up to 15 per cent; chattel mortgages commanded up to 18 per cent. The Middle West land bubble had burst, and many dispirited farmers turned homeward, to the South or East, their wagons bearing such slogans as "Going home to the wife's folks" and "In God we trusted, in Kansas we busted."[2]

Oscar Micheaux, in a novel about a black settler in the prairie country, described the return East of broken, dispirited farmers during the drought years: "Fine horses that marched bravely to the land of promise, drawing a prairie schooner, were returning east with heads hanging low from long, stringy necks, while their alkalied hoofs beat a slow tattoo as they wearily dragged along, drawing, in many cases, a dilapidated wagon over which was stretched a tattered tarpaulin; while others drew rickety hacks or spring wagons, with dirty bedding and filthy looking utensils."

Of forty-seven houses passed along the way, only one was occupied.[3] Micheaux's hero, by unbelievable perseverance and resourcefulness, weathered the bad times.

Conditions did not improve, and the spirit of protest grew. J. Rogers Hollingsworth suggests as underlying causes of farmer suffering and revolt that the nation's economic growth rate was too low to accommodate a rapidly increasing farm population of producers for a much more slowly increasing urban population of consumers; and that to many of the western settlers, especially recent migrants and more particularly the older ones, this world of new neighbors, new ideas, and new values, of sudden obsolescence of traditional crafts and tools, was bewildering and created a need to reaffirm identities and values.[4] Black migrants to the frontier Middle West from a tradition-bound South must have been as bewildered by their new life, as sorely in need of fellowship and help and identity, as any peasant from Sweden or Poland.

They needed, in sum, to organize in a group with appropriate and stable values that they could understand. Such an organization was the Patrons of Husbandry, or Grange, in existence since 1867 and active in both the South and Middle West. At first mainly social and recreational in its programs, the Grange ventured into politics in the 1870s and achieved a reduction of freight rates. Also, there was the Greenback Labor party, founded in 1875, which attracted farmers with its demand for cheaper money and free silver coinage. The Granges in the North seem to have admitted blacks to membership and to have urged southern Granges to do the same, but there is no evidence of blacks in the regular organization or in separate chapters. The Greenbackers of Texas, however, declared at their first state convention in 1878: "The object of our republican government is to protect alike the rights of every individual in the union, irrespective of section, state, riches, poverty, race, color, or creed." There were that year 70 black groups among the 482 Greenback organizations in Texas. In 1880, although by then the federal troops of the Reconstruction no longer protected black voters, Texas Greenbackers said their party "denounces the attempted disfranchisement of citizens as a crime, whether committed by Republicans in Massachusetts and Rhode Island or Bourbon Democrats in Texas. . . ."[5]

When the Greenback party collapsed in 1884, the Farmers' Alliance took up the agrarian causes and, to an extent, the Greenbackers' liberal attitude on race. The main organization of the Alliance, active in southern and border states, was formed of many local farmers' co-operative and protective groups. Commonly called the Southern Alliance, its full name was the National Farmers' Alliance and Industrial Union. Its counterpart in the North and Middle West was the National Farmers' Alliance, or Northern Alliance. The Southern Alliance was white, but it sponsored the formation in 1886 in Houston, Texas (conformably to Texas Greenbackers' policy) the formation of a separate black group, the Colored Farmers' Alliance and Cooperative Union, called for short the Colored Alliance (CA). The Northern Alliance, most numerous in the Middle West, was a mixed black and white group.

By 1888 the CA was a national organization with educational, social, and economic programs through a network of co-operative exchanges; in 1890 two blacks sat as representatives of the CA on a standing committee of the Southern Alliance, the State Business Agents Association. Friendly relations were maintained between the white and black Alliances in the South, although they sometimes parted on important issues. When, for instance, Senator Lodge was pressing for the passage of the Force Bill to protect black voters, the CA enthusiastically supported the bill at its 1890 convention, but the Southern Alliance as vigorously opposed it.[6] When Lodge's bill died in committee, the victim of a Republican deal with southern Democrats in which the party of Emancipation bartered black rights for a high tariff, many black farmers quit the Republican party to join the Alliance's infant political offspring, the Populist party.[7] Again the following year, 1891, the CA and the Southern Alliance disagreed on a matter of importance. When the CA called for a strike by cotton pickers, Colonel Leonidas L. Polk, former Grange leader in North Carolina and then president of the National Farmers' Alliance, advised whites to break the strike, on the ground that it was designed to benefit blacks at the expense of whites. "Reforms should not be in the interest of one portion of our farmers at the expense of another," Polk said. The *Advocate* of Kansas was more tactful in its columns: "The Alliance third-party movement will also settle the race question of the South, and black and white will vote together for the common interest of all."[8] Color seems to have been only peripheral to the point of this matter, which was a strike of hired agricultural workers—the cotton pickers—against farmer owners; what the Grange was opposing, therefore, was a strike of labor against capital, a class conflict. Most blacks in agriculture were not owners but tenants, sharecroppers, or mere hands. The Alliance had no wish to be involved in labor troubles, although it included between one million and one and one-half million members in the CA.[9]

In spite of the strike controversy, at the Alliance convention that year an effort to segregate the black delegates was defeated, and the fourteen hundred present heard Terence V. Powderly urge justice and equal rights for blacks. The CA mentioned in its newspaper that its members were invited to Southern Alliance camp meetings, and urged them to go, saying, "It will do you good."[10]

With the approach of a presidential election in 1892, the Alliances formed a third party dedicated to the protection of farmers' interests, instead of simply backing sympathetic candidates of other parties, as they had been doing for some years. As usual with third parties, the Populist party attracted a variety of reformers, moderate to radical, along with some assorted monomaniacs and hate-mongers. Old Free Silverites and Green-backers found themselves in the company of socialists, suffragists, prohibitionists, and single-taxers; also nativists, Anglophobes, anti-Semites, and vegetarians. "I once was a tool of oppression," ran an 1890 Populist campaign song of obvious inspiration,

> "And as green as a sucker could be
> And monopolies banded together
> To beat a poor hayseed like me.

> The railroads and old party bosses
> Together did sweetly agree;
> And they thought there would be little trouble
> In working a hayseed like me.
>
> But now I've roused up a little
> And their greed and corruption I see,
> And the ticket we vote next November
> Will be made up of hayseeds like me."[11]

The black vote became the Populist party's dilemma. Over considerable apathy or opposition among white Populists, it could try to win the black vote; or it could try to eliminate the black vote altogether, lest the Bourbons by unscrupulous practices of trickery, force, and bribery should lead the blacks to the polls to vote for the old-line Democratic candidates.[12] In the early Populist elections the black vote was generally sought. A Louisiana call to a third-party conference in October 1891 made a clear appeal: "To the voters of the State of Louisiana irrespective of class, color, or past political affiliation. . . . Both of you, white and colored, know that the Republican party has degenerated into a machine controlled by the money kings. . . . And you Democrats, . . . can you disguise from yourselves that this much vaunted democracy has degenerated into a name to conjure by. . . . The specter of negro supremacy has been used to keep you in the toils of scheming machine politicians."[13]

This was pretty heady stuff, but the black Alliancemen were by then educated in the rhetoric of party politics. Their delegates took an active part in the convention of 1892 at St. Louis, where the Populist party—which was to save them from both Democrats and Republicans—was officially founded. With only one negative vote, William Warwick of the Virginia CA was elected the convention's assistant secretary; a Georgia delegate, white, who had moved to make the vote unanimous, said, "We can stand that down in Georgia."[14] At a convention get-together of the Blue and the Gray, "E. C. Cabel, a negro, was brought forward on the platform, and shook hands, laughing, with everybody sitting in front."[15]

Was the Alliance as liberal as its motto, "Equal rights for all and special privilege for none," or was it merely courting the black vote? The answer seems to be, both are true. Abramowitz, in his study of the movement, was convinced that the Alliance was looking for new paths in race relations; other scholars have noted that the Southern Alliance often took a firm antiblack stand to attract white members.[16] Whatever motivated the fair treatment usually accorded blacks, through the CA, black farmers had gained the experiences of joint action with whites for interests common to all, and of power through their own organized numbers; they had sat as delegates to state and national conventions; they had worked on committees with and without whites; they had learned to reserve their votes for those who pledged desired legislation; they had found they could differ openly with white men and be heard. Also, they had tried to guarantee to the next generation continued progress in the national community: "Thousands of their public free schools have been wonderfully improved in character of teaching," claimed an Alliance leader; they kept school open for longer sessions by the levy of a small tax on all CA members, and higher education was available at a number of academies and high schools.[17]

The political education of black Alliancemen was not yet over. In 1890, the Alliances had helped elect senators, congressmen, and state legislators who supported their demands. Black and white Alliancemen, voting the Populist line in the presidential election of 1892, swelled that party's vote for James B. Weaver to more than 1 million, winning 22 electoral votes to Harrison's 145 and Cleveland's 277. Intimidation of black Populist voters by southern Democrats had not split the Alliance vote, even though whiskey and dollar bills flowed freely and large planters herded their black croppers to the polls to vote for the Bourbon candidates. Again black voters were a potent force in local elections; and in 1894 the Populists increased their vote by 42 per cent, mainly in the South.[18]

But by 1896 it was clear that the Populist party was finished, not in spite of but because of its rapid rise. The Lodge Force Bill fight had brought out racism, regionalism, and suspicion of the Negro among many white Populists, and general hostility was exacerbated by resentment toward blacks, some of whom, herded to the polls by the Democrats, had cut into the Populist vote.[19] The Democrats played on race hatred and fear of black domination, a fear to which white Populists in the South were no more immune than other white Southerners. White men hastened to disclaim interest in black advancement. By 1896 a southern white man's place in his community and among his friends was threatened if he voted the Populist ticket, which according to Democratic propaganda was a "nigger" ticket.[20] Populist leaders like Tom Watson began to realize that white supremacy was the sure-fire political issue in the South, and that any party that allied itself with blacks on a basis of equality could not win. Watson wrote: "No matter what direction Progress would like to take in the South she is held back by the never failing cry of 'Nigger!'"[21] Any interest in the cause of blacks was such a political embarrassment that when the Republicans formed a fusion party with the Populists in an effort to defeat the resurgent Bourbon Democrats, Republicans too had to ignore Negro rights. So the black farmer, who at the beginning had contributed substantially to the success of the Populist party, was also, ironically, a cause of its failure and end.

But black farmers were moving ahead, and, because of their advance, the campaign of 1898 was openly a white supremacy campaign. In North Carolina, white Populists denied the charge of endorsing black equality, declaring that wherever the white race lives it rules, and competing with the Democrats to show who was most anti-Negro by spreading scare stories of rape and miscegenation; a group calling themselves Red Shirts ambushed and beat or shot blacks at political rallies. The Republicans were playing the same game in North Carolina in 1898, bidding for the white supremacy vote through propaganda such as its *People's Party Handbook*, a sensational fusion pamphlet. While pretending a lofty attitude about the rights of blacks, the handbook claimed Democrats were responsible for the election and appointment of black officials. Each section of the handbook points to some Democratic scandal, negligence, or tie-in with big interests, and concludes thus: "While all this is going on the Democratic machine is squalling 'nigger,' with the purpose of diverting the attention of the people from it."[22]

These last efforts of the Republican-Populist fusionists said too much and too little—too much to keep the loyalty of blacks, too little to attract the loyalty of white supremacists. What white people in the South wanted were plain statements of white supremacy to rally 'round, thus removing any lingering Populist taint of brotherhood with blacks. White leaders fell into the popular posture. Tom Watson of Georgia as a courageous and equalitarian Populist had won, with the help of the black vote, first a place in the state legislature and then, in 1890, a seat in Congress. As the Populist leader of Georgia, he had chosen several black organizers and speakers, and had been loyal to them. He told the small farmers, black and white, that the big-money interests deceived and blinded them into hating one another, and that "race antagonism perpetuates a monetary system which beggars both."[23] His Populist state platform in 1896 denounced lynching and the Ku Klux Klan and called for an end of the convict lease system, which was a curse to blacks. But by then the tide of white supremacy was running strong, and no politician could afford to ignore it. With the fusion attempt it became clear to many whites that the white vote might be split, leaving the blacks with the balance of political power. Neither party dared court the Negro vote for fear of being branded "nigger"; therefore the only course was to make it impossible for the black man to vote, and pressure began to build to disfranchise him altogether. Watson turned his steps along that path. By 1904, when he ran for President on the Populist ticket, he was supporting most discriminatory legislation on grounds that the small southern white farmer, Watson's particular interest, could be served only by sacrificing the black man.[24]

South Carolina had its Populist-turned-racist in "Pitchfork" Ben Tillman, although Tillman had never been so outspoken for equal rights as Watson, and his conversion came earlier. By 1890, when Tillman was elected governor on a Populist ticket, his inaugural speech insisted on absolute white supremacy; he also called for an end to lynch law, saying it was "simply infamous" considering that all juries and the whole machinery of the law were in white hands—a fine piece of political cynicism, calculated to reassure both black and white voters. Tillman grew more racist with the years, easily swimming with the flood tide of white supremacy. Governor William C. Oates of Alabama, although a conservative Democrat, nevertheless went along with black suppression to insure the election of Democratic candidates: "I told them [the whites] to go to it, boys, count them [the Negroes] out. We had to do it. Unfortunately, I say it was a necessity. We could not help ourselves."[25] A Georgia Democrat echoed Oates in 1894: "We had to do it. Those damn Populists would have ruined the country."[26] The old southern conservatives may have had more regrets about depriving blacks of their constitutional rights, but most of them did as good a job of it as the newly arrived rough, plain, "Pitchfork" Ben Tillman.

Feeling morally justified by the necessity of beating the "damn Populists," Democrats bought or forced black votes, or counted them whether the blacks voted or not. In Augusta, Georgia, the home district of Tom Watson, vote tampering was so successful that the final recorded vote in 1892 totaled twice the number of legal voters; and Watson complained that his Democratic opponents brought in wagonloads of blacks from South Carolina to vote.[27]

Race hate flamed throughout the South at the end of the brief Populist threat. Tom Watson cried vainly: "You are made to hate each other because upon that hatred is rested the keystone of the arch of financial despotism which enslaves you both . . . perpetuates a monetary system which beggars you both."[28] That was a cerebral and philosophical appeal, harder to grasp and much less gratifying to the exasperated white farmers Watson was addressing than the race hate that was being given such a hard sell. Frustrated white men were easily swayed to barter their own and their children's best interests, and to weaken the moral fiber of their country, for the mindless pleasure of hating the black man; even those who were not swayed had to go along or lose face in their community. So by 1900 the black man, especially the black Southerner, was so bloodily trodden to earth that it did not look as if he could ever again raise his head.

Yet Populism had put into the minds of blacks certain higher expectations of life, and these could not be beaten out by the boots of any Secret Nine or Red Shirts or other terrorist groups. Incorporated into the blacks' past by 1900 were not only the heady power given to them and protected for them by Reconstruction governments but the more sober experience of Populism. In the Populist movement black people got a sense of being equal participants in the political process, rather than mere recipients of federal favors; of gaining their ends by the power of the vote. Numbers of blacks had worked and socialized with white people of similar interests on a level of relative equality if not actual integration; had had the experiences of organizing and campaigning, of committee work, party politics, national conventions; of listening to and talking and reading about advanced economic ideas such as co-operatives and unions. They could not have come out of the movement unchanged in their hopes and goals.

So although the future blacks faced in 1900 was if anything less promising than at any time since abolition, their taste of a fuller citizenship under Populism must have altered their attitude toward the renewed political, economic, and social injustices that followed. It seems probable, therefore, that a major cause of discriminatory *laws*, which came in such quick succession after the collapse of Populism, was the refusal of black people to be governed again by discriminatory *customs*, customs that had been discarded in the striving years of the Alliances and Populism. With the failure of the reform movement, laws, ordinances, and court decisions strove to put a seal of legality on racial discrimination, unnecessary earlier because the black people before Populism had expected and accepted, for the most part, different treatment than whites. The Plessy *v.* Ferguson decision segregating seating on trains would in all likelihood never have occurred except that by 1896 enough blacks had indicated that they meant to sit where they liked instead of congregating in one car out of the white man's way. Disfranchisement need not have required modification of state constitutions except that by the 1890s enough blacks were daring to use their vote, and were using it to their best advantage. In sum, Jim Crow legislation appears not to have been an impulsive, repressive vengeance by the white

South for the mortification of Reconstruction control so much as a gradual effort by the South to block loopholes through which a substantial number of black people had been continually trying, for the thirty years since Emancipation, to exercise their constitutional rights. Black people suffered greatly by Jim Crow laws, but those laws measured their efforts and progress. And at least laws are matters of record and can be challenged and changed, whereas custom, which can be as effective as law, is much more elusive and resistant to change.

By 1900, both law and custom were attacking black people with incredible ferocity. Certainly there can be little doubt that the unscrupulousness, violence, and terrorism of political campaigns after 1896 undermined national morality to such an extent that otherwise decent white people could look unmoved upon the abysmal condition of black people in the South as the new century began.

Neither discriminatory law nor discriminatory custom was a phenomenon, of course, in 1900. The vanquished southern leaders after the Civil War had at once begun to build a new society on the model of the old slave society, and consequently the Black Codes had come into being, restricting the life of black people by state laws which defined and regulated such matters as vagrancy, work contracts, business pursuits, and roles in court proceedings. When the Fourteenth and Fifteenth amendments and the Force bills that implemented them invalidated those state codes, repression was maintained through extralegal means, including the terrorist tactics of the Ku Klux Klan; thus much of what had been law under slavery and immediately after the war passed into the region of unwritten law, or custom. Many blacks who would not accommodate tried migrating to the North and West; but there, as Woodward and other historians have observed, although the distinctions made between black and white were less sharp than in the South, there was also less intimacy and liking between the races; and in the absence of custom based on a mutual understanding of master-slave positions, there was more formal and legal Jim Crow to keep the races separate.

Perhaps another way of saying this is that the blacks who were liked in the South were those who played the complaisant darkies and mammies demanded by slavery and such southern folkways as the Klan, and who remained menials or farmers or practiced one of a few sanctioned "Negro" businesses, usually of a service nature; whereas north and west of the old slave states, blacks were generally more independent and often dared to compete economically and politically with whites, behavior that would make them much less likable and that would call for legal regulation. However, although intimacy, liking, and mutual understanding might make life smoother and less tense, they did not fill the belly except with broken meats toted from the southern white man's table; so many blacks chose to be less liked and less understood in exchange for a greater variety of ways to earn a living and to get ahead.[29]

The Supreme Court of the United States, in its Plessy *v*. Ferguson decision of 1896, opened the door to systematic and legal discrimination against blacks at a point where they were demonstrating through Populism that custom was not enough to keep them in their place, even in the South, and that they had the power to rock the white man's world.

The case of Plessy *v*. Ferguson was a test of the constitutionality of a Louisiana law of 1890, which had aroused controversy when it was passed, segregating railroads within that state (interstate travel came under federal law and could not be segregated). In 1892, a very light-skinned Negro named Homer Adolph Plessy rode the train from one point in Louisiana to another in a coach designated as white. The conductor insisted that Plessy move to a Jim Crow car, although he was almost indistinguishable from the white passengers. Plessy refused and was arrested. Eventually the case came before the Supreme Court. The plaintiff argued that "the enforced separation of the two races stamps the colored race with a badge of inferiority," but the Court held that "if this be so, it is not by reason of anything found in the act, but solely because the colored race chooses to put that construction upon it."[30] The Court reached the historic decision that "legislation is powerless to eradicate racial instincts or to abolish distinctions based upon physical differences"[31]—in short, it upheld as constitutional laws separating the races on railroads, and by extension anywhere else desired, as long as "separate but equal" facilities were provided for both races. Justice John Marshall Harlan, described by a biographer as a "Southern gentleman and a slaveholder, and at heart a conservative,"[32] dissented from the majority decision, declaring the Louisiana law clearly "inconsistent with the personal liberty of citizens . . . and hostile to both the spirit and letter of the Constitution of the United States."[33] As to the broad effect of such laws, Harlan asked: "What can more certainly arouse race hate . . . than state enactments which in fact proceed on the ground that colored citizens are so inferior and degraded that they cannot be allowed to sit in public coaches occupied by white citizens? That, as all will admit, is the real meaning of such legislation as was enacted in Louisiana. . . . The thin disguise of 'equal' accommodations for passengers in railroad coaches will not mislead anyone, or atone for the wrong this day done." Harlan predicted that the doctrine of "separate but equal" would "stimulate aggressions, more or less brutal and irritating, upon the admitted rights of colored citizens."[34]

The decision was, as Justice Harlan prophesied, a signal for "racial instincts" to do whatever was felt necessary to close all gates, by force of law, against the black people who at the very same time were being obnoxious and dangerous as Populists. The door that had opened a crack in Alliance times in the South was slammed shut, locked, and double-barred against the black man who had committed the crime of advancing himself, a thing intolerable to the white ruling class, and destructive of the liking and understanding that had formerly existed. In past times, when the door of opportunity could safely be left ajar because of the assumption that few blacks were likely to go where they weren't wanted, Jim Crow restrictions except as a local and occasional phenomenon had been unnecessary. By and after 1896, however, when blacks dared take the matter of their rights in the South all the way up to the highest court in the land, it clearly appeared that Jim Crow *was* necessary. That was probably the chief reason for what Woodward calls the South's "capitulation of racism"

—or, at least, to institutionalized racism implemented by Jim Crow legislation.[35]

That there were exceptions to the late arrival of Jim Crow cannot be denied, but what they show, Woodward suggests, is that the South was from the end of the Reconstruction until about 1900 in a period of experimentation and transition to total segregation, and that the pattern had not yet jelled in the earlier years. In Georgia, for example, the first Jim Crow law establishing separate railroad facilities for blacks was passed in 1891; soon after, Georgia towns and cities began to adopt Jim Crow ordinances regulating streetcar travel, but the big city of Savannah did not Jim Crow streetcars until 1906. There was no genetic date, in short, on which the command rang through the South, "Let there be darkness," and darkness instantly descended.

Perhaps Jim Crow might have been better synchronized except for one element sometimes overlooked, which is that, until after the Bourbons recaptured the South at the end of the 1890s, blacks had frequently defied discriminatory legislation. Meier and Rudwick point out that streetcar segregation was attempted in Savannah several times before 1906, but failed because of black action. In 1870, 1899, and 1906 blacks boycotted streetcar lines that established Jim Crow seating, in the earlier instances forcing the companies to capitulate. In the 1906 boycott one of Savannah's black leaders is quoted as pleading: "Let us walk! walk! and save our nickels. . . . Do not trample on your pride by being 'jim crowed.' Walk!" Nor was Savannah the only city in which blacks delayed streetcar Jim Crow. For several years after 1900, respectable black businessmen led boycotts lasting from a few weeks to a few years in more than twenty-five southern cities, although in the end Jim Crow won out.[36] In connection with Woodward's likely thesis that there was an era of experiment before Jim Crow became rigid and consistent, it is important to remember that experiments need be repeated only if they fail at first, and that the most probable reason they failed was black resistance. The early streetcar boycotts illustrate the repeated effort of black people to shape their fate.

But Jim Crow was eventually the victor, from the border state of Maryland in which by 1900 segregation was the rule in public transportation, housing, and places of public accommodation, to states farther South, where every human activity was segregated.[37] Ray Stannard Baker, an excellent observer and reporter, said of Atlanta, Georgia, in 1906: "After I had begun to trace the colour line I found evidences of it everywhere—literally in every department of life."[38] Streetcar segregation, Baker commented, was especially irritating. The cars bore signs: "White people will seat from front of car toward back and colored people from rear toward front," thus drawing a color line somewhere in the middle, but, Baker remarked, "neither race knows just where it is."[39] Friction and bitterness, he noted, resulted from this uncertainty. Georgia by state law had segregated streetcars in 1891, and by 1907 such state laws had been adopted in North Carolina, Virginia, Louisiana, Arkansas, South Carolina, Tennessee, Mississippi, Maryland, Florida, and Oklahoma. In most southern cities, streetcars were segregated by the Atlanta system, with whites in front and blacks in back of the same car, but in Montgomery, Alabama, possibly to alleviate the friction created by the Atlanta system, separate cars for whites and blacks were mandatory after 1906. Motormen and conductors had police powers for enforcing Jim Crow rules.[40]

Wherever Jim Crow settled, it must have occasioned considerable annoyance, delay, and expense to whites as well as blacks, but evidently the white South counted the gains worth the losses, and in a short time virtually all public facilities were segregated. Trains were segregated throughout the South, Virginia being the last to pass such laws; railroad waiting rooms were segregated in almost all southern states before 1910. Coastal states segregated steamboats. Jails were generally segregated; Arkansas, for example, in 1903 separated black and white prisoners in state and county jails, stockades, workhouses, convict camps, and other correctional institutions. In Mobile there was a curfew for Negroes; in Oklahoma separate phone booths were the rule; in North Carolina there had to be separate copies of schoolbooks for black and white pupils, and the books had to be stored separately; South Carolina had separate schools for blacks and whites, and still a third class of schools for mulattoes. Factory workrooms, public parks, hospitals, mental institutions, and

homes for the aged, orphaned, and handicapped—all were segregated. There was soon nothing a black and white could le-
gitimately do together in the South, where signs saying "Whites
Only" or "Colored" guarded entrances and exits, elevators, theaters, libraries, boarding houses, toilets, drinking fountains, ticket
windows, and pay windows. In North Carolina and Virginia the
law prevented blacks and whites from going to lodge meetings
together, because of a ban on fraternal organizations that permitted blacks and whites to address each other as brother. Housing segregation was prohibited by Supreme Court decisions, but
it was accomplished in many devious ways in most southern
cities; in Richmond, for example, city blocks were designated
as black or white according to the color of the majority of residents, and no one was permitted to live on a block where there
were residents "whom said person is forbidden to marry." Blacks
and whites could not pray together, because churches were definitely white or black; and when New Orleans segregated black
and white brothels in separate districts, they could not even sin
together (legally) in that city famous for sin. As for more permanent sexual arrangements, concubinage between the races became a felony in Arkansas in 1911, and intermarriage was
prohibited by state law throughout the South.[41]

What must have been particularly galling to black people was
that, whereas most laws affect only those who commit misdemeanors or crimes, Jim Crow surrounded with restrictions and
penalties anyone who was black—to whatever degree the state
declared constituted blackness—no matter how respectable, law-
abiding, or valuable a citizen one might be. Even in the relatively
free District of Columbia, well-known citizens such as Frederick
Douglass, former Senator Blanche K. Bruce, and Mary Church
Terrell found it very difficult to shop in stylish and convenient
stores.[42] And in the border state of Maryland, although voting
rights of blacks were protected, trains and boats were Jim
Crowed, and the first residential segregation law in any city was
that passed in Baltimore in 1911.[43]

It must be remembered that in addition to Jim Crow legal restrictions in public life, there remained the "understandings," or
private restrictive customs, in their hundreds and thousands and

effectively as binding as laws. A black entered a white home by
the back door; removed his hat to a white man on the street, and
stood on the outer side of the pavement to let him pass; always
addressed a white person by some title of respect, such as Mrs.,
Mr., or the more flattering Captain or Colonel; might not engage
in sports or games with whites (except in childhood), might not
eat or drink at table with them in their homes, and so endlessly
on and on.[44]

Between law and custom, as the black novelist Charles Chesnutt said in 1903, "the rights of the Negroes are at a lower ebb
than at any time during the thirty-five years of their freedom,
and the race prejudice more intense and uncompromising."[45]

The purpose of the franchise being to give every voter the
power to use his vote toward the furtherance of his interests, it
was essential to deprive blacks of that recourse by taking away
their right to vote. In the 1890s, black voting power was being
demonstrated in the Populist movement, and the Democrats on
their return to rule made swift and potent moves to prevent a
recurrence of that threat.

Not surprisingly, the thrust for disfranchisement came first and
most vigorously from localities where blacks outnumbered
whites, as in a number of counties in Mississippi and Alabama;
and in those counties with the largest black majorities, whites
turned out in greatest numbers to push through the new state
constitutions that disfranchised blacks. In the end, however, there
was no polling place anywhere in the South, no matter how few
blacks lived in the area, where a Negro could safely and legally
cast his ballot. White supremacy, which demanded an end to
black voting, was such a popular issue that the political careers
of a number of Democrats—James K. Vardaman, Coleman Blease,
Hoke Smith, and others—were based on open, sometimes obscene, embrace of black disfranchisement. Nor was the Republican party eager to be branded as the "nigger party" by opposing
disfranchisement. In some places it called itself "lily white," and
before 1900 white Republicans were making mighty efforts to
exclude blacks from the polls. In most of the South what Re-

publicans did was of so little effect as to be negligible; to get any votes at all, the party had to espouse the Democratic platform. Only in Maryland, which had a viable two-party system, and where the votes of blacks were important to the Republican party, a series of disfranchisement efforts from 1900 to 1912 all failed. But Maryland did not have the bitter heritage of defeat and Reconstruction, and was therefore not really southern; in the former Confederate states, the issue was not whether to disfranchise blacks, but how to accomplish it without disfranchising poor whites as well, as a poll tax might do.[46]

Although there was no way of achieving this honestly, southern politicians insisted, seriously or with tongue in cheek, that there was nothing fraudulent in disfranchising blacks only. Ben Tillman said, "There is no particle of fraud or illegality in it. It is just simply showing partiality, perhaps, or discriminating. Ah, you grin."[47] Carter Glass, also of South Carolina, who in the Wilson administration would be one of the outstanding southern Progressives in the Senate, made probably the frankest and fullest statement about the means and the ends of disfranchisement: "By fraud, no; by discrimination, yes. . . . Why, that is precisely what we propose . . . to discriminate to the very extremity of permissible action under the limitations of the Federal Constitution, with a view to the elimination of every Negro voter who can be gotten rid of, legally, without materially impairing the numerical strength of the white electorate."[48] A Mississippian defended the Mississippi Plan for disfranchisement, which served as a model throughout the South, in this way: "Every provision in the Mississippi Constitution applies equally, and without any discrimination whatever, to both the white and the negro races. Any assumption, therefore, that the purpose of the framers of the Constitution was ulterior, and dishonest, is gratuitous and cannot be sustained."[49]

Beginning with Mississippi in 1890, all southern states disfranchised blacks by one or another legal device. Mississippi, South Carolina (1895), Louisiana (1898), Alabama (1901), Virginia (1901), Georgia (1908), and Oklahoma (1910) accomplished disfranchisement through new state constitutions; North Carolina achieved the result by amendments to its constitution in

1900 and 1905. The constitutional changes also embodied Jim Crow regulations in such facilities as streetcars, jails, and schools. The rest of the southern states disfranchised by statute rather than by constitutional changes.[50]

The easiest and most obvious method of disfranchisement, one with an ancient tradition to support it, was the poll tax. Most states adopted it. It was not, however, wholly satisfactory because a money requirement for the privilege of voting—$1.50, for example, in Alabama—militated against all the poor of both races; it was, however, common practice for politicians to ignore or pay the poll taxes of needy whites. Politicians in a tight race might be tempted to pay the poll taxes of blacks, too, in exchange for their votes, and to prevent this, most states required payment of the tax many months in advance of an election, before candidates had announced. This device proved so effective that Florida, Tennessee, Arkansas, and Texas depended entirely on the poll tax to keep blacks from voting.[51]

In states with larger black populations, a "grandfather clause" was an additional and more watertight method of stopping the black vote, although more vulnerable than the poll tax to challenge as unconstitutional. The usual form of the clause followed the model set in the Louisiana Constitution of 1897, which specified that a person might register and vote if his father or grandfather had been eligible to vote on January 1, 1867, or if he or an ancestor had served in either the Confederate or the United States Army.[52] That effectively eliminated practically all blacks in the South.

Such loopholes as were left by the grandfather clause and the poll tax were almost entirely closed by the most generally adopted method of all, the literacy or "understanding" requirement. This test ranged from writing one's name and the year, month, and day of one's birth, to reciting from memory or interpreting portions of the federal or state constitution, or answering questions about law and government. The virtue of the understanding requirement was that it was the most susceptible to fraud in its administration and the hardest to prove fraudulently administered. The Mississippi Plan, which established the understanding test as well as the poll tax, proved so effective that in the first election after the new 1890 constitution went into effect, the electorate of Mississippi was reduced from over 250,000 to less than 77,000. In New Orleans the black electorate was reduced from 14,000 in 1896 to 408 in 1908. In Louisiana as a whole, there were 130,344 registered black voters in the 1896 national election (the last election before disfranchisement), and more black than white voters in 26 parishes; in the 1900 election there were only 5,320 registered blacks, and in no parish were they a majority of the electorate. That is a drop of 96 per cent among black voters after only two years of the new constitution of 1898. White voters in Louisiana in the same period of time fell off from 164,008 to 125,437, or about 24 per cent. In Alabama, it is estimated that in 1900 only 3,000 of the 181,471 black males of voting age were registered, less than 2 per cent.[53] Nor was it only in the Deep South that disfranchisement measures were successful. Between the understanding test and the tax requirement, disfranchisement was very effective in Virginia. Of the 147,000 black men of voting age on the books prior to 1902, only 21,000 (14 per cent) remained registered by 1905.[54]

Not only was the law corrupted by unconstitutional efforts to eliminate the black voter, and the administration of that law corrupted in order to keep the black out and let the white voter in, but corrupt law and corrupt administration were both thwarted by corrupt politicians throughout the South. Even in Mississippi, it is probable that disfranchisement was not consistently and rigidly administered in regard to blacks who were going to vote "right." Kirwan says that in 1899, nine years after disfranchisement, blacks helped swing a bitterly contested gubernatorial election, and he draws the conclusion that when the black vote was needed it could be produced, even if the political parties had to pay the poll taxes—not too different a situation, he says, from the predisfranchisement role of black voters in Mississippi, where they had always been herded to the polls when wanted.[55]

Because in most states only regular voters were called for jury duty, disfranchisement deprived blacks of this right also. Even in counties with a black majority, in such states as Alabama, Florida, Georgia, Louisiana, and Mississippi, no blacks whatever served on juries after disfranchisement. An interesting side effect of disfranchisement pointed out by Ray Stannard Baker was that other parts of the country were victimized by southern disfranchisement of blacks, because although blacks were not constituents, they were counted in the allotment of congressmen. In 1906, this made for the outstanding inequity that the four states of Alabama, Arkansas, Georgia, and Mississippi, which together cast only 413,516 votes, were allotted 35 congressmen because the count for representation included disfranchised blacks, whereas Massachusetts, which alone cast 445,098 votes, was allotted only fourteen congressmen. In 1920, it was calculated by Herbert J. Seligmann that a reapportionment of congressional representatives on the basis not of population but of actual votes cast would have cost southern and border states 64 representatives: Alabama would have lost 7; Arkansas, 3; Florida, 2; Georgia, 9; Kentucky, 1; Louisiana, 6; Maryland, 1; Mississippi, 6; North Carolina, 3; South Carolina, 6; Oklahoma, 2; Tennessee, 3; Texas, 9; and Virginia, 6.[56]

To succeed in disfranchising the black man, southern politicians did not hesitate to whip up race hate. Hoke Smith, editor of the Atlanta *Journal* when he was running for governor of Georgia in 1906, played up stories of Negro atrocities in his paper so successfully that his victory in the election was followed by four days of mob rule and lynching.[57] Smith ran on a strictly white-supremacy platform, promising: "Legislation can be passed which will . . . not interfere with the right of any white man to vote, and get rid of 95 per cent of the Negro voters."[58] Even the moderates, who favored giving back the vote to a few high-level blacks like Booker T. Washington, agreed with Thomas Nelson Page that general black disfranchisement was "a measure of high necessity."[59] But radicals like Vardaman said, "I am just as much opposed to Booker Washington as a voter, with all his Anglo-Saxon reinforcements, as I am to the cocoanut-headed, chocolate-colored, typical little coon, Andy Dotson, who blacks my shoes every morning. Neither is fit to perform the supreme function of citizenship."[60] It was frequently alleged that disfranchisement would benefit blacks; Congressman Thomas Spight of Mississippi said that "the negroes of Mississippi have understood that they were not to be allowed to participate in State or county government, and as a result we have had but little trouble with them, and they have been better satisfied and more prosperous than at any time since their emancipation."[61] The loftiest note was struck by Representative William C. Langford of Georgia: "White supremacy is not oppressive tyrannical supremacy, but is compassionate, God-like supremacy exercised for the good of our nation, the happiness of the human race, and the civilization of the world."[62] And bluntest of all was Governor Vardaman of Mississippi, who declared in 1907: "If it is necessary every Negro in the state will be lynched; it will be done to maintain white supremacy. . . . The XV Amendment ought to be wiped out. We all agree on that. Then why don't we do it?"[63] The Atlanta *Constitution*, referring to a legislator who opposed disfranchisement as contrary to the Fifteenth Amendment, said, "Why let a small obstacle like an oath to support the Federal Constitution stand in the way? Shall 'conscience make cowards' of the legislature? Surely the public conscience is entitled to some consideration."[64]

The false logic, overblown rhetoric, homespun coarseness, immorality, deception, and self-delusion expended in the cause of disfranchisement do not conceal the one big ugly truth behind it all: the white South was terrified lest blacks use the vote to better their condition and secure their rights as citizens.[65] So disfranchisement was everywhere jubilantly hailed in the white South. As the Richmond *Times* rejoiced when Virginia's new law went into effect: "At the hour of noon today (July 10, 1902) the dark cloud will be lifted, and peace and sunshine will come to regenerated Anglo-Saxon people as a result of the organic law made with its own hands."[66] It was the next best thing to winning the War.

Against the steamroller of the solid white South there was little blacks could do at that time. Here and there an isolated gesture of protest was made, as when in 1899 the black people of Boston appealed in an open letter to President McKinley for protection of black rights. In Maryland blacks formed the Negro Suffrage

League, which worked with other organizations in the early 1900s to oppose disfranchisement. In southern states, educated and well-to-do blacks tended, it seems from various statements, to support the principle of literacy tests provided they were fairly administered. But among the great masses of blacks there seems to have prevailed a feeling of frustration and lethargy about disfranchisement, something the law had done to them and that they were powerless to change.[67] W. E. B. DuBois, emerging as a black leader, did not oppose denying the vote to incompetents, but he knew and said that the real purpose of the new laws was "the elimination of the black man from politics."[68]

But the South so often and so plaintively yearned for the "old-time" black man that one is led to suspect there was more black opposition to Jim Crow and disfranchisement than has been recorded. If competition between blacks and whites were eliminated, Hoke Smith said, and blacks could content themselves with a position of inferiority, they would be treated with greater kindness.[69] Smith meant the kind of old darky whom the black novelist Gustav Mertins portrayed in his 1905 novel The Storm Signal—old Uncle Ephraham, the faithful, cheerful, and loyal servitor. Vardaman meant that kind of Negro when, after calling black men the vilest names, he said he did not hate them but they ought simply to give up the vote and remain servile.[70] John Sharp Williams of Mississippi had this sort of Negro in mind when he declared "the very best friend the darkey has ever had in this world or ever will have is the Southern gentleman."[71] Professor George T. Winston of North Carolina, another old-time conservative, also deplored the passing of the friendliness that had existed between the races when "Southern whites were familiar with and very tolerant of the Negro's weaknesses and petty vices. They looked upon him with sympathy and sorrow, with friendship and affection, rather than with anger, resentment, and hostility."[72] The villains were the Northerners (like Julius Rosenwald) who sent money South to set up Negro schools that would educate blacks to demand equality.[73] Booker T. Washington, eager to educate blacks without upsetting whites, said, "We are trying to instil into the Negro mind that if education does not make the Negro humble, simple, and of service to the community, then it will not be encouraged."[74]

Generalization about a class basis for hostility toward blacks is further challenged by the fact that the conservatives of pre-1890 were in many cases the politicians of 1900 and after, men like Senator John T. Morgan of Alabama, Hoke Smith, John Sharp Williams, and Furnifold Simmons of North Carolina; and these men did not hesitate, whatever their own feeling may have been, to whip up the hostility of the lower-class whites. Many of these politicians were Progressives, and fought for measures that would benefit the poor man—but not the poor black man. If the black had to be ground to dust to better the condition of the white South, then that was what had to be done, and wealthy, prominent, old-line conservatives rarely boggled at it. Indeed, Newby and other students of southern racism claim that the upper classes were at least as antiblack as any peckerwood or sandhiller, but they were probably more restrained in expressing their feelings; and also, because they were less often in contact with Negroes except as servants, they had fewer occasions to state their positions and sentiments.[75]

To cut down the black man required sharpening the blade of race hatred, and this presented the South with another dilemma. As Baker commented in 1906, "One of the most significant things I saw in the South—and I saw it everywhere—was the way in which white people were torn between their feelings of race prejudice and their downright economic needs."[76] Benjamin Brawley calls it the great fallacy underpinning the prosperity of the industrializing New South that "the labor of the Negro existed only for the good of the white man."[77] In 1900, although there must have been enough demonstrated black discontent to explain white yearning for the old contented darky, the southern Negro by and large subscribed to the fallacy, and in any case had little choice of doing anything except labor for the good of the white Southerner. This did not mean, however, that when an alternative presented itself some years later the black man would choose to continue his role in the southern economy and society, a role in which he had no more rights nor dignity than the mule that drew his plow.

According to the 1900 census figures there were in the South more than 2,620,000 farmers (the majority of the population), of whom 741,000 were black and 1,879,000 were white. Among white farmers, there were better than two whole or part owners for every tenant farmer; among blacks, there were three tenants (552,401) for every whole or part owner (186,676). The census did not enumerate the third agricultural class, sharecroppers, until 1920, at which time there were sixteen white owners for each white cropper, but only three black owners for each black cropper. The number of black croppers in 1900 can be roughly estimated on a basis of figures supplied in that census, which show that 82 per cent of the 8,000,000 southern blacks—about 6,560,000 persons—lived on farms or in small rural towns. Allowing for an average black farm family of six, this would mean that there were 1,100,000 black farmers, heads of those farm families. Subtracting from this total the 741,000 represented in the census of 1900 as owners, managers, and tenants, the remaining 359,000 farmers, unenumerated by type of farm occupancy, must have been sharecroppers or hired laborers; that is, for every two black men who were owners, tenants, or managers of farms, there was one black man who worked the land for shares or wages.[78]

Among the approximately 187,000 blacks who owned their farms, although most had small holdings, there were some who owned several thousand acres. Booker T. Washington cited among his favorite success stories two Georgia farmers who owned 2,000 and 3,000 acres respectively of fertile land, and had as many as fifty Negro farm families as tenants; the 1906 census figures showed that the total black landowning in Georgia amounted to 1,400,000 acres worth over $28,000,000, and in Mississippi there were blacks who had owned farms of several hundred acres in the delta country since 1870. In Texas, where the Colored Alliance had been very active, in 1908 the 9,256 members of a black farm co-operative, the Farmer's Improvement

Society, owned in common more than 71,000 acres of land and livestock valued at $275,000.[79]

As the price of cotton climbed from an average of $.0717 a pound between 1890 and 1902 to $.1062 between 1903 and 1915 and as high as $.2154 in the next decade, the efficient farm-owner beloved of Booker Washington theoretically stood a chance of improving his condition and adding to his holdings. But, as Ray Stannard Baker pointed out, in actuality most of the 552,400 black tenant farmers were very poor and rarely got an opportunity to better their situation;[80] in fact, they almost never ended a year free of debt. Ignorant and illiterate, they signed (or X'd) contracts that they could not read or understand, and from which the law offered them no relief because, as Woodson says, "for them law is the will of the particular planter with whom they may be dealing."[81] According to the usual arrangement, tenants had to buy their seed and supplies on credit from the plantation owner, paying him back with a quarter to a third of the crop they made. Exorbitant charges for purchases and interest usually ate up any remaining profit, and before the next crop the tenant was deeper in debt than the year before.[82] Farmers kept their tenants in line more or less roughly; when Ray Stannard Baker asked one landlord how he managed his tenants, the man picked up a hickory wagon-spoke and said, "When there's trouble I just go down with that and lay one or two of 'en out."[83] Hopeless poverty and ill treatment did not encourage tenants to put down roots, or to take an interest in school, church, co-operative ventures, and causes concerning the community or nation.[84] Their tendency to move on from one place to another in search of a livable life for themselves and their children might, if they had been white, have been approved of as showing ambition; but when blacks moved along, they won the reputation of being natural migrants and drifters.

Between tenant farming and sharecropping there was a fuzzy, sometimes all but invisible line. The cropper was by contract obligated to work the owner's land part of the time; in return, he was permitted to cultivate in his free time a plot set aside for his use, with seed and other essentials furnished by the owner. The cropper got a percentage, sometimes half, of the proceeds of the crop he made for his employer. An unscrupulous boss could easily cheat on what the crop brought, because he never showed the bill of sale to his croppers and they had no idea what their share should amount to. It is obvious that, by such a system, the cropper almost always ended the year not just broke but owing the owner so much money that he could never catch up with his debt. His condition was so hopeless that a black farmer rented if he possibly could, rather than sharecrop. With no chance to better himself, the sharecropper had even less incentive than the tenant farmer to put down roots in any one community. But generally he had no option about staying or going, because with a debt that grew more mountainous year after year he either stayed bound to the land in a fruitless effort to pay off what he owed or was subject to arrest. To make his bondage still more complete, his debt as part of a planter's assets could be sold by one landlord to another, and the cropper would have to work for the buyer to pay off his indebtedness. So the cropper was nothing but a peon, tied to the land as irrevocably as any serf.[85]

A tenant, too, might find himself in peonage because without realizing it he had signed a contract that obliged him to farm the landlord's acres virtually for the rest of his life. For cropper or tenant saddled with such an obligation, it was work or jail. Sometimes he was deprived even of that choice by a sheriff who, in conspiracy with the landlord, terrorized the black man but instead of putting him in jail forced him to stay and work the land. Peonage continued unchecked by a Supreme Court decision of 1911 that struck down a law sentencing a tenant to jail and a large fine if the landlord said he had defaulted on a debt or contract.[86] But for the Supreme Court decision to be invoked, such cases would have had to be taken to court, which the tenant rarely had the means of doing; contracts were personal arrangements between landlord and tenant or cropper, and the final word about the terms of contract was the landlord's.

A simple way in which a planter could get cheap labor for an almost indefinite period was through the system of work fines administered by local courts. A black man found guilty of vagrancy or any trivial offense—and in most courts he was presumed guilty unless he could prove his innocence—would be fined instead of jailed, and any planter who paid his fine would have the right to the black man's labor until he had worked out the amount advanced. The planter could pay the man what he chose, perhaps $.50 a day, and charge what he chose for necessaries supplied. By this system, it might take months or years for a black laborer to pay back the amount of his fine. The work-fine arrangement was so profitable, evidently, that planters would regularly show up in court on Monday mornings and pay the fines of Negroes who had been rounded up during the weekend.[87]

Debt slavery and peonage were quite destructive of morality or faith in the law. Baker observed of the black farm worker, "He comes to the belief that if the white man wants him arrested, he will be arrested, and if he protects him, he won't suffer, no matter what he does." The system, Baker felt, "discourages justice and confuses the ignorant Negro mind as to what is a crime and what is not,"[88] because often a landlord would shield a hard-working tenant from punishment unless his crime were very serious, rather than lose his services.

There were some honest planters who rejected the system. "I've quit paying fines," Baker quotes a prominent Mississippi planter as saying; "my Negroes, if they get into trouble, have got to recognise their own responsibility for it and take what follows. That's the only way to make men of them."[89] He would better have said that was the only way not to unmake their manhood, but it is unusual to find even this patronizing kind of admission of white guilt. One hears more about the planters who, to quote the Mississippian again, "exploit the Negro by high store prices," and the still lower element of whites who "sell him whiskey and cocaine; they corrupt Negro women"; such whites this planter declared "worse than the meanest Negro that ever lived."[90]

The remaining 18 per cent of the South's black population lived in larger towns or cities doing a wide variety of work. Urban growth had taken a large stride in the 1890–1900 decade as many rural blacks began to seek better opportunities than they could hope for as tenants or croppers. There was an increase of 31 per cent among black people in domestic and personal-service jobs in southern cities during that decade, of 39 per cent in trade and transportation, and of 12.9 per cent in manufacturing. Frenise Logan found that, in North Carolina cities before 1900, although almost 25 per cent of blacks were in service jobs, many were employed in industry, primarily as makers of cigars and cigarettes but also as sawmill workers, carpenters and joiners, blacksmiths and wheelwrights, and stone cutters. There were also sizable numbers of black miners, more than 15,000 in 1890, and almost 4,500 painters; in the personal-service jobs there were about 17,500 barbers, 7,500 dressmakers, 5,000 shoemakers, and 1,300 tailors. Businessmen and manufacturers were fewer, Logan says, with only 175 blacks in these fields in all of North Carolina, half of the firms worth $500 or less; in the same state, there were 2,036 black professionals, but of these, 95 per cent were in teaching or the ministry, professions that did not require special training.[91]

Black workers almost never got equal pay with white workers on the same job. The chief reason for inequities was the antiblack attitude of many unions. Although the national union organizations claimed to have no color prejudice, their locals in many trades did discriminate. DuBois listed forty unions that at the turn of the century officially barred blacks, and twenty more that had only a few black members.[92] The reason for this, it was said, was that few blacks had the qualifying skills; very often this was true, because they had been effectively prevented from learning them—a type of circular logic that becomes familiar to any student of black opportunity whether economic, educational, or political. There were, however, many skilled black workers, and a number of unions, including those of some skilled trades, freely admitted blacks at that time: barbers, brick and tile workers, carpenters and joiners, carriage and wagon workers, coopers, longshoremen, miners, and tobacco workers. The reason blacks were taken into those unions was a quite pragmatic one, as a white official of the barbers' union explained: "We have to recognize them to hold our prices and short hours. . . ."[93] Or, as Samuel Gompers said, "a labor union is primarily a business institution and very little sentimentalism enters into its make-up."[94]

But there was less common sense in the great resistance to black members in many unions. One white labor leader in Virginia said ignorant prejudice against blacks was "one of the greatest obstacles to the labor movement in the South. . . ."[95] Of nine strikes reported by the Labor Department between 1894 and 1900, seven were by white workers in the South against the employment of blacks; there were also antiblack strikes in New York and New Jersey. In Pittsburgh in 1890 the Iron and Steel Workers ordered out 500 men when blacks were hired; they stayed out six months and failed in the end.[96] So time, energy, and money that might have been expended in securing for all workers better hours, pay, and conditions of labor were squandered on the unproductive luxury of race hatred.

The tide away from the farm was running strong by 1900, when 72 urban areas had black populations of 5,000 or more. Mulattoes particularly were attracted to the cities, and their broader range of employment opportunities. In cities mulattoes formed a much larger proportion of the Negro population than in the country—it might be three to five times as large—and there was a continual "passing" of very light mulattoes from the black to the white count. Nevertheless, rural blacks like rural whites still far outnumbered their city brothers and sisters.[97]

Much of the movement toward towns and cities lay within the South, which, like the rest of the nation, was experiencing rapid industrialization. Booker T. Washington wrote in 1898: "In many respects the next twenty years are going to be the most serious in the history of the race. Within this period it will be largely decided whether the Negro will be able to retain the hold which he now has upon the industries of the South or whether his place will be filled by white people from a distance"[98]—European immigrants. The "New" South, the industrial South, was the high hope of white southern leaders and of Booker T. Washington and his friends.

Between 1903 and 1917 the South doubled its steel production, and blacks who were employed in that industry made a degree of progress. Birmingham, Alabama, was third among iron-shipping points in the world. The most marked increase in production, however, was in the textile industry, particularly spinning mills. By 1900, Charlotte, North Carolina, was the center of a spinning industry that had more than 2,000,000 spindles within a radius of 100 miles; Columbia, South Carolina, lately a small town, numbered 500,000 spindles and employed 12,000 people.[99] But this prosperity did little for blacks, because practically none were employed in the textile industry.

Of the total of 3,769,000 black workers in 1900, almost one third (1,185,000) were women, as compared with slightly less than 11 per cent women in the white labor force. Most working black women were in domestic and personal service, a large number in the professions (chiefly teaching) and in agriculture, and smaller numbers in trade, transportation, and manufacturing and mechanical jobs.[100]

According to Oscar Micheaux, it is clear that there were no great work opportunities in the North, either, for the average black man early in the century. Micheaux describes an exceptionally hard worker who was paid $1.25 a day for rough work at a car manufacturing plant in Ohio, which employed 800 blacks out of a total of 1,200 workers; in an all-black town in the area he earned $2.25 per twelve-hour day bailing water in a mine under frightful working conditions. When the worker moved to Chicago in hope of advancement, he found fierce competition among thousands of unskilled laborers for jobs at common labor that paid $1.50 a day; and in a Joliet, Illinois, steel mill, for the heaviest sort of work cracking and heaving coal, he earned $1.50 for each twenty-five tons heaved into the chutes—a backbreaking day's work for which he competed with many immigrants whose only English words were the digits of their laborer's number.[101]

Such earnings were not inordinately low for that time. It was a period of widespread poverty, when seven eighths of the country's wealth was held by only one eighth of the people. In 1900, the average daily wage was under $2.00. Two thirds of the male workers earned less than $12.50 a week, and only a few workers earned as much as $18 a week. Prices, too, were low: $.21 a dozen for eggs, $.14 a pound for pork, $1.14 a bushel for potatoes, $4.69 for a barrel of flour, and $6.00 a ton for coal.[102] Nevertheless, the average worker could barely meet these costs. So an article on money in an encyclopedia of 1901, extolling thrift, seems somewhat unrealistic: "If the head of a family earns two dollars a day, and finds that, by rigid economy, he can save twenty cents a day" he will save over $60 a year, which compounded at 4 per cent interest "offers a 'fortune' at middle age that is worth having saved for."[103] An ambitious white man might have been able to follow such a Spartan program during his early working years; but as for the black man, he was not earning that $2.00 a day, and, as DuBois pointed out in his study of Philadelphia blacks at that time, since a black man almost could not hope to rise above menial status regardless of skill or training, he did not have the incentive needed to sustain such self-denial. By contrast, Micheaux describes a "flashy" city Negro in Chicago who was flat broke but wore a $5.00 hat, $15 made-to-measure shoes, a $45 coat and vest, $11 trousers, $50 tweed coat, and a diamond or two—all probably bought on credit. Small wonder that when such gloriously turned-out figures went back home to South Carolina or Georgia to dazzle kinfolk on the old farm, cities like Chicago seemed like suburbs of heaven.[104]

By 1900 and shortly thereafter, at the time when systematic Jim Crow segregated blacks in every activity of life, one small gain from an inverse working of the system was that more black people began to "buy black." This produced a marked increase in the number and value of businesses owned by blacks. Many of these enterprises were members of the National Negro Business League organized by Booker T. Washington, and doubtless drew strength from it. At the League's first convention in 1900, delegates reported enthusiastically on black businesses in various southern cities. In Montgomery, Alabama, for instance, with only 2,000 black residents, there were twenty-three Negro-owned grocery stores, three drugstores, twenty restaurants, a dry-goods store, thirty shoemakers, twelve contractors and builders, fifteen blacksmith shops, wood and coal yards, butcher stalls, greengrocers, draymen, insurance and real estate agents, a lawyer, a jeweler, a dentist, "four hundred preachers, five physicians and two undertakers all doing well."[105]

Nor were all black businesses small ventures. Booker T. Washington reported on a Montgomery undertaker who did $40,000 worth of business a year and a baker in Jackson, Mississippi, who took in $30,000 a year; among black-owned banks in the South, numbering forty-seven in 1908, Washington named two with capital of $100,000, but noted that a number of banks failed because of poor management. Nevertheless, many did not fail, and by 1916 there were reported to be nearly seventy banks owned by blacks. Among other big businesses were insurance firms, such as the North Carolina Mutual and Provident Association, which as of 1909 had paid out $500,000 in benefits.[106]

Ray Stannard Baker mentioned an increase in Atlanta's Negro drugstores, which he attributed to an increase in black doctors and dentists.[107] Perhaps that was so in Atlanta, but Kelly Miller, dean of Howard University, stated that although black professionals were increasing about 1900, there were as of that date scarcely enough of them to list as a professional class. Miller wrote that in Texas there was one black doctor per 9,000 black residents and one black lawyer per 40,000; in South Carolina, one doctor per 22,000 and one lawyer per 29,000. Booker T. Washington's count of black professionals included 207 black inventors who held U.S. patents as of 1899, and 350 doctors belonging to the (black) National Medical Association in 1900; and he mentioned that black women contributed to the professional ranks in almost incredible numbers: 160 physicians, seven dentists, ten lawyers, as well as 164 ministers, assorted journalists, writers, and artists, 1,185 musicians and teachers of music, and 13,525 teachers.[108] It is difficult to reconcile Miller's and Washington's figures.

Certainly the job opportunities, the businesses, and the professionals were concentrated in the cities of the South rather than in its rural areas; but rural or urban, southern blacks formed such a low-power group in 1900 that the numerous measures designed to "keep them in their place" appear to constitute quite excessive overkill.

The lifestyle of southern blacks was in keeping with their position at the very bottom of southern society. On the farm, tenants, croppers, and probably most small owners as well lived in old log cabins or flimsy houses made of upright boards with batten filling the cracks. Such a house would rest on four corner supports of piled-up stones, and under it would shelter the dogs, a couple of pigs, and some chickens. Water came from a broken-down well. Windows were holes in the walls and were boarded up in winter, so about the only light inside came from the fire-place. In a dog-run house—two rooms connected by a roughly floored open passage where the family lived and ate in summer —the mother and father usually shared one room with the younger children and the older children slept in the other room, which was also used for cooking and eating.[109]

In cities, certain areas were set aside for blacks, by custom if not by law, although as Kelly Miller pointed out, there was more formal segregation in northern cities than in the South. One rea-son for greater mingling in the southern cities dated back to slave days when blacks lived in quarters behind the master's house. However, by the early twentieth century there were black ghettos in every southern city, where the poorest blacks lived. DuBois deplored this arrangement, pointing out that although there might be a black slum bordering a good white neighbor-hood, or a white slum in a good black neighborhood, upper-class blacks and upper-class whites never lived in proximity; and so each race knew only the lowest element of the other.[110]

Smaller towns made it clear, sometimes painfully clear, that they did not want black residents. As a result, all-black settle-ments sprang up in practically every southern state and also in California, Illinois, Kansas, Michigan, and New Jersey. There were also exclusively black suburbs of many cities including Birming-ham, Raleigh, Columbia, Chattanooga, Houston, and Norfolk. Robert Abbott, editor of one of the most influential black news-papers, the Chicago *Defender*, had grown up in the Negro town of Yamacraw, a suburb of Savannah, which had been established before the Civil War by an elite group of free Negroes.[111]

Health conditions in both city and country were deplorable, probably owing chiefly to the shortage of black doctors noted by Miller. Rural areas were particularly deprived, because the younger and better-trained doctors tended to migrate to the cities. Public health agents did little or nothing for rural blacks; hospitals were nonexistent, and in any case, Woodson says, black farmers were too backward to appreciate their use. They also knew nothing of the prevention or treatment of gonorrhea and syphilis, and treated them lightly as ordinary complaints. Health facilities were not much better in the cities, where, although there were some hospitals, doctors, and visiting nurse services, these never filled the need for medical attention, and most blacks depended on the druggist and patent remedies when they were ill. In Savannah, in 1908, four out of five deaths among black people were unattended by a physician.[112]

There is considerable testimony pointing to the concern of even the most backward black rustics about education for their children, a goal all but unattainable in the South of 1900. The reason was not simple negligence on the part of the white community, but quite deliberate prevention of black education by white Southerners who had no intention of improving black schools, which might enable blacks to read their contracts, seek better jobs, and pass literacy and understanding tests at the polls.[113] A bill to give $15,000,000 of federal funds to the school systems of ten southern states was proposed by Senator Henry W. Blair of New Hampshire in 1884 and again in 1886 and 1888; it was finally voted on and killed in 1890 by a coalition of southern Democrats and of Republicans opposed to using up the budgetary surplus. So ended one of the bright hopes of southern blacks for social and political improvement.[114] White children also suffered by the defeat of the Blair bill, but that was apparently thought worthwhile in order to keep blacks ignorant.

Public education was deplorable throughout the South. No state had a compulsory education law, and it was estimated that less than 40 per cent of all school-age children attended regularly. Also, the school term was about one third shorter than the national average, and the number of teachers about one third less. Only one out of ten pupils completed fifth grade; one out of seventy reached eighth grade. Illiteracy in the adult population ranged between 30 and 45 per cent.[115]

Whatever school funds were available, black children got far less than their proportionate share. In 11 southern states, Booker

T. Washington reported, although blacks formed 40 per cent of the population, they received less than 15 per cent of educational appropriations. In Mississippi—57 per cent black—blacks got 22 per cent of school moneys; in Louisiana—43 per cent black—they got less than 9 per cent. In South Carolina, for every $1.00 spent on educating black children, the expenditure per white child was $6.00 in 1900, and $12.37 by 1915.[116]

Separate schools for blacks had been established by law in the South and were prevalent in the North as well, although in the North they appeared "quietly and naturally," Baker says, without legislation.[117] Baker thought it was to the advantage of blacks to have their own schools, provided that states spent the same amount of money on black schools as on white schools. It was not yet axiomatic in the thinking of liberals like Baker that separate could not possibly be equal, but this truth was amply demonstrated by the deplorable conditions in black schools, from the dilapidated, unsanitary, crowded one-room building in which school kept to the inadequate, poorly trained, and poorly paid teachers and the almost total lack of equipment. In 1900, the South Carolina superintendent of education recommended doubling the salary of black teachers so that it would amount to $160 a year. If teachers wanted maps, charts, globes, or other teaching tools, they were obliged, even in the relatively generous system of Virginia, to buy them out of their own money.[118] "Much of the prejudice in the South against Negro education," Baker says, "is unquestionably due to the wretched school system, which in many places has not really educated anybody"; it has only taught both blacks and whites to despise work, Baker continues; it "has made the Negro 'uppish' and 'bumptious,'" and has given white men illusions of superiority unsupported by accomplishment or usefulness.[119] All this could have been changed by federal appropriations under the Blair bill, but that might have enabled a few blacks to drop a ballot in the box.

City schools for blacks were in general superior to rural schools, although so crowded that in many places black children had to attend in shifts. Even in the cities, there were practically no black high schools before the end of World War I. In the black schools of southern cities attendance was higher than in rural black schools, where children were often kept at home to work in the fields, but much lower than in the rural schools of the North and West. Furthermore, the school year for southern blacks was much shorter than the standard 180-day school year elsewhere in the country, and up to seventy-eight days shorter than the school year in white schools in the same state. In South Carolina, black schools were open only seventy-eight days a year, and white schools 156 days. But a little education, Baker to the contrary notwithstanding, seems to have been better than none, because illiteracy declined significantly among southern blacks; even in South Carolina, with its very brief school year, black illiteracy dropped from 78.5 per cent in 1880 to 52.8 per cent in 1900.[120]

White Southerners who could tolerate the idea of any education for Negroes considered mechanical, industrial, and agricultural schools the least obnoxious. The 1862 Land Grant Act had made no provision for Negro schools, but Virginia gave part of its land grant proceeds to Hampton Institute, South Carolina to Claflin, and Mississippi to Alcorn. Tuskegee Normal and Industrial Institute, of which Booker T. Washington was president, was the recipient of private gifts from Julius Rosenwald and other philanthropists. The agricultural and mechanical schools for southern blacks were sufficiently well accepted by the community to increase from fourteen in 1893 to seventeen in 1914.[121]

Education of black people was another of the southern dilemmas. At the Southern Sociological Congress of 1913, presided over by the governor of Virginia, one speaker's point was that southern prosperity depended on educating, improving, and cooperating with the Negroes.[122] On the other side, there was the Vardaman point that educating or improving the Negro was inimical to the best interest of the South. Hortense Powdermaker, studying Mississippi blacks in the 1930s, found the southern dilemma still unresolved; the general feeling was, " 'If you educate the niggers, you ruin the South; if you don't educate them, you ruin it too.' "[123] Most people, probably, or at least enough people to influence the politicians, favored not educating them. The granting of private moneys by John D. Rockefeller, and by the

Jeanes, Slater, Rosenwald, and other northern foundations to supplement public funds for black education was considered vicious by the many white Southerners who agreed with a Montgomery lawyer, quoted by Baker, that they "never saw a Negro benefited by education, but hundreds ruined. He ceases to be a hewer of wood and a drawer of water . . ." which, the lawyer was confident, is what the Creator intended the Negro to be.[124] Vardaman said: "What the North is sending South is not money, but dynamite; this education is ruining our Negroes. They're demanding equality."[125]

Disfranchised and uneducated, often illiterate, hedged about with Jim Crow do's and don'ts and such Black Code holdovers as vagrancy laws, black Southerners frequently found themselves in trouble with the law, particularly when white Southerners stood to gain by their trouble.[126]

The peonage and debt slavery systems were extremely profitable to white planters. The convict lease system was another means of exploitation, by which private companies or the state itself could use the labor of convicts while they were serving their terms. The Supreme Court ruled out convict lease along with peonage in 1911, but that did not stop either of them. The system encouraged locking up blacks for the most trivial offenses and sentencing them to outrageously long terms. In 1903, Missouri made chicken stealing a felony punishable by five years in prison and/or a $200 fine; the following year Kentucky passed an almost identical law.[127] It became a frequent complaint of whites that blacks refused to turn in felons or criminals of their own race; a white leader in Atlanta explained to Baker with unusual insight that this happened because "the Negro has too little confidence in our courts."[128]

Under such circumstances it is not surprising that blacks formed a disproportionately large part of the jail population. In 1890, the state penitentiary at Raleigh had in it 408 whites and 1,625 blacks, Logan says, the reason being that North Carolina was embarking on a vast program of internal improvements and needed the convict labor; furthermore, it was understood from the beginning that "the system of convict leasing was to be confined in the main to the use of Negro prisoners."[129] In the same year, of 1,184 persons in South Carolina state prisons, 1,061 were blacks, so it seems probable that the same understanding held in South Carolina. Francis Butler Simkins, in his not notably pro-Negro history of the South, confirms that with the expansion of road building in the South more blacks were sentenced to long terms to keep them on the state road gangs.[130]

But the uninformed or self-deluded white Southerner drew from the large number of Negro arrests and the severity of their sentences the inference that blacks were naturally criminal. He did not take into account—and probably did not even know—such facts as that in Atlanta, where 60 per cent of those arrested were black, although blacks were only 40 per cent of the population, most arrests were for misdemeanors such as disorderly conduct, that convenient catch-all charge, and drunkenness, not for felonies. People also did not take into account, although they did know this very well, that a white man was rarely charged with an offense against a black, and if charged and tried would almost certainly be dismissed, while the black complainant might quite possibly find himself on the chain gang for making false charges.[131]

When the state leased its convicts to private farms or industries, the proceeds enriched the state treasury. In 1906 Georgia made a profit of $354,853.55 from leasing out convicts, most of them black. Baker explained how the system worked. Agents of Alabama firms would gather in Montgomery several days before the sentencing of fifty or so blacks, and by competitive bidding each agent maneuvered to get some of them for his company. With little or no supervision by the state of the treatment of leased convicts, one can imagine how dreadful must have been their conditions of life and work. In South Carolina, when the horrors of the system were exposed, leasing was forbidden in 1897, and instead convicts were restricted to work on the state farms; but conditions there were often no better than in private companies or on privately owned farms.[132]

For a black man charged with fornication or adultery with a white woman, the law of the South saved its utmost severity.

The Alabama Supreme Court explained that this was not the ordinary crime of fornication or adultery, and thus the sentence was not discriminatory "against the person of any particular color or race, but against the offense, the nature of which is determined by the opposite colors of the cohabiting parties."[133]

Concubinage or prostitution of black women, however, was accepted as a traditional part of the southern system. Brothels were restricted to the Negro quarters of almost all southern cities. And since, at least officially, all prostitutes in the South were black, prostitution, like criminality, gained the reputation of a race trait. Certain black houses, such as the Stanley Club in Memphis, were famous for their plush accommodations, and were protected by the corrupt police force of that crime-ridden city. There were in Memphis about a dozen drugstores that made almost all their profits by selling cocaine to Negroes and poor whites; a $.05 or $.10 box of it would produce a high for the evening, so it was an escape within the reach of all but the absolutely stony broke. Cocaine and opium use was increasing in the early 1900s, not only in Memphis but in Atlanta and doubtless all large cities in the South. Atlanta law officials stated that a large percentage of black crimes were committed by drug users. With all the drunkenness, drug use, prostitution, and pimping that was deliberately concentrated in the Negro quarters of big towns and cities, it was inevitable that growing black children would quickly learn how to get themselves in some sort of trouble. Youth crime, DuBois says, was one of the worst black problems. To prevent twelve-year-olds from landing on chain gangs with hardened criminals, DuBois pleaded for improvement in the southern school system and for recreational facilities such as a well-equipped YMCA.[134]

The average black child or grownup had no wholesome way of spending leisure time; parks, playgrounds, and other public facilities were closed to them, and home surroundings did not encourage them to stay off the streets. Music was a refuge, and had been since slave days. Booker T. Washington was outraged to find in a hovel where there was only one fork for the whole family, a parlor organ that was being paid for in $60 monthly installments. But many a black musician, including W. C. Handy

and Eubie Blake, learned to play on such a parlor organ, at home
or in church. Church and camp meetings with their singing,
shouting, marching, stomping, and shuffling, with services, meetings, and sociables, provided almost the entire respectable social
life of southern blacks; the importance of music to black people
and their competence in it are reflected in Booker Washington's
count of almost 1,200 black musicians and music teachers, by
far the largest group of black professionals except for school-
teachers. Black musicians might stay with spirituals or folksongs,
as did the highly trained singer Harry Burleigh, who provided
Anton Dvorak with inspiration and themes for his Symphony
No. 5, "From the New World." Or they might in much greater
numbers convert the rhythms they knew to dance music and jazz,
from which they could make a living by playing in the dancehalls, brothels, and honky-tonk dives of darktown alleys. The
larger the red-light district, the more opportunities for black
players of ragtime, that syncopated music in which the thumping
left-hand accompaniment recalled the foot thumping of camp
meetings, and later for the jazz pianists who fused ragtime with
the old spirituals and other forms to get a new exciting kind of
music. And in black dancehalls, to the old-new ragtime beat,
black dancers lifted their feet high in the cakewalk, another survival of plantation days when the slaves on festive occasions were
called to "walk for the cake" that was given as a prize to the
highest stepper. Of all the South's red-light districts the most
fabulous was New Orleans' "Storyville," as it came to be called,
an all-black quarter set apart in 1897 under the sponsorship of
Alderman Sidney Story in order to segregate vice in one portion
of the city. Black musicians flocked to Storyville's Basin Street,
and played together in bands which then toured the country and
spread New Orleans jazz everywhere.[135]

Black music, genuine or imitated, grew enormously popular
with whites in the early 1900s. *Colliers Cyclopedia and Compendium of Profitable Knowledge* of 1901, under "Popular Songs
of All Nations," listed for America Stephen Foster's "O Susanna,"
"The Old Folks at Home," and "Uncle Ned," and Will S. Hays's
"Keep in de Middle ob de Road," along with "Glory, Glory! Hal-
lelujah," "Hail Columbia," and the national anthem. As enter-

tainers, blacks were accorded their full merit by whites, South and North; but an entertainer is a person hired to please, and thus another kind of menial. At least this has been true in America, possibly because of the large number of black entertainers, who, being black, had to be regarded as menials.

No picture of the environment in which black people lived in the South of 1900 can be complete without the shadow of the lyncher lurking behind the door. In the 1880s, when data on lynching were first collected, reports showed more whites lynched than blacks; the figures for lynch victims from 1882 to 1888 showed 595 whites and 440 blacks.[136] By 1889 the trend had reversed, and in the 1890s lynching of blacks soared as the ultimate expression of Jim Crow. As E. Franklin Frazier put it: "Lynching has been one of the fruits of the crusade to establish 'white supremacy.'"[137] According to one source, in 1900, of 115 lynchings throughout the nation (as against 114 legal executions that year), more than 100 were in the southern states; and of those lynched, 8 were white, 107 black. In the years following 1900, about 90 per cent of lynch victims were black.[138]

Despite hard evidence to the contrary, it was commonly claimed in the South, and probably believed, that the overwhelming reason for lynchings was rape of white women by black men. Figures, however, show that of all Negroes lynched between 1889 and 1941, less than 17 per cent were even charged with rape.[139] Murder and felonious assault were the most usual charges, according to one study, with rape the second most frequent. Among other offenses for which blacks were lynched were several that might, by a wishful mind, be construed as rape or at least intention to rape: insulting a white woman, writing to or paying attention to white women, proposing to or eloping with a white woman. But there were also such totally unrelated charges as testifying in court for another black or against a white, practicing voodoo, slapping a child, throwing stones, rioting, introducing smallpox, or disobeying ferry regulations.[140] Any charge at all, however remote from rape, might fire up a lynch mob; as one black observer wrote, "The temptation of the lyncher is the weak administration of the law when the Negro is to be protected and the helpless position into which the colored race is forced by disfranchisement and other forms of oppression."[141]

Booker T. Washington said any study of the facts would reveal that four fifths of those lynched were not even suspected of sex crimes, and Baker wrote that in 1903, out of 104 lynchings, rape was charged in only 11 cases and attempted rape in 10. In the years 1914 to 1918, only 19.8 per cent of Negroes lynched were accused of rape or attempted rape of white women; in 1919, a year of particularly great urban violence, only 18.2 per cent were so accused.[142] Still, the idea that a black offender of any kind was a living threat to white womanhood was an underlying reason for all lynchings. As Cash wrote in *The Mind of the South,* "What Southerners felt . . . was that any assertion of any kind on the part of the Negro constituted in a perfectly real manner an attack on the Southern woman."[143] Herbert Seligmann had made similar observations twenty years before Cash. The South's color psychosis, Seligmann observed, was rooted in sex jealousy; such easily aroused emotionality was a convenient tool for political and industrial purposes, and could be used against any black man who had got ahead a little, or any white man accused of being a "nigger lover." "It is upon the pretext of the necessity for maintaining the 'purity' of the white race," Seligmann wrote, "that the white supremacy of Southern states is based. It is with this dogma dominant, and the emotions which cling to it, that the South and the nation must face the dilemma of open and deliberate violation of the letter and the spirit of the federal Constitution and its amendments."[144]

Much has been written about the southern psychology of sex: the elevation of southern women by their men, the consequent terror of rape of white women by black men, and the fury unleashed against black men as a result of this self-induced terror.[145] But there are still unanswered questions as to why mob killings of black people, whom almost all Southerners would say they did not dislike as Northerners disliked them, became such a devastating force in the American South.

It would be interesting to know more about why southern

white womanhood had been made so pure, sweet, and unapproachable. Was it because, as Cash said, the southern white woman was regarded as the vessel from which would issue future members of the superior race, and must therefore be guarded like a vestal virgin who keeps the sacred flame alight? This seems too intellectual a concept to operate in the sphere of sexual relations. Could it have been invented as an excuse for seeking the sexual services of black women by white men who thus convinced themselves that white women were too pure and holy to be so used, and who convinced white women that chastity and coldness were adorable virtues?[146] Would not this charade, costumed by Sir Walter Scott and with props by Tennyson, have had a destructive effect on white southern women? Would they not have become so dehumanized by the rare atmosphere surrounding their pedestals that in fact they could no longer stimulate or satisfy their men the way black women could, normal women who had not been chilled by statuary status? Then, if sex became the work of black women, white women not only could not but would not wish to engage in it, any more than white men would do a "Negro job" like shining shoes or barbering. Repugnance for sex would be final proof of the purity of white womanhood; this would make it excusable for their men to resort to black women and obligatory for them to protect their marble goddesses from the contaminating touch, glance, or even presence of a black man. It seems possible that the myths of black male hypersexuality and extraordinarily large sex organs were simply materializations of the concept of the black as ravisher; also possible that black men were believed necessarily endowed with great sexual prowess in order to satisfy black women, who in their natural response to sex must have seemed prodigiously sexual to white males who fled to them from their frigidified wives.

These questions are important in connection with lynching. The black man, once established as lustful, could be believed to lust after any white woman he passed on the street; so being on the same street with a white woman would constitute intended rape and thus justify lynching. Viewing the sex theme as inseparable from lynching may help to explain the psychology of the lynch mob. Seligmann wrote: "The emotion which animates the mob has a large component of sex jealousy. Yet lynchings take place on any one of dozens of pretexts."[147] Did lynching itself take on the attributes of rape, granting an emotional release comparable to sexual fulfillment? That would explain why a lynch mob would so quickly gather at the scent of a victim, regardless of the actual offense; why otherwise decorous citizens would come from fifty miles around to enjoy the climactic act, however horrible; and why law-and-order authorities, even if they tried, found it practically impossible to disperse a lynch mob until it had been satisfied.

There is no question, in any case, that in the popular mind lynching and rape became so synonymous that to oppose lynching was to condone rape. Southern politicians could not act conscientiously and still keep public support. Vardaman, running for governor of Mississippi in 1903, straddled the issue: "If I were the sheriff and a negro fell into my hands, I would run him out of the county. If I were governor and were asked for troops to protect him I would send them. But if I were a private citizen I would head the mob to string the brute up."[148]

Black people in the South in 1900 lived every moment, through every act of their days, in fear of the lynch mob. Many years after, when Charles Johnson was gathering material for the Myrdal study, a Nashville black man explained to him that he always raised his hat to white women as a sign of respect, adding, "It is another reason for respecting them when you know that they will get you killed for disrespecting them."[149] And Seligmann summed it up thus: "So long as the relations of Negro and white man in this country are conceived in the terms of the black man's encroachment upon the white man's sexual preserve there will be embittered hostility between the races."[150]

"If only colored women could be equally safe in the hands of white men," William Pickens wrote in sorrow and anger.[151]

These were the blacks of 1900, and this was their life. What sort of man could serve as leader to such deprived and frightened people? Not a Moses, nor a Joshua, as Andrew Carnegie mistakenly called Booker T. Washington,[152] because although the black people were in bondage in the South there was nothing better beckoning, no land of plenty and opportunity for them to go to; Robert Abbott could be that sort of leader ten years later. Not an Alexander, leading them to establish outposts of their civilization across seas; Marcus Garvey could lead them that way, twenty years later. Not a Sequoyah, to lead them to freedom through the power of the written word; few heard DuBois's voice urging higher learning. Not a George Washington to bring them to armed victory against their oppressors, those who took their tax money and gave back nothing for it; any attempt at rebellion would have been ruthlessly cut down by the law of their own land.

The leaders of black people in 1900 were appropriate to the time: Jesus Christ, who promised them rewards in heaven; and Booker T. Washington, who told them that they could have peace and prosperity on earth if they would cast down their buckets where they were, in the South; that they could become valuable to the white community by learning to do a job well, to accommodate to white authority, and to "throw aside every nonessential and cling only to essentials—that this pillar of fire by night and pillar of cloud by day shall be property, economy, education, and Christian character."[153]

Whether Washington was a superevent, as he was hailed by followers, or merely an opiate, as radical young blacks called him when he died in 1915, he was the powerful man among black Americans in 1900 because he was appropriate to his time, a time of static low fortune in the tightening grip of Jim Crow. Perhaps he was not so much an important leader as a powerful individual; perhaps there was truth in what Marcus Garvey said twenty years later, that Washington was not a leader of the black people at all, but simply the man whom white people chose to consider the leader of blacks[154]—at a time when blacks did not have the power to challenge what the white man chose for them. But Garvey said that in 1921; to view Washington in terms of the New Negro of the World War I generation or to judge him in terms of what a black leader can do today is to miss the importance of what he did *then*. The whites who recognized him as a leader gave their financial support to black education—mostly trade education, to be sure, but Robert Abbott learned the printing trade at Hampton Institute, Tuskegee provided many of the black officers who served in World War I, and Rosenwald schools brought literacy to thousands of rural blacks. Washington was mistaken in his fervent belief that through wealth black men could crack the Jim Crow code, but he was merely echoing the current American faith in the power of money to do anything— near the truth, provided you were white. The Russian revolutionary Peter Kropotkin thought it very funny that there were, as he was told, conservative Negroes. "What on earth do they have to conserve?" he is said to have asked.[155] But conservatism was the faith of the day, and Washington was a man of his time. He inspired a number of men like Oscar Micheaux, who said that blacks used slavery and white prejudice as excuses for lethargy, which may have stung a few black men out of inert despair. He brought race pride to black men at a time when their self-esteem was at a low ebb by his famous dinner with the newly sworn President of the United States, Theodore Roosevelt.[156] To Roosevelt, a Northerner, the dinner was mostly a matter of politics, and he undoubtedly did not understand the power of the taboo he had violated by sitting at table with a black man. To the shocked white South the dinner party was "the most damnable outrage ever";[157] Roosevelt had turned the White House into a "nigger restaurant." Blacks everywhere felt a thrill of hope.

Every black in the South knew Booker T. Washington, down to the elderly Georgian rustic who described him as a "pow'ful big nigger."[158] Many of them deserted him as soon as they got the chance, seeing no reason to believe they could find salvation by the conservative route. But in the dreadful years around 1900, years of hunger, suffocating discrimination, political impotence, and the ever-present fear of noose and faggot, no other leader could have done more for them. Booker T. Washington was a name to cling to, a manifestation of black worth through whom, vicariously, the poor southern blacks could participate in American society, and because of whom, perhaps, they were able to retain enough self-respect to seize opportunity when it came.

CHAPTER 2

The Great Migration

Some are coming on the passenger,
Some are coming on the freight,
Others will be found walking,
For none have time to wait.

From a poem, *They're Leaving Memphis,*
published in the Chicago *Defender*

American blacks had always been moving from one part of the country to another, and also out of the country, looking for freedom and opportunity. In colonial times slaves fled to the French-governed Northwest Territory, a number settling in what is now Pittsburgh. Others were brought or sent to the northern country by Quakers when the Quaker meeting very early outlawed slavery. When the British evacuated America after the Revolutionary War, 14,000 former slaves went with them to Canada, in addition to 5,000 who had already escaped there or to East Florida, also British territory; others emigrated to the West Indies, Nova Scotia, or England. A few years later, about 1,200 blacks went on from Canada to Africa, to settle the country of Sierra Leone; the name of its capital, Freetown, tells the story. When East Florida was ceded to Spain some blacks went from there to the British West Indies; others joined those already in Canada and were resettled in Africa by the Sierra Leone Company. Although some were brought back to slavery in Georgia and South Carolina, others found their way to the upper Mississippi area. From the early nineteenth century, fugitive southern slaves found free friends in Pennsylvania, New York, Massachusetts, Ohio, Indiana, Michigan, Illinois, and Canada. The newer black settlers, fresh from slavery, were not always cordially welcomed by state governments, immigrant laborers, or established Negro citizens, but despite discrimination and some racial violence, blacks managed to make economic and social progress in such northern cities as Cincinnati, New York, and Boston. And by the end of the century the American Colonization Society had sent almost 8,000 blacks to establish Liberia.[1]

At the end of the Civil War there was a great scattering of southern blacks. Around 72,500 southern refugees were living in government camps and settlements in the District of Columbia, New York, Pennsylvania, and Massachusetts. There was also some movement in the opposite direction as northern blacks went South for what opportunities Reconstruction might offer. Soon after the sellout of the blacks by the Republicans and the removal of protective federal troops from the South, it was clear that there would be precious few opportunities in that part of the country, and so blacks began moving westward; there were between 5,000 and 10,000 blacks in the 1879 stampede under "Moses" Singleton of Tennessee and Henry Adams of Louisiana, and by April of that year about 60,000 blacks had found their way to Kansas and Nebraska, and to Texas, Arkansas, and Oklahoma.[2]

In the years from 1890 to the early 1900s, although blacks continued to trickle from South to North and West, migration seems to have been greater from country to town within individual regions. Those were bleak farm years in many parts of the country, and farmers moved not only out of the drought-stricken prairies of the Middle West but off the land in the southern, northeastern, and Middle Atlantic states. Especially they moved off the worn-out soil of the poorer lands of the Old South, where in order to make a crop the farmer had to invest heavily in fertilizer and equipment he could not afford. Many of these southern black farmers went to the richer new lands of Arkansas and Texas in that period. A relatively small number journeyed to the Far West, only about 35,000 between 1890 and 1910. More tried their luck in the cities. In 1890, only 15.3 per cent of southern blacks were city people; by 1910, the percentage had increased to 22.[3] Also, in the early 1900s a number of northern blacks returned to the South, probably many of them to southern cities, because they could not compete with immigrant labor at a time when European immigrants were flooding into the country—from an average of less than 500,000 a year from 1890 to 1900, to over 1,000,000 a year in 1905, 1906, and 1907. Between 1900 and 1910 the black population gains in southern cities include a 215.6 per cent increase in Birmingham, a center for mining and steel industries; 212.5 per cent in Fort Worth; 137.3 per cent in Jackson; and gains between 45 per cent and 99 per cent in Atlanta, Charlotte, Dallas, Houston, Richmond, and Shreveport.[4]

This story of movement in the black population says clearly that many blacks did not sit quietly in one place waiting for things to change under them; that, in fact, they shared in the general American pattern of mobility.[5] But early migrations were dwarfed by the surge of black people northward after 1900, and especially after 1910. According to various contemporaneous estimates, between 1890 and 1910 around 200,000 black Southerners fled to the North; and between 1910 and 1920 another 300,000 to 1,000,000 followed. The Department of Labor reported that in eighteen months of 1916–17 the migration was variously estimated at 200,000 to 700,000. Abraham Epstein, in his 1918 study of migrants in Pittsburgh, gave the figure for 1916 alone as somewhere between 300,000 and 700,000, but he did not have the benefit of the 1920 census. Baker said 400,000 had gone North by 1917, and DuBois estimated somewhat more conservatively 250,-000 by the summer of that year. Whatever the exact figures, 1916 and the two war years that followed brought the northward Negro movement to its peak.[6]

What precipitated the mass migration of that period is succinctly expressed in this verse:

> Boll-weevil in de cotton
> Cut worm in de cotton,
> Debil in de white man,
> Wah's goin' on.[7]

Drought, then heavy rains, and the boll weevils that flourish under wet conditions had ruined cotton crops in 1915 and 1916. Tenant farmers and croppers were desperate. Too, injustice, disfranchisement, and Jim Crow—"debil in de white man"—grew more severe and galling each year, until life in the South was intolerable for a black man. And at the same time, finally, there was a reasonable hope of escape from this suffering because of the Great War, as it approached and while it was going on. At precisely the time war production needed all the labor it could get, immigration was sharply curtailed, dropping from 1,218,480 in 1914 to 326,700 in 1915, to under 300,000 in 1916 and 1917, and finally to 110,618 in 1918—less than 10 per cent of the 1914 figure.[8] If immigration had continued at the 1914 rate, almost 5,000,000 more immigrants would have entered the United States by the end of the war, and war production could probably have employed almost all the workers among them. It seems reasonable to believe, therefore, that even if one accepts the top figure of 1,000,000 black migrants during that period, they and the immigrants who did manage to enter the country during the peak production years could not have filled the void. Such friction, then, as developed between black and white workers was probably not based on economic competition so much as on racism.

Woodson claims that even before the unskilled and semiskilled black laborers went North, there was a substantial movement in that direction by educated and professional-level black people— the group that DuBois named the Talented Tenth—who could no longer bear the violence, intimidation, and suppression that were part of everyday life in the South.[9] The increasing callousness of the Republican administrations of Roosevelt and Taft badly shook their faith in the party of liberation. The Brownsville incident of 1906, when President Roosevelt and Secretary of War Taft arbitrarily punished 167 black soldiers, may have been final proof that blacks were deserted by the federal government and must look after themselves. These political facts may have motivated some of the poor, uneducated blacks also to leave the South, although by and large they clung to their faith in the party of emancipation. When Ray Stannard Baker asked a black man why he was leaving Atlanta (after a riot there in 1908) for Washington, D.C., the answer was: "Well, you see, I want to be as near the flag as I can."[10]

According to several contemporaneous studies of the motives of migrants, most blacks left the South simply to be able to feed themselves and their families. George Edmund Haynes, one of the Urban League founders, reported in 1912 that of southern black migrants in New York City, 47.1 per cent had come for better jobs.[11] In a 1917 study made for the Secretary of Labor, again the economic motive came first. In the light of what has been said in previous pages about the condition of southern blacks, a rundown of all the reasons given in that study is interesting:

1. low wages: "The Negro . . . appears to be interested in having some experience with from four to six times as much pay as he has ever had before" even if, in buying power, 50¢ to $1 a day in the South should equal $2 to $4 a day in the North;

2. bad treatment by whites—all classes of Negroes are dissatisfied with their condition;

3. injustice and evils of tenant farming—difficulty of getting a planter to settle accounts, about which his word cannot be questioned; also, the high prices charged by planters and merchants for necessary supplies;[12]

4. more dissatisfaction than formerly with these conditions, in the light of the world movement for democracy.[13]

Poor pay was the leading reason for migration in a survey of 1917 in the *Crisis*, followed by bad treatment, bad schools, discrimination, and oppression.[14] Abram L. Harris, an economist and informed student of Negro migrations, concluded that all the movements away from the rural South, from the Civil War on, were "fundamentally the result of the growth of machine industry, and of the lack of economic freedom and the non-assurance of a margin of subsistence under the one-crop share system of the agricultural South."[15]

There were undoubtedly some migrants who moved about simply for adventure or to see new places. Out of the 400 interviewed by Epstein, 85 said they were just traveling to see the country. Gilbert Osofsky in his Harlem study speaks of some who were just wanderers, criminals, hoodlums, or adventurers. But most evidence shows, as Louise Venable Kennedy wrote in her study of Negro urbanization, that blacks move about for the same reasons as other American groups—for jobs, education, better conditions—and not because of a racial trait of rootlessness, as many believed.[16] John Daniels in his 1914 book on black people of Boston spoke of the "excessive migratoriness which is inherent in the Negro character." He added, "Obstacles in the environment are not opposed by a quality of rootedness," explaining why almost 2,000 blacks left Boston between 1900 and 1910.[17] But such an attack on character was hardly necessary to explain why numbers of blacks left Boston. Daniels himself mentions a notable decrease of interest and tolerance on the part of white Bostonians. Even more important was the scarcity of any but menial jobs in nonindustrial Boston. Howard Odum, also, spoke of migratoriness as a race characteristic of blacks, claiming that they have little attachment to home, siblings, or parents.[18] Dillard, however, said that migration was motivated by an effort to improve their condition of living, and as such deserved "commendation not condemnation."[19] And the Atlanta *Constitution* stated bluntly: "The Negro does not move North because he is of a restless disposition. He would prefer to stay in his old home if he could do so on a wage basis more equitable to his race."[20]

The industrial cities were magnets. To farm workers in the South who made perhaps $.75 a day, to urban female domestics who might earn from $1.50 to $3.00 a week, the North during the war years beckoned with factory wages as high as $3.00 or $4.00 a day, and domestic pay of $2.50 a day. As the Dillard report pointed out, blacks longed to get more money into their hands, even if more went out of them; and though living was higher in the North, it was generally not 400 per cent higher, as wages might be. A migrant who had gone to Cleveland wrote that he regularly earned $3.60 a day, and sometimes double that, and with the pay of his wife, son, and two oldest daughters, the family took in $103.60 every ten days; the only thing that cost them more than at home, he said, was the rent, $12 a month.[21]

In Pittsburgh in 1918, black migrants were earning between $3.00 and $3.60 a day; only 4 per cent of them had earned that much in the South. A 1919 study showed that only 5 per cent of migrants in Pittsburgh earned less than $2.00 a day; 56 per cent of them had earned less than $2.00 a day in the South. A migrant working in a Newark, New Jersey, dye plant made $2.75 a day plus a rent-free room, and the company had paid his fare North; back home he would have earned less than $1.00 for a long day's work on a farm. Tenant farmers in the Deep South often made less than $15 a month; in 1920, the average annual income of a rural Negro family in Georgia was $290. Even where there was some industry, as in the foundries around Birmingham, unskilled workers got a top of $2.50 for a nine-hour day, while the same sort of worker could make $4.50 a day in Illinois. In Haynes's survey of Negro migrants in New York City, the great majority reported earning from 50 to 100 per cent more than they had in the South.[22]

In the complex of motives active upon most migrants it is hard to assess the weight of better educational opportunities for their children. Letters of potential migrants to Emmett Scott and others often speak of this motive. One such letter, written by a representative of a group of 200 men in Mobile, said the men didn't care where they went "just so they cross the Mason and Dixie line" to "where a negro man can appreshate beaing a man" and give his children a good education.[23] Southern politicians of the Vardaman stamp were constantly trying to reduce the little schooling black children got. As governor of Mississippi, Vardaman told the legislature in 1906: "It is your function to put a stop to the worse than wasting of half a million dollars annually" —the cost of black schools—"to the vain purpose of trying to make something of the negro which the Great Architect . . . failed to provide for in the original plan of creation."[24] The black man had no vote, and without a vote he was not likely to enlist any politician in the cause of black education. When Powdermaker's study of Mississippi was made in the 1930s, black schooling was still brief and inadequate; she found fifth-grade children, in that grade because of automatic promotions, who could not read; and she found black parents, especially mothers, with a burning desire to give their children an education at whatever sacrifice to themselves.[25]

Also, it is hard to assay a motive like wishing to appreciate being a man, or wanting to go "where a man's a man" or any place "where a man will Be anything Except a Ker . . . I don't care where so long as I go where a man is a man."[26] The theme is repeated over and over again, and it is a difficult thing to say, a hurtful thing, much harder than simply saying one wants better pay. But it was possibly the overriding reason for leaving the South. W. T. B. Williams, the writer of the report of the Dillard team and its only black member, pointed out that although better pay was most frequently named as a reason for migrating, "the Negro really cares very little for money as such. Cupidity is hardly a Negro vice." He quoted a Florida woman as saying: "Negroes are not so greatly disturbed about wages. They are tired of being treated as children; they want to be men."[27]

Southern blacks were tired of "bene dog as [if] I was a beast";[28] of never, never being addressed, as they must always address the white man, with a title of respect. Powdermaker says that in Mississippi whites will address a black grade school teacher as "doctor" or "professor" to avoid the Mr., Mrs., or Miss; the consistent withholding of those titles endowed what is a mere polite form with such symbolic force that blacks felt the values of the whole system were concentrated in that Mr. or Mrs. or Miss, and not to be called so meant to be outcast by the system.[29] The sense of being outside the society was reinforced by the equally consistent practice of better-class whites of addressing even the meanest, most illiterate white laborer or loafer as Mr., a cheap way of flattering him into docility by giving him, through the magic of the title, assurance that he was a white man and that as such he shared the superiority of other white men to blacks. This was most damaging to the black man's sense of who he was; because if he, a respectable black, perhaps well educated and fairly prosperous, was not treated like even the dregs of white society, then perhaps he was a different species, not a man at all.

In the many bitter complaints of blacks that they were never Mr. in the South although the white man always was, and in the boast of a migrant writing home that in the North you didn't have to "sir" the white men you worked with—in these there is the cry of the dispossessed and disinherited, a summing up of all the reasons for the black migration. A black minister in Philadelphia put it this way to Ray Stannard Baker: "Well, they're treated more like men up here in the North, that's the secret of it. There's prejudice here, too, but the color line isn't drawn in their faces at every turn as it is in the South. It all gets back to a question of manhood."[30]

Scott said that fear of mob violence and lynching were frequently alleged reasons for migrating, and Booker T. Washington had said that "for every lynching that takes place . . . a score of colored people leave . . . for the city."[31] In the statements of migrants themselves, however, these reasons are not mentioned nearly so often as jobs, pay, justice, better living, and education. Charles Johnson came to the conclusion that persecution, and its ultimate expression in lynching, were not nearly such dominant stimuli to migration as the hope of economic betterment. He claimed that many black migrants—almost 43 per cent of them—had gone not North but Southwest, mostly to Arkansas, Oklahoma, and Texas—where economic opportunities might be better but where mob violence was far from uncommon; and that Jasper County in Georgia, and Jefferson County in Alabama, both with fearsome lynching records, had increases rather than declines of black population during the migration period. Kennedy's findings indicated that insecurity of property and life was more likely a supporting cause of migration than a fundamental one, underlying the frequently named reasons of social and educational inequities, humiliations, and insults. In Dutcher's analysis of changes during the 1910–20 decade is the statement that "social grievances appear never to have been sufficient of themselves to produce any considerable movement of the Negro population," and that economic betterment had much greater force.[32] It is amazing, if true, that fear of lynching should not have been a chief reason for flight, considering that ninety-three blacks were lynched in 1908, and fifty, sixty, seventy, or more each year (except 1917) from then until 1920; but the fear may have been too terrible to be given expression in so many words.

Also, there appears to have been a generation gap that made for different motives among older and younger blacks. Many of the older generation, although desperately in need of financial succor, were not so rebellious against "keeping their place." But their sons, who had some schooling, who could read, did not take kindly to the old customs. They were not going to endure being knocked about and beaten on the job "to an extent hardly believable," as the Labor Department reported, and hit with anything that came to the white man's hand, a tool or a piece of lumber. Particularly they resented abuse when their women were with them, and black women were so terrified of what their men might do and what might happen to them as a result, that often the women defended themselves rather than expose their husbands or male friends to danger.[33] A young black said to his father, who was trying to persuade him not to migrate to Chicago: "When a young white man talks rough to me, I can't talk rough to him. You can stand that; I can't. I have some education, and inside I has the feelin's of a white man. I'm goin'."[34]

Words and phrases in the letters of those who hoped to migrate convey their feelings of despair, urgency, and sometimes fear for their lives:

. . . twenty families want to leave "this hard luck place. . . . Please find someone that need this kind of a people and send at once for us. . . . We can't talk to you over the phone here we are afraid to. They don't want to hear one say that he or she wants to leave here if we do we are apt to be killed. . . ."[35]

"I am so sick I am so tired of such conditions that I sometimes think that life for me is not worth while. . . ."

"things is afful hear in the south. . . ."

"this tormenting place. . . ."

"our chance here is so poor. . . ."

"We are sick to get out of the solid south. . . ."

"the people is getting so bad with us black people down south hear . . . help me get my family away. . . ."[36]

Help, help, help. Over and over again in the letters written to Scott, to Robert Abbott, to anyone who might tell them what to do, there is the cry for help in getting a job, decent wages, decent treatment, education for the children, appreciation of one's manhood.

Those who had left early wrote home about freedom and jobs in the North. Labor agents came South recruiting for the big industrial companies, especially the railroads. The Chicago *Defender* carried northern help-wanted ads and detailed accounts of southern lynchings in its "national edition," widely read in the South, thus both pulling and pushing black people. The idea of "exodus" became surrounded with religious fervor. Many believed that God had opened a way for them to escape oppression. Scott described a group of 147 Mississippi blacks who, when they crossed the Ohio River to freedom, knelt, prayed, and sang hymns; they stopped their watches to symbolize the end of their old life.[37] "Exodus" was a matter of excited secret discussion among southern blacks. Anyone who advised against going was suspected of being in the pay of whites. If a black businessman opposed migration, his customers began to vanish; a minister who preached against it from the pulpit was stabbed the next day.[38] Rumors of jobs and of transportation to them increased unrest. Incautiously, many blacks sold or gave away their belongings and followed any crowd of migrants without an idea of their destination. Some rural areas emptied out so thoroughly that one old woman complained she hadn't enough friends left to give her a decent funeral.[39]

"I should have been here twenty years ago," a man wrote back from the North. "I just begin to feel like a man. . . . My children are going to the same school with the whites and I don't have to humble to no one. I have registered. Will vote in the next election and there isn't any yes Sir and no Sir. It's all yes and no, Sam and Bill."[40] A man wrote from Philadelphia telling of good pay, $75 a month, enough so he could carry insurance in case of illness, and added that there you "don't have to mister every little white boy comes along" and that he hadn't heard "a white man call a colored a nigger" since he'd been North; what was more, he could sit where he chose on the streetcars—not that he craved to sit with whites "but if I have to pay the same fare I have learn to want the same acomidation"; still, this far from rootless wanderer would always "love the good old South," he said.[41] A Columbia, South Carolina, Negro paper reported that a migrant brother had come home for a visit with "more than one hundred dollars and plenty of nice clothes."[42] All this was hallelujah news to the home folks. They could easily ignore the occasional cautionary letter, like one from a Cleveland migrant who warned of loafers, gamblers, and pickpockets and said the city streets weren't safe at night.[43] An unnamed but allegedly widely respected black educator is reported to have said: "Uncle Sam is the most effective [labor] agent at this time. All who are away are writing for others to come on in, the water's fine."[44]

Stimulating the urge to "vote with their feet," as the migration was sometimes called, were the solicitations of northern labor agents. In 1916, the first year of large-scale movement, most agents were representing railroads or the mines. Baker reported: "Trains were backed into several Southern cities and hundreds of Negroes were gathered up in a day, loaded into the cars, and whirled away to the North." For example, in February 1917 a special train was sent to carry 191 black migrants from Bessemer, Alabama, to Pittsburgh at a cost to a coal company of $3,391.95.[45] So great was the excitement, Baker said, that Negroes "deserted their jobs and went to the trains without notifying their employers or even going home."[46] Between 75,000 and 100,000 got to Pennsylvania that way, Baker said, many of them to work for the Pennsylvania and Erie railroads, and still more for the steel mills, munitions plants, and other heavy industries.[47] As might be expected, men so hastily and haphazardly gathered up included a good share of shiftless characters, and in addition, the companies had not prepared for their sudden arrival the necessary housing or facilities; because of this combination of circumstances, many of the labor recruits drifted off the job before they had worked out the railroad fare the companies had advanced.[48]

Some of the labor agents were salaried employees of large industrial companies, and these included some blacks. Others were independent employment agents who charged the migrants from $1.00 to $3.00 for placing them in jobs, and collected from the companies as well if they could get anything. Often the labor recruiters gained access to Negro quarters in the cities where they worked by disguising themselves as salesmen or insurance agents. There were probably some honest men among them, but others were flagrantly unscrupulous in their promises. An agency soliciting workers in the Birmingham and Bessemer areas advertized in such phrases as: "Let's go back north where there are no labor troubles, no strikes, no lockouts; Large coal, good wages, fair treatment; Two weeks pay; Good houses; We ship you and your household goods; All colored ministers can go free; Will advance you money if necessary; Scores of men have written us thanking us for sending them; Go now while you have the chance."[49] Some of the "agents" were downright crooks who collected fees from men wanting to migrate and then failed to be at the depot where they were supposed to rendezvous with their clients. Such was the fate of 1,800 Louisiana blacks who paid $2.00 each to an agent who promised them jobs in Chicago but never made good on the promise. The hardship was greatest when men had quit their jobs in the expectation of leaving the South.[50] Micheaux described one agent who, after collecting $3.00 from a man, sent him to several places in search of imaginary jobs; in the end, the agent refused to refund more than $1.00, although he had done nothing for his client. Another racket was to induce ignorant black girls to sign contracts they could not read that obligated them for the cost of their journey plus a placement fee; in many cases the agents were recruiting for brothels, although what they promised the girls was domestic service.[51]

Alarm spread throughout the white South as farm laborers and city menial and domestic help drifted off in twos, twenties, and two hundreds. State laws and city ordinances were passed to oust or curb the agents who were taking most of the workers. In the light of complaints against the agents by a number of migrants, it seems believable that licensing laws for agents were meant at first to protect black workers as well as their white employers. In South Carolina, for example, an 1891 law requiring all labor agents to pay $500 for a license might simply have been aimed at assuring the reliability of the man promising work out of the state; but when in 1907 the fee was raised to $2,000, it was due simply to panic on the part of whites who saw their cheap labor force dwindling. According to Scott, a license cost $1,000 in Jacksonville, under penalty of a $600 fine and 60 days in jail; in Alabama the state, city, and county fees totaled from $1,000 to $1,250; in Macon, a license cost $25,000, and the applicant had to be vouched for by 10 local ministers and 35 local businessmen, which seems not so much regulatory as prohibitive, as the Atlanta *Constitution* called such licensing. In Montgomery, recruiting labor for out-of-state jobs was punishable by a $100 fine and 6 months at hard labor on a convict gang. Force was not infrequently used to prevent the taking of blacks North, Scott says. Labor agents were arrested. Trains carrying migrants were stopped, the blacks forced to return, and the agents beaten. Blacks might be terrorized or lynched on suspicion of trying to leave the state.[52] "But they might as well have tried to stop by ordinance the migration of the boll-weevil," Baker said;[53] by ordinance, or by hitting them on the head, one by one.

Robert Abbott, editor and publisher of the Chicago *Defender* and himself a migrant from the "Negro town" of Yamacraw, was the loudest single voice calling for the northward flow of black labor, but not the only one.[54] Many other Negro papers also encouraged migration, Baker reported. The Richmond *Reformer* spoke out against Jim Crow, segregation, and living conditions "like cattle, hogs or sheep, penned in" as evils that black people in the South must continue to endure "until they rise up in mass and oppose it openly"; self-respecting Negroes, said the Timmonsville (South Carolina) *Watchman,* should take a hint from a recent lynching and "get away at the earliest possible moment."[55] But it was Abbott who fleshed out the vision of escape, who gave it a definite and dramatic form—even a birthday: the Great Northern Drive of May 15, 1917. Carl Sandburg wrote in the Chicago *Daily News:* "The Defender more than any other one agency was the big cause of the 'Northern fever' and the big exodus from the South."[56] A Georgia paper called the *Defender* "the greatest disturbing element that has yet entered Georgia." The U. S. Department of Labor said that in some sections the *Defender* was probably more effective in carrying off labor than all the agents put together: "It sums up the Negro's troubles and keeps them constantly before him, and it points out in terms he can understand the way of escape."[57]

Abbott was, according to one's lights, either the founder of and greatest force in Negro journalism or a sensationalist and showman. Abbott's biographer Roi Ottley says that to Chicagoan Julius Rosenwald, admirer of the old conservative leader Booker Washington, Abbott was "a monkey with a shotgun, who will hurt anybody"; but to Charles S. Johnson he was "a man with a sense of crisis."[58] A very black black man, Abbott was fiercely dedicated to improving the life of black people; he was also determined to build for the *Defender* the largest circulation of any Negro newspaper. Through the migration he fulfilled both purposes. Between 1916 and 1918, the circulation of the *Defender* increased from 10,000 to 93,000.

Abbott put out a "national edition" of his weekly, aimed at southern blacks. It carried in red ink such headlines as: 100 NEGROES MURDERED WEEKLY IN UNITED STATES BY WHITE AMERICANS; LYNCHING—A NATIONAL DISGRACE; and WHITE GENTLEMAN RAPES COLORED GIRL.[59] Accompanying a lynching story was a picture of the lynch victim's severed head, with the caption: NOT BELGIUM —AMERICA.[60] Poems entitled *Land of Hope* and *Bound for the Promised Land* urged blacks to go North, and editorials boosted Chicago as the best place for them to go. Want ads offered jobs at attractive wages in and around Chicago. In news items, anecdotes, cartoons, and photos, the *Defender* crystallized the underlying economic and social causes of black suffering into immediate motives for flight. Repeated stories of those who were leaving the South or who were already in the North conveyed the excitement of a mass movement under way and created an atmosphere of religious hysteria; the *Defender* called the migration the "Flight out of Egypt" and the migrants sang "Going into Canaan." The more people who left, inspired by *Defender* propaganda, the more wanted to go, so the migration fed on itself until in some places it turned into a wild stampede. Even illiterate people bought the paper, as a status symbol.[61] A black leader in Louisiana was quoted as saying, "My people grab it [the *Defender*] like a mule grabs a mouthful of fine fodder."[62] Sandburg wrote that there was in Chicago "a publicity or propaganda machine that directs its appeals or carries on an agitation that every week reaches hundreds of thousands of people of the colored race in the southern states."[63]

Soon a number of towns prohibited the sale of the paper and confiscated any copies that arrived by mail or express. "A colored man caught with a copy in his possession was suspected of 'Northern fever' and other so-called disloyalties," Carl Sandburg wrote.[64] Young black students were arrested for reading aloud "migration poems" from the *Defender*. Two southern agent-correspondents for the paper were killed, Roi Ottley says, and a dozen others were run out of their hometowns.[65] How then did the "propaganda machine" work, in the face of suppression, intimidation, and violence? How did the paper reach the South without being mailed or expressed? It is one of the great stories of newspapering, as Ottley tells it.

Abbott enlisted the aid of two very mobile groups of black people, the railroad men and the entertainers. Chicago was the end of the North–South railroad lines, and a great junction. Hundreds of Pullman porters, dining-car waiters, and traveling stage people passed through it, some of them on their way to remote whistle-stops in the South. The *Defender* paid many of them to pick up bundles of the newspaper in Chicago and drop them along their routes at points where local distributors would meet the trains, get the bundles, and circulate them. In a town where the *Defender* was unknown, the porters would give copies away to any black person they saw. Stage people took bundles of papers and distributed them free in the theaters. The well-known concert singer Sissieretta Jones, who was called the "black Patti" in the patronizing style of the day, asked the ushers in theaters where she performed to give out free copies to all comers.[66]

By such devices the circulation of the *Defender* soared to 283,-571 by 1920, with about two thirds of its readers outside of Chicago. This was by far the largest circulation any black newspaper had ever achieved. If each copy reached five readers, a reasonable guess, about 1,500,000 blacks saw it.[67]

Abbott's master stroke in materializing a migration that in 1916 was more rumored than real was the setting of a date, a specific month and day in 1917, for what the *Defender* called "the Great Northern Drive." The incendiary message spread that on May 15 railroad cars would back into the stations of southern towns prepared to carry North any who wanted to go, at a very low fare. The word struck southern blacks with messianic force. There was to be a second coming of freedom on May 15, and it behooved everyone to be ready.

Letters poured into the *Defender* office. "We will come by the thousands." . . . "I am expecting to leave the South about the 15th of May and will bring my family later on. Answer soon." . . . "I want to come North on 15th of May, & I would like to get a job at once." . . . "I seen in it where cars would be here for the 15 of May. . . . I am a poor woman and have a husband and five children living and three dead. . . . This is my native home but it is not fit to live in . . . will you please let me know where the cars is going to stop . . . hoping to hear from you soon from your needed and worried friend." . . . "Since the Northern Drive has begun I have decided to return to Chicago." . . . "We want more understanding about it for there is a great many wants to get ready for that day & the depot agents never gives us any satisfaction when we ask for they dont want us to leave here . . . please publish . . . just what the fair will be on that day." . . . "hearing that the excursion will be $6.00 from here north on the 15 and having a large family, I could profit by it if it is really true. . . . Nearly the whole of the south is getting ready for the drive. . . ."[68]

They went with whatever possessions they could carry, "wearing overalls and housedresses, a few walking barefoot," Ottley says.[69] Although it is hard to see how they took their goats, pigs, chickens, dogs, and cats along, as he claims, they certainly must have carried provisions for their long, long journeys, a thousand miles or more for many of them, days and nights of travel with no prospect of any creature comforts along the way. To Chicago from Savannah was 1,027 railroad miles; to New York from San Antonio, 1,916 miles; to Cincinnati from Jacksonville, 822 miles; to Newark from Vicksburg, 1,273 miles; to Detroit from New Orleans, 1,096 miles; to Cleveland from Mobile, 1,046 miles. Some stopped at Chicago for a time before going to their destinations, but most went straight through: from Florida and Georgia to Pennsylvania and New York; from Alabama, Mississippi, Tennessee, and Louisiana to Illinois and Michigan.[70] Most of these people had probably never been more than twenty miles from their homes.

The regular passenger fare was $.01991 per mile in 1915, $.02051 at the end of 1916; then $.02097 in 1917, $.02421 in 1918, $.02648 in 1919, and $.02755 in 1920—an increase of 40 per cent in five years. In 1918, for example, it would have cost $22.52 per person from New Orleans to Chicago, or over $135 for a family of six. A relatively short trip, Norfolk to Pittsburgh, would have cost a family of six $73. Obviously, very few migrants could afford this kind of money. Many workers traveling to definite jobs had their fares advanced or paid outright by waiting employers. Among almost 500 Pittsburgh migrants, however, over 80 per cent said they had paid their own fares. Often these were special excursion rates, usually offered by the railroads during slack summer months. So, for instance, a man from St. Petersburg had heard that $19 would take him to New York; less likely was the rumor the New Orleans woman reported that for the Great Northern Drive the fare to Chicago would be $6.00. Some believed the *Defender* would send them free tickets on request. A Mobile man wrote the *Defender* that a labor agent had promised him a ticket to Detroit and a job there for a $2.00 cash advance and payment of $24.92 after he started work, a bargain but believable because the fare would have cost around $22, leaving almost $3.00 for the agent's fee. Another way of getting one's fare advanced was through "Justice's Tickets," which were given to young women by agents who collected fees from both the women and their waiting employers. In exchange for such a ticket, a girl would agree to pay the agent an amount equal to one or two months' wages, and would sign a contract promising to work for the person who paid her transportation expenses and to bind over her personal belongings as collateral until the agent's fee was paid. Most of the girls had no idea what they contracted for. All they knew was, they were promised easy work, a good time, and good pay.[71]

One cheap way to travel was in a group. The *Defender* encouraged the formation of "clubs" of ten to fifty persons and arranged special fares and travel dates with the railroad companies.[72] Many people wrote to the newspaper that they could bring "about 8 or 10 men" or "a family of (11) eleven more or less" or "15 or 20 good men" or "25 women and men," and so on up to "300 or 500 men and women" and finally "as many men as you want." Some of these correspondents sent stamped return envelopes and asked the paper not to publish their letters—"whatever you do, don't publish my name in your paper"—or asked that, if an answer was sent by wire, there should be no mention of the number of people because "if you say 15 or 20 mans they will put me in jail." "This is among us collerd," says one letter offering to bring 20 men and their families.[73]

With so many concerned for secrecy, many must have been too frightened to write at all. They never revealed the presence among them of labor agents. Migrants described how they had to slip away from their homes at night, walk to some railroad station where they were not known, and there board a train for the North. If they were found to have tickets, the police confiscated them. If three or four blacks were discovered together it was assumed that they were "conspiring to go North" and they would be arrested on some trumped-up charge.[74]

For migrants to New York from a coastal city in the South—and most of those who went to New York were from the South Atlantic States—the cheapest and most direct passage was by boat. Steerage fare from Virginia, from which most New York migrants came, was $5.50 or $6.00, including meals. The Old Dominion Line ran boats twice a week from Virginia to New York, and the Baltimore, Chesapeake & Atlantic Railway ran steamers from Baltimore, Washington, and as far south as Florida. By train it would have cost at least $7.50 from Norfolk to New York City, without meals. So the boat was a good buy, although blacks might find themselves in a separate section of the vessel with the household pets of white travelers.[75]

Toward the end of the peak migration period another category of southern blacks settled in northern cities: soldiers returning from France. Rudolph Fisher, a writer of the period, spoke in a short story of a family of Waxhaw, North Carolina, whose son "had gone to France in the draft and, returning, had never got any nearer home than Harlem."[76] There were many such men whose fare, in a roundabout way, had been paid by Uncle Sam. "How're you gonna keep 'em down on the farm,/ After they've seen Paree?" a popular song asked.

The rapid flow northward of black people, especially from 1916 when war production went into high gear, aroused much concern and discussion among whites and blacks, North and South. The word "exodus" was apparently so current that Octavus Roy Cohen used it as both noun and verb in his spurious Negro stories of the early twenties: "the merrymakers exodusted" from a party, he wrote; and, there was a "complete exodus from Decatur."[77] Census figures show that in 1900 only 15.6 per cent of black people (1,373,996) lived in a state other than that of their birth, whereas in 1910 the percentage born elsewhere had increased to 16.6 (1,616,608), and in 1920 to 19.9 (2,054,242).

Of the 300,000 to 1,000,000 blacks estimated by contemporaries to have gone North, almost all went to urban centers. In 1900, 22.7 per cent of Negroes lived in cities, North and South; in 1910 this had increased to 24.4 per cent, and in 1920 to 34 per cent, in numbers totaling more than 3,500,000. By 1920, almost 40 per cent of the black population in the North was concentrated in the eight cities of Chicago, Detroit, New York, Cleveland, Cincinnati, Columbus, Philadelphia, and Pittsburgh, although those cities contained only 20 per cent of the total northern population. The city with the most dramatic percentage increase in black population between 1910 and 1920 was Detroit, by an astounding 611.3 per cent; Cleveland came next with a 307.8 per cent increase; then Chicago, 148.2 per cent; New York, 66.3 per cent; Indianapolis, 59 per cent; Cincinnati, 53.2 per cent; and Pittsburgh, 47.2 per cent. In numbers Chicago gained nearly 65,500 black residents, New York 61,400, and Detroit 36,240.[78]

A question that immediately comes to mind is: what did these southern people know how to do that would earn them a living in the North? Since so much of the South was rural, it is amazing the number of occupations represented by the migrants whose letters are in the Scott collection. But indications are that about half the migrants came from towns, a Labor Department survey found. The largest number said they wanted work as laborers at unspecified common labor, with some longshoremen, stevedores, freight handlers, stokers, miners, packers, and warehousemen; many of these men had experience in southern industries such as lumbering, railroading, iron and steel foundries, sawmills, and turpentine stills.[79] The next largest category was the semiskilled or skilled craftsman: plumbers and roofers, painters and plasterers, cleaners and pressers, hotel waiters, brickmakers and bricklayers, machinists and machinists' helpers, caulkers, carpenters, woodworkers, cabinetmakers, mailmen, auto workers, engineers, blacksmiths, glaziers, lumber graders and inspectors, foundry workers, and a large number of molders. The majority of women who wanted to migrate, and some of the men, sought menial or domestic jobs: cooks, laundresses, baby nurses, housemaids, butler-chauffeurs, janitors. Among the businesses represented by migrants were insurance man, barber, hairdresser, laundry owner, merchant, and packer and mover—memorably, the moving company owner who called himself "the Daddy of the Transfer business" of Rome, Georgia. In the much smaller class of professionals and white-collar workers the majority were teachers, including the Alcorn College graduate who was four feet, six inches tall and weighed 105 pounds—a woman, presumably, as were many of the teachers who wanted to leave the South. There were also a sixty-three-year-old graduate of Howard University Law School, an eighteen-year-old artist and actor, and a fifteen-year-old cartoonist; also printers, a college-educated bookkeeper, and a stenographer-typist. Many of the educated class expressed their willingness to do any kind of work, even common labor, if only they could get jobs in the North. Only a few who wrote of their wish to migrate described themselves as farmers, and two of these wanted to go to Nebraska and Dakota to farm.[80] But probably many of those who were looking for laborers' jobs were tenant farmers, sharecroppers, and farm workers; and probably also many other rural people could not write or were afraid to, so we do not know about them—they simply disappeared off the farms and took their chances of finding work in northern cities. Baker says that whole tenant-farming areas of Georgia and Alabama were emptied of prime-age workers. A small number wound up in the tobacco fields of Connecticut,[81] but the great majority must have gone to industrial cities. The black rural population of the South dropped by almost 250,-000 between 1910 and 1920.

As the trains and boats pulled out week after week and month after month, the South began to hurt from a loss of the black labor force, especially the Deep South. For the first time in their history, Mississippi and Louisiana showed a decrease in Negro population between 1900 and 1910; and between 1910 and 1920 Mississippi suffered a loss of 129,600 blacks, Louisiana a loss of 180,800. In that decade the black population of the East North Central states increased by 71 per cent, and that of the Middle Atlantic states by over 43 per cent, although the national increase was only 6.5 per cent.[82]

Contemporary estimates by observers such as Baker and Epstein of a million or so migrants seem wildly out of line with the 500,000 figure to be calculated from 1920 census figures, which were not available to them, but it may be that their estimates were more nearly correct than figures arrived at from census returns. For one thing, it has been and remains a fact, substantiated by recent studies by the Census Bureau of its own operation, that black males are significantly undercounted.[83] As this study proceeds to examine the circumstances of migrants in their new homes, a number of reasons will emerge why the census provides no direct, reliable count of the number of black people who went North, and why the early, higher estimates of such informed and interested people as Baker and Epstein, based on direct observation and unofficial inquiries, may very well be nearer the mark.

Another reason to suspect that the number of migrants exceeded census figures is the difficulty or impossibility of achieving a correct count of mulattoes. Mulattoes, for demographic purposes, are "all persons, except full-blood Negroes, with any perceptible trace of Negro blood."[84] This is, in effect, the way most southern states defined a Negro in their new Jim Crow laws around 1900, so that in the South the fairest-skinned person of mixed ancestry was legally subject to every restriction put upon the blackest man in the state. In the light of this, it is interesting that in the first two decades of the Jim Crow constitutions, the census reported a smaller percentage increase of mulattoes in the North and West than in the South. In 1890, according to the census, mulattoes formed 28 per cent of the black population in the North and 13.7 per cent in the South; in 1900 the percentage was 26.6 in the North and 20.1 in the South; and in 1920 the proportion had dropped to 16.5 per cent in the North—a drop of 11.5 per cent since 1890—although in the South it was 15.7 per cent, slightly higher than in 1890. It is not likely that in the North, where miscegenation was not nearly so taboo as in the South, the proportion of light-skinned Negroes to black-skinned would in fact diminish; it is also unlikely that southern mulattoes would not take the opportunity to get out of the South in large numbers when jobs were available in the North. It is far more probable that the percentage of mulattoes in the Negro population only appeared, in census counts, to decrease, while in actuality mulattoes in considerable numbers chose the material advantages of being counted with their white relatives rather than their black ones in the northern cities to which they went and in which, unlike their southern hometowns, they and their family histories were not known.[85]

Between these two circumstances—the undercount of black males by the census and the absorption of mulattoes by the white population—a large error in enumerating southern blacks who went North was not only probable but inescapable.

It is nothing short of amazing that the migration continued and increased, considering the discouragement, intimidation, and harassment the migrants met on every hand. The spirit of the opposition changed as more blacks vanished from the southern scene. In 1911 the New Orleans *Picayune* could still summon bravado and compare the migrants to the "Goths, Huns, Vandals and other barbarians" who had "swarmed into the dominions of ancient Rome,"[86] but as the drift northward swelled, thinking and language became less romantic. Many newspapers openly admitted that the loss of the black labor force would be disastrous:

Everybody seems to be asleep about what is going on right under their noses. That is, everybody but those farmers who have awakened up of mornings recently to find every male Negro over 21 . . . gone—to Cleveland, to Pittsburgh, to Chicago. . . .
Macon (Georgia) *Telegraph*[87]

The black laborer is the best labor the South can get, no other would work long under the same conditions.
Columbus (Georgia) *Enquirer Sun*[88]

Mississippi, hardest hit by the black exodus, with the disappearance of an estimated 130,000,[89] turned against James Vardaman, whose rabble-rousing racist speeches when he was running for governor were believed to be scaring blacks out of the state. The Biloxi *Herald* called Vardaman "the most dangerous man that ever aspired to the governorship of Mississippi." It was unwise to excite prejudice against Negroes, the most valuable labor supply in the state, said the *Herald* editor. The Hazelhurst *Courier* feared that Vardaman's words and actions would disturb these valuable laborers "who are docile and contented." The Natchez *Democrat* went so far as to scorn the issue of race mongelization, a favorite bugaboo of Vardaman's that he counted on to bring out the white vote for him. "What home is threatened with social equality with the Negro?" the *Democrat* scoffed. Very few, in fact; and it is instructive how realistic Mississippi could be when push came to shove.[90]

European immigrants might have served as surrogates for the vanishing black laborers if the South had known how, or really wanted, to attract them. But the southern states were always ambivalent about "foreigners," especially southern, central, and eastern Europeans, as most immigrants were at this time. By 1900 southern states had set up immigration bureaus and even sent labor agents abroad, but immigrants were not attracted as they were to the North. If Baker's information is correct, this is not surprising. A distaste for Italians and others of the "new" immigrants, as those not of northern European derivation were called, was general throughout the country; but in the South these people were treated as badly as Negroes, because they did the same work. In Louisiana, Italian women resented being set to work under black foremen. Mississippi tried to keep children of Italian immigrants out of white schools, and an Italian community leader was taken to the woods and whipped.[91] The Mississippi stand was echoed in the words of the Honorable Jeff Truly, candidate for governor in 1907: "I am opposed to any inferior race. . . . Italians are a threat and a danger to our racial, industrial, and commercial supremacy. . . . As governor of the state, I promise that not one dollar of the state shall be spent for the immigration of any such."[92] With Vardaman damning the blacks and Truly the Italians, the wonder is that Mississippi kept any labor force at all.

Again the paradoxical nature of southern thinking was demonstrated. Young blacks, born a whole generation after Emancipation, were scorned as a worthless lot compared to the old-time darky, who was diligent, faithful, and "orderly"—he knew his place and kept it. "That the 'old-time Negro' is passing away is one of the common sayings all over the South," gently lamented Thomas Nelson Page in the very early years of the century; their former masters, he said, reminiscing about these wonderful old servants and associates "turn away to wipe their eyes."[93] The younger Negroes, Page said, expressing a general opinion, are taught to be rude and insolent, and have lost their skill as workmen.[94] The race situation was less acute and complex, Odum wrote, in sections where the Negroes assumed a submissive attitude than where they were aggressive and obstinate; race relations were less strained where they made a special effort to pass on the outside of a sidewalk.[95] Nevertheless, Southerners did everything they could, according to their various lights, to prevent these rude, insolent, aggressive, obstinate, worthless workers from leaving them. An organization called the Southern Negro Anti-Exodus Association was established in Virginia as early as 1905, to preach contentment to Negroes. White folk warned their black workers of the hardships they would meet in the North: the cold climate and the chilly welcome of prejudiced whites, the crowded dwellings and high rents, the unaccustomed city ways, and the city scalawags both black and white who would cheat them. The sympathetic and liberal-minded Baker wrote that the migrants "do not know how to shop at the stores, they blow out the gas [instead of turning it off], they wear insufficient clothing and catch cold and have pneumonia"; instead of the accustomed "easy-going tasks of the South" they find hard work and "the savage competition of white men."[96]

Baker was too knowledgeable to believe that the black man's tasks in the South were "easy-going."[97] On the contrary, their tasks were rough, long, hard, and ruthlessly disciplined. He was right, however, in commenting that in the South blacks had little competition from white men. Where was the white man who wanted to "work like a nigger" at those "easy-going" tasks?

Baker's affectionate concern and his sentimental fallacies were shared by many decent and wise white Southerners who were honestly worried about how "their" Negroes would make out in the hostile North. Also, they deplored the use of whip and rope to persuade the Negroes to stay in the South, when those were the very reasons they were leaving it. Stop the police roundups, the beatings and the lynchings, and pay the Negro a just wage, said these advocates of reform, and "our" blacks will not desert us. White men who "have allowed negroes to be lynched, five at a time, on nothing stronger than suspicion . . . have allowed whole sections to be depopulated of them,"[98] wrote an outraged Georgia citizen to the newspaper. In Columbia, South Carolina, a newspaper asked its readers: "If you thought you might be lynched by mistake, would you remain in South Carolina?"[99] A Savannah paper said: "The lack of legal protection in the country is a constant nightmare to the colored people."[100] The Atlanta *Constitution* put it bluntly: "This loss of her best labor is another penalty Georgia is paying for her indifference in suppressing mob law."[101] And, said the *Constitution,* setting prohibitive taxes on labor agents "fails to touch the core of the matter" because what the blacks want is a fair wage. "It seems to us," the paper added, "that the subject is too serious, too fraught with menace to our local industries, to be dismissed lightly. The Chamber of Commerce could do no better work than . . . investigate the grievances of the Negro, decide upon the proper remedy, and see that it is enforced."[102]

There was a kind of awakening of appreciation of the Negro as a man rather than a stereotype, but it came too late. An editorial in the Macon *Telegraph* summed up:

Everybody seems to be asleep about what is going on right under our noses—that is, everybody but those farmers who waked up on mornings recently to find every Negro over 21 on their places gone—gone to Cleveland, to Pittsburgh, to Chicago, to Indianapolis.

Better jobs, better treatment, higher pay—the bait held out is being swallowed by thousands of them about us. And while our very solvency is being sucked from underneath us we go about our affairs as usual—our police raid pool rooms for "loafing Negroes," bring in 12, keep them in the barracks all night, and next morning find that 10 of them have steady jobs and were there merely to spend an hour in the only indoor recreation they have; our county officers hear of a disturbance at a Negro resort and bring in fifty-odd men, women, boys, and girls to spend the night in jail, to make a bond at 10 per cent, to hire lawyers, to mortgage half of two months' wages to get back their jobs Monday morning, although but a half-dozen could have been guilty of the disorderly conduct. It was a week following that several Macon employers found good Negroes, men trained in their work, secure and respected in their jobs, valuable assets to their white employers, had suddenly left and gone to Cleveland, "where they didn't arrest 50 niggers for what three of 'em done."[103]

One can see what is meant by the "bait." In northern cities, too, police would "arrest 50 niggers for what three of 'em done" at the time of riots of 1919; but by then a few years of getting ahead socially and economically would have changed these "niggers" into black men, and they would respond differently.

There were southern whites who would have reformed the system if they could. But as one black leader said, "Frankly, the thing that discourages me most is the helplessness of the southern white man who wants to help us," but who feared reprisals if he tried to get fair dealing for blacks in the courts or elsewhere and had to work in secrecy, which was not very effective.[104]

For each calm and reasonable voice there were many racist outcries, ego-satisfying, perhaps, but self-destructive. The Nashville *Banner* advised letting the blacks migrate freely, "to relieve the South of the entire burden and all the brunt of the race problem. . . ."[105] The Vicksburg *Herald* said that "a more equitable distribution of the sons of Ham will teach the Caucasians of the northern States that wherever there is a Negro infusion, there will be a race problem. . . ."[106] These were popular sentiments.

Perhaps every southern point of view was summed up in a statement by Theodore Bilbo, governor of Mississippi in 1920, when the mayor of Chicago inquired of him whether it would be possible to send some of Chicago's surplus of Mississippi migrants back to their home state. Bilbo wired back:

> Your telegram, asking how many Negroes Mississippi can absorb, received. In reply, I desire to state that we have all the room in the world for what we know as N-i-g-g-e-r-s, but none whatever for "colored ladies and gentlemen." If these Negroes have been contaminated with Northern social and political dreams of equality, we cannot use them, nor do we want them. The Negro who understands his proper relation to the white man in this country will be gladly received by the people of Mississippi, as we are very much in need of labor.[107]

"Your neck has been in the yoke," said the *Defender* to its southern black readers. "Will you continue to keep it there because some 'white folks' nigger' wants you to?"[108]

By the term "white folks' nigger" Abbot might have been referring to Dr. Frissell of Hampton Institute, to Kelly Miller or Emmett Scott, or to the greatest of the older leaders, Booker T. Washington himself. Washington was dead (1915) before the *Defender*'s great migration drive, but his was still the big name, especially in the South, although DuBois, James Weldon Johnson, Monroe Trotter, and other younger blacks were becoming known. Washington had fervently advised Negroes to stay in the South, but despite his great reputation and power, some half a million to a million ignored his pleas; nor, in fact, is there evidence that the encouragement to come North voiced by the recently organized NAACP moved any to go who were not so minded. Among the leaders only Robert Abbott, it would appear, who spoke to the poor southern black man and woman in terms of exodus, of jobs, of security of person and property, had any direct or considerable influence on the migration.

Frissell, although he chided southern whites for not properly appreciating the "kindly, helpful body of colored people among them," nevertheless told Negroes that "the very best place for the great mass of the colored people is in the South," and that "the very best educational institute is the small home in the country" and "that little piece of land."[109] But half a million suppressed and seething blacks were not moved by Frissell's argument. For them the *Independent*, a black newspaper in Atlanta, spoke more to the point: "And yet they [our white neighbors] claim to be our best friends; in heaven's name, how can they be or how can they convince us that they are when they treat us in such a manner? They talk about our migration and are asking the leading Negroes to join with the best white people in persuading our people to remain South; that this is the best place for them! Neither the leading Negroes nor the best white people can ever convince the Negroes that the South is the best place for them in the face of such treatment and discrimination as are meted out to him. . . ."[110]

When Booker T. Washington said that "the Negro is at his best in the South," that in the South Negroes would find their best economic opportunities and highest moral life, who could keep a straight face except his white patrons and supporters? Washington's famous "gospel of the toothbrush" was wasted on the grits-and-gravy masses who didn't need teeth so much as something to chew. His assurance that "there are few places in the South now where public sentiment would permit such organizations [as the Ku Klux Klan] to exist" would be cold comfort to a stiffening corpse on a rope. His philosophy that "the individual who can do something that the world wants done will, in the end, make his way regardless of his race" suited Washington himself perfectly, but would not inspire hope in a convict laborer even though he was building a road that Georgia wanted built.[111] To those with enough leisure time so that the work ethic was only an intellectual exercise, Booker T. Washington and his gospel of salvation through achievement came "within the realm of those great super-events which seem to come providentially at rare intervals in the world's history," to quote one of his admirers, John Daniels of Boston.[112] To Theodore Roosevelt, who dined with Washington, he was "a genius such as does not arise in a generation," and to another great achiever, Andrew Carnegie, he was "the combined Moses and Joshua of his people."[113] He was "a wise counselor and safe leader" to the Atlanta *Constitution,* "an advocate of high morality, sublime ethics and bath tubs"[114] to the Memphis *Commercial Appeal,* but also, to the same paper—alas for Washington's faith that by achievement blacks could transcend the barriers of race—he was just another "Alabama coon."[115]

Although the very pro-Washington Negro newspaper, the New York *Age,* warned skilled southern black workmen to "think carefully" before migrating where skilled jobs were hard to get;[116] and although Kelly Miller declared that "the Negro's industrial opportunities lie in the black belts" and that the South was his "Land of Goshen";[117] and although Emmett Scott was heartened by the sentiments and promises of reform-minded Southerners to make the South flow with milk and honey for its black people;[118] nevertheless, the newer leaders called on blacks to pick up their buckets—full of a bitter draught, not the fresh, sweet water Washington lauded in his Atlanta Exposition speech[119]— and get out of the South. DuBois, whose history of the Negro was published, portentously, the year Washington died, urged blacks not only to fight obstructions to equality, such as capitalist oppression, but to make their own way to power, including a planned migration from southern mob rule and robbery. But DuBois's influence was not at that time strong enough in the South to stimulate the march to jobs and a very qualified freedom, any more than Washington's considerably greater influence could prevent it.

If there was finally a black Joshua it was Robert Abbott, blowing the trumpet call of jobs through a rolled-up *Defender;* his troops were the Pullman porters and road shows, with labor agents as mercenaries. Half a million blacks followed behind. Where the metaphor breaks down is that their Jericho was a dirty, crowded, sickly, dangerous city ghetto, which must often have seemed scarcely worth the trouble of getting to.

But the getting there was a tremendous feat of initiative, planning, courage, and perseverance—qualities never appearing in any catalogue of Negro traits drawn up by white people, yet here demonstrated incontestibly not by one or two "exceptional individuals," as blacks were called who did not fit the stereotype, but by at least five hundred thousand perfectly average southern Negroes. They were not passive reactors, waiting for something to happen to them; they made it happen.

CHAPTER 3

City Within a City

Ever since a traveling preacher had first told him about the place, King Solomon Gillis had longed to come to Harlem. . . . In Harlem, black was white. You had rights that could not be denied you; you had privileges, protected by law. And you had money. Everybody in Harlem had money. It was a land of plenty.

City of Refuge
by Rudolph Fisher, 1925

Negroes in Illinois are legally entitled to all the rights and privileges of other citizens. Actually, however, their participation in public benefits in practically every field is limited by some circumvention of the law.

Report of Chicago Commission on Race Relations, 1922

As United States involvement in the war neared, booming northern industry could absorb any amount of cheap black unskilled labor, but the industrial cities to which the migrants swarmed became less and less receptive as more and more arrived. White communities responded with fear and hostility. Whatever abolitionist sympathies an earlier generation of Northerners might have had, "the men of the newer generation are not only not interested, but are impatient of being worried with a problem so essentially disagreeable," Baker wrote in 1916; "They dislike, quite frankly, to see Negroes crowding into Northern cities. . . ."[1] Considering that about 14 million people had come to the United States from foreign countries between 1860 and 1900, people who had to get along themselves in a new country, who had no involvement with black people, slavery, or abolition, and who almost all settled in the cities of the North, it is hardly surprising that they were uninterested, and impatient with the "problem." But regardless of their feelings, black people were crowding in—black Southerners who knew no more about foreign-born Northerners than the immigrants knew about them.

Baker had the foresight to warn that the black migrants could not be allowed to "fester and stew in city swamps without endangering the whole body politic."[2] He sounded a sensible note of alarm: "On wide Southern farms they can live to themselves; in Northern cities they become part of ourselves."[3] Surely many white Northerners realized this with a shock of horror, as they looked at the poor, ignorant, often sick blacks from the southern backwoods who appeared on their cities' streets—people who did not know the use of a flush toilet or bathtub, or the value of privacy, or the need for refrigeration and sanitation, for air and light and space and proper clothing and medicine and rest and wholesome recreation. A more reforming age might have tried to teach and heal and provide for the newcomers, so that they might benefit, not harm, the body politic. But the common response to Baker's tocsin was to lock the gates, to insure that these people did *not* infect the whole society, did *not* "become part of ourselves." The response was to shut them off in inner cities or outer cities, ghettos where they would not have to contend with the things they were not used to, neither the toilets nor the privacy nor the iceboxes nor even, sometimes, a bed to call their own. But what was ignored was that the migrants came out of their ghettos every day to work in the white city, bringing the smell of the swamps with them, and returned every night to fester and stew, a little more aware of how other Americans lived and earned, a little more resentful of their own condition. Rage smoldered, at intervals erupting into violence. Ghetto containment proved no answer at all, but only a buying of time—which has now run out. Now the cities must grimly face the question they locked the ghetto gates on fifty, sixty years ago.

"Generally speaking," Baker commented in 1908, "the more Negroes the sharper the expression of prejudice."[4] Other students of the black migration made the same comment. Of San Francisco, where there were very few blacks, James Weldon Johnson said in 1905 that the black community there agreed it was the best city in the United States for Negroes. "I found it a freer city than New York. I encountered no bar against me in hotels, restaurants, theaters, or other places of public accommodation. . . ."[5] This perhaps had partly to do with the frontier personality of San Francisco, and partly, no doubt, with the kind of people in Johnson's set—no backwoodsmen in overalls and housedresses, one may assume. But certainly the chief reason for acceptance was a matter of numbers. Not even the most cultured black in New York, into which black people were pouring, could say of it what Johnson found true in San Francisco.[6] In the West, there were so few blacks that whites had no reason to fear becoming the minority group; so the restrictions that express that fear, and are rationalized into attitudes of prejudice, were not appropriate.

The same thing was true in the Middle West and the East in the early stages of the migration. There was no great buildup of pressure in Chicago as its black population grew from 30,000 in 1900 to 44,000 in 1910 and to 50,000 in 1915. The white population, too, was growing, and so the proportion of blacks to whites increased almost imperceptibly, from 1.8 per cent in 1900 to 2 per cent in 1910. But by 1920 the proportion of blacks to whites had doubled to 4 per cent, and the number of blacks had more than doubled, to 109,000. Between 1910 and 1920 the white population increased by only 21 per cent, as the war slowed and then virtually stopped immigration; but the black population in that decade increased by close to 150 per cent. Then the boiler burst. After a very bloody riot in 1919, the alarmed city of Chicago somewhat late in the day felt the need for a Commission on Race Relations. New York City went through a similar if not quite so dramatic experience. Its black population grew by over 66 per cent in the 1910–20 decade, from 91,700 to 152,400. And then race violence erupted in New York, too, in serious form.[7]

The Chicago Commission on Race Relations found that in some neighborhoods blacks and whites lived together in reasonable harmony; trouble occurred where blacks and whites were battling for control of an area, and especially where the whites who felt threatened had time and money to organize an opposition, as in Kenwood and Hyde Park.[8] The Kenwood and Hyde Park Property Owners' Association in October 1919 sponsored a mass meeting of 2,000 persons. When the treasurer of the organization asked all to stand who would work to free the district of Negroes, the Chicago *Herald-Examiner* reported, "with one accord, every man and woman arose with shouts."[9] But at a meeting that same month in another part of Chicago threatened with a black influx, the group was an integrated one and there was a friendly interchange of ideas; a black lawyer was quoted by the Chicago *Tribune* as telling the meeting: "If your property values go down, it is your own fault. If a Negro family moves into a white block, every one else sacrifices his interests in a panic and runs away. You ask what you can do for the colored man. You must offer him a better place to live at a more reasonable price than he is now paying. Then he will be glad to move. He does not want to invade the white district because he wants white neighbors, but simply because he wants the most comfort and the best home he can get for his money." The *Tribune* said, "a vote of thanks was tendered the Negroes for their spirit of fairness and open-mindedness."[10]

A ghetto, as Blair Justice defines it in a recent study of urban violence, is "any place that people live because they do not have any other choice *and* because the conditions that provide them with opportunities for options are either missing or have appeared so recently that they still do not belong to the mainstream of society."[11] Spear in his study of the black ghetto in Chicago asserts that ghettos were not caused primarily by poverty nor by a deliberate choice of blacks to cluster together, but by white hostility and refusal to rent to black tenants. The black inner city, Spear believes, bears no resemblance to the ethnic neighborhoods of European and other immigrants. Blacks did not congregate voluntarily in an area in order to enjoy a common linguistic, cultural, or religious tradition, Spear says; they lived in the ghetto because discrimination gave them no choice; they were bound together less by a common set of cultural values than by a common set of grievances.[12]

Ghettos took time to develop. In Chicago, for example, in 1900 no ward was more than 10 per cent black, and as late as 1910 Negroes were less segregated than Italian immigrants. Black neighborhoods began to emerge, but up to the peak wartime migration no neighborhood was more than 60 per cent black. There was as yet no clear-cut ghetto. Around 1915, a black family could rent an average four-room dwelling for about $16 a month. But as a neighborhood grew blacker it deteriorated, mainly because of landlord neglect. At first rents were proportionately reduced. That same apartment, in much worse condition, would in 1916 rent for $12 or $13. Then came the peak migration period, 1916 to 1918, and landlords no longer had to lower rents or make any repairs or improvements to fill their by now dilapidated apartments.[13] In fact, they could raise rents if they wanted to, because despite the enormous influx of migrants "pouring into Chicago at the rate of ten thousand a month," according to the Chicago Real Estate Board,[14] the physical boundaries of the ghettos—by now quite clearly defined—were unable to expand. Organized white opposition effectively prevented that. So more and more black people simply had to crowd into the two established black areas, a large one on the South Side and a smaller one on the West Side. Deterioration of housing, services, and facilities is characteristic of the ghetto, because crowding like this puts an intolerable strain on private and public facilities. The pace of decay quickened as migration reached its peak. The Chicago Real Estate Board predicted that city property would suffer damage in the amount of $25,000,000 or more.[15] The Board did not comment that this loss would result largely from the gross neglect of ghetto areas by city officials and politicians, with consequent falling off of such municipal services as police protection, sanitation, and lighting.

Official neglect, Woodson believes, is the final step in the degradation of the ghetto; after that, he says, come constructive moves, the development of community awareness leading to self-help projects. For example, in 1920 Chicago blacks formed the Protective Circle of Chicago, its aim being to challenge legally, with Urban League support, the repressive actions of white groups such as the Kenwood and Hyde Park Property Owners'

Association. But Woodson omits one important factor in ghetto decay, true in Chicago, New York, and other cities: the concentration of vice in the black area, with the acquiescence and connivance of police and city officials. Langston Hughes described the Chicago ghetto when he was going to high school in 1918. He lived on the South Side, next to the elevated, with his mother and brother in a one-room apartment. South State Street, he said, was a teeming Negro street full of crowded theaters, restaurants, and cabarets, where midnight was like noon. The night street was full of gamblers, prostitutes, and pimps mingled with workers from respectable families who were trying to bring children up decently.[16]

Northern ghettos were *de facto,* Southern ones *de jure,* even after the laws creating them had been several times struck down by the Supreme Court. The cities to try legal segregation were: Baltimore, struck down in 1911; then, between 1912 and 1913, Birmingham, Atlanta, Richmond, Norfolk, and several others; Louisville in 1914, with a law that served as a model for St. Louis, Dallas, and several smaller towns in Texas and Oklahoma, but that was held unconstitutional by the Supreme Court in 1917. In spite of Supreme Court reversals, many southern cities retained residential segregation laws on their books, slightly reworded from the Louisville code to circumvent the Court's decision. Other cities achieved segregation after the northern plan, by private restrictive covenants and homeowners' or tenants' associations. Legal segregation was not unthought of in the North, although it did not occur; Spear says that in Chicago some white residents were pushing for a segregation law as early as 1910.[17]

Ghetto containment by one means or another was believed essential by many whites who feared that if black migrants penetrated white neighborhoods, property values would tumble. The Chicago Commission on Race Relations held: "No single factor has complicated the relations of Negroes and whites in Chicago more than the widespread feeling of white people that the presence of Negroes in a neighborhood is a cause of serious depreciation of property values. To the extent that people feel that their financial interests are affected, antagonisms are accentuated."[18] The extraordinary twelve-man commission, six whites and six blacks, whose insightful report was written by the black sociologist Charles S. Johnson, could hardly have hit nearer the mark. Actual Negro presence was not necessary; property values fell if blacks only seemed about to or were said to be about to encroach on a white block, usually one already deteriorating, with realtors manipulating the situation by the well-known methods of blockbusting. Realtors would introduce a Negro family into a neighborhood deliberately to clean up large profits as whites in panic sold cheap and blacks bought dear. Actually, as the Chicago Commission pointed out, property values are driven up, not down, when black families are brought by realtors into white areas, and the white seller who is not panicked into immediate sale can make a handsome profit.[19]

Few whites, however, had such cool heads and strong nerves. Terrified of a collapse of values, many sold quickly at bottom prices; others bombed homes of Negroes who had just moved into white streets, and also the homes of agents who sold or rented to blacks.[20] Herbert Seligmann wrote in 1920 that financial considerations alone would not have led to the bombings: "It is true that the influx of Negroes had caused real-estate values at first to become depreciated. But the bombings would never have taken place if the Negro himself, as a human being, had not been depreciated in the esteem of his neighbors by a hostile propaganda." This hostile propaganda, Seligmann believed, was promulgated by the South. The southern dogma teaches that "the South is a 'white man's country'" and is affirmed with "bullets and whip." And, Seligmann was convinced, "The Southern dogma colors the opinions of the rest of the country."[21]

Violence accompanied the early black occupation of neighborhoods destined to become ghettos. In Chicago, the violence occurred when blacks tried to push out boundaries that would no longer contain their numbers. There were at first only sporadic bombings and beatings as the ghetto seemed about to spill over into white streets; whites were facetiously reported to deal with Negro residents or potential residents by "the judicious use of a wagon-load of bricks."[22] Later they used bombs. In New York City, in order to find a place to live, blacks had to take over a previously all-white area, Harlem. Bricks were the heavy artillery in New York, too, as various groups battled for tenancy of Harlem streets. A character in a novel by Rudolph Fisher says: "Those were the happy days. People kept kettles of hot lye on the stoves and carried them to their doors whenever the bell rang. And you could go upon the roof of your house and not see a chimney within four blocks: they'd all been knocked down and the bricks stacked at front room windows for ammunition."[23] White policemen patrolled in threes, and blacks and Irish fought pitched battles for the turf of 134th Street. When James Weldon Johnson wrote in *Black Manhattan* that "it should be noted that Harlem was taken over without violence," he must have forgotten the "happy days" Fisher described so vividly.[24]

New York had had black neighborhoods long before Harlem. At first, most blacks lived in lower Manhattan, in the squalid shantytown of the Five Points district, the neighborhood of the present City Hall. As waves of European immigrants arrived, blacks were pushed northward on the island. By 1860 the Irish had supplanted them in Five Points, and the blacks were pioneering in Greenwich Village, "Old Africa," as it was called. Then the Italians occupied the Village, around 1890, and the blacks moved farther uptown. In the area from Twentieth to Sixty-fourth streets, on the West Side, small enclaves of blacks lived surrounded by Irish and German immigrants. The lower part of this area was known as the Tenderloin, and the upper part was called San Juan Hill—an area from Sixtieth to Sixty-fourth streets, between Tenth and Eleventh avenues, with a population in and around 1900 of 3,580. Blacks and Irish fought bitter battles for control of that area. By 1906 the New York *Tribune* was commenting on the "general exodus of Negroes from all other neighborhoods to Harlem,"[25] but at the same time many blacks were going over to Brooklyn, to the Brownsville and Bedford-Stuyvesant areas, which were developing their own ghettos. In 1910 there were 60,500 blacks in all of Manhattan; by 1914, 49,-500 blacks were living within a 23-block-area in Harlem, and by 1920 some 73,000 people, almost all black, lived between 130th and 145th streets, from Fifth to Eighth avenues—two thirds of Manhattan's entire black population.[26]

Typical of ghettos almost everywhere, most of Harlem was deteriorating before the arrival of blacks. An exception was the beautiful and expensive area of 138th and 139th streets, where brownstones designed by Stanford White rented for $80 a month and up, compared to working-class rents of $10 to $18. The first residents in this luxury area were native-born Americans or successful immigrants from northern Europe, including some German Jews. This desirable neighborhood was fringed, however, by low, marshy land; one such area was headquarters for a bunch of young toughs who called themselves the Canary Island Gang, and other swampy areas were used as garbage dumps. At the turn of the century, eastern European Jews moved to Harlem to escape the crowded Jewish quarter on the Lower East Side.[27]

Harlem seemed a coming area, and enjoyed a building boom around 1902. But overbuilding made the boom go bust in 1904–5. Rents tumbled, mortgages were foreclosed, and property was going begging. It was only after this slump that blacks could afford Harlem. Black realtors, especially the Afro-American Realty Company owned by a very astute Massachusetts black realtor, Philip Payton, Jr., bought and rented to blacks; white realtors did the same. Also, white owners were willing to sell or rent to blacks to retrieve a part of their investments. There was, naturally, vehement white opposition from some white owners to the black influx, but it could not be effectively organized (as it was in Chicago) to keep blacks out of the deteriorating white streets; the wealthier whites were gone, and few white owners could resist the offers they got from black churches and other organizations, which then rented to blacks. The two streets of Stanford White houses remained for some time a white island in Harlem, but in 1919 the Equitable Life Assurance Society sold the houses there to wealthy blacks. That neighborhood was irreverently called "Striver's Row" by the less bourgeois and prosperous black residents of Harlem.[28]

One unusual and complicating feature of the New York ghetto in Harlem was the presence of two quite different nonwhite populations. By far the larger was the group of southern migrants, but a minority not to be ignored had originated in the Caribbean islands, chiefly the British West Indies, with some from the Dutch West Indies, Cuba, and Puerto Rico. To the 5,000 foreign-born blacks who lived in New York in 1900 were added 28,000 more during the war decade. In 1917 the New York *Times* estimated that they formed one quarter of the population of Harlem, although Haynes in 1912 had found them to be only 5.8 per cent.[29] A man of James Weldon Johnson's status could write noncompetitively of the West Indians that they were "soberminded and have something of a genius for business, differing almost totally, in these respects, from the average rural Negro of the South."[30] But Fisher voiced the opinion of the typical southern migrant that there were "too damn many" of these smart, "tricky" West Indians—"monkey chasers"—in Harlem. "Any time y'can knife a monk," Fisher has one of his characters say in a short story about Harlem, "do it. They's too damn many of 'em here. They're an achin' pain."[31] Dislike and competition often caused violent incidents between the southern blacks and those from the islands who had had a so much more propitious history. But they were all black, all the same, to whites; and all were caught in the black ghetto, outside the mainstream of New York society.

In Philadelphia, Boston, Pittsburgh, Minneapolis, Columbus, and Detroit, ghetto development followed the Chicago pattern of gradual concentration in certain neighborhoods. DuBois wrote at the turn of the century that the majority of blacks were scattered in every ward of Philadelphia, although the Seventh Ward was the heart of the Negro community. Even the Seventh Ward concentration, he explained, was not the result of discrimination, but had occurred because the ward was the old pre-Civil War black area and in it were most Negro churches and social facilities. The implication is that clustering in the Seventh Ward was voluntary and convenient. But the question remains, why, if not because of discrimination, were the pre-Civil War blacks, their churches, and their social halls all in one district? DuBois admitted that the Seventh Ward became very overcrowded, with insufficient sanitation and consequently a high death rate; and that more prosperous migrants from out of state headed for the Thirtieth and Thirty-sixth wards, where there were blacks in lesser numbers.[32] So the theory that blacks voluntarily congregated in the Seventh Ward does not stand up very well. They went, it seems, wherever they could find the best living conditions within their means in a neighborhood they were permitted to occupy, even if they had to travel a way to get to church.

"The Negro in Boston, as in other cities," Baker reported, "is building up 'quarters' which he occupies to the increasing exclusion of other classes of people,"[33] which seems an odd way of saying that black ghettos were forming where whites moved out and let the black migrants take over. John Daniels pointed out an interesting Boston variant of the usual pattern of ghetto formation, which is that by 1914 Jews had taken over the old Negro section, the West End, converting two Negro churches to synagogues. Daniels said prosperous blacks as well as whites were already moving to the suburbs, an option blacks did not have in other cities.[34]

Race relations deteriorated as the ghettos decayed and became breeding grounds of disease, vice, and crime. The unsavory characteristics of the ghettos were transferred, in white minds, to their unfortunate inhabitants; and blacks were less welcome than ever in the outer community. Places of public accommodation were not legally segregated, but there were many ways of impressing on blacks that they were not welcome. Eating places often ignored Negro customers, served them spoiled food, and overcharged them; in theaters an effort was made to seat them in the balcony or on the extreme side aisles; in at least one Chicago department store, the clerks are said to have been instructed to be cool to black customers and to direct them to the cheaper merchandise sold in the basement. Yet some white establishments treated black clients courteously.[35] When blacks ventured out of the ghetto, therefore, they "could never be certain when they might be embarrassed or humiliated by discriminatory practices."[36] Such uncertainty would become a facet of the ghetto mind, and would make blacks timorous of accepting opportunities for options when, rarely, these were offered. Most black migrants preferred to avoid the chance of humiliation outside by trading within the ghetto, which made it corruptingly easy for ghetto stores to charge high prices for shoddy merchandise. The extra markup was a price worth paying for one's dignity.

Not only recent migrants but second- or third-generation

northern blacks were caught in the ghetto trap. The established, middle-class black neighborhoods, like Philadelphia's Seventh Ward, were the first to be invaded by the homeless newcomers. Most of the older residents had no option but to stay in the deteriorating neighborhoods, although a few might be able to afford the suburbs if these were open to them. From the early 1900s these people were complaining bitterly about crime in the ghetto, being the principal sufferers. In 1900 the New York *Age* complained about the undesirable southern blacks who were ruining the city. Many New York black leaders and the black press there did their best to discourage migration. So alarming a personal threat did the migrants present that even followers of DuBois joined Booker T. Washington in singing the praises of the small southern farm.[37] In some black churches, old members opposed admitting migrants to membership, showing that there were indeed conservative Negroes, however amazed Kropotkin may have been.

Probably the most convincing indictment of how Negroes were treated in the South is the fact that, despite all the strangeness, discrimination, and danger, blacks continued to trek to the northern ghettos. Langston Hughes summed up the migrant's attitude in one of his Simple stories, "A Toast to Harlem." Certainly there was plenty wrong with the ghetto, Simple admitted; and certainly the South had a lot to recommend it—ideally. "You're talking about what ought to be," Simple tells his friend. "But as long as what *is* is—and Georgia is Georgia—I will take Harlem for mine. At least, if trouble comes, I will have *my own window* to shoot from."[38]

CHAPTER 4

Life and Death in the Inner City

... a slow, chronic contest
against everlasting odds ...

Russell Sage Foundation, 1914

... the babies die like flies ...

Mary White Ovington,
Half a Man, 1911

The people walled into the ghettos were of every social and economic class, and of all kinds. There was the Talented Tenth, the upper 10 per cent of the black population, consisting of professionals, successful businessmen, and skilled artisans, whose prewar migration DuBois felt had robbed the South of black leaders. They included the intellectual blacks who, Woodson says, were driven out of the South because they set bad examples for menial and manual labor, the black role in southern states.[1] But such people formed a small minority in the ghettos, into which poured the untrained and uneducated.[2] The "solid, well-placed land-owning Negro people" of the South had scarcely been touched by the migration, Baker believed; those who filled the northern ghettos were mostly discontented tenant farmers, urban people, and unsettled youths.[3] They must certainly have formed the majority; and another of Baker's observations must also be correct, that migrants represented the worthless, ignorant, semicriminal and criminal classes, as well as the self-respecting, hard-working people who sought a better life for themselves and their children.[4]

In its population of every class and character the inner city was like the city as a whole, with the notable difference that the ghetto, by its absence of options, forced all sorts of black people to live in close proximity: the wealthy and the poor,[5] the virtuous and the vicious, the respectable workingmen side by side with "desperadoes, gamblers, and moral lepers," as the New York *Times* put it.[6] The Chicago Commission on Race Relations found four classes of homes: Type A, occupied by black professionals and prosperous businessmen; Type B, occupied by clerks, mail-workers, artisans, and various skilled workers; Type C, occupied by ordinary working-class blacks; and Type D, the worst slums, occupied by the poorest class.[7] From A through D, all were contained by the narrow precinct of the ghetto, which differentiates the black ghetto from the white slum that reaches out into better neighborhoods.

About three quarters of those who lived in the ghettos in 1912 were between their late teens and early fifties, the prime working years; of the rest, only a few were beyond their middle fifties.[8] By 1918, at the peak of the migration, three quarters of the blacks in Pittsburgh were within a narrower and even more employable age range for heavy labor, between eighteen and forty years of age; almost half of them were single, and more than a quarter of the married men had left their families behind.[9] In 1920, the northern ghetto population was still more than half in the twenty-to-forty-four-year age group, although that group comprised only slightly more than one third of the southern black population. In the South, almost half the black people were under twenty; in the North, less than one third.[10] Old people were few in the ghettos, which is not surprising in a group that had migrated chiefly to find work; also, as Spear and other students of the ghettos point out, older Negroes were much less likely to pick up and leave their traditional southern home than young blacks who had not grown up under slavery or Reconstruction. So ghetto people were by and large young, ready and able to work hard, unattached, and relatively unencumbered by a slave past.

What is surprising, and requires examination, is the census

finding of more black women than black men in the ghetto population as also in southern cities and in the nationwide black population, whereas census figures for whites consistently show more males than females. These are the national population figures for the migration period:

	White		Black	
	MALES	FEMALES	MALES	FEMALES
1900	28,686,450	27,908,929	4,386,547	4,447,447
1910	34,654,457	33,731,955	4,885,881	4,941,882
1920	40,902,333	40,205,828	5,209,436	5,253,695[11]

The preponderance of women in the black population was particularly noticeable in cities, from which Kelly Miller drew the conclusion that, women being unequal to the heavy work on the farm, they went in larger numbers than men to urban areas where they might expect to find lighter labor.[12] That may have been true to some extent in southern cities, but it does not seem a satisfactory explanation of why more women than men should have made the arduous, dangerous journey to cities hundreds of miles from their homes. Also, almost all the jobs advertised and offered by labor agents were for men, not women.

Yet there is no question but census takers found more black women than men in the northern ghettos, especially in New York, where they counted 810 men for every 1,000 women in 1890, 809 men for every 1,000 women in 1900, 850 men for every 1,000 women in 1910, and 926 men for every 1,000 women in 1920.[13] The question is: Was the count correct? Even with today's improved demographic techniques, the Census Bureau has announced that it misses a considerable part of the black male population in each count. The undercount in 1960 was greatest in the young adult age group, 15 to 24, where, the Bureau estimates, about 15 per cent of males were missed. The 1970 count is believed to be more accurate, but still imperfect. Urban experts point out that among poor blacks, the "'street corner men' who have only odd jobs, casual addresses, and a distrust of government that extends even to census takers," to quote the New York *Times,* some undercount is inescapable.[14] In a recent study of "street corner men," Elliot Liebow finds the poor black men characteristically "absent" from the household when the census taker appears; when they are not at work they shun their uninviting homes, preferring to visit with their friends on street corners, with the result that officially many of them do not exist because their names never get on official records of any sort, although black women are known to the welfare and school authorities.[15] If this takes place today, with the much higher degree of organization and communication within a community, it must have been much more operative when migrants were pouring into strange cities, homeless or transiently housed, seeking work, changing rooms and jobs, and even more likely to distrust a white person who came around and asked questions. From the ignorance, the inexperience, and the fear of getting into trouble that migrants brought with them from the South, it is more than likely that black men were substantially undercounted, and that Louise Kennedy's finding of more men than women in black ghettos (except for New York, she said) was more reliable than the census.[16] Kennedy commented in her 1930 study that the preponderance of young adult single males in urban surroundings—the group most likely to be undercounted—increased major social problems such as unstable family life, immorality, and crime.[17] The undercount may also mean that there were fewer women heads-of-households and fewer fatherless children than the agencies and schools knew of.

The settled black northern population viewed with distaste the street-corner men and other newcomers who turned old respectable black neighborhoods into ghettos. Among those aghast was the Chicago *Defender,* which had brought so many of the migrants North; it now took them to task for their appearance and behavior, which, although doubtless resulting from "ignorance of law and customs necessary for the maintenance of health, sobriety and morality," nevertheless gave white people grounds for complaint. Appended to this scolding was a list of do's and don'ts about apparel and conduct in public.[18] The Chicago Urban League had a similar list printed on a placard, providing a kind of migrant's creed for the guidance of newcomers and pointing out the black draftees as shining examples:

> I realize that our soldiers have learned new habits of self-respect and cleanliness.
>
> I desire to help bring about a new order of living in this community.
>
> I will attend to the neatness of my personal appearance on the street or when sitting in front doorways.
>
> I will refrain from wearing dust caps, bungalow aprons, house clothing, and bedroom shoes out of doors.
>
> I will arrange my toilet within doors and not on the front porch.
>
> I will insist upon the use of rear entrances for coal dealers, etc.
>
> I will refrain from loud talking and objectionable deportment on street cars and in public places.
>
> I will do my best to prevent defacement of property by either children or adults.[19]

One offense attributed to migrants, which neither the *Defender* nor the Urban League mentioned, was drinking. DuBois had deplored the rising beer consumption among Philadelphia blacks long before the big migration years, not that he felt drinking to be a major black social problem, but because of the money wasted on drink.[20] In Pittsburgh, Epstein found no significant drinking problem even in 1918, particularly among married men; he pointed out that 15 per cent of ghetto families had savings, and that where the family had been left in the South, a large majority of migrant husbands sent money home to them. These were not the actions of drunken wastrels. Still, drink was so popularly considered a black weakness, Epstein said, that people were saying Negroes had gone North chiefly because southern states had adopted prohibition. Some increase in drinking was to be found, Epstein reported, among single men in the ghettos, who did not even have a room to themselves but rented a turn at a double-shift bed and had no place except the saloons or brothels in which to spend their waking, nonworking hours.[21]

Ghetto children made as poor an impression as their elders on northern white and also black society. Fresh from the black schools of the South, especially the rural South, with their brief sessions, lax attendance rules, disorder, noisiness, ignorant teachers, and lack of equipment, children of migrants found northern schools an entirely new world. Many of them had never been to school at all, and even those who had were severely retarded by comparison with northern children, black and white. Harlem schools got fourteen- and fifteen-year-old youths who did not know as much as average eight-year-old New Yorkers. Although there was no significant discrepancy in school performance between northern black and white children—indeed, some teachers said these black children did better than children from certain groups of whites, both native-born and immigrant—still, the retardation of the migrants' children convinced many that all black children were retarded. Figures were cited in proof, although all they really proved was that southern migrants were retarded; but geography and color were easily confused by prejudiced minds. The figures showed that among black children as a group, migrants included, 74 per cent were overage for their grade compared with 49 per cent overage among white children; also, most of these white children were less than a year below proper grade level, while most of the retarded black children were two to five years below, so it was not unusual to have eighth graders who were in their late teens.[22]

Certainly some of the problems of migrant children resulted not just from their backgrounds but from the irregular, unpredictable family life in the newly forming ghettos. DuBois from his elevated position taxed poor Negroes with "lack of respect for the marriage bond, inconsiderate entrance into it, and bad household economy and family government."[23] In regarding these faults as in any way racial, DuBois did not differ too much from John Daniels of Boston, who in 1914 wrote of sexual laxity among blacks as "an innate weakness or failing,"[24] although Du-

Bois did explain that the poverty, youth, and single status of many urban blacks tended to foster illegal sexual arrangements and immoral activity rather than marriage and a stable home life.[25]

Although the high proportion of women to men in the ghetto was apparently a census inaccuracy, many ghetto families must have been effectively, if not actually, fatherless. In one Harlem school, almost half the children were reported to have no father at home, which would not necessarily mean that there was no man in the house. Women were (or seemed to be) heads of households in more than 20 per cent of Chicago ghetto families. In a great number of cases the family unit was a loose and changing structure, and children often had to shift for themselves; if their mothers went out to work, as many of them did, the children would go to school with the house key on a string around their necks. Ovington estimated that between 20 and 50 per cent of ghetto mothers were workingwomen; and she found that almost one third of the black children who were arraigned in Children's Court were brought in because of improper guardianship—about twice as high a percentage as among children of Russian immigrant slum dwellers. But black ghetto mothers worked because they had to, to support or help support their families; most of them were in domestic service, with long and irregular hours. It has often been stated that black women were the "backbone" of the indigent ghetto family, without taking into account that even in a family with a steady, sober, hard-working father, the mother also had to work to keep a decent home and send the children to school fed and clothed. DuBois's complaint about women who worked only to keep some "well-dressed loafers" as lovers may have been true of a few, but economic necessity was surely a more common reason.[26]

Belief in black traits of immorality and indifference to family ties, of vagrancy and drunkenness among black men and industry among black women, has acquired respectability more through age and frequent repetition than through solid documentation, and has by mere familiarity convinced not only white racists but a number of white liberals and some black spokesmen; any student of black history or society, however, has found that neither longevity of belief in stereotypic traits nor impeccability of motive in those who hold such beliefs can guarantee their accuracy. Theories about common characteristics among people as poor, reviled, threatened, hurt, disinherited, and deliberately invisible as the migrants in the ghettos cannot possibly be conclusive. That the "plantation tradition" weakened the black concept of home life, as DuBois says,[27] or that the high percentage of working females deprived black men of the essential symbol of manhood in our society, as Osofsky says,[28] are propositions that cannot be ignored but are not necessarily true. Against them one must weigh the facts of ghetto life; statistics concerning black workingmen, which will be studied in a later chapter; and the tendency to evade, lie, or simply disappear of men who had learned in the South the dangers of being honest or merely of being present.

What was common to almost all in the ghettos was poverty. At least one quarter of a man's earnings—totaling perhaps $15 to $20 for a forty-eight to sixty hour week when he had the luck of being employed—went to the landlord. The man's wife might add a few dollars to the family income, but withal few could have seen more than $25 come in each week. What was left after paying the rent had to get the workers to and from their jobs, feed and warm and clothe maybe six people, pay the doctor, the druggist, the insurance man, the lodge dues (or who would bury you?), and perhaps buy a bottle or a few beers or a packet of cocaine on Saturday night. And these were the lucky ones, the ones who had jobs at least part of the time. Many were virtually paupers.

The penalty for poverty was not only physical want but also humiliation, because being poor was (and still commonly is) believed to be one's own doing, a "self-inflicted mortification" that was the result of bad habits, chiefly drinking. In the early 1900s, in tune with emerging Progressive reform ideas, social thinkers like Walter Rauschenbusch began to investigate the causes and effects of poverty; pioneering works like DuBois's Atlanta University studies, Jacob Riis's *How the Other Half Lives,* and reports of the Department of Labor and the U. S. Industrial Commission cast a little new light on poverty, replacing some of those ideas no less wrong than venerable. The reformers insisted it was not the fault of the poor man that he was poor, but of a social and economic order that operates in such a way that some people become poor and remain poor.[29] John Daniels in a study of poverty in Boston and other cities found that among blacks such misconduct as drinking, immorality, and shiftlessness was responsible for only 13.76 per cent of poverty cases, compared to 27.35 per cent among native white Americans, 16.67 per cent among German-born, 30.43 per cent among Irish-born, and 28.01 per cent among English-born; and that misfortune—no job, poor pay, accident, illness—accounted for 83.31 per cent of poverty cases among blacks, a higher percentage than in any other group.[30]

Of the effects of poverty, Rauschenbusch said early in the 1900s: "Constant underfeeding and frequent exhaustion make the physical tissues flabby and the brain prone to depression and vacillation, incapable of holding tenaciously to a distant aim." In a Russell Sage Foundation monograph of 1914 it was said of poverty: "It does not kill perhaps but it stunts. It does not come as an overwhelming catastrophe; but steadily it saps the vigor of the young as well as of the old. . . . With the less fortunate, poverty takes the form of a slow, chronic contest against everlasting odds."[31] A few social scientists and reformers saw the poor man as, in most cases, the victim through misfortune of the most debilitating misfortune of all, poverty, which robbed him of the vigor to overcome it. But such thinking was exceptional at the time. Much more accepted were such ideas as that poverty, dirt, and crime were due to the poor human material in the lower classes; and that, as David Starr Jordan, president of Stanford University, expressed it, "Not the strength of the strong but the weakness of the weak . . . engenders exploitation and tyranny."[32] The idea that poverty and weakness might be the fault of society did not take general hold until the depression of the 1930s, when all the thrift, industry, and sobriety of the middle class proved shockingly inadequate to save it from the bite of need.

For the poor black ghetto people newly arrived from the South, the interesting question was not how they had gotten poor nor what poverty was doing to them, but, as the song asked:

"Rufus Rastus Johnson Brown,
What you gwine ter do when de rent comes roun'?"[33]

One thing to do was to take in lodgers, no matter how cramped home was, especially in periods of unemployment. This was a traditional ghetto means of boosting the family income. Du-Bois had reported before 1900 that taking lodgers was very common in Philadelphia, and an important source of funds for many black property owners. At about the same time, the Federation of Churches reported at least one third of black families as taking in lodgers or boarders, and later reports, at intervals from 1912 to 1930, named the same percentage or a bit higher in the ghettos of all big northern cities.[34] In describing the wealth and status of a black society matron of Harlem, Langston Hughes has his character Simple say she lives "so high up on Sugar Hill that people in her neighborhood don't even have roomers. They keep the whole house for themselves."[35]

The Chicago Commission on Race Relations noted that, although taking lodgers is common practice among all poor people, immigrant families were less likely to share their homes in this way than blacks.[36] Again, it would be easy to interpret this as meaning that blacks placed less importance on home and family privacy; but there is an economic reason that is far more probable, which is simply that blacks were charged higher rent than whites for the same accommodations. When a Chicago paper advertised "seven rooms, $25.00" and "seven rooms for colored people, $37.50,"[37] it is a safe bet that the apartment labeled "colored" was not worth $12.50 more than the other. Baker reported that in the Indianapolis ghetto known as Bucktown, landlords got $25 a month for flimsy one-story frame row houses that would have rented to whites for $18.[38] In 1900 Jacob Riis wrote that "the old robbery goes on" and that where "the Negro pitches his tent, he pays more rent than his white neighbor"—anywhere from 25 to 50 per cent more for the same tent.[39] Chicago surveys in 1909 and 1919 showed blacks paying 100 per cent more. The situation prevailed in every big city except Washington.[40]

Another circumstance that led Negro families to take in lodgers was that, as whites hurriedly vacated streets that became part of the ghetto, the newly available houses and apartments were often of large size, and consequently expensive. With housing at a premium, it was easy to find a lodger or two to use the extra space and make up the rent money. In some instances a family had enough income to pay the rent, but took lodgers so they could tuck away a little savings and sometime perhaps buy a house. This was the pattern especially in Washington, where blacks earned better, had more options, and therefore had higher expectations. But in most cases it was to meet the rent that single young men just off the train or boat from the South, or married men arrived ahead of their families, were crowded into already cramped quarters.[41] There is absolutely no evidence that blacks welcomed a diminution of their little privacy and comfort any more than white people would; if the blacks accepted necessity with a better grace, it can more reasonably be laid to their long schooling in want than to that native cheerfulness and light-heartedness, which alternated, in the racist's catalogue of Negro characteristics, with sullenness and meanness.

Surely it was better to sacrifice comfort and privacy than to live in the street because one couldn't pay the rent; but the effects on family life and morals of keeping lodgers were devastating. Woofter commented on how overcrowding "saps the vitality and the moral vigor of those in dense neighborhoods" and leads to high incidence of crime, prostitution, gambling, and every other vice.[42] About 70 per cent of the black men in New York City were unmarried, and probably a similar percentage elsewhere. About 80 per cent of dwellings that let rooms to lodgers were those of families headed by black women without husbands, according to an Urban League report.[43] Sometimes the revenue from a room was increased by renting it to two, three, or more male lodgers. In Pittsburgh, with its particularly unwholesome and overcrowded ghettos, half of the single men lived three or four to a room. Less than 40 per cent of them had a bed to themselves; half slept two in a bed, and the rest three or more in a bed. In the most crowded sections, beds were rented on a double-shift basis. And beds were put not only in bedrooms but in attics, basements, dining rooms, and kitchens. More often than not the sleeping space was damp, dark, and airless. Water and toilets were usually out in the yard. In fact, living conditions in Pittsburgh were so intolerable that few of the migrants stayed a year. But new men arrived to fill up the beds. About ninety-eight out of every hundred dwellings in the Pittsburgh black ghetto were shared by lodgers or multiple families.[44] In the ghettos of all major cities there were many dwellings where members of the family, including the children, had to share their sleeping space with newly arrived migrant families or single men.[45] It is hard to imagine a situation more destructive of family life and morality or more distorting of a child's view of right and wrong. In the light of such conditions, the Urban League placard enjoining cleanliness, neatness, and decency appears quite out of touch with reality.

The housing in which families and lodgers lived ranged from rundown to uninhabitable. Again, Pittsburgh was outstandingly bad. About half of all ghetto families lived in one-room apartments, about 20 per cent in two rooms, and only a little better than 10 per cent in three rooms. Epstein thus described homes in the Pittsburgh black belt in 1918: "The sections formerly designated as Negro quarters, have long since been congested beyond capacity by the influx of newcomers, and a score of new colonies have sprung up in hollows and ravines, on hill slopes and along river banks, by railroad tracks and in mill yards. In many instances the dwellings are those which have been abandoned by foreign white people since the beginning of the present war. In some cases they are structures once condemned by the City Bureau of Sanitation, but opened again only to accommodate the influx from the South."[46] From such homes, every day, exhausted men, women, and children emerged to mingle briefly with the rest of society, which found them stupid and dirty.

Housing, any housing, was so short in the ghetto that landlords could rent anything. On a single day in 1917, Chicago real estate brokers had 664 black families apply for housing, with only 53 units available. An easy and profitable recourse for landlords was to chop up larger places into smaller units, often with no decrease in rent. All space was filled with human bodies. In a study of forty-one families in Chicago, it was found that thirty-nine were living in one room. The population density in the black ghetto of Cleveland was thirty-five to forty persons per acre, contrasted with a citywide density of twenty-one. In some cities the Negro districts had a population density four times that of white districts. In the Philadelphia of 1900, a toilet in the backyard served the people living in the house in front of it; but already landlords were beginning to build additional housing in the backyards, so not one or two but a number of families had to share the one outdoor toilet. DuBois blamed the high death rate in the black Seventh Ward on this inadequate sanitation. Later, Kennedy reported ten families in one three-story house in Philadelphia, with one bath and one toilet for all, which would probably number at least thirty to forty men, women, and children; all rooms, including kitchens, doubled as bedrooms. Negro housing, Kennedy says, was substandard everywhere, and there was no enforcement of health and sanitation regulations.[47] Still, housing in the Newark ghetto must have been outstandingly evil. In fifty-three families closely studied by the Negro Welfare Committee, the number of persons occupying each room averaged 4.3. The Committee's report included such comments as: "Wife and three children living over a stable. Husband earning $11 a week." "Three families in four rooms." "A little house, not fit for a chicken-coop." "A sorry-looking house for so much money—$15 a month; doors off the hinges; water in the cellar; two families in five rooms." "Indescribable; so dark they must keep the light burning all day." "This family lives in three rooms on the second floor of a rickety frame house built on the side of a hill, so that the back rooms are just above the ground. The entrance is in a muddy, disorderly yard and is through a tunnel in the house. The rooms are hard to heat because of cracks. A boy of eighteen was in bed breathing heavily; very ill with pneumonia; delirious at times."[48] New York's Harlem was exceptional in that many of the houses there, formerly occupied by middle-class whites, were "substantially built" and designed "with regard for sanitation and convenience."[49] But ghetto housing, even if originally good, quickly deteriorated under the abnormal pressures put upon it; and, because demand for housing consistently exceeded supply, landlords could let their tenements rot and still raise the rent. The consequent disrepair and filth, however, did not in the public mind reflect on the landlords, but merely confirmed the common belief, long held and often repeated, that blacks destroyed property and diminished its value.[50]

The best return on one's investment came from renting single rooms, furnished or unfurnished, in a house one owned or leased. Thus, in Chicago in 1919, a three-story building rented by a man for $65 a month brought him over $200 a month from letting its individual rooms, unfurnished.[51] Woofter describes the furnishings in a typical furnished room: an old iron bed with a cheap mattress and two pillows, all black and greasy from use by previous tenants, who slept in their soiled clothing because they had no sheets or covers; a filthy two-holed stove; a table soiled with food customarily eaten out of the paper in which it had come wrapped; oil lamps for light, which had to be used even in the daytime; floors, walls, ceiling, and windows thick with dirt, because roomers are generally temporary tenants and do not clean their premises.[52]

Still, there was something perhaps worse, and that was the labor camp. A number of big industrial firms, especially railroads and steel mills, built camps for their workers. Some railroad camps consisted simply of boxcars, with four to eight beds to a car. Conditions in some were so inhumanly crowded and foul that they can be compared only to slave ships. In a camp of the Lukens Steel Company, 225 black workers lived in unsanitary, dilapidated shacks unfavorably situated behind a slag pile; the mattresses on the bunk beds were filthy and verminous, and the food sold by the commissary was ill-smelling and bad. "A score or more of Negroes loitering about the camp evidently belonged to an unruly crew," the Labor Department commented of this place, which is not really surprising. Not all work camps were that bad, however. Those of the Pennsylvania Railroad were the best, according to the Department of Labor. They were wooden sheds, covered with tarpaper, steam heated and furnished with tiers of cots; separate sheds contained toilets, showers, and an eating room. Lodging was a nominal $1.00 to $2.00 a week, and good, clean food might cost an additional $4.00 to $7.00 a week.[53]

With such unlivable conditions and high costs in rented housing, it was the dream of many black families to buy their own homes. This was not easy to accomplish. A survey of Chicago in 1919 showed that about 5 per cent of blacks owned their homes as against 19 per cent of Polish immigrants in some districts and almost 24 per cent in the Lithuanian neighborhood. In New York City's five boroughs, Woofter says, blacks in 1920 represented a little more than 3 per cent of all home owners; in individual boroughs, the black owner group formed over 30 per cent of all owners in Queens, almost 18 per cent in Richmond (Staten Island), and down to a low of under 1 per cent in Manhattan, where land was scarcest and costliest. Considerable numbers of blacks also managed to own their homes in outlying areas of other cities, as in Morgan Park, Chicago, and Douglass Park, Indianapolis. But even when outlying areas were not restricted, lack of public transportation prevented all but a few blacks from moving out of the inner city. More affluent New York blacks were aided in buying or renting decent housing by the black churches, such as St. Marks Methodist Episcopal and St. Philips Protestant Episcopal, both in Harlem and both active in acquiring better-class real estate; also in Harlem were about 20 black realtors, notably Philip Payton's Afro-American Realty Company, which was well capitalized and which catered to middle-class black buyers and renters.[54]

The main importance of the churches as intermediaries for home buyers was that black individuals had great difficulty getting mortgages at reasonable interest. Micheaux, speaking of

Chicago in 1910, told of annual interest of $300 on a $2,000 mortgage, or 15 per cent—out of a family income of $18.50 a week, or a maximum possible income of $962 a year.[55] The Chicago Commission on Race Relations explained: "An important factor in the housing problem is the low security rating given by real estate loan concerns to property tenanted by Negroes. Because of this Negroes are charged more than white people for loans, find it more difficult to secure them, and thus are greatly handicapped in efforts to buy or improve property."[56] So with the circularity typical of black suffering, crowding and owner neglect in the ghetto resulted in deterioration of property, which in turn gave blacks the reputation of being such poor security risks that they could not borrow money to buy a house of their own and put it in livable condition. Making the down payment on a house, toward which end many black families took lodgers into their crowded flats, must have been for most an insurmountable first hurdle. And yet, despite all the very apparent handicaps of blacks in buying property, the conclusion commonly drawn by whites from the small number of black home owners, said the Chicago Commission, a conclusion "not shaken even by the satisfactory experiences of those who have dealt with them, [is] that Negroes have no financial resources, and are thriftless and improvident."[57] Here again, it was easier to invoke the stereotype than to examine the individual; and by the naming of stereotypic traits that were believed to make the black responsible for his own condition—in spite of much evidence to the contrary—the stereotype was reconfirmed.

Living as they did, ghetto people were a sickly lot, and they brought their sickness into the outer city each day when they went to work in white factories and kitchens, or took back the white washing they had done in the filth of their crowded tenements. Tuberculosis was common in the ghettos, and also pneumonia and venereal diseases. It was reported that the syphilis death rate among Philadelphia Negroes before the peak migration years was 12.5 per 100,000; later it rose to 78.6 per 100,000. The Labor Department pointed out that the highest rates of syphilis and other venereal diseases were found among the migrants who had been swept up off the streets by labor agents, but that among carefully selected workers only 5 per cent were venereally infected. Plants began to give physical examinations to job applicants and to men already hired. At an eastern railroad camp, doctors found that 560 of the 800 men working there had tuberculosis or venereal diseases, and of those, 448 were venereals.[58] Tuberculosis spread throughout the cities at an alarming rate, and accounted for over half of all deaths among blacks. Philadelphia, Pittsburgh, and Cleveland had outbreaks of smallpox that were believed traceable directly to the migrants, and labor camps and plants had to undertake wholesale vaccination programs. The black population menaced all cities where they stewed in unwholesome ghettos, overworked and undernourished, ignorant of health rules and of preventive measures, and ignored by community health and sanitation services.[59] And, as the Labor Department commented, "The high Negro mortality rate is no more his problem alone. Eventually the community pays the price in money and life, in loss of work, and in taxes for hospitals and pauper burials. . . . The public-health function of northern cities is in process of rapid expansion, and the departments of health are beginning to undertake constructive work."[60] But meanwhile, sick black men were working in sugar refineries; and their wives had jobs in food processing plants, or as cooks for their husbands' bosses.

In 1896, the first of the Atlanta University studies headed by DuBois deplored the circumstances that brought such killing diseases as tuberculosis and infant cholera to urban blacks: poverty, dirt, ignorance, and carelessness; failure of the cities to provide health care, public hospitals, and free dispensaries for blacks; lack of black doctors and nurses, and reluctance of white doctors to care for black patients; and the indifference of prosperous blacks to the needs of their poor brothers. One of the reports in this first study, however, flatly stated that drink was a principal factor in the high black death rate; and although the tone of the report is more moralistic than scientific, the picture of ghetto dangers for children rings true: "How long shall our poor and untaught children, tempted on every corner by the cigarette seller, the beer shop and the brothel, be arrested and placed in the chain-gangs with hardened criminals, to be steeped in iniquity and schooled in crime, and hastened to death of body and soul?"[61]

In the second Atlanta study, published a year later, Professor Eugene Harris of Fisk University took a similar high moral stand about sickness among urban blacks, insisting that not environment so much as the poor moral and social posture of black people accounted for most diseases and deaths. Granting all political, social, and economic handicaps of the black man, Harris said that nevertheless "he is at perfect liberty to be abstemious or intemperate, chaste or licentious, cleanly or filthy." And he believed that sanitary regulations were less needed by blacks than "social reconstruction and moral regeneration."[62] In today's thinking this seems naïve and self-righteous, considering the difficulty of being cleanly in the ghetto, and the lack of any escape from its dreariness except sex and the saloon.

The "cigarette seller" may also have pushed drugs. Black people were long accustomed to their use. Southern rural blacks had been sold cocaine by whites, and the use of cocaine and opium was increasing alarmingly in the black quarters of all southern cities in the early 1900s. In Memphis around 1900, about 80 per cent of the city's Negroes were said to use cocaine, a scarcely credible figure; there were a dozen drugstores said to make nearly all their profits in drug traffic. A $.05 or $.10 box furnished "a comfortable drunk for four or five hours," the Memphis Commercial Appeal reported; some blacks, it said, held "coke parties," where the participants would sit in a circle, sing a slow song to get into the mood, and then pass the cocaine. In 1900 the Memphis chief of police admitted that "the sale of cocaine has reached such an alarming extent that the department is unable to cope with its ravages." In 1905 the Commercial Appeal again said drug use was growing, and that opium was being used as well as cocaine.[63] At the same time, Baker found extensive use of cocaine among Atlanta blacks, and police officials said a good part of black crime was committed by men who took drugs.[64] According to Dollard, white drug addicts in the 1930s put great pressure on black doctors in southern towns to supply them with drugs, using both bribes and threats. "Since the Negro physician's income is likely to be small anyway," Dollard commented, "there must be a great temptation to sell narcotics."[65] Blacks, too, presumably, could get drugs from the hard-up black doctors.

Many migrants must have come North equipped with the drug habit, even if the 80 per cent addiction in Memphis was an exaggeration. Cocaine seems to have been available in ghetto drugstores to pushers who sold it in small quantities. Rudolph Fisher's story "City of Refuge" is about drug pushing in Harlem in the twenties and a pusher who found that "there were any number of people who would buy and pay well" for as many little white pills as he could get from the druggist.[66] So although drink is frequently mentioned as a cause of poverty and sickness among blacks, and drugs almost not at all, there can be little doubt that many sought escape through "coke" as well as whiskey, and that some of the omnipresent illness would have been a result of drug addiction.

The nature of the chief killing diseases in the ghettos—tuberculosis, pneumonia, and other pulmonary and bronchial ailments—has convinced most investigators that the chief causes of sickness among ghetto blacks called not so much for moral regeneration as for social reform. Practically all commentators agree that the Negro's susceptibility to these diseases was not racial but environmental. Crowded, unsanitary housing; hard work for long hours, often exposed to the weather; insufficient food, clothing, and rest; confinement and lack of ventilation; and the strain of urban life; these weakened the ghetto dweller's resistance to disease. It was not that blacks were unable to withstand a cold climate, most agree, but that housedresses and overalls were inappropriate for a Chicago or New York winter. Poverty and lack of experience prevented Negroes from dressing, eating, and heating their homes as a cold climate required. In Pittsburgh, bad housing and pace-setting labor as well as the change of climate were declared responsible for a 200 per cent increase in deaths from pneumonia and a 100 per cent increase in deaths from heart diseases at the peak migration period. Baker cites a black physician who mentioned as additional causes drink, reliance on patent medicines and "hoodoo" cures, and "immorality," but since lack of morals does not in itself kill, he presumably meant sexual promiscuity without attention to cleanliness or prophylaxis. A later investigator found a high rate of mental illness among urban blacks, which also appears to be not a black trait but a ghetto hazard, because it has been shown that indigenous populations have lower crude rates of mental disease than migrants who are suddenly confronted with a whole new set of circumstances to which they must quickly adjust.[67]

With all this sickness, 125 per cent more blacks than whites in Philadelphia required hospital care, Baker reported. He found that sickness was at least twice as prevalent among blacks as among Germans, Irish, or native white Americans; and he believed that sickness was the chief cause of black poverty, just as poverty was a chief cause of sickness. In almost all hospitals, blacks met with discriminatory treatment; one outstanding exception was Provident Hospital in Chicago, which was staffed by blacks and which catered to blacks. But almost everywhere, hospital facilities for black people were very insufficient. Not only was it hard to get a bed, but the typical ghetto dweller from the South was afraid of hospitals and preferred to die in peace at home—with some help, perhaps, from patent cures and "hoodoo."[68]

Although death rates for both blacks and whites declined steadily from the beginning of the century, the black death rate was consistently higher and diminished less rapidly. In 1910 the white death rate was 14.5 per 1,000, the nonwhite 21.7; in 1920 the white rate was 12.6, the nonwhite 17.7. In Pittsburgh between 1915 and 1917 Negro deaths almost doubled, although the black population increased only 78 per cent. In Detroit in 1920, 776 blacks per 100,000 of population died of pneumonia, and 208.2 whites; 232.6 blacks died of heart diseases, and 106.6 whites. Statistics of Chicago, New York, Cincinnati, Pittsburgh, Indianapolis, St. Louis, and Kansas City showed about the same proportions.[69]

As black deaths in northern cities increased with the increase in population, birth rates went down, so that in most cities there was less than zero rate of increase. In New York State Negro deaths exceeded births by about 400 a year from 1895 to 1915. Among Pittsburgh blacks, deaths exceeded births by 55 per cent, while in the total population of the city, births exceeded deaths by 30 per cent. Among both blacks and whites in the North the death rate soared in 1917–18 when epidemic diseases, especially Spanish influenza, carried off great numbers of soldiers and civilians. Meanwhile, the birth rate among northern and western urban blacks dropped much below that of southern rural blacks. Undoubtedly this had largely to do with the unsettled conditions during periods of migration and readjustment; also, as Powdermaker points out, in the rural South a large family was an economic asset; in the North, children were extra mouths to feed, extra bodies to house, clothe, and care for, to mothers who in many cases went out to work six or seven days a week. In addition, during the transitional years in urban ghettos, there was, as mentioned, a large percentage of single men and women, and there were many men whose wives had not yet joined them; in the irregular alliances such a situation would encourage, babies would not be eagerly welcomed. Still, however, blacks continued to have more children than whites. In 1900 there were 27.4 per cent of black children under 10 in the population, to 23.3 per cent of white children; in 1910, 25.5 per cent black to 21.8 per cent white; and in 1920, 23.0 per cent black to 21.5 per cent white.[70]

Before reaching the age of ten, five, or even one, however, a staggering number of black children died. More than one quarter of these children never reached one year of age, an infant death rate that was twice that of white infants. Between 1915 and 1919, 149.7 black babies died among each 1,000 born, compared to 92.8 white babies per 1,000.[71] In Pittsburgh, the figures for the first seven months of 1917 show that of 356 infants born, 87 died. Infant mortality was at its highest in the summer months in the steaming, overcrowded ghettos; it was then, as Ovington said, that "the babies die like flies,"[72] of convulsions due to unidentified diseases, of the "summer complaint" they got from contaminated food and milk; and all year long they died of whooping cough, tuberculosis, and pneumonia, weakened and rickety from improper diet and lack of sunshine.[73]

That the high death rate among black babies was not a racial but a ghetto weakness was demonstrated by the New York Bureau of Child Hygiene in the Health Department, when Dr. Jacob Sobel brought together all community resources in a crash program to reduce infant mortality. Sobel went after what he called "the triad of 'baby-killers'—poverty, ignorance, and neglect," which he said worked even more havoc among black children than among white children. Sobel attacked not merely symptoms but causes. His dramatic effort combined baby clinics, visiting nurses, a "Little Mothers" group, educational lectures and slides, newspaper articles, a Health Department bulletin, day nurseries, home inspection visits, improvements by the Tenement House Department, free ice and milk, and jobs for men so that women could stay home and care for the children. As a result of this program, deaths among black infants dropped from 202 per 1,000 (white rate: 96 per 1,000) in 1915 to 173 per 1,000 in 1917 and then to 151 per 1,000 in 1919.[74] Sobel's work demonstrated what could be accomplished by marshaling community resources in a generous and intelligent use of knowledge, effort, money, and compassion.

Mental and physical health in the ghettos suffered from an almost total lack of wholesome recreation, particularly needed where home was so cramped and depressing that no one cared to spend time there. The Urban League, social agencies, and churches tried to provide for this need, but existing public facilities were as inadequate as existing housing to accommodate the influx of migrants. Also, although there was no legal Jim Crow, there was plenty of a menacing unofficial kind at parks, beaches, theaters, and dance halls. In a study of forty northern cities in the late 1920s, it was found that two thirds practiced some form of segregation in settlement houses, movies, theaters, and amusement parks. The YMCA and YWCA were strictly segregated, as in southern cities. Where blacks were admitted at all, they had separate swimming days and separate classes. New York had the first black YMCA, established in 1900. Two years later a private company, Consolidated Coal, built a $20,000 Y in the company town of Buxton, Iowa, for its mostly black miners. In 1906 John D. Rockefeller pledged $25,000 toward a Negro Y building in Washington, D.C., and a few years later, Julius Rosenwald offered $25,000 to any city that would put up the rest of the money for a black Y. In 1913 an all-black Y was established in Chicago with the help of Rosenwald's gift and other moneys, including some from the national Y itself. This building helped fill a vital need in the migration time, when no black could get a bed or use any of the facilities of the regular Y's, the Salvation Army, or the Mills Hotels.[75]

The Crime Commission of Chicago said in 1919: "The answer to the lack of a sufficient number of well-ordered places of recreation and amusement is to be found in the thriving condition of Chicago's cheap dance halls, underworld cabarets, unsupervised movie theaters of the cheaper class and the large number of pool-rooms scattered throughout the city."[76] While this was true to an extent for all the poor of Chicago, it was particularly true in the black ghettos.

The Negro churches, always social centers in the South, played the same role for the ghetto dweller in the North. DuBois reported this in the Philadelphia of 1900, and it continued to be true. Church services, with their spirited preaching, singing, and praying, were refreshing in themselves, and in addition there were frequent lectures, banquets, box suppers, receptions, plays, and concerts. Crowding gave churches a problem, too, and until new ones were organized (thirty-four in Chicago alone, between 1915 and 1920; thirty-nine in Detroit in 1919), some churches held double services. In addition to religious and recreational functions, the busy and fast-growing churches set up employment and welfare agencies. In the migration years, at least half of northern blacks were church members. Pittsburgh reported 76 per cent church attendance.[77]

The form of recreation in which blacks had had most experience and opportunity was music, and this was the staple entertainment in and outside of church, with no sharp line between sacred and profane. Spirituals had borrowed from folk songs; gospel music borrowed popular song tunes and forms, and was the church counterpart of city blues music; popular music borrowed back from church music, and many of the famous black composer-musicians emerged from church playing. Pianist Tom Dorsey migrated about 1919 from Georgia, where his father was a country preacher, to the steel mills in Gary, Indiana; he began by composing church songs, and then joined the band that accompanied the blues singer Ma Rainey.[78]

An event that gave a great lift to black music in northern cities was the closing down of Storyville, the New Orleans redlight district, in 1917. New Orleans jazz bands had been touring the North for some ten years, but at the peak of the migration, ousted from New Orleans by the Storyville cleanup, many black musicians headed for Memphis and points north, chiefly Chicago. Among the greats were Louis Armstrong and King Oliver. The jazz diaspora brought badly needed entertainment of a high order to Harlem and other northern inner cities. Harlem particularly grew outstanding for entertainment, because at about the same time as the jazz bands arrived, black musical comedy moved up from Broadway, where it had for some years been popular with white theatergoers. Black artists like performer Will Marion Cook, singer Harry Burleigh, poet Paul Dunbar, composer Bob Cole, the lyrics and music team of James Weldon Johnson and his brother J. Rosamond, and others of their level had formed an élite creative circle in New York when the center of "Black Bohemia" was in mid-Manhattan, at the Marshall Hotel on West Fifty-third Street; but the excitement of Harlem attracted and inspired them and a crowd of other black writers, musicians, and performers.[79] White New Yorkers began to drift up to Harlem to see black shows and dance to black bands, and ghetto people who had the price could get first-class entertainment in Harlem theaters, dance halls, and nightclubs.

To ghetto dwellers deprived of many of the usual social and recreational outlets, lodge night gave a wonderful outlet. The elaborate secret rituals, splendid regalia, and pompous titles these lodges favored have been laughed at by upper-class blacks as well as whites. Rudolph Fisher said Negro organizations tried to include in their names "delineation, history, and prophecy," and to make them "encompass a society's past, present and future";[80] and Octavus Roy Cohen poked fun in many of his spurious Negro stories at "The Sons and Daughters of I Will Arise." But titles of this kind were the style in both black and white lodges. The "Star Order of Ethiopia and Ethiopian Missionaries of Abyssinia"[81] is succinct and factual compared with "Supreme Council, Mystic Order Veiled Prophets of the Enchanted Realm" or "Imperial Council of the Ancient Arabic Order of the Nobles of the Mystic Shrine for North America."[82] Ritual and regalia as well as titles may have been copied from white lodges, but were not much more elaborate, if at all. The vital role of lodges to the ghetto man puts in question Myrdal's theory that the black lodge was a pathological replica of white society in which blacks displayed exaggerated manifestations of the American norm.[83]

No phase of Negro life grew so rapidly as the fraternal society. It gave the ghetto-bound black man his own organization, where he could identify his interests with those of his own people and satisfy a social want ignored by the white community. Many of the migrants had been lodge members in the South, where fraternal orders were thriving by 1900. At that time black lodges were estimated to be worth between $5,000,000 and $6,000,000. By 1906, 80,000 black lodge members in Mississippi alone had paid more than $550,000 in dues and assessments, of which $450,000 was paid back in death and burial benefits. Boston in 1914 had at least 30 to 40 black lodges, including Odd Fellows, Masons, Elks, Knights of Pythias, and smaller orders. Black members founded a Masonic temple in Harlem in 1916, and there were also by that time many black Elks and Odd Fellows lodges in New York.[84]

Lodges in their thriving time early in the century were far more than social clubs; for both blacks and whites, they were insurance companies and burial societies. DuBois pointed out that the burial function of Philadelphia lodges was particularly important because blacks could not be buried in white cemeteries. One burial lodge owned eight acres of ground and was worth over $100,000. With burials insured, black funerals became costly and lavish affairs, which must have helped make black undertakers one of the most prosperous groups of Negro business-men. The insurance program of the lodges, which brought in very substantial amounts of money, is said to have been the start of most Negro banks, organized as depositories for lodge funds; and part of the insurance funds was invested in real estate.[85]

The most outstanding and successful black fraternal society was the Grand Fountain United Order of True Reformers, founded in the South in 1881 for the usual social and insurance purposes. Before 1900 it owned a great deal of property, pub-lished the *True Reformer* (circulation 8,000), established the True Reformers Bank and the Old Folks Home of the Grand Fountain, and began large-scale co-operative business and farm-ing ventures; within a short time after 1900 it opened the Hotel Reformer in Richmond, Virginia, and founded a building and loan association.[86]

The banking function of the lodges gradually passed into the hands of black-owned banks, as more black businesses in the ghettos needed more funding than they could get from white banks. And as more black institutions sprang up in the ghettos—banks, insurance companies, hospitals—the savings and "benefi-cial" functions of the lodge became less essential and more diffi-cult to maintain against commercial competition. But its social functions were vitally important for the ghetto man, providing as it did a meeting place of a respectable kind, companionship, splendor, and excitement, which relieved the dreary monotony of ghetto life.[87]

DuBois contrasted with his Talented Tenth the group at the opposite end of the social spectrum, which he called the "sub-merged tenth" and described as "the lowest class of criminals, prostitutes and loafers."[88] It was a large class, to judge by the not too reliable evidence of arrests, convictions, and jail popu-lation. From 1900 to 1910, although Negroes constituted only 10 to 11 per cent of the population, blacks in jail constituted about 30 per cent of the prisoner group.[89] Also, blacks were likely to be in for longer terms. In 1910, for example, of persons sentenced to a year or more, 40.9 per cent were black; of persons sentenced to death, 37.7 per cent were black; but of persons sentenced to terms under a year, only 13.4 per cent were black. By population, more blacks than whites were arrested, but the percentage of those whose cases were dismissed was also very high, about one third of those arrested. The high dismissal rate suggests hasty, unwarranted, mass seizure of blacks, often only on suspicion, perhaps merely because of being found near the scene of a crime. Many of those picked up for vagrancy were simply recent arrivals in the ghetto who were wandering in search of a job or a bed.[90] As to the large number of blacks convicted and sentenced, the Census Bureau itself warned against taking this as proof of black criminality, because "an offense committed by a Negro is perhaps more likely to be punished than the same offense committed by a white man."[91] Other reasons why many blacks went to jail and why many drew long sentences were linked with poverty; they could not take the option of a fine instead of imprisonment, nor could they afford good lawyers. Considering the number of arrests for such minor offenses as gambling, being drunk or disorderly, or violating minor city ordinances, many could probably have got off with a fine if they had had the money. The number of arrests in Pittsburgh for such offenses increased 80 per cent from 1915 to 1917, although arrests for graver crimes like larceny and rape remained stable or even declined.[92] A peak number of migrants arrived in 1917, which suggests that minor offenses were due largely to ignorance of city ways on the part of the newly arrived Southerners.

In view of the popular linking of Negroes with sex crimes, it is particularly significant that, although nationwide more than 25 per cent of those committed for rape were black, the percentage in the South was over 66, while that in the North was less than 13; in both North and South, the percentage of blacks committed for rape was lower than the percentage committed for other serious crimes, such as homicide, assault, robbery, and burglary. It is probable, however, that rape by black men of black women rarely got on the books, just as, in the South, crimes of violence committed by blacks upon blacks seldom received official attention. The city fathers of Memphis, for instance, in response to the accusation that their city had the highest homi-

cide rate in the country, said most of the murders were of Negroes by Negroes, so the police and government could not be
held responsible. That would explain why, when black migrants
in Pittsburgh found they might be sent to jail for "cutting" another black man, they were very much surprised.[93]

Many people were willing to believe Vardaman when he said
in 1904 that the Negroes "are deteriorating morally every day"
and that "they are increasing in criminality with frightful ra-
pidity. . . ."[94] But social scientists were beginning to understand
why there was, or at least seemed to be, a higher percentage of
law-breakers among blacks than their population percentage—
about three times higher. In the first place, as the Chicago Commission on Race Relations pointed out, crime committed by
blacks had to be seen in the total context of their history and
existence: "The traditional ostracism, exploitation and petty daily
insults to which they are continually exposed have doubtless
provoked, even in normal-minded Negroes, a pathological attitude toward society which sometimes expresses itself defen-
sively in acts of violence and other lawlessness."[95] Then, as
Reuter observed, Negro fear of whites led to resentment and a
daring attitude toward violating white laws; in addition, crime
and punishment have only a tenuous connection for people who
have suffered the undeserved penalties of debt slavery and convict lease.[96] "Crime," Kelly Miller said in 1914, "is a question
of condition, not of color." He added: "If the entire Negro population should withdraw from the South and its place be supplied
with whites occupying a similar status, the crime rate of the
South would *not* be appreciably affected."[97] He might have said
the same of the North. John Daniels, commenting on the fact
that 3.3 per cent of convicts in Massachusetts were Negroes
although they formed only 1.1 per cent of the total state population, pointed out: "If the Negroes were of an exceptionally criminal bent, such an innate proclivity combined with the social
and economic adversities with which they have had to cope,
would make their percentage of convicts much more than three
times as large as their percentage of the population."[98]

Still, the average white resident in northern cities was convinced that blacks had an innate proclivity toward crime. Many

social workers, and some Negroes themselves, talked loosely about black criminality, with no facts to back up their talk.[99] According to a Labor Department statement: "A colored probation officer in Pittsburgh, for example, believed that the juvenile delinquency among her people had at least doubled during the past year, and was much surprised when an examination of the records revealed that it had considerably decreased."[100] The press fed popular beliefs with sensational stories. Negro crime was news, and so it was one of very few aspects of black life that made the white newspapers. Herbert Seligmann, himself a journalist, castigated the press for playing up sensational stories without regard for accuracy. There was much talk, Seligmann said, "that the Negro is racially and by nature a criminal. Statistics of crime are adduced in proof. Then the social scientist investigates and discovers that a far larger percent of Negro mothers than white must leave their families during the daytime in order to earn money, thus contributing to juvenile delinquency. He discovers that in Southern courts Negroes are convicted on evidence on which any white man would go scot-free." And, most significantly, he added: "He finds that Negro vice, of which there is so much talk, is much more closely involved with the 'superior race' than the reports of the newspapers would indicate."[101]

Years later, Myrdal echoed Seligmann's accusation of 1920. He found that much of the crime in the ghettos, although committed by blacks, existed because of whites; that the ghettos were unprotected by police; and that crime flourished in the ghettos because police and politicians profited by bribes to let it flourish.[102] In one mining town, the Labor Department reported, the police acted in collusion with local lawyers; the policemen get $2.00 per head for picking up blacks for petty offenses, such as gambling, from lawyers who would then offer to defend them for a fee of around $50.[103] Roi Ottley reported that in Chicago's red-light district black men, women, and children catered to a white clientele; and he quoted an unnamed black leader as saying that "a good deal of the vice in the 'colored belt' is the white man's vice, thrust there by the authorities against the protest of the colored people."[104] So in two ways, it appears, black vice was "closely involved with the 'superior race.'"

New York's Tenderloin, and Harlem, when that succeeded the Tenderloin as the city's major black ghetto, were thriving vice areas, full of saloons, gambling joints, prostitutes, pimps, and drug peddlers. The ghetto was the best graft area in the city; so much in bribes or protection money was handed out that, it was said, any police captain in the precinct a year "could live on tenderloin steaks the rest of his life."[105] Many of the vice resorts were owned or run by blacks who had grown rich by peddling flesh, booze, or dope. One such appears in a story by Rudolph Fisher; he is a black man named Edwards, a former Pullman porter, the owner of a seedy basement cabaret in Harlem during Prohibition, who "stands in with the police, with the political bosses, with the importers of wine and worse." Edwards is a big wheel in the dope racket and has lieutenants who pass the drugs on to addicts. "Dope," one of them pleads in the story, "coke, milk, dice—anything. Name your price. Got to have it."[106] Then, as now, the price was most likely come by through crime, and perhaps accounted for many of the assaults, robberies, and burglaries. But the political bosses could not concern themselves with crime. They were paid off by men like Edwards; and if they in turn paid back a small part of that money to ghetto men for the votes that kept them in a position of power, it was no more than these migrants from the South had learned to expect.

Social scientists noted the significant correlation between the crowded conditions of the ghetto and crime, especially fighting and brawling, assaults, and sex crimes. In Pittsburgh, a few tenements notorious for overcrowding showed an extraordinarily high incidence of arrests; one house with over a hundred families living in it had eighty-four arrests in seven months during 1914–15, and over a hundred arrests in seven months of 1917. The Chicago Commission on Race Relations observed that, because of the enclosed nature of the ghetto, perfectly respectable black people had no choice but to live in these breeding grounds of crime, close to the saloons, brothels, and other dives where vice flourished; further, they had far too little political power to effect a cleanup of the vice that so richly rewarded corrupt officials.[107]

So they had to bring up their children in this vicious atmosphere, surrounded by the crime that paid for the indulgence of vices. Yet when more Negroes, proportionately, than white people were arrested and jailed, the commonplace reaction was that blacks had by nature a streak of criminality.

Most arrests of women were for prostitution. White prostitution, said the Chicago Commission on Race Relations, was likely to be "more or less clandestine," but black prostitution was more observable because blacks were confined to ghetto areas. A much larger proportion of black women than white women landed in jail, especially young women between eighteen and twenty-four. In that age group, by population, eleven to sixteen black women were jailed for each white woman, whereas among men, the ratio was three to four blacks for each white. There might not have been quite so many black women in jail if there had been more correctional facilities for them of the reformatory type, to which many white women were sent instead of being put in prison.[108] The New York *Age* was complaining indignantly by 1911 that Harlem was becoming "infested" with "the dance-hall harlot and the diamond-decked lover,"[109] and the infestation increased as the migration quickened. Some of the women may have been prostitutes before they came North, but many, apparently, were simply ignorant, gullible girls recruited by labor agents on the promise of easy jobs and good pay. Some of them were recruited deliberately for prostitution; others went expecting to find domestic or industrial jobs that never materialized, and they too landed on the streets.[110] Girls lucky enough to get jobs discovered they were at the bottom of the wage scale, and sometimes had to moonlight on the streets to live. Some must have been encouraged to try their luck because of the great number of unattached young males in the ghettos, many of whom were making more money than they had ever dreamed possible.

The children in the ghettos, exposed to all the vice and crime that flourished there, and many of them thrown on their own while their mothers worked, might be expected to get into trouble, and many did. As Seligmann observed, many more of their mothers worked than white children's mothers. At home there was grinding poverty, and so little space as to preclude any privacy. Children often shared their rooms and even their beds not just with family members but with lodgers. They had no play place beyond what the schools and streets offered. The schools were new and strange, and the academically retarded southern child got little help in adjusting to them; they felt inferior and tended to become "incorrigibles," then truants, and finally juvenile delinquents. Often the truancy that landed them in children's courts was not known by them or their parents to be against the law, because where most migrants came from school attendance was not compulsory.[111]

Census figures show that 20 per cent of all juvenile delinquents were black, a high rate but lower than the 30 per cent of blacks among adult criminals. This relatively low percentage may be explained in part by the fact that where correctional facilities did not exist, or were overcrowded, black delinquents were allowed to remain at large and thus were not represented in official counts.[112] Or did the police ignore a certain amount of black juvenile delinquency, as they ignored a certain amount of black adult crime, if the only people who suffered by it were themselves black? Most petty larceny and mischief done by black youths must have been restricted to the ghettos, so perhaps the police winked at it. Still, from the way these children lived, one would expect that more of them would have gotten on the police records. Perhaps the premises of black immorality and of the looseness of black family structure should be re-examined. Or perhaps ghetto children were a tougher and more resilient lot than anyone has said, most of them able to deal with immorality and an irregular home life without serious damage to themselves.

Gradually the white community became aware of the appalling conditions within the cities, and the reform spirit of that Progressive era moved a number of white people to try to help the migrants. Sociological studies set forth the facts of Negro life in the ghettos, including such important books as Frances Kellor's *Out of Work* (1904), Baker's *Following the Color Line* (1908), Mary Ovington's *Half a Man: The Status of the Negro in New York* (1911), Daniels' *In Freedom's Birthplace: A History of the*

Boston Negro (1914), Epstein's *The Negro Migrant in Pittsburgh* (1918), and Seligmann's *The Negro Faces America* (1920). Ground had been broken for these urban studies by DuBois's *The Philadelphia Negro* in 1899. One of the most distinguished of the later studies was also by a black scholar, George Edmund Haynes, whose *The Negro at Work in New York City* (1912) was exceeded in importance only by the later reports on the migrants when he was director, during the war, of the Division of Negro Economics in the U. S. Department of Labor, reports whose outspokenness would perhaps not have been tolerated except during a period when the mounting needs of war production made people willing to try anything that might help keep the black laborers working.

Progressivism brought social respectability to social consciousness, and many middle- and upper-class white women dedicated themselves to the betterment of the urban Negro. Baker mentions especially Misses Bartholomew, Hancock, and Wharton in Philadelphia, Miss Eaton in Boston, Mrs. Celia Parker Wooley in Chicago, and Miss Mary White Ovington in New York. It was through Mary Ovington's urging, when she discovered the horrors of ghetto conditions, that steel magnate Henry Phipps in 1907 built the model Phipps Houses in New York's San Juan Hill district, houses that were fireproof and had steam heat, and where Miss Ovington herself was a tenant for a time—the only white person in the development.[113] Through the concern of these women and others like them, settlement houses proliferated in the ghettos. In 1906 Lillian Wald opened Stillman House, a branch of her Lower Manhattan Henry Street Settlement, in the San Juan Hill area. New York also had Mary Kingsley Simkovitch's Green House. The Mary F. Walton Free Kindergarten for black children gave working ghetto mothers some relief and drew support from such prominent New Yorkers as Mrs. Walter Jennings, wife of the Standard Oil Company millionaire; Jacob Riis; Professor Morris Loeb; and, again, Mary Ovington. Lillian Wald's Lincoln Day Nursery also helped. One of the oldest and most useful ghetto agencies was the New York Colored Mission, a biracial group founded by Quakers after the Civil War, which during the migration period served as an employment bureau and provider of temporary housing, medical care, and food for the newly arrived blacks; the Mission also founded several boys' clubs. In Philadelphia, DuBois gave special mention to the Home Missionary Society as particularly friendly to black people. The Travellers' Aid and YMCA also helped.[114]

But despite the efforts of social workers, agencies, and missions, there were never enough facilities or enough money or enough anything to meet the rapidly increasing needs of the ghetto as the migration came to its flood tide. There was much waste and duplication of effort on the part of these agencies because of a lack of organization and co-operation among themselves. Besides, the patronizing Lady Bountiful attitude of some of the social service groups irritated ghetto people so much that they rejected their help. In general, few black people were invited to sit on the boards of these groups. The Flanner Guild seems to have been an exception; founded and funded by whites, it was black-controlled.[115]

Black people themselves, however, worked for ghetto welfare. Sometimes they did this in co-operation with white individuals or agencies, as in the Hope Day Nursery for Colored Children, founded in New York in 1902 by a group of black mothers whose children were rejected by a white day nursery. An outstanding example was the White Rose Industrial Association, which operated the White Rose Working Girls' Home, its purpose to "check the evil of unscrupulous employment agents who deceived the unsuspecting girls desiring to come North."[116] Mrs. Victoria Earle Matthews, who had been a slave in Georgia, founded the organization in 1897. In Norfolk, Virginia, where many black girls embarked for the trip North, White Rose stationed agents who tried to explain to the girls the perils to which they were exposing themselves. In New York other agents met the boats, helped the girls find a place to live or housed them temporarily in the White Rose Working Girls' Home, tried to place them in decent jobs, and taught them domestic science and "race history." Frances Kellor's Out of Work aroused pity for these young black women, so many of whom were going to land on the streets and in the police stations. In 1905, a year after the Kellor book appeared and possibly as a result of it, Mrs.

Matthews' organization became part of the New York League for the Protection of Colored Women, which soon became a national organization with branches in many cities and a distinguished roster of both black and white patrons.[117]

The black or mostly black organizations to help ghetto people that sprang up in every city indicate that not all northern blacks were hostile to the migrants, and that black people were active in improving their own conditions. Black churches did relief work, especially the African Methodist Episcopal, and tried to bring the newcomers into their congregations, said Emmett Scott, although the churches drew criticism from some for spending more on new buildings and show than on good works. The black church was also active in the temperance movement, and ministers denounced the evils of drink, which was held responsible for the high crime rate. Black liquor dealers, in self-defense, formed the Negro Liquor Dealers Association to improve the image of the saloon, and Boston had the Harriet Tubman WCTU Home. In Detroit, Negro college men formed the Young Negroes' Progressive Association to organize recreation and summer camps for young people. The work of the New York Colored Mission has already been mentioned. There was in New York also the Young Men's Industrial League, founded by T. Thomas Fortune, publisher of the New York *Age,* in 1895, which helped black youths train for and find jobs; later organizations for the same purpose were the Associated Colored Employees of America and the interracial Committee for Improving the Industrial Conditions of Negroes, both in New York. In all big cities, blacks formed state clubs—the Sons and Daughters of South Carolina, Georgia, Alabama, and so on. These helped migrants find friends and relations from their home states, and thus relieved the loneliness of the strange big city. Toward the same end, churches held special services for people of each southern state. And as businesses sprang up in the ghettos, migrants had the comfort of being able to go to southern-style barber shops and saloons, and to groceries and restaurants that specialized in regional southern food; many migrants quickly made small fortunes by catering to their fellow Southerners in such enterprises. Booker T. Washington's National Negro Business League helped these businessmen, and, later, so did DuBois's Negro Cooperative League. The National Medical Association provided a center for black medical men, who were not acceptable to the segregated American Medical Association. George Haynes was active, while he worked for the U. S. Department of Labor, in establishing in a number of cities a Negro Advisory Committee, an organization where employers could discuss problems with their workers, both black and white. And in all the city ghettos, black women formed clubs for operating day nurseries and kindergartens, for instructing and helping migrant mothers, and to train women in such skills as sewing in order to place them in jobs. The Colored Women's Conference of Chicago represented over half a dozen such clubs.[118]

Lodges, clubs, churches; nurseries, kindergartens, homes for girls and orphans; uplift, welfare, business and professional groups—all helped mitigate the sufferings of the migrants, but they did little to broaden their horizons. Two organizations, however, born as the migrants began to fill the inner cities, had the long-range goal of getting them out. In the two years between 1909 and 1911, both the National Association for the Advancement of Colored People and the National Urban League were formed. They were manifestations of the break from the old leadership of Booker T. Washington and his philosophy of the virtues of the rural life, of salvation through lowly labor well and willingly done, of cultivation of decency, sobriety, and manual skills so as to win the acceptance of the white world, of gradualism by such small steps that it seemed blacks could never reach social or political equality. The new organizations showed the ascendancy of DuBois's leadership, of a whole new school of blacks who taught self-respect and insisted on equal rights and opportunities in education, labor, and every other field of life. The new leadership will be discussed later; what is pertinent here is its impact on the migrants in the ghettos.

The NAACP encouraged southern blacks to migrate and served as a clearinghouse for information about migration and the ghettos, but its chief purpose, from its inception, was to safeguard the constitutional rights of black people and to combat legislation that threatened these. The average ghetto man was rarely directly touched by its work, and many had probably never heard of the organization, which in 1913 had only one southern branch and by 1916 still only six. The Urban League, however, worked directly with the needs of ghetto people for better housing, cleanliness, and health, better training and employment opportunities, better pay, and better relations with the labor unions; and also with their need to adjust their country manners to the quite different circumstances of city life. The purpose of the Urban League's parent group, the Committee on Urban Conditions among Negroes, was to encourage co-operation among all social service organizations active in ghetto affairs and to provide them with information and help. When the Urban League emerged, its major function was to improve conditions and relations of labor. It worked with the migrants, instructing them, training them, and investigating their complaints; at the same time, it worked with white employers, helping them to train and screen potential workers. It was also from the very first deeply concerned with the problems of women migrants, and the National League for the Protection of Colored Women was absorbed into the National Urban League as early as 1911.[119]

But neither the two major organizations nor all the smaller ones together could give the mass of blacks a decent life in the ghettos. Their needs were simply too great. In their ignorance and helplessness they were materials for exploitation by greedy landlords and businessmen, and by vicious characters, both black and white; they were victims of indifference in the schools and city departments, of a corrupt police force and discriminatory judges; and they bore the sicknesses visited on them by poverty, ignorance, and filth with an almost complete absence of health and medical services. Most of all, they were victims of poverty, of unfulfilled needs so broad and deep that the wonder is they survived.

Still, dreadful as conditions were for blacks in the North, there was always the possibility of achievement for extraordinarily strong, gifted, or lucky people, a possibility that the South had cut off with disfranchisement, systematic Jim Crow, and the attitude even among enlightened whites that the Negro must be kept in his place. The list of migrant blacks who made good in the North is long and significant. Among them one might mention William Lewis Bulkley, from rural South Carolina, who became a school principal and was one of the founders of the National Urban League; James Weldon and J. Rosamond Johnson, from Florida; T. Thomas Fortune, also from Florida; wealthy and successful business people like Lillian Harris in real estate, Madame C. J. Walker who invented a hair-straightening process, manufacturer H. C. Haynes, James C. Thomas and Henry C. Parker in real estate; bankers and money lenders Jesse Binga, J. Franklin Smallwood, J. S. Montague, and Henry White; and New York politician Ferdinand Q. Morton. The list could be doubled or trebled, but let it suffice to add two internationally famous migrants, W. C. Handy, born in Alabama, and Jack Johnson, born in Texas.

Of course, these are "exceptional" people, as are great achievers of whatever color. The point is, although it was not easy to rise in the North, it was possible. For the less gifted and fortunate migrants, there was the possibility that their children might make good. And, bad as things were in Harlem or Bucktown or Chicago's black belt, you didn't get lynched on 135th Street, you didn't have to "mister" every little white boy, and you could put your ballot in the box the same as John D. Rockefeller.

Many migrants must have been homesick for the South, but few went back. One black man wrote this to the Chicago *Defender:* "After twenty years of seeing my people lynched for any offense from spitting on the sidewalk to stealing a mule, I made up my mind that I would turn the prow of my ship toward the part of the country where the people at least made a pretense at being civilized. You may say for me, through your paper, that when a man's home is sacred; when he can protect the virtue of his wife and daughter against the brutal lust of his alleged superiors; when he can sleep at night without the fear of being visited by the Ku-Klux because of refusal to take off his hat while passing an overseer—then I will be willing to return to Mississippi."[120] While James K. Vardaman was governor, and then senator, there was little chance of such changes in Mississippi. Migrants came to the ghettos, stayed, and began to find a place in the economy and society of northern cities.

CHAPTER 5

Pushing Ahead in the Economy

. . . the young white man starts in
life knowing that within some limits
and barring accidents, talent and application will tell. The young Negro
starts knowing that on all sides his advance is made doubly difficult if not
wholly shut off by his color.

W. E. B. DuBois,
The Philadelphia Negro, 1899

Of course, as a Negro said to me,
"there are always places for the coloured man at the bottom." He can always get work at unskilled manual
labour, or personal or domestic service—in other words, at menial employment. He has had that in plenty in the
South. But what he seeks as he becomes educated is an opportunity for
better grades of employment. He
wants to rise.

Ray Stannard Baker,
Following the Color Line, 1908

The first decade of the century was a promising time for those who sought to rise in the American economy. Following the Spanish-American War, industrial production steadily increased, farm prices rose, and unemployment diminished, even though European immigrant workers were arriving in larger and larger numbers, from half a million in 1900 to more than a million in 1914. The national wealth nearly doubled in the decade after 1900; total physical production leaped by 75 per cent to 90 per cent. United States investments abroad in 1914 were five times as great as in 1897. Money was becoming concentrated in fewer hands; by 1909, close to half the nation's manufactures were produced by only 1 per cent of the industrial firms.[1] But two forces were struggling to control unbridled capitalism: the Progressives in politics, and the labor unions. When Europe became involved in the Great War, the already booming economy surged still higher, and the struggle among government, labor, and capital became more intense with the vastly increased demand for more goods and a broader distribution of wealth. Great industrialists and businessmen shared their fortunes by philanthropy while obstinately defending their right to increase those fortunes without controls, at the expense of competitors and of the poor who were the objects of their philanthropy.

The Department of Labor summed up the situation of 1917 as it referred to the people of the ghettos: "That the present economic stability of the Negro worker is low is evident; but consideration must be given to the fact that these newcomers are handicapped, as were the foreign immigrants, by an almost universal attitude of 'laissez faire' and individualism in the northern cities. The communities have assumed almost no control of his living conditions, and the burden of his success or failure in establishing himself has rested on his own weak shoulders."[2]

In this striving, cutthroat world of big and expanding business, most of the migrants became the smallest cogs in the great money machines of railroading, coal, oil, steel, meat packing, and manufacturing. At least 90 per cent of black industrial workers were common laborers in huge and growing plants.[3] While European immigration dropped, as the result of the war in Europe, from the 1914 peak of 1,200,000 to an average of about 235,000 for the next five years, southern blacks were moving in to fill the labor vacuum. Depending on how well they had been selected for their jobs, and what were their wages, conditions of labor, and relations with employers and unions, they succeeded or failed, just like white workers.

Polls of employers produced the whole range of opinion about blacks. The Urban League of Pittsburgh found that the Negro laborer could do anything the white could do, and a poll of employers in Cleveland yielded the same result. The Division of Negro Economics in the U. S. Department of Labor reported that semiskilled black workers in the auto industry in Detroit—molders, dippers, punch press operators—were doing well; a report quoted one automobile company in Detroit as saying that the 1,200 to 1,500 blacks in its employ were very satisfactory, and another auto manufacturer who employed a group of blacks for such semiskilled work as riveting, drilling, filing, and pressing in hangers and bushings said they proved 300 per cent more efficient than white workers who had preceded them. In foundry work, the Department of Labor published the general opinion of owners and managers that black molders gave complete satisfaction even under the pressures of war production and that the Negro was making good. In other polls of employers in Cincinnati, Chicago, and Detroit, at least three quarters of the responding companies found black workers satisfactory. One unusual group of migrants, young students from Hampton Institute who went to work for tobacco planters in Connecticut, were highly praised as being well-behaved, industrious, thrifty, pious, clean, and thoroughly successful. Employers of black women as domestics had long expressed the belief that they were much more likely than white girls to become attached to the family, to be loyal, stanch, and affectionate friends, to stay in one job, to be respectful and obliging and well-mannered. Now black women were found satisfactory workers by employers who hired large numbers of them in industry and manufacturing, reported the Women's Bureau of the Department of Labor, and they were as successful as could be expected considering their handicaps of background and training, and the discrimination practiced against them.[4]

Good opinions of black workers were fairly general but not universal, and employers who found in them the stereotypic characteristics of stupidity and laziness, shiftlessness and undependability, seldom bothered to look for the qualities of ghetto life that might make for such traits and try to alleviate them.[5] Seligmann quoted an officer of the Labor Department as saying: "It is unreasonable to expect 100 per cent efficiency from a man who is obliged to sleep in a public park, in a sub-basement, or in a ten-by-twelve foot room with half a dozen other men."[6] Instead, the exhaustion resulting from chronic lack of sleep was taken to mean that blacks were naturally lazy and sleepy. A mill owner said: "A Negro can't work in a mill. The hum of the machinery would put him to sleep."[7] Another problem, it has been said, was that southern migrants, especially rural people, were not accustomed to the rigid hours and six-day work week of industry, and some had difficulty adjusting to their employers' expectations in regard to prompt, daily attendance.[8]

It is scarcely surprising that the black workers who were least satisfactory—those Baker said the bosses found "undisciplined, irresponsible, and sometimes actually dishonest"[9]—were those migrants who had been picked up by labor agents at random off southern street corners and crossroads, and simply herded into boxcars for a ride North with the promise of a job at the end of the trip. The railroads and steel companies acquired a lot of their labor force that way, and many of the unselected, single, young black men they scooped up were indeed shiftless drifters or irresponsible youths. The companies housed these men in camps under the more or less dreadful conditions that have been described, and then complained that most of them stayed only long enough to collect a first paycheck. The Pennsylvania, Baltimore & Ohio, New York Central, and Erie railroads all had trouble with the tremendous turnover rate of their black migrant laborers. One road brought more than 13,000 southern blacks up North between July 1916 and July 1917, but in a few months had only 1,880 left. At the Carnegie steel plant in Youngstown the employment department had to hire five men to keep every two jobs filled. It is quite clear that the worse the living conditions, the greater the turnover. In Pittsburgh, with its notorious ghetto conditions, plants could not keep their workers; one company lost 700 out of 1,000 it brought North; another lost 10,000 out of 12,-000. As to the lack of selectivity on the part of the labor agents, whether they were unscrupulous and knowingly hired unqualified help (for example, representing farm laborers as experienced miners) or whether they were so harassed by southern police and officials that they couldn't take time to be selective, the results in many cases were bad, and nourished prejudices against blacks as workers.[10]

To say that black workers responded well to decent, fair treatment seems to have racially patronizing overtones, but the same was true of white workers. The employer who listened to complaints, adjusted grievances, and gave equal pay and opportunity to his black workers was naturally the one who found them most satisfactory and co-operative; difficulties between black and white workers were often created by white gang bosses and supervisors who refused to give blacks any job except common labor. Segregation within the plant—separate workrooms, washrooms, and so forth—was resented by blacks who thought they had left Jim Crow behind. Another and perhaps greater cause of dissatisfaction was that the 90 per cent of black migrants in industry who were employed at common labor could see no way out of this dismal rut, no chance of promotion no matter how punctual and regular they were, no matter how well they performed. In the Chicago stockyards the highest position a black worker could hope to reach, and that was a dim hope only, was subforeman of a gang of black workers. There advancement was blocked, because promotion beyond that point would create the intolerable situation of a black man supervising white workers. As Baker commented, "there are always places for the coloured man at the bottom," but he wants to be "judged at his worth as a man, not as a Negro," and he can't find a job that will let him advance according to his ability and training. The same lack of incentive held back black women of ability.[11]

The inferior job stamps the holder of that job with its quality of inferiority, John Daniels wrote, especially when the job is of a personal-service nature, such as bellboy, bootblack, or waiter, where the physical service rendered another connotes inferiority, and where the worker is never dignified by a title but is called by his first name or merely "boy." The tips given service people show a lack of respect in the tipper and a loss of self-respect by the recipient, Daniels noted. Further, in the case of waiters and bellboys, he believed that their constant exposure to white people at their worst—extravagant, vulgar, drunk, and immoral—would lower the black worker's own standards. However, true apostle of Booker T. Washington as he was, Daniels added to these insightful remarks that no stigma necessarily attached to menial work, because "any task done honestly and well is creditable."[12]

In northern cities as earlier in the southern countryside, what the black man was chiefly wanted for was common labor; he could always get some dirty, exhausting, low-paid work, and if he got tired of it and quit there was always another shoveling job somewhere else, and another pair of hands to pick up the shovel he had dropped. Many migrants were therefore what the Labor Department called "real peripatetics of industry,"[13] who let an employer pay their fare North, stayed in the company camp and ate company food for a few days, and then disappeared; who drifted from one city to another, from one employer to another, and from one company to another; and who eventually landed in jail for riding the freight cars.[14]

Liebow, in his study of ghetto men in the 1960s, learned that the laborer "puts no lower value on the job than does the society around him," and knows exactly what that value is "every pay day, [when] he counts in dollars and cents the value placed on the job by society at large."[15] Society has no esteem for the dishwasher, janitor, or ditch digger, and neither does the boss nor the worker himself, Liebow says, because the jobs are low-paid and dead ends: "Neither hard work nor perseverance can conceivably carry the janitor to a sit-down job in the office building he cleans up."[16] As for the unskilled industrial worker, the digger or hauler, he is just as far from becoming "the apprentice who becomes the journeyman electrician, plumber, steam fitter or bricklayer. . . ."[17] He is not "future oriented," like the white world around him, because for him there is no future; so he gets drunk, quits the job, and idles until he absolutely has to have money to eat, at which point he takes another job that's going nowhere.[18] Among the early migrants, as with Liebow's street corner men, a great number must have held these attitudes. Since nine out of ten were in low-status, dead-end jobs, and great numbers were unencumbered by families, there must have been drifters as well as many steady workers. This, in addition to race prejudice, explains the broad range of opinion among employers as to the value of black workers.

Whatever they thought of their jobs, the black migrants had to eat, and that took quite a lot of money. Prices kept rising right through the migration period. One could buy a pound of bread for a bit over $.06 in 1914, but by 1920 the same loaf cost over $.11—almost a 100 per cent increase. Coffee went from $.297 a pound to $.47, sugar from $.295 for 5 pounds to $.97, a dozen eggs from $.353 to $.681, 10 pounds of potatoes from $.18 to $.63, bacon from $.275 a pound to $.523, and a quart of milk, brought to your door, from $.089 to $.167. As to stove-size anthracite coal to heat and cook with, a bag worth $.371 in 1914 cost $.536 in 1919.[19]

Wages, however, were increasing also, particularly as more jobs in industry opened. In 1900, blacks in New York had average earnings between $12 and $15 per family, and that only if there were multiple wage-earners. George Haynes in his study of the New York black reported even lower earnings in 1906-9; under $6.00 a week for nearly 70 per cent of male workers, and less than $5.00 a week for nearly 90 per cent of the women. But these jobs had been mostly menial or personal service—butlers, bellboys, janitors, houseworkers, laundresses. Then industrial jobs became available, and by 1917 the Department of Labor could report that of 58 male wage-earners studied in Chicago, only 4 (or about 7 per cent) were earning less than $12 a week; 22 were earning between $12 and $14.99; 27 were earning $15; and 5 were earning between $15 and $20. These men worked in the stockyards, in a fertilizer plant, as car cleaners, and for the railroads and the Pullman Company. A single man earning $15 would have a comfortable amount left even if he paid $3.00 a week for a room, or $7.00 or $8.00 for room and board. The job of Pullman porter was particularly lucrative and sought-after. His wages were only about $25 a month, but tips might come to as much as $100—or as little as almost nothing—so a Pullman porter could average $75 a month with most of his expenses paid; and if he were dishonest, by sharing with conductors unreported money paid on the train for berths, he could make another $75 a month.[20]

Semiskilled and skilled blacks in Chicago could earn $3.50 a day or more in a foundry, and a bricklayer or plasterer could make $30 for 40 hours' work, if he could land a job in his trade. In Duluth steel mills, a man was paid $3.60 for 12 hours' labor, and U. S. Steel in Pittsburgh raised its pay to $.33 an hour, or $3.96 for a 12-hour day. There was practically no unemployment for able-bodied men who wanted work, the Labor Department reported. In Epstein's study of Pittsburgh, he found that only 5 per cent of those he questioned earned under $2.00 a day, compared with 56 per cent of workers in the South. In Chicago, a pay envelope containing $25 was not unusual for a 48-to-60-hour work week, which is between $.40 and $.50 an hour.[21]

The wife of a black worker, and perhaps a daughter or son or two, could considerably augment the family income. A capable laundress or cook in a northern city could command $1.50 to $2.00 a day plus carfare and a meal, which was only a little less than she would have earned in a week in Mississippi. Or a woman employed in industry might make about $3.00 a day, compared with $.50 a day picking cotton, in the season, down home. A young unmarried woman in domestic service got about $8.00 a week and her room and board, just twice what a house servant earned in Mississippi, where she would live in a house in the yard.[22] It was possible, therefore, for a Negro family's earnings to meet the 1919 figure of $43.51 set by the Bureau of Labor Statistics as the weekly income necessary to maintain an acceptable standard of living for a family of five.[23] In Philadelphia in 1919, a study showed that half the families investigated met the acceptable income standard, but in less than half of those families did the father alone earn that much.[24] If his wife worked, the income standard could be met, but there would be no one at home to take care of the children and keep them off the vice-ridden streets. True, a family in which everyone of working age had a job could set a bit aside each payday toward buying a house; but such forethought is more typical of the "future oriented" white middle class than of the black laboring class that had no future, no hope of advancement. Some black laborers did save and buy houses, but for many, since there was no tomorrow, money's only use was to buy pleasure today: cheap, showy clothes; bought meals and sweets; beer, whiskey, and perhaps drugs; women and crap games. So a new stereotype emerged, that of the "flash" Negro who couldn't keep money in his pocket —useful as an excuse for paying him less than white wages.

A survey made in Pennsylvania in 1925, when the economy had recovered after a postwar slump and a new wave of black migrants was streaming in from the South, showed that the average Negro in Pennsylvania was then earning 91 per cent more than he had been earning back home, and that his cost of living was 23 per cent higher than in the South. It is clear from this that the gain in real wages was enormous, about 70 per cent.[25] The warnings of white Southerners that sky-high prices in the North would cancel out higher wages, whether sincere or part of antimigration propaganda, were simply not borne out by facts. Blacks were financially better off in the North. Very few went back home.

DuBois had said in 1899 that Negroes had fewer job offers and were accustomed to low pay, so "the first thought that occurs to the average employer is to give a Negro less than he would offer a white man for the same work."[26] The New York Urban League corroborated this, and Scott Nearing insisted that wherever blacks and whites worked together, there was wage discrimination. There was, however, some evidence to the contrary. An investigating group in Detroit and the Chicago Commission on Race Relations both reported almost no wage discrimination. Actually, wage equality is difficult to assess, because blacks and whites so rarely filled identical jobs. The black certainly seemed to be paid less, but that may have been because he always held the lowest-paid job, and in piece-work operations was given the least desirable, most time-consuming tasks; thus his earnings were kept down.[27]

It is generally agreed, however, that black men earned less than whites, whatever the cause, and that this is reflected in the greater number of working women among blacks; also, that the advance of black men in the economy by 1920 is evidenced by the decrease in working black women by that date.[28]

Census returns show these percentages of gainfully employed women over 10 years of age in different population groups:

	1910	1920
Native white	19.2	19.3
Foreign-born white	21.7	18.4
Black	54.7	38.9[29]

A 1910 survey in New York City showed that over 30 per cent of married black women worked, as against 3.4 per cent of married white women.[30]

Two other reasons why there were more workers among black women than among white women, besides the low earnings of black men, are the larger number (although probably not so large as census counts show) of black women who were heads of families, and the greater equality of the sexes among blacks because so many black women had always been breadwinners, as John Daniels pointed out. But, although Daniels was impressed by the capability and responsibility of black women, nevertheless in his city of Boston in 1900, 76 per cent of the women in menial jobs were black women; still, a fair number of black women were seamstresses, dressmakers, and boarding-house keepers, and small numbers were engaged in skilled crafts, professions, and clerical work. Throughout the North prior to 1915, 80 per cent of black workingwomen were in domestic or personal service. More of them would have broken through to upper-level jobs, Daniels believed, except that white women who would have been fellow employees were even more prejudiced racially than white men in the same situation.[31]

Although relatively few black women got teaching or clerical jobs, possibly for the reason alleged by Daniels, a large number of them entered the manufacturing and mechanical industries in the second decade of the century. Many became unskilled laborers in the tobacco industry, garment trades, paper-box factories, munitions factories, meat packing plants, and tanneries in such cities as Philadelphia and Chicago; in Detroit a number found work in the automobile industry, although more worked in hotels, laundries, and restaurants. Employers in northern cities admitted they hired black women only because of the labor shortage during the war, so black women formed the most marginal group of industrial workers, hired only when and where there was acute need. Victims of sex discrimination as well as race discrimination, in industry they got the least desirable jobs at the worst pay, with practically no chance of advancement. Many of them, therefore, resorted to domestic work, and some to prostitution. Nevertheless, the percentage of black working-women in domestic service declined significantly between 1910 and 1920, from 86 per cent to 71.5 per cent in New York, from 78.4 per cent to 63.8 per cent in Chicago, and from 81.1 per cent to 77.8 per cent in Cleveland. In the same interval, black working-women in industry increased from 9.2 per cent to 22.6 per cent in New York, from 11.2 per cent to 21.5 per cent in Chicago, and from 10 per cent to 14.1 per cent in Cleveland. Similar shifts of occupational field occurred in Philadelphia, Detroit, and Cincinnati, but in smaller cities almost all black workingwomen were still servants. Even in domestic jobs many of the migrant women had difficulty because of their inexperience with northern standards and methods. The Urban League and other institutions worked to train women for both domestic and factory work.[32]

New techniques and conditions increased opportunities for black women migrants in certain nonindustrial jobs. More of them than ever became trained nurses, teachers,[33] boarding-house keepers, laundry workers, and waitresses. The highest percentage increases were among hairdressers and manicurists, clerical help, and elevator operators (from two black women op-

erators in 1910 to 3,073 in 1920). Almost as prestigious and re-
munerative for women as the Pullman porter job for men was
a post as maid in a theater lounge or on one of the "limited"
luxury trains.[34]

A job almost closed to black women was that of salesclerk in
a store, with only two blacks per thousand saleswomen by 1930,
but some did find employment as mail clerks and order fillers in
the nation's two great mail-order houses, the Montgomery Ward
Company and Sears, Roebuck and Company, both in Chicago.[35]
Julius Rosenwald, who became president of Sears, Roebuck in
1909, was like his friend Booker T. Washington in beatifying hard
work and in seeing right and wrong as moral absolutes; he was
a businessman of the old school of rugged individualism and
laissez-faire, but with a social conscience to the extent of helping
people who strove to help themselves. In his lifetime he gave
more than $63,000,000 to worthy causes, a good part of it going
to help train black people so they could succeed. Washington's
Tuskegee Institute was a frequent beneficiary, and when Rosenwald and his wife paid an annual visit there they were welcomed
by cheering students, torchlight processions, singing, and craft
demonstrations. As a member of the Chicago Vice Commission
in 1910, Rosenwald was well aware of the extent of prostitution
in the city, which according to the Commission's report involved some 5,000 women, black and white; and of the question
raised by the Commission whether, if legitimate jobs paid them
a living wage, these women would be walking the streets.
Women were at that time earning an average of $6.00 a week
in the city's "mercantile establishments."[36]

In 1913 an Illinois state body, the O'Hara Committee, investigated the connection between low wages and prostitution, calling
Julius Rosenwald as its first witness. He testified that 119 girls
under sixteen years of age, employed by Sears, Roebuck, were
paid $5.00 per week; that 1,465 girls got less than $8.00 a week;
and that the average pay for women employees of Sears was
$9.12 a week. He would raise wages, Mr. Rosenwald testified,
if he felt girls could not live decently on what the company paid
them; but he remained unshaken in his belief that immorality
was unrelated to pay, saying, "The girl that gets $10 a week

would be just as likely to use that as a subterfuge as the girl who gets a less wage."[37] This opinion was no doubt generally shared by Chicago business people. A woman of twenty-five, Rosenwald said, whether or not she was living in her parents' home, "could be honest and might live on $8.00 a week."[38] A little later this interchange took place:

"Could you, Mr. Rosenwald, live on $8.00 a week?" Senator Juul [of the O'Hara Committee] asked. "That is pretty hard to tell without trying." "Have you ever tried?" "No, I don't think I have ever tried."[39]

The questioning developed the information that in 1911 Sears, Roebuck had a net profit of over $8,000,000.[40]

Rosenwald was never swayed from his opinion that there was no connection between wages and vice, and refused to pay higher wages than other employers did. In 1916, however, Sears, Roebuck instituted one of the earliest profit-sharing plans, which helped the kind of employee Rosenwald admired, the one who skimped to plow back 5 per cent of earnings into the stock of the company as a savings and pension fund.[41] But how many girls and women who had to support themselves on $8.00 or $10 a week could afford the $.40 or $.50 per pay envelope to become shareholders? A shopping bag filled with a week's supply of bread, coffee, sugar, milk, potatoes, bacon, and eggs would cost about $2.50, without any coal to cook them; room rent would take another $3.00 or $4.00; and what of carfare, clothing, insurance, and the doctor's bill?

It is certainly no matter for wonder that so many women turned to prostitution as, literally, the only viable alternative, especially black southern women who, untrained and inexperienced, and always subjects of discrimination, would rarely be able to rise above $5.00 or $6.00 a week in a commercial establishment. It is impossible to interpret correctly the preponderance of black women over white women in the jail population without taking into account what mercantile houses like Sears paid their low-level workers.

Frederick Douglass observed in 1853: "Every hour sees the black man elbowed out of employment by some newly arrived immigrant whose hunger and whose color are thought to give him a better title to the place. . . ."[42] By 1916 the situation was different. Labor was arriving in the North by internal migration in larger numbers than by international migration. In that year, about 250,000 immigrants of working age came into the United States from abroad;[43] about as many black migrants went North at that time from Georgia, Mississippi, and Alabama alone.[44] In authorizing the Labor Department's report of the migration in 1916–17, Secretary of Labor W. B. Wilson said the influx of black workers aroused "the fears of wage earners in the North on account of the potential competition for opportunities to work and consequent depressions of wages which it threatened. . . ."[45] Yet there was employment for all, especially at the lower levels, and it was scarcely the fault of the black man if an employer would not pay him the same wage as a white. Whether or not it had to be, labor competition was a cause of friction between white workers and black migrants, but perhaps a greater cause was the wave of racism that had been building up since the 1880s, not merely white racism toward blacks but American "racism," in which many blacks shared, toward foreign-born immigrants.

Booker T. Washington, warning the South against immigrant labor, had pleaded that "those of foreign birth and strange tongue and habits" not be allowed to displace black Americans who for centuries had supported the economy of the South "without strikes and labour wars."[46] Black leaders and the black press pointed to the foreigners as disturbers of the peace and causers of urban crime, and said that increased immigration would result in a loss of status, jobs, and civic recognition for blacks. The New York *Age* claimed immigrants were teaching black people to be lawless; and it was held by some race leaders that these "socialist agitators" would undermine the capitalist system and would never adjust to the American way of life.[47] These attitudes were typical of conservative Americans at that time, a reminder that black people, especially the migrants who had absorbed southern white conservatism even while they languished under it, were very conservative Americans until the migration and the war changed them. Also, xenophobia among blacks was encouraged by whites who feared that these lowest men on the social ladder, Negroes and immigrants, might form an alliance against their native white exploiters.[48]

Nativism, although basically conservative, was to some extent shared by almost all Americans, including such liberals as Woodrow Wilson, people who were working to improve the lot of the masses and who feared the job might grow impossible if immigrants continued to flood in. Especially were they dismayed by the "new immigrants" from central, southern, and eastern Europe—Italians, Poles, Russian Jews, Greeks, and such—who, as Wilson said in the 1880s, were displacing the "sturdy stocks" from northern Europe, the British, Germans, Irish, and Scandinavians. The fear grew as these "new immigrants," whose skins tended to be somewhat darker than those of the "sturdy stocks" and who were considered stupid, dirty, and dangerously radical, outnumbered northern European immigrants by three to one from the Spanish-American War to World War I. Between 1900 and 1915 over 13,000,000 immigrants, mostly of the "new" kind, entered the United States, at least 80 per cent of them settling in northern cities.[49] Wilson called them "men out of the ranks where there was neither skill nor energy nor any initiative of quick intelligence."[50] Italians were among the most scorned, and, as already mentioned, those who immigrated to the South were treated like the blacks.[51] The early intelligence tests, which will be discussed later, appropriately if unscientifically found Italians very stupid.

The tide of nativism was running strong throughout the country in the late nineteenth and early twentieth centuries, but especially and most consistently in the South, and in the Far West to which yellow peoples were immigrating. It seeped through the whole fabric of American society, but was most conspicuous among native-born workingmen and patrician intellectuals.[52] Edward A. Ross, a leading sociologist of the time, called the immigrants "these oxlike men [who] are descendants of those who always stay behind."[53] Francis Walker, president of the Massachusetts Institute of Technology, declared that the birth rate had declined among native Americans because they chose not to bring forth children who would have to compete in "labor and the walks of life with those whom they did not recognize as of their own grade and condition"—the socialistic, improvident, over-fecund "new immigrants."[54] Frederick Jackson Turner thought the influx of Italians, Poles, Russian Jews, and Slovaks "a loss to the social organism of the United States."[55] He particularly deplored the immigration of Jews, because, he explained in an inverse Social Darwinian proposition, generations of living in bad urban quarters had "produced a race capable of living under conditions that would exterminate men who centuries of national [sic] selection had not adapted to endure squalor and the unsanitary and indecent conditions of a dangerously crowded population."[56] Jews were condemned, that is, for their fitness to survive. These and many other intellectuals were joined by southern racist politicians. Senator Tom Watson, who in 1906 characterized immigrants as "Goths, Huns, Vandals" (in fact, northern peoples of the "sturdy stocks," unfortunately for Watson's metaphor) "who lust for loot," and scarily prophesied that the day would come in America "when the order would go out for those defending the ramparts, 'Put none but Americans on guard tonight.'"[57] Small wonder that Wilson and other Americans in 1917 had trouble accepting the fact that Germany was the enemy and that the ramparts had to be defended against Germans, not against Italians or Poles or Russian Jews.

Basically, then, nativism was a racist creed rather than an anti-immigration movement, discriminating not against all foreigners but only those groups considered inferior to white "Anglo-Saxon" (or "Nordic" or "Teutonic") peoples. By 1900 the "Yellow Peril" consisted mostly of Japanese, because Chinese immigration had been stopped by the various Chinese Exclusion acts before that time. Labor unions on the West Coast demanded Japanese exclusion as well, claiming that the low money requirements of Japanese workers threatened union wages; but it was racism, not the low standard of living of the Japanese, that moved San Francisco to segregate all Japanese children in one school, and California to pass laws preventing Japanese from buying or leasing real estate.[58] Jews also were subjected to discrimination; they were barred from certain neighborhoods by residential restrictive covenants, and many employers refused to hire them. Where there was no traditional racial difference between undesirable immigrants and Americans, new "races" were carved out of the Caucasian, viz., the Mediterranean and the Alpine, to account for those European peoples who were felt to be of inferior stocks. What it all added up to was that the native-born white Anglo-Saxon American believed himself to be, by virtue of nativity and "stock," superior to anyone else, although he could tolerate foreign-born people of his own derivation. The division of superior and inferior peoples according to race or stock is plainly racism, not merely nativism. The concept was applied against the most native of all Americans, the Indians, who were not treated at all as equals by the inept, corrupt, and worthless government officials of the Bureau of Indian Affairs nor by white men in the West who were tricking or forcing them into selling their land holdings.[59] When black Americans lined up with white Americans who were pressing for immigration restrictions, believing that their American nativity gave them the status of co-equals, they were tightening the chains of racism around themselves. John Higham in his study of American nativism concluded that gradually, "in every section, the Negro, the Oriental, and the southern European appeared more and more in a common light."[60] Race, once a pressing problem only in the South, was now in the forefront of the national consciousness wherever the black migrants settled.[61]

In the prewar period, however, there was employment for everyone who was content to work on the level assigned him in the racial hierarchy. In 1910, 71 per cent of the total black adult population (over ten) was employed, compared with 60.3 per cent of foreign-born and 49 per cent of native-born whites. The larger percentage of blacks employed is accounted for mainly by the much higher proportion of women workers among blacks than in either of the other groups. Among male workers, 90 per cent of the foreign-born were employed, as against 87.4 per cent of black Americans and 77.9 per cent of native-born white men. By 1920, after the war was over, the percentage of male black workers over ten had dropped to 81.1 per cent; this may have been because compulsory education laws in northern states kept boys in school longer[62] and because increased earnings of black men made it unnecessary for their children to work at a very early age. Higher earnings of black men probably also explains why there were fewer black women workers in 1920 than in 1910. A decrease in the percentage of foreign-born women workers indicates that immigrant men, too, were earning more by 1920. In the same period, as the war opened many new kinds of employment to white women, it is interesting that the percentage of native-born white workingwomen increased, which indicates probably that many women in this group worked not entirely from necessity, but by choice, as more interesting, diversified, and rewarding careers became available to them.[63]

For black workers, the decade from 1910 to 1920 brought changes not only in the percentages employed but in the kinds of work they did. In New York, for example, 50.3 per cent of male black workers in 1910 were domestics; this had dropped to 37.4 per cent by 1920. The percentage of the male black work force employed in manufacturing, on the other hand, rose from 13.9 per cent to 21.3 per cent, an increase of about 50 per cent in black men so employed. The percentage of black men employed in trade and transportation increased from 30.3 per cent in 1910 to 35.1 per cent in 1920, and of black professional men from 4.7 per cent to 5.9 per cent. In the same period in New York, among foreign-born workingmen, domestic employment dropped from 11.4 per cent to 10.4 per cent; manufacturing rose from 49.8 per cent to 50.2 per cent; trade and transport rose from 33.1 per cent to 33.4 per cent; and the professional group increased from 5.1 per cent to 5.6 per cent of employed males.[64] Although the direction of change away from domestic jobs toward industry, business, and the professions was common to both groups, the extent of change was much greater among blacks.

More visible at the time, probably, than these shifts in broad fields of work was the increasing presence of white immigrants in what had been thought of as "Negro jobs." Italians, Sicilians, Greeks, and other "new" immigrants by 1910 were replacing black barbers, bootblacks, and draymen; western Europeans, especially French and German, were taking traditionally black jobs as cooks and waiters; Swedes and Germans were filling up the better-grade janitorial jobs, especially in office buildings.[65] Undoubtedly these usurpations by foreigners of "strange tongue and habits" irked black workers and created friction between them and immigrant workers; but such friction was trivial compared with the irritation and frustration caused by unequal treatment of the two groups by the labor unions.

In the all-pervading atmosphere of racism, it was easy for white unionized workmen to believe it when they were told that blacks by strike-breaking and undercutting union wages were endangering the labor movement. The whole white public was incensed and frightened by race riots like the one at East St. Louis, caused, they were convinced, by black scabs taking the jobs of white union men. This was a great oversimplification of a most complicated segment of American labor history.

At least 90 per cent of blacks in industry were in unskilled jobs, which with few exceptions were nonunion, although efforts were being made to organize this level of worker. It was, therefore, on this level that most job competition took place, where neither whites nor blacks were organized. The dilemma of the unions was that, because of race prejudice, they did not want to organize blacks, but blacks' availability in large numbers impeded the organization of whites. As the 1919 report of the Department of Labor said:

> Of course it must be admitted that any hostile attitude of the labor unions is probably based upon the fear that Negro labor may ultimately be used to batter down the standards of the labor movement, and may be grounded

in the deduction that if unskilled Negroes can be used to fight the organization of unskilled whites, skilled Negroes may be used to break down the craft unions. As we have shown, the number of skilled Negroes employed in the North seems as yet to be so small that this is a groundless fear. . . . Indeed, the number of Negroes taking the place of striking whites and of skilled white workers is so small that it can hardly be noticed. They are . . . largely taking the places that were left vacant by the unskilled foreign laborers since the beginning of the war, and the new places created by the present industrial boom. These unskilled people, whose places are now being taken by the Negro, worked under no American standard of labor. The fear of these unskilled laborers breaking down labor standards which did not exist is obviously largely unfounded.[66]

According to this report, the violence that so enraged the public against black workers "seeemed to have had its basis in saloon politics"[67] and to have developed not because of labor competition so much as from friction between bad elements in both black and white groups.

Facts bear out, however, and there seems no reason to doubt, that employers sometimes used blacks to impede union efforts. Labor leaders accused employers of importing blacks wholesale to break up the labor movement, and this seems to have been true in a few instances. Subway contractors in New York in 1903 brought in 2,000 black laborers from Maryland and Virginia. In 1901 John Mitchell, president of the United Mine Workers, testified before the United States Industrial Commission that black labor was being imported by bosses in order to keep down miners' wages, even though the UMW was one of the few unions that freely accepted black members.[68]

The stockyards story illustrates very clearly the relations between blacks and the unions throughout the migration period. In 1904, the Amalgamated Meat Cutters and Butchers Union called a strike. The stockyards and packers brought in 2,000 black workers, and in 1905 the strike was cracked. The strikers predictably blamed their failure on blacks, and Ben Tillman encouraged this by saying: "It is the niggers that whipped you into line. They were the club with which your brains were beaten out."[69] But the defeated strike was only a temporary interruption in the progress of Amalgamated, and the black workers who were brought in were not scabs in the sense of union men crossing a picket line of their fellows, for the very good reason that the union would not at that time let them join. Many of the blacks did not know when they were recruited what their role was to be; and at least one group refused to work when they found out. Once inside the plants, however, the blacks had no choice but to obey orders and work. They were herded into the factories under guard and not permitted to leave. The living conditions provided for them were so bad that a member of the Armour meat-packing family, visiting one of the plants, is quoted as having exclaimed: "My God, I can't stand that."[70] Although white stockyard workers hated blacks as enemies and scabs, the black workers were in fact only ignorant troops being pushed around in the power battles between employers and the union. As the war years approached and the demand on the stockyards increased, yard bosses continued to hire blacks, so that eventually there were so many black workers in the yards that Amalgamated had to organize them in self-defense. But acceptance came too late and too grudgingly to excite many black workers about becoming union members. They knew they could work whether they joined or not, and only about one third of them did join.[71]

Just before and during the war, black workers generally were cool toward unionism. Booker T. Washington explained this not very convincingly by saying that many of the southern migrants did not grasp the advantage or necessity of belonging to a union; they were accustomed to work for persons, not for wages, and did not like or understand an organization based on hostility to employers. Washington's conservative National Negro Business League was procapitalist, as was most of the black middle class; and although the centrist NAACP favored black participation in unions, the old Washington school of conservatism was still a potent force in forming black attitudes.[72] Opposed to these conservatives was a just emerging group of socialistic blacks, spearheaded by Asa Philip Randolph and Chandler Owen, who wanted to see black labor organized but in a much more radical, class-conscious grouping than the American Federation of Labor. With no unanimous leadership position on unions, no firm push from above to join when the chance was offered, black workers did not stampede the union gates when they opened a crack.

Chiefly, however, blacks were indifferent to the labor movement because, as one worker is quoted, "Unions ain't no good for a colored man. I've seen too much of what they don't do for him."[73] Under the circumstances, it was not worth bucking the opposition of white union workers to having blacks join their locals, which in itself had caused a number of strikes. AF of L policy, as handed down from headquarters, was expressly nondiscriminatory, and in its early years the federation made an effort to enforce this policy; it refused, for example, to recognize the International Association of Machinists, which organized in 1888 with a white-only clause in its constitution, until in 1895 the clause was dropped (although segregation was continued by other methods).[74] AF of L president Samuel Gompers stated prior to 1900 that "organized labor is decidedly in favor of maintaining and encouraging the recognition of the equality between white and colored workers,"[75] and officially that stand remained unchanged. All unions wishing to join the Federation were required to pledge that they would not exclude workers on grounds of color, creed, or national origin, but in practice they did exclude on color ground, and Gompers, howbeit reluctantly, gradually admitted segregated unions rather than damage the movement as a whole.[76] In 1904 Gompers earned the hatred of black workers by calling those brought into the Chicago stockyards "hordes of ignorant blacks . . . possessing but few of those attributes we have learned to revere and love," and by insisting that blacks were excluded from unions only because they could not meet skill standards, which was often a downright lie.[77]

In the absence of an enforced national policy, there were four kinds of unions: those whose constitutions prohibited black members, such as the Machinists, Boilermakers, Railway Mail Association, Railway Telegraphers, Railway and Steamship Clerks,

and Switchmen; the many that did not constitutionally bar
blacks, but simply rejected their applications for membership or
admitted a few outstandingly qualified individuals; those that
would not take black members but organized separate "lodges"
for them under the jurisdiction of the nearest white local that
would approve their charters, such as the Amalgamated Association of Steelworkers, Brotherhood of Carmen, Hotel Employees,
and Tobacco Workers; and finally those that accepted black
members freely, like the UMW, Teamsters, Longshoremen, and
Hodcarriers and Building Laborers, trades in which so many
blacks worked that the unions had to include them or lose control over employers. In the coal fields of West Virginia, for example, almost half of all miners were black.[78] In New York,
where half the longshoremen were Negroes, one black worker
said: "We are in the union today because the white man had
to take us in for his own protection. Outside of the organization
the Negro could scab on the white man. Inside he can't."[79] Black
women who worked in the needle trades, numbering a great
many by wartime, had the advantage of dealing with the exceptionally liberal International Ladies' Garment Workers' Union;
when in 1917 black women were brought into Chicago to break
a garment strike, the ILGWU solved the problem by organizing
them into the union on a basis of full and equal participation.[80]

If black workers were such thorns in the side of the labor
movement, why did not more unions take the path of the UMW,
Teamsters, ILGWU, and others that simply accepted the black
competition? The usual answer is that top-level policy favored
this, but that within the locals, at the contact level, whites refused
to work with blacks. That whites did work with blacks in some
of the biggest unions indicates that locals took their cue from
the leadership and that there lay a racist reluctance, not an inability, to make integration work.

In 1920 Herbert Seligmann reported: "If many Negroes are
not now good union men, it is because they have never, despite
their interest and desire, been given opportunity to have an effective part in the American labor movement."[81] He quoted Roger
Baldwin, director of the Civil Liberties Union, as saying that the
black scabs imported into the steel mills at Homestead, Pennsyl-

vania, "were all for the union and all for a strike at the right time," but the union had never made a move to absorb blacks in the Pittsburgh steel district and blacks "felt they owed nothing to white men who had so long ignored and oppressed them."[82] Having always been victims of white discrimination, why should they fight the white unionists' battles by declining jobs offered them? As long as they could get work at a living wage, why should they struggle for the advancement of unions in most of which they were welcome only as segregated locals?[83]

Every kind of white authority in the United States had some more important objective than doing justice to black people. Gompers said that the surrender of his early liberal principles was "theoretically bad but practically necessary,"[84] because he could not let the race issue prevent the accomplishment of his goal of organizing all American unions into one great federation. Similarly, Secretary of War Newton D. Baker, although also a man of liberal principles, when pressed on the troublesome question of equal opportunity for blacks, said it was not the job of the Army to solve the race question but to win the war.[85] Looking backward, it seems clear that if priority had been given the race issue, and if the AF of L and the Army had both in their separate spheres firmly and forcefully integrated blacks, their other goals would have been accomplished nevertheless and with incalculable saving of blood and suffering from then until now. Much of the race violence of the period, which will be discussed in a later chapter, was the result of racism in the field of labor.

Besides the many black workers alienated by organized labor's racism, there were many others so determined to "better their condition"—the reason most migrants went North—that they accepted unionism on its own segregated terms if this would advance them in the economy. Black unions were organized in a number of trades and crafts, either as independent bodies or as black lodges attached to white locals. Among these were the United Hodcarriers, the Colored Caulkers, Colored Waiters, National Association of Negro Musicians (although there were some black members in ASCAP, the American Society of Com-

posers, Authors, and Publishers, formed in 1914), and the Afro-
American Steam and Gas Engineers and Skilled Laborers, which,
formed in 1903, was the first independent black union and for
a while very successful.[86]

A new black leader was emerging at this time: Asa Philip Randolph, college-educated, a labor man and a socialist, who was
as appropriate to an era when blacks began to assert themselves
in industry as Booker T. Washington, self-made, conservative,
and capitalistic, had been in the previous era. Randolph and
Chandler Owen were editors of a socialist publication, the *Messenger* (originally the *Hotel Messenger,* organ of a waiters' union), in 1919 described by the United States Attorney General
as "by long odds the most able and most dangerous of all the
Negro publications . . . representative of the most educated
thought among the Negroes."[87] The *Messenger* called for a federation of all Negro workingmen—railroad porters and firemen,
longshoremen, masons, farm hands, elevator operators, and all
others in whatever trade or craft—not simply because these workers were black and excluded by most AF of L unions, but also
because they represented the most exploited social class. However, the response of black workers to radical philosophies was
generally cool. The socialist workers' federation, Industrial Workers of the World, from early in the century had been offering
black workers an equal chance in industrial organization. IWW
leader "Big" Bill Haywood said its doors were wide open to every
workingman, "all races, regardless of religion, color and skin,
shape of skull or kinks in the hair. As long as they are wage
workers and can straighten out the capitalist kinks in their brains,
the IWW welcomes . . . every one of them."[88] Such early success as the IWW had in organizing blacks was due more to black
exclusion by the AF of L unions than to any deeply felt radicalism. The mass of black workers, like the mass of white workers,
was interested in unionism for increased pay and opportunities
that would advance laborers within the capitalist system. The
IWW had gained some advantages for black dockworkers, longshoremen, and lumbermen, especially in the South, but it did not
have a broad appeal to black workers.[89]

Randolph and Owen became officers in the National Brotherhood of Workers of America, formed in 1919 by T. J. Pree and R. T. Simms with the purpose of organizing and federating all black workers, which was Randolph's goal. At first the National Brotherhood had the support of longshoremen and stevedores, and was enough of a threat so that the AF of L Longshoremen's Union liberalized its policy to admit blacks. That knocked the pins out from under the National Brotherhood, and in 1920 it collapsed.[90]

Randolph then concentrated on black railroad workers, who were rejected by AF of L railway brotherhoods but were organized into a number of independent black unions. The Railwaymen's International Benevolent and Industrial Association had been formed by Robert L. Mays in 1915 in an attempt to federate those unions. The Association had considerable success during the war, when, with the railroads under federal control, it was able with government co-operation to improve the working conditions and pay of its members. But once that had been accomplished, and the railroads were back under private control after the war, the Association lost membership support and power.

However, with the AF of L railroad brotherhoods still refusing to accept black railroad workers, black railroad men were forced to rely on their own independent organizations, such as the Brotherhood of Sleeping and Dining Car Employees, the Association of Train Porters, Brakemen, and Switchmen, and the Association of Colored Railway Trainmen. It was out of their membership that Randolph in 1925, after a fierce struggle with the Pullman Company, organized the most powerful group of black workers in any field, the Brotherhood of Sleeping Car Porters, most of whose members were not interested so much in Randolph's socialist ideals as in the very real benefits he won for the Brotherhood through his brilliance and dedication.[91]

Marxian class struggle is an intellectual concept; for most Americans the class struggle is an effort to get up from a lower class to a higher one. Unions spelled discrimination, trouble, race hatred, and violence. Many black people turned their backs on all this and went into business instead, a course to which they were continually exhorted by most black leaders, the black press, and organizations such as the National Negro Business League, the Professional and Business Men's Social Club, and smaller local businessmen's groups.[92] DuBois joined Washington in applauding black business enterprise, though perhaps with more restraint. A report on business in the fourth Atlanta University Study said: "For a Negro to go into business means a great deal. It is, indeed, a step in social progress worth measuring."[93] Professor John Hope at the Atlanta conference enunciated probably the most significant value of black business, its role in helping blacks to shape their lives and their future: "We must take in some, if not all, of the wages [of black workers], turn it into capital, hold it, increase it. This must be done as a means of employment for the thousands who cannot get work from old sources. Employment must be had, and this employment will have to come to Negroes from Negro sources."[94]

It was 1899 when John Hope said that. Soon after, blacks began to flood into northern cities in search of jobs; but, alas for Hope's good idea, few black businesses were large enough to offer any great amount of employment. At the time of this fourth Atlanta conference, 5,000 blacks were reported to own businesses in which they had an investment of $500 or more. Grocery stores were most numerous in that category (432), followed by barber shops (162), undertaking establishments (80), saloons (68), hotels (30), catering enterprises (24), and building and loan associations (13), followed by smaller numbers of banks, real estate firms, dry goods stores, photographers' studios, millinery shops, and so on. Very few businesses represented investments of more than $1,000, and those were mostly real estate, building and loan companies, banking companies, and saloons.[95]

In 1909, when the northward movement was developing, Haynes reported about 300 black businesses in New York City alone, of which about 20 per cent were owned by West Indians; they were mostly in the categories above, but with significant numbers in new, urban categories: tailoring and pressing, coal and ice, employment agencies, moving companies, and pool halls.

About 80 per cent of the businesses were small retail establishments with low overhead and limited inventories, employing less than three in help; so they were not of much importance in providing jobs for other black people. In 1920 there were about 70,000 black people engaged in business throughout the country, in the previously mentioned categories but with significant numbers of truck gardeners, peddlers, butchers, and junk dealers, none of which promised large-scale employment for workers.[96]

For black businesses to be successful, the Atlanta study had stated flatly, "The mass of the Negroes must learn to patronize business enterprises conducted by their own race, even at some slight disadvantage. We *must* co-operate or we are lost."[97] Speaking in New York City in 1914, Booker T. Washington made the same appeal for race patronage, and in the same year Adam Clayton Powell warned that the race problem would never be solved "as long as Negroes talk race loyalty and race rights and then spend their money with white business and professional men."[98]

The advice was good, but too few buyers were willing or could afford to accept the "slight disadvantage" of buying black, and black businessmen had their troubles. Few of them had had enough business experience. They were limited to ghetto locations and hence to a poverty-ridden ghetto clientele; and even in the ghettos they had white competition. In the heart of Harlem, for example, although in 1915 the customers were 98 per cent black, only 12 per cent of the businesses were black-owned; in the Chicago ghetto, about the same time, less than one third were black-owned. The small capital of most black businessmen limited the choice of products they could offer, and also made it impossible to extend credit to customers. Credit and variety of goods attracted a large part of the black market to white stores, and successful black businesses, except in a few special fields, were rare. An outstanding but exceptional enterprise was a Negro film company, Oscar Micheaux Pictures, with studios in New York making movies designed to attract black audiences both North and South.[99]

The business fields in which blacks could and often did succeed were those in which whites would not serve blacks: hotels, restaurants, and other eating places; insurance and undertakers; tailors, barbers, and beauty parlors—the so-called "decorative" trades; cabarets, dance halls, pool rooms, and saloons. The southern migrants, accustomed to strict segregation in these services, gravitated without urging to the black enterprises; and owners of such businesses, mostly migrants themselves, did better than other black businessmen because their customers couldn't "buy white" if they wanted to, as they could in such lines as furniture, dry goods, groceries, clothing, or hardware.[100]

Insurance was one of the most rewarding businesses. White companies did not want black clients, Myrdal reported, both because they simply didn't want to deal with blacks and because high mortality made ghetto blacks a poor risk. Here was one business in which blacks had a long history, dating back to pre-Civil War times, when most insurance was connected with churches. Some of the later insurance companies were linked with banks, and those in turn with lodges and their sickness and burial funds. Such was the True Reformers Insurance Company, connected with the True Reformers Bank, the largest black bank of its time in Virginia and probably in the whole country, which as previously noted was founded as the repository for funds of the Grand Fountain United Order of True Reformers, a fraternal organization. Following its migrating clients, the True Reformers Insurance Company in time opened a branch in New York City.[101]

Black-owned banks filled a desperate need for ghetto people, especially home buyers and businessmen who could almost never get loans from white banks and who might be charged 30 to 40 per cent interest by a loan shark. Banks were absolutely essential if black business enterprises were to expand.[102] In the South before 1910, small Negro banks "sprang up like mushrooms but died as rapidly as they were organized," Abram Harris reported.[103] Their chief problems were poor capitalization, inexperience, poor management, too many long-term speculative real estate loans and too few short-term business loans, too low a ratio of funds on hand to deposits, and occasional carelessness or dishonesty in dealing with bank funds. Between 1908 and 1920 there were usually about twenty to thirty Negro banks operating, but many failed and were replaced by new ones. Even the True Reformers failed in 1910, when an audit showed unrepaid loans to various projects of the organization amounting to $200,000. Two other respected banks that failed were the Binga State Bank of Illinois, founded in Chicago in 1908 by Jesse Binga, a southern migrant who rose from Pullman porter to real estate owner and then to bank owner, which operated for almost twenty years; and the Douglass National Bank, also in Chicago, which went under at about the same time as Binga's bank. These two banks represented more than one third of the assets of all black banks in the country, and their failure was a shattering blow to Negro efforts in business and finance, and caused great suffering to the poor workingmen who were their depositors. A later (1928) alternative to the wholly black-owned bank was the Dunbar National Bank in Harlem, a project of John D. Rockefeller, Jr., but staffed and run by blacks; this, too, failed when after ten unprofitable years Rockefeller withdrew his support.[104]

A business closely tied in with banking was real estate, and the migration period offered blacks great opportunities in this line. New York's Harlem was perhaps the most fruitful field, because in New York masses of blacks were moving into a white middle-class area, and consequently the buying, selling, leasing, managing, building, and alteration of houses proceeded at a frantic pace. By 1914, 37 per cent of Negro tenements in Harlem, although mostly white-owned, were managed by black agents. Philip Payton, Jr., got his start managing white-owned houses; his big break came when one white landlord, in a spite move against another, told Payton to fill his house with Negro tenants. After this initial blockbusting, Payton's Afro-American Realty Company (founded in 1904) did a brisk business buying up or leasing properties and filling them with blacks, at high rents, and became the most important real estate firm in Harlem. Two other realtors who got rich in Harlem were John E. Nail and Henry C. Parker; after Payton's firm went bankrupt in 1908, the firm of Nail and Parker was Harlem's biggest realty company. Church money also went into real estate. St. Philips, when it moved in 1911 from the Tenderloin quarter to Harlem, invested the $640,000 realized from the sale of its former site in ten apartment houses on West 135th Street, which it then rented to black tenants.[105]

The undertaking business thrived not only because white undertakers would not serve blacks but also because, as Langston Hughes's Simple explains, "Negroes don't have much in this world so we might as well have a good funeral."[106] Funerals tended to be lavish out of all proportion to the means of the bereaved family, because, as noted earlier, in most cases a lodge burial fund took care of expenses. The most successful business ventures in Chicago were the cemetery associations.[107]

Like undertakers, restaurant and saloon owners also had a captive clientele because blacks were not tolerated in white eating and drinking places. Also, black migrants were happy to assuage their homesickness with familiar southern food like the pigs' feet, hog maws, and chitterlings sold by "Pig Foot Mary" on Harlem streets out of an old baby carriage fitted up with a boiler; after she had grown rich on the proceeds, well invested in real estate, she was known more respectfully as Lillian Harris. Cooking was a field in which a number of southern blacks had experience and skill, and catering became a road to riches. DuBois mentioned the large number of black caterers in Philadelphia around 1900. The same was true in the District of Columbia and in New York, apparently, and in many cases the children of those who grew wealthy in catering became the doctors, lawyers, teachers, and businessmen of the next generation.[108] Rudolph Fisher in his illuminating novel of Negro life, *The Walls of Jericho,* published in the 1920s, presented as one of his upper-class characters the heiress of a Philadelphia catering fortune. As for saloons, although John Daniels reported few in Boston because there they had great trouble being licensed, New York's Harlem abounded in them, and saloon-keeping was very profitable.

Ghetto drugstores made a living from patent medicines, usually of high alcoholic content, which the poor took for their many ailments instead of going to a doctor, and perhaps in a few cases from the sale of cocaine or morphine; also, from toiletries such as the products of the Chemical Wonder Company of New York, which promised to erase the "racial" characteristics that whites seemed to find offensive. The Chemical Wonder Company claimed to be the true friend of the race because its products improved the body "as Dr. Booker Washington improves their minds."[109] Its ads declared: "If colored people groom themselves daintly [sic], destroy perspiration odors, remove grease shine from the face, and use our new discoveries for improving the skin and dressing their hair they will be better received in the business world, make more money, and advance faster."[110] Hair preparations were much in demand, and one of the biggest success stories among southern migrants is that of Madame C. J. Walker, as she styled herself, from Louisiana, who invented a hair straightener that made her vastly wealthy; residents of the then very wealthy white New York suburb of Irvington-on-Hudson were awed by the gleaming Greek-revival mansion she built there and furnished magnificently, the feature being a "gold" grand piano.[111]

Not only druggists but barbers and hairdressers flourished because of the popularity of grooming products and processes to dekink hair, lighten skin, and in every way help black men and women migrants advance by imitating that paradigm of success, the white world, in which now they were not merely servants but competitors. Photographers played the game, too, Langston Hughes says, for a slight extra charge tinting portrait photos to make the subject's complexion any desired shade—chocolate instead of black, or sepia instead of chocolate.[112]

A revolutionary change in the philosophy of black business occurred around 1920 with Marcus Garvey's black nationalist movement, which will be discussed later. Black, Garvey preached, was beautiful, so perhaps the hair straighteners and skin bleaches became less popular. Blacks bought black because products were aimed at their pride, not their shame. Harry Pace's Phonograph Company put black jazz on disks; the black firm of Berry and Ross manufactured black baby dolls for black children to mother; and the Black Star Line was established to take Afro-Americans back to their ancestral Africa.[113] Ghetto people so recently out of the South had an exciting few years until this new business world, created in Garvey's shining black image instead of mimicking a dull, conventional white model, tottered and fell.

A lack of race co-operation held back black professionals as it did black businessmen. Nationwide, whereas 5.7 per cent of the native white population was in the professional class in 1910, only 1.3 per cent of blacks were professional people, even including a great number of clergymen (more than among whites, by population) many of whom had no professional training. Still, by 1920, when the white professional group had increased to 6.4 per cent, blacks in professions had also increased slightly, to 1.7 per cent. The professional fields in which greatest percentage gains were made by blacks between 1910 and 1920 were among the following: chemists, assayers, and metallurgists (123 in 1910; 207 in 1920); college instructors, professors, and presidents (242 in 1910; 1,063 in 1920); dentists (478 in 1910; 1,019 in 1920); and technical engineers (none listed in 1910; 184 in 1920). There were also gains, but smaller, among librarians, clergymen, lawyers, physicians, teachers, musicians and music teachers, trained nurses, and every other professional group. By 1920, it would seem, a substantial number of southern migrants had advanced enough economically in the northern cities to avail themselves of, or make available to their children, the increased opportunities for professional training. There had been 47,219 professional-class blacks in 1900; by 1920 there were 80,183—a 70 per cent increase—most of them in the urban North. But there were still far too few dentists, doctors, lawyers, too few blacks in every profession except preaching, to serve the black community.[114]

Numbers and percentages tell only how many blacks were practicing professions, not how many were equipped and qualified to do so. Among the migrants were a number of business and professional people who worked at first at whatever jobs they could get to support themselves. William Lewis Bulkley, an educator and one of the founders of the Urban League, worked as cook, janitor, and waiter. James C. Thomas, first president of Philip Payton's Afro-American Realty Company, was a cabin boy and then a steward in private clubs in New York; Payton himself had worked as porter and barber. Adam Clayton Powell worked as a waiter even after he was ordained. Langston Hughes worked for a truck farmer and as mess boy aboard ships.[115]

Those who tried to live on their professional earnings alone had a thin time of it. DuBois had reported before 1900 that a few black doctors and dentists in Philadelphia had some white patrons, but as the ghetto gates closed, professional people like business people would have to depend for a living on the other blacks shut in with them.[116] Still, they need not have done too badly if all blacks had patronized them; but black professionals, except possibly nurses, did not have the confidence of fellow blacks. It is not difficult to understand why a poor southern migrant, brought up on the image of blacks as born menials and propagandized into believing it, could not trust a Negro to be as professionally trained and therefore as competent as a white professional. In many cases, Carter Woodson says in his study of Negro professionals, they were indeed not competent, because of educational and economic handicaps. Black doctors and dentists had almost all trained at Howard, Shaw, and Meharry, which could not at that time compare with good white professional schools; in the case of dentists, less than one third had completed work for a degree. This was also true of lawyers, about 80 per cent of whom had gone to Howard but who had not all completed the law curriculum. Most pharmacists and nurses had only a high school education, and less than 10 per cent of clergymen were graduates of accredited divinity schools. Black teachers were exceptional in often being better educated than white teachers, Woodson says, one reason being that among blacks many extremely talented and well-educated men and women taught because other fields were closed to them because of their color—not, as with many white teachers, because of their poor qualifications for other fields.

Except for teachers and nurses, blacks entered their professions later than whites because of the difficulty of completing their educations and accumulating the capital necessary to begin practicing. And once in practice, it was no easy matter to stay in practice. They were deprived of the advantages to be gained from membership in the major professional associations, from which they were barred. Doctors, dentists, and pharmacists could not afford adequate and modern equipment, nor lawyers an up-to-date law library. Doctors were excluded from many hospitals, and consequently had to send their patients to second-rate ones. Black lawyers often hired white lawyers to plead their cases in court, to give their clients a better chance before more or less bigoted judges and juries. Black doctors preferred not to have prescriptions filled by poorly equipped and often poorly trained black pharmacists. Not even teachers, although generally of a high order, had the trust of the community to act as leaders in the social welfare and race betterment projects to which many of them dedicated themselves.

So handicapped, black professionals usually had to augment their incomes in some way. Doctors often served as medical examiners for the many fraternal orders and insurance companies, and some lucky lawyers were retained by such groups as legal advisers. Dentists relied so much on the cosmetic and status dentistry favored by blacks at that period, consisting of as many gold teeth as one could afford, that they were known as "glorified blacksmiths."[117] Druggists sold five-and-ten-cent-store merchandise, and lived largely off the profits of their soda fountains; because blacks were not welcome at white soda fountains or lunch counters, the black drugstores were social centers of the ghettos.

Black theater people also found that Jim Crow had its profitable aspect. Forced to work mostly in black theaters for black audiences, actors and musicians had an easier time finding jobs in the ghettos as theaters and cabarets multiplied than they would have outside the ghetto in competition with white entertainers. An additional plus was that the high quality of black entertainment began to attract whites to black quarters, especially New York's Harlem, so that still more night spots were opened and more work was available to actors, singers, and bands. Actors could also get jobs in road companies sent by the Theater Owners' Booking Association, a black group, to small towns in the South and Midwest. It was a golden age for those in the theatrical profession.[118]

The field of journalism expanded phenomenally during the migration and war period, as blacks became urbanized, more literate, more interested in and concerned with what was going on in the race and the world. About 1900, Dubois enumerated black publications as 3 papers, 136 local weeklies, 11 school papers, and 3 monthly magazines, almost all of them produced in southern or border states. By 1908, Ray Stannard Baker reported more than 200 black newspapers and magazines; in 1916 he said there were more than 450 such publications, and in 1917 he said they totaled more than 500. Most of the important periodicals were now produced in the North, such as the *Age* and the *News* in New York, the *Courier* in Pittsburgh, the *Gazette* in Cleveland, and the sensationally successful *Defender* in Chicago, which in 1916 had a circulation of 10,000 and in 1918 of nearly 100,000. In addition, Randolph and Owen brought out the *Messenger* in 1917, and in 1918 there appeared Cyril Briggs's *Crusader*, both calling for radical social change; also in 1918 Hubert Harrison brought out the literary and cultural *Negro Voice*. Among the most influential periodicals before 1920 were *Crisis* and *Opportunity*, the organs of the NAACP and the National Urban League, respectively; and finally, by 1920 Marcus Garvey's black nationalist *Negro World*, begun in 1917, had not only an American but an African circulation.[119]

The civil service was not a promising field for black people, either in the federal city, where one by one, government departments became segregated during the Wilson Administration, nor in the other cities. The post offices, under the federal civil service, still offered the most jobs. There were 500 blacks in the postal service in Chicago in 1910, although mostly as carriers or low-level clerks, with promotion virtually unattainable. At about the same time, the post office in New York employed about 175 to 180 black people, and the District of Columbia had about 135 black postal employees out of a total force of 880.[120]

As for urban civil service, the District of Columbia had about forty black policemen and Chicago had fifty, but as late as 1918, New York had only five. There were practically no black firemen except where they were organized in Jim Crow platoons, as in the District of Columbia and in Chicago after 1919. These segregated units had the advantage, frequently pointed out by the whites responsible for them, of providing blacks with a better chance of promotion than in integrated units. The cities also had a scattering of blacks in their departments of docks, parks, and sanitation, and a few black messengers, drivers, and low-paid clerks. New York City, however, in 1910 had a black assistant district attorney, a black city corporation counsel, and three black doctors on the Board of Health; it also had a powerful black politician, Ferdinand Q. Morton, a migrant from Mississippi, who bossed what was called "Black Tammany" for many years.[121] But such successes were exceptional because, as a black man said of the civil service, it "is run by friendship . . . and under that sort of arrangement, Negroes won't come out on top."[122]

In a summary view of the economic activities of black migrants, failures and frustrations pale in the light of the enormous advances made. By 1920, 34 per cent of black people were urban; and whereas ten years earlier, 55.2 per cent of all black workers (58 per cent of black male workers) were agricultural—in almost all cases working white-owned land in the South—by 1920 black farm workers had dropped to 45.2 per cent (48.2 per cent of male workers). The 10 per cent loss can be found in the North in manufacturing and mechanical work chiefly, and in mining, transportation, trade, public service, professional service, domestic and personal service, and clerical occupations. The percentage of working black women holding clerical jobs doubled between 1910 and 1920; and the number of men in clerical jobs increased by three times in New York and Philadelphia, four times in Pittsburgh, five times in Cincinnati and Chicago, twelve times in Cleveland, and thirty times in Detroit.[123]

The war and the draft opened to black women "occupations not heretofore considered within the range of their possible activities," said the Department of Labor survey in 1918. Hotels began to take them on as cooks and waitresses; many found work in the new steam laundries; and others got jobs in food processing and packaging plants.[124] But for the war, undoubtedly most of these women would have been servants.

Wartime dearth of labor also opened new jobs to black men who were not taken by the Army. In 1910, 51 per cent of Chicago black men were in service trades; by 1920, only 28 per cent. Meanwhile, the 16 per cent of male black laborers in Chicago rose to 39 per cent, and the percentage of semiskilled workers rose from 1 per cent to 6 per cent; by 1920 factory work was the major employment field for Chicago black men, although by far the greatest number were, and remained, in unskilled jobs.[125]

The pattern was pretty much the same throughout the country. Black men were in industry, although almost all were low-level workers. Partly this was due to the kinds of industries blacks entered in greatest numbers—mining, iron and steel mills, stock-yards, and automotive, chemical, and textile factories—where almost all labor is unskilled. What is important is that blacks broke out of domestic and personal-service categories and into fields where advancement was at least possible, even if extremely difficult. In Pennsylvania, blacks in domestic and personal service declined by 23.3 per cent between 1915 and 1920, while increasing by 151.1 per cent in manufacturing and mechanical jobs. In Chicago, the increase in the latter fields was 148 per cent in the same period. In Detroit automobile factories, which in 1910 employed only seventeen black workers, there were 3,870 in 1920.[126]

Before the war, one third of the black steelworkers were employed in Alabama; by 1920 the number of blacks in this field had trebled, and only one quarter of them worked in Alabama. The others were scattered from Maryland to Illinois. Pittsburgh iron and steel plants in 1910 employed only 100 black workers; by 1915 they had 2,550. In the war years, Carnegie Steel went from 1,500 to 4,000 black workers, and Jones & Laughlin from 400 to 1,500. In the stockyards and meat packing plants of Chicago, the approximately 1,500 blacks employed in 1915 increased to 7,000 in 1918. In the electrical industry, black help increased at Westinghouse from 25 in 1916 to 1,500 in 1918. Comparable gains were made in the chemical industry, and in car and railroad shops.[127]

Not only were there all these jobs, but they paid better and better. Wages, real wages in terms of what the money could buy, were the highest Negroes had ever earned. A foundry worker who had thought himself lucky to be earning $2.50 for a ten-hour shift in Alabama or Tennessee could get the same job in Illinois or Ohio at $4.00 for an eight hour shift.[128]

It was hard for the skilled black worker, rejected by the craft unions, to get ahead as a mason, painter, plasterer, or plumber; but, despite the unions, there were a few blacks who made their way in as at least semiskilled workmen in rolling mills, and as cranemen and derrickmen, and especially in the automobile factories of Detroit, whose eight semiskilled black employees in 1910 increased to 809 in 1920.[129]

Black workers seized the opportunity offered by wartime labor needs to make a hairline crack in the unions' rigid exclusion. At the 1918 annual convention of the AF of L, a number of black union representatives demanded more organizing of blacks and better co-operation between the national union and black locals. The 1920 convention promised some substantial gains, with the executive council agreeing to promote better understanding between black and white workers, and to hire more black organizers in areas where they would be most effective. Even more encouraging was the council's acceptance of a resolution presented by black delegates calling for full recognition of black workers, on the ground that black men deserved this for having done their share in the war and having died in the cause of freedom.[130] The Negro sharecropper of 1900 could not have dreamed that in 1920, as a worker in industry, he would be demanding equality of this powerful white organization, much less that his demands would be acknowledged as justified.

And meanwhile, what had been happening back in the South that this sharecropper had left? Emmett Scott spoke of a vast increase in wages, claiming that black farm workers were earning $1.50 a day and common labor in the mills $2.00 or more; that unions were organizing as many workers as possible; and that race relations had improved.[131] To Scott, however, the South was the proper homeland for Negroes, and his vision of it was generally rose-tinted. The Labor Department saw things differently. It found that $2.00 was the very top pay for common labor in the mills, but that the average was nearer $1.50; and that farm laborers "receive from 50 to 75 cents and rarely $1 per day," with $.35 and $.40 per day the usual wage of women and children.[132] The Department's report in 1919 quoted a North Carolina newspaper editor on the "outrageous wages" of $1.25 a day that some farmers had to pay to keep their hands; and in Georgia, the report said, $1.00 or $1.10 a day was far above average pay.[133]

The pay situation did represent some improvement over pre-migration conditions, and the labor dearth by the time of the war scared southern employers into certain other efforts to hang onto the dwindling black work force, the lifeblood of the southern farms and mills. But the efforts reported by the Labor Department seem about as useful as trying to stop a spurting artery with a paper tissue. Farm bureaus started some educational campaigns, some farm demonstrators were sent around, and in some places leading blacks met with white employers to discuss community problems. In the Alabama coal district, which, as we have seen, had lost such an alarming portion of its labor force to mines in Ohio and Illinois, some reforms were made in the treatment of Negroes by foremen and by instituting a regular monthly pay envelope instead of the scrip and discounted store-check system.[134] Some employers were reported as "coming to the conclusion . . . that they must give the Negro better treatment and a more nearly square deal. Owing to the scarcity of labor, a Georgia farmer near Albany this year laid aside his whip and gun, with which it is reported he had been accustomed to drive his hands, and begged for laborers. . . ."[135] But no southern white would beg when he could command. A Loyalty League formed by white civilians in Louisiana during the war, and backed by state "work or fight" laws, practically revived the Black Codes of pre-Reconstruction years; the avowed purpose of the League was to insure that every able-bodied man—and this meant black man—would work at any wage, any job, for any number of hours required by employers.[136]

Such reforms as were made in the treatment of southern farm workers were admittedly the result of the farmers' need at a time when the war opened other options to blacks, and do not appear to have been more than temporary expedients. A recent motion picture, *Sounder,* concerning the life of a black tenant-farmer family in 1933, shows the same conditions of starvation, injustice, and abuse under which southern black farm workers suffered in 1900.[137] Hortense Powdermaker's study of the lives of blacks in a Deep South town in the 1930s shows the same white attitudes and institutions that had made so many blacks go North twenty or thirty years earlier.[138] What temporary respite from the whip and gun the southern black enjoyed in 1920 he owed to brothers who had been desperate enough and brave enough to try for a better life in strange northern cities.

Scott was also overoptimistic about the future of blacks in unions in the South. It seems that more white workers than in 1900 were gradually realizing, as in the North, that it was to their eventual economic advantage to include blacks in the labor movement, but "any such general change of front by white workmen would menace the very foundations of the color line as it is drawn in the South,"[139] Herbert Seligmann commented, so extraordinary measures were taken to prevent a color coalition. In Bogalusa, Louisiana, in 1919, three white men were shot dead because they walked down the street with a black labor organizer. The excuse given for the shooting was that the organizer was inciting blacks to riot. And the Great Southern Lumber Company, which controlled Bogalusa, using the muscle of the Loyalty League (although by then the war by which it justified its existence was over), ordered 2,500 union men to destroy their union cards. "The black man had dared to organize in a district where organization meant at the least exile, at the most death by lynching," Seligmann quotes from an article by Mary Ovington.[140] At whatever cost, black people were daring to change their future.

It is hard, however, to see any chance in the South for the black man who wanted to better himself. Whatever improvement Scott may have seen, the hunger-level of life for blacks in the South was attested by the terrible ravages of pellagra, the killer that followed every bad crop year.[141] The northern ghettos had their killers, bronchitis and pneumonia and tuberculosis; but the migrants could adjust, could get better jobs at better pay—perhaps even union pay—so they could live, dress, and eat better, and envision not too improbably a future in which they and their children would be happier and healthier people, respected and self-respecting. There was violence in the North, bloody violence, especially after the war, when a letdown in production intensified job competition between blacks and whites; blacks suffered, but they had gained enough by leaving the South to nourish hope of some really good time ahead. Hope was the most significant difference between the black worker who had migrated North and his brother who had stayed behind.

CHAPTER 6

Paths to a Place in the Society

The surest way to incite a people to
meet the material demands of life is to
teach them that life is more than meat.

Dean Kelly Miller,
Howard University

Tuskegee Institute and similar southern black schools were not educating Negroes for social equality. Booker T. Washington had promised that in his lauded Atlanta Exposition speech: "In all things that are purely social we can be as separate as the fingers. . . ."[1] But Washington was not one of those who pulled up roots and moved North; those who did were showing that they did not intend permanently to be separate—that is, inferior—socially or any other way. Through schools, church, communications, talents, new leadership, and organized effort, great numbers of the migrants pushed ahead toward a self-respecting and respected place in American life. World War I, a unique factor in black advancement, will be treated by itself in a later chapter.

One way to crack the Booker T. Washington syndrome of separateness-and-service was to get an education. As the statements of so many migrants showed, a major reason for their leaving the South was to insure that their children would be literate. Rural blacks were bitterly aware of the handicap of illiteracy every time they bound themselves to a contract they could not read, or paid accounts they could not tally. Blacks in many cases had moved into the southern cities because city schools, although perhaps not good, were better than backwoods schools; and so city blacks, having a taste of better education, moved North in even greater proportion than their country cousins to seek the much better education they were told they would find there. The Labor Department's report on the migration commented that "in whatever else Negroes seem to differ they are one in their desire for education for their children."[2] There was, Negroes knew, no upward mobility in America without education; one had to have it to get a better job, live in a better house, use the vote, know what was going on, choose among leaders, and eventually get into the leaders' class oneself.

William Pickens, Yale-educated son of a South Carolina sharecropper, wrote: "Is not the inferiority of the Negro's educational status and progress amply explained by the inferiority of his educational advantages?"[3] No, resoundingly answered James K. Vardaman of Mississippi: "God Almighty created the negro for a menial—he is essentially a servant. . . . At any rate, that is all that he will ever accomplish in Mississippi, and as it is in Mississippi, so will it be in all the states ultimately."[4] "Does education make Negroes more criminal and less useful?" Pickens asked; "If this were true, the Negro would be a contradiction to the experience of all mankind in all previously recorded history."[5] It was indeed true, Vardaman answered, supporting his point with a fallacious, self-serving syllogism: "If, after forty years of earnest effort and expenditure of fabulous sums of money to educate his head, we have succeeded only in making a criminal of him and impairing his usefulness and efficiency as a laborer, wisdom would suggest that we make another experiment and see if we cannot improve him by educating his heart and his hand."[6]

Here Vardaman was of course giving the nod to Booker T. Washington's thesis for industrial and moral education. DuBois, with his Harvard Ph.D., like Pickens pleaded for academic education as fervently as Washington rejected it in favor of "the proper training of head, hand, and heart. . . ."[7] Vainly Washington insisted that he did not preach the accumulation of wealth as an ultimate purpose, but only as a means to an end;[8] the erudite DuBois cried, "If we make money the object of man-training, we shall develop money-makers but not necessarily men."[9] Stung by what must have seemed unfair criticism, Washington made his often quoted thrust against academic education for blacks: "When a mere boy, I saw a young colored man who had spent several years in school, sitting in a common cabin in the South studying a French grammar. I noted the poverty, untidiness, the want of system and thrift, that existed about the cabin, notwithstanding his knowledge of French and other academic studies."[10] This, in turn, stung DuBois to fury. Washington kept hammering home his point: "It is little trouble to find girls who can locate Pekin or the Desert of Sahara on an artificial globe, but seldom can you find one who can locate on an actual dinner table the proper place for the carving knife or the meat and vegetables."[11]

The controversy forced the two leaders into extreme positions that oversimplified their thinking. Washington did not oppose higher education for those who would be leaders; thirty of his chief teachers at Tuskegee were college-educated. DuBois in his Atlanta University studies showed himself fully aware of the importance of industrial skills to lift the mass of black people out of the common laborer category. Their difference was mainly a matter of horizons. Washington, slavery-born and totally a man of his time, could not envision a girl as a reporter or business executive to whom it would be much more important to know where Pekin is than where the mashed potatoes go; nor could he imagine a black man in the Army in France whose knowledge of French might make him indispensable, nor, certainly, a black tourist enjoying a vacation in Paris. DuBois, northern-born to freedom and privilege, had a much broader horizon; he saw black people emerging from the lower depths to take their place alongside whites in American society. Dean Kelly Miller, of Howard University, one of the few black leaders not completely polarized in this struggle between men and philosophies, commented: "The one-eyed advocates aligned themselves in battle array. . . . Men of sane and sober judgement on ordinary issues seem to lose all logical balance and composure on this problem. Where passion enters, reason takes flight. The war between the hand and head went merrily on."[12]

Unfortunately, whether Washington was the great pragmatist or only the great compromiser, his position on the beauty and dignity of humble labor only too strongly buttressed the plans of southern whites of every stripe of racism—but, of course, appealing to those whites was the most important component in Washington's success in getting support for industrial education. Early in the 1900s Governor Vardaman was saying: "Literary education—the knowledge of books—does not seem to produce any good substantial results with the negro, but serves rather to sharpen his cunning, breeds hopes that cannot be gratified, creates inclination to avoid honest labor, promotes indolence, and in turn leads to crime."[13] Edward Alderman, president of Tulane University, said that at the blacks' current stage of development, a higher education would be wasted, and that they must "start in the very kindergarten of racial development"—mechanical training, training of the hand.[14] Thomas Nelson Page argued warmly the evils of higher education and the virtues of industrial training, which, he pointed out, would benefit both the South and the Negroes without raising blacks unsuitably high on the social ladder.[15]

Black leaders lined up in Washington's camp or DuBois's. Kelly Miller leaned toward DuBois in defense of higher education for Negroes, especially to prepare leaders and professional people.[16] J. J. Pipkin, a black of Washington's generation, supported the old leader with the Page-like argument that the mechanically trained Negro "becomes a citizen who is able to add to the wealth of the State and to bear his share of the expenses of educational government,"[17] whatever exactly he meant by that. But Pickens, with clear-sighted bitterness, pointed to the insult lurking behind all the different educational theories; common to the various schools of thought, whether they claimed that industrial education made blacks better workers, or that higher education made them better leaders, or that any education at all made them dissatisfied with their condition, was that they all simply "view the Negro as a commodity" and not as a free, equal, dignified human being.[18]

Not only Vardaman but Bilbo, Blease, Watson, and Williams, southern Progressives all, were convinced of the dangers and the waste involved in educating black children; so as the first ten and then the second ten years of the century passed, politicians in the South continued to short-change blacks in the apportionment of tax moneys to education. In country areas, bad schools grew even worse as the migration took away many blacks, leaving large pockets where those who remained were without funds to support local schools or to pay competent teachers.[19]

The migration, although disastrous to the schooling of blacks left stranded in the South, did to a degree realize the dreams of those parents who fled North to give their children a better education. Many more black children went to school in the North. In 1920, 93.1 per cent of black children between 7 and 13 years of age attended school in New York, 95.8 per cent of that age group attended school in Ohio, and 93.7 per cent in Illinois, as contrasted with 70.2 per cent in Georgia, 69.2 per cent in Alabama, and 61 per cent in Louisiana. Not all those enrolled in school got there every day, to be sure; often older children had to take the place at home of working mothers, and there was also a lot of casual truancy, Mary Ovington found, absences which would have gone unnoticed in the South but which in the North, with its compulsory education laws, would bring the truant officer to the door—an attention quite unexpected by southern migrants.[20]

Whatever the imperfections in northern schools, they were greatly superior to schools in the South, in many cases even to white schools. About 1910, more than half the black schools in Alabama and Georgia and nearly all those in Louisiana were in rented homes, churches, lodge halls, or abandoned buildings. These were all grade schools. Even in Memphis, which did make an effort to expand schools to house a rapidly growing school population, there was no black high school until 1910, when an old white grade school was converted to this purpose. As noted earlier, black schools never got anything like their proper share of tax-based school funds; most southern states spent about $1.00 per black child for each $8.00 to $10 per white child. The severest handicap caused by insufficient funds was an inability to pay good enough salaries to attract qualified teachers. The average annual wage for black teachers in Alabama, Florida, Georgia,

Louisiana, the Carolinas, and Virginia was under $200 a year; white teachers earned about double that amount for teaching half as many students. Even in 1916, when the outflow of labor had persuaded whites that they must improve conditions to keep blacks in the South, these are the amounts appropriated in sample states as pay for teachers, white and black:

	WHITE	BLACK
Alabama	$ 9.41	$1.78
Arkansas	12.95	4.59
Georgia	9.58	1.76
Louisiana	13.73	1.31
Mississippi	10.60	2.26
South Carolina	10.00	1.44[21]

It seems no matter for surprise that South Carolina had trouble finding enough qualified black teachers who would work for such wages. The solution to this problem found by the state superintendent of education is astonishing, like so much black-problem solving, in its disingenuous ingenuity: lower the qualifications for black teachers. And so South Carolina did, with the further saving that, while the state one summer spent nearly $9,000 training white teachers, the cost of the now pared-down training of black teachers was under $2,000. No state could get well-qualified teachers for such pay. In the black belt, 70 per cent of the teachers had no more than a sixth-grade education.[22]

What the migrants found who had gone North to give their children a better education was indeed better, although in many places not really good. Segregation of schools by neighborhoods was almost as restrictive as the southern segregation by law, but not quite, and the absence of a rigid legal barrier makes a vast difference psychologically if not materially. For instance, many schools, like Chicago's Wendell Phillips High School, were largely but not exclusively black; and at Wendell Phillips there was one black teacher on an otherwise white staff. A black teacher in a mixed school was exceptional, the Chicago Commission on Race Relations found; but in the exception resides hope. New York, like Chicago, had no officially segregated schools; Philadelphia, Indianapolis, Gary, and Dayton had forms of segregation established by school boards. Everywhere, however, as the ghettos became more sharply defined, neighborhood schools had less mingling of blacks and whites; and in mixed fringe-ghetto areas, it became school policy to transfer children to schools outside their own neighborhoods, if necessary, to keep blacks and whites separated. Even where there were mixed schools, as in New Jersey, segregation was sometimes maintained within the school by separate classes and separate rooms, with white teachers for white students and black teachers for blacks. Playgrounds were often divided by a heavy wire fence. In schools with mixed classes, the status of black students was unpredictable; acceptance varied from one room to another and from one teacher to another, so that one class might have a black student president while in another blacks might have to sit in the back rows.[23]

One of the most disturbing problems of black migrants was this uncertainty about what role they would be expected to play from one situation to another. At home in the South they had known who they were and exactly how they were expected to act with the white man, but in the North they could never be sure. Certainly it makes for tension to have to probe another's eyes to see one's image—despised menial, pitied inferior, applauded although handicapped achiever, or culturally deprived equal—and to see all those selves and many shadings of them within a single day, perhaps. But was it better in the South, where one's image was clear and immutable, that of beast of burden, intended by God Almighty for the white man's service and commended to his care, kind or cruel? Apparently it was not better, or more blacks would have returned to the Land of Goshen. But a child who must give a large part of his attention to playing all the different parts and never missing his cue is not likely to do the best he is capable of in his studies.

Segregation in schools, as in housing, increased as the numbers of black migrants increased. By the flood tide of the migration, twelve Philadelphia schools were 100 per cent black, including teachers and principal; Negro children from outside the district were brought into those schools, and whites within the district were sent out. In the nonsegregated schools of Philadelphia all black students, regardless of grade, were assigned to "Union Rooms." New York's segregation was much less rigid. A 1913 report showed that although there were some black students in every school in Manhattan, more than 70 per cent of Negro children were concentrated in nine of the sixty-four schools investigated; however, there was some flexibility about placing black teachers in mostly white schools, and William Bulkley (over some faculty protest) was appointed principal of a white-majority school. Chicago schools were used as a weapon by whites determined to discourage the influx of black southern migrants; efforts were made to segregate schools by law, and when this failed, irate parents prevailed on sympathetic school staffs to achieve the same result by such devices as keeping white children at the main school building and sending blacks to a branch school. In Indianapolis, by 1918 more than 80 per cent of all black elementary school students were in segregated schools, and by 1920 almost 90 per cent. The Chicago Commission on Race Relations found what must have been true in every city where schools were black or white, that the black schools were the oldest buildings; in Chicago, only one out of the ten serving the majority of black children was built after 1890, whereas more than half the white schools had been built since 1899. Part of the reason for this, of course, was that the neighborhoods where black migrants settled were old, run-down neighborhoods, while whites pushed out into newer areas where new schools had to be built. The old schools abandoned to the black children had the worst facilities; rarely was there such a thing as a gymnasium or an assembly hall.[24]

Private schools generally made their own rules about segregation in their admissions policy, but in some southern states—Florida, Kentucky, Oklahoma, and Tennessee—even private schools were segregated by law, and in Georgia and Texas private-school segregation was assured by making state aid available only to racially separate schools. In Minnesota the exact opposite was true, state law specifying that no state aid would go to a racially segregated school. Minnesota's extraordinarily liberal race policy in all areas was undoubtedly related to the small size of its black population; in Minneapolis, for example, there were only 3,927 blacks, or 1 per cent of the whole population, in 1920, a figure virtually unchanged from 1900.[25]

Most school segregation took place on the grade school level, probably because so few black children stayed in school beyond eighth grade. In 1915, there were only ninety-one black high schools in the country; the number increased to 179 by 1922, indicating that the migration, with better jobs and better pay for black parents, enabled many more of their children to get a secondary education, even if in segregated schools. Above the high school level there was little problem, because of the relatively small number of black students who had the qualifications, time, or money to go on to higher education. In 1917, 455 blacks earned bachelor degrees, mostly from Negro institutions but with a sprinkling from Harvard, Yale, Cornell, Ohio State, the University of Chicago, Northwestern, the City College of New York, and other northern institutions, including, for women, Oberlin. Black professional schools, all in the South and the District of Columbia, were few and small, only three law schools and three medical schools by 1924; a few black doctors and lawyers got their professional training at northern universities.[26]

Life may have been happier and easier for black college students at one of the many southern institutions—a large number of which were church-controlled—than at a northern university, but the black schools could not give the same quality of education as northern nonsegregated institutions. In the South, both black and white colleges were on very slim budgets. It was reported that, early in the century, the combined funds available to sixty-six southern colleges and universities did not equal the income of Harvard University. In 1900 an Atlanta University study found that most students in the thirty-four black colleges were in fact doing only secondary-school work, and the same was very likely true of many of the smaller white colleges of the South. Northern colleges did not have to segregate black students, there were so few who could afford it or who met entrance qualifications.[27] Charles W. Eliot, president of Harvard University, said in 1907: "At present Harvard has about 5,000 white students and about thirty of the colored race. The latter are hidden in the great mass and are not noticeable. If they were equal in numbers or in a majority, we might deem a separation necessary."[28] There we have one very influential educator's thoughts on the question: how many are too many?

The occasion on which Eliot spoke was the meeting of the Twentieth Century Club of Boston, convened to consider the case of Berea College in Kentucky, which a year or so later would be the subject of a most destructive decision of the U. S. Supreme Court. Berea had been founded by the American Missionary Society before the Civil War as a one-room district school. After the war it was chartered as Berea College, for the purposes of "promoting the cause of Christ" and giving integrated, nonsectarian instruction to "all youth of good moral character."[29] Founded mainly for the benefit of poor mountain whites of the surrounding area, Berea nevertheless accepted black students from its inception. In 1904, when the college had 174 blacks in a student body of 927, the Kentucky legislature—aiming directly at Berea, the only mixed school in the state—made integrated schools illegal. The school found funds to send its black students to Fisk, Hampton, and other black institutions. The white students protested indignantly when their black schoolmates were removed, declaring: "We realize that you are excluded from the class rooms of Berea College, which we so highly prize, by no fault of your own, and that this hardship is a part of a long line of deprivations under which you live."[30] It might be noted that these students were not the sons of aristocrats, but of very poor, disadvantaged whites; their response to injustice weakens the common-sense myth that compassion is the exclusive badge of the blue blood, and is not found in the white masses whose social and economic level puts them in competition with black people.

But despite the objection of white students, the Kentucky courts upheld the segregation law, and the Supreme Court of the United States upheld the Kentucky Supreme Court. Justice Harlan, who had distinguished himself by his wise and learned dissent twelve years earlier in Plessy *v.* Ferguson, again disagreed with the majority opinion, saying: "Have we become so inoculated with prejudice of race that an American government, professedly based on the principles of freedom, and charged with the protection of all citizens alike, can make distinction between such citizens in the matter of their voluntary meeting for innocent purposes simply because of their respective races?"[31] Harlan a dozen years earlier had predicted that the doctrine of separate but equal, laid down in the Plessy case, would "stimulate aggressions, more or less brutal and irritating, upon the admitted rights of colored citizens," and how right he had been, this aristocrat who shared the compassion of the poor whites of Berea. The majority opinion of the U. S. Supreme Court in the Berea case concorded with racial feelings which, at about the same time, barred Chinese and other oriental children from San Francisco's public schools.[32] "It may be," President Eliot told the Twentieth Century Club, "that as large and generous a work can be done for the Negro in this way [i.e., by segregated schools] as in mixed schools."[33]

Eliot's speech was a severe blow to liberals, black and white. It provided a highly reputable quote to any school board chairman or college administrator who wanted to get rid of the Negro problem. Perhaps it was partly in response to Eliot and the Berea decision that a stiffening of black consciousness became noticeable. "Negroes are meeting prejudice with self-development," Ray Stannard Baker wrote in 1908, the year of the Berea decision. "It is a significant thing to find that many Negroes who a few years ago called themselves 'Afro-Americans' or 'Coloured Americans,' and who winced at the name Negro, now use Negro as the race name with pride. . . . The pressure for separation among the Negroes themselves is growing rapidly stronger. Where there are mixed schools in the North there is often pressure by Negroes for separate schools."[34] There were neither enough qualified black educators nor enough money for an adequate system of separate black schools. But black men who could desire independent black education, impracticable as that was at the time, had advanced socially a long way from the dependent stance of an older generation.

Despite all the educational inequities in the North, migrants' children did learn far beyond their parents' accomplishments. In

1900, 44.5 per cent of the nonwhite population was illiterate; illiteracy dropped dramatically to 30.5 per cent by 1910 and to 23 per cent by 1920, a decrease of about 48 per cent in the twenty years. In the same span of years, illiteracy dropped also among whites, native-born and immigrant, but less sharply: from 6.2 per cent in 1900 to 5 per cent in 1910 and to 4 per cent in 1920, a decrease of a little more than 35 per cent in the two decades. It has been pointed out that the amount of illiteracy among both blacks and whites is roughly in inverse proportion to the amount spent per capita on education; and this could surely explain to a large degree why by 1930 the illiteracy rate among New York City Negroes was lower than that of whites in Louisiana, Virginia, South Carolina, Mississippi, Kentucky, Georgia, or Alabama. Also pointing to the great advantages of a northern education is the much higher illiteracy among older Negroes, mostly southern-educated, than among their children who had gone to school after their parents migrated North. In the forty-five to fifty-four year age group, 68.1 per cent of Negroes were illiterate in 1900, 47 per cent in 1910, and 34.1 per cent in 1920; in the ten to fourteen year age group, however, illiteracy dropped from 30.1 per cent in 1900 to 18.9 per cent in 1910 and to 11.4 per cent in 1920.[35]

Still, despite great gains, many of the children of the migrants seemed to show the ill effects of early years of poor schooling or none at all. In the peak migration years, most of the migrants' children in Pittsburgh were in the first four grades, but 16 per cent of them were overage for their grades (eleven years old or more), as against 4.7 per cent overage white students. Also, almost all school principals in Pittsburgh agreed that in the first four years of school, black children kept up well with their classmates, but that thereafter they fell behind. This convinced many educators that a program of practical and industrial education, geared for black children who were believed to be more motor-minded than white children, would solve the overage problem and help prepare students for jobs.[36] It was not characteristic of the time to look for other reasons than capability why culturally deprived and psychologically hurt children might slip behind as studies began to require a larger frame of reference and greater self-assurance.

The church, being the most important black social institution, was forced to broaden its functions beyond the purely religious as black participation in the society broadened. But to provide the migrants with the emotional-religious outlet they were used to and needed, a new kind of church sprang up in the ghettos.

Established churches, such as St. Philips Protestant Episcopal and the Abyssinian Baptist in New York, grew very big and wealthy in the migration years. In 1920, St. Philips, reputedly the richest, had assets of nearly $1,000,000; the combined assets of the twenty-six largest black churches in Chicago totaled over $1,677,000. A frequent criticism was that there were too many churches; the census count of 1916 reported over 39,000 separate black church organizations in the country, with more than 37,000 church buildings, and owning property valued at about $86,-810,000. Another criticism often voiced was that the churches did not use enough of their wealth on social services needed by the community. James Weldon Johnson repeatedly complained that there were too many churches draining off money that should have been used to build and maintain hospitals, old people's homes, and similar institutions essential for ghetto people, and using that money instead on magnificent buildings and accouterments. The Zion African Methodist Church of Boston, for example, for many years required more than $10 a year per member to pay off indebtedness for a church building that had cost $59,500. The failings of the churches were probably exaggerated; almost every church in New York, for instance, had some sort of charitable and educational program for members even if it did not do extensive social work, and in Chicago it was noted that many churches were making an effort to expand their social programs. In any case, there was one notably exceptional church, the Institutional Church and Social Settlement founded in Chicago in 1900 by the Reverend Mr. Reverdy Ransom; it was more settlement house than church, some black ministers protested, with its stress on Christian service through a day nursery, employment office, and similar institutions to the neglect of conventional religion.[37]

Desperately as migrants needed social services, they suffered almost as severely from privation of the kind of emotional, ecstatic, salvation religion they had grown up with in the South, quite different from the solemn, conventional religion of the regular sectarian church services. Mushrooming storefront churches satisfied this need of the less-educated, poorer, and especially rural migrants, and presented a serious challenge to the solidly established churches with their large debts for handsome buildings. In every ghetto, the evangelical groups that met in stores or a preacher's parlor soon outnumbered the regular churches. Services tended to be fervent and noisy, with emotional chanting, which might be accompanied by tambourines to set a rhythmic beat. The most outstanding of these sects in Harlem was the Church of Christ, Apostolic Faith, founded in 1919 by Rev. M. R. C. Lawson, who deplored the sedate kind of religion that imitated the white man's style, and gave his congregation the fire-and-brimstone preaching they loved.[38] The migrants were more than happy, on the whole, to leave behind their old jobs, old farms, old cabins, old ramshackle one-room schools; but they brought the old religion with them, changing in this way the northern cities that were so profoundly changing them. And here, too, even more than Baker had observed in other areas of life, black consciousness was asserting itself.

The urbanization of black people when they moved North had the effect, as at other times with other groups, of developing a middle class as the result of expanded education, communication, job and business opportunities, and sense of identity. That middle class provided most of the black leaders of the period and sired later ones.

In every northern city there had been an earlier black elite, founded on property, family, and, usually, degree of color. William Hannibal Thomas, a mulatto who was a lawyer, Civil War veteran, and once member of the South Carolina legislature, at the turn of the century presented in his book *The American*

Negro a typically elite, censorious appraisal of his fellow but lower-class blacks. He declared Negroes superstitious, ruled by passion, addicted to showy shams, lacking in honor, truth, integrity, discretion, and affection for others of their kind, recklessly vindictive, fickle, unstable, criminal by instinct, and endowed with practically every other bad quality that the most vicious white racist attributed to them. Thomas's conclusion was that it was pointless to give Negroes, through book learning, a glimpse of a way of living they could never pursue, when what they needed was moral and mechanical training.[39]

Among successful Negroes like Thomas, who had such a poor opinion of lower-class Negroes, many were of brown or lighter complexions rather than black. Their lightness had no doubt contributed to their success, not for the reason alleged by racists that their white genes gave them superior endowments, but because the more they looked like the ruling race the more acceptable they were to it and the more opportunities came their way. The price the mixed-blood person paid for his advantages was that he lived in two different and antagonistic cultures, neither of which would completely embrace him; blacks regarded him rather hostilely as of a higher status than their own, while to whites he was of a lower status, however successful.[40]

Southern migrants found elite Negro enclaves in Philadelphia, Chicago, and every other northern city. In New York there was the old and aristocratic Negro Society of the Sons of New York. Washington, D.C., long a place of opportunity for black people, had probably the largest and most snobbish elite of all, with an almost-white "Four Hundred" at the top and a substantial prosperous group just below it;[41] Langston Hughes spoke of the Washington elite of about 1920 as "on the whole as unbearable and snobbish a group of people as I have ever come in contact with anywhere," and said that they "drew rigid class and color lines within the race against Negroes who worked with their hands, or who were dark in complexion and had no degrees from colleges."[42] These people did not agitate for political or legal relief from discrimination; they counted on building their own exclusive social, civic, and economic institutions. Like any white immigrant group that has established itself in American society, the entrenched black elite on the whole furiously resented the intrusion of uncouth new arrivals from the South who crowded into their cities and raised ghetto barriers where none had been before. They objected to what they considered the vulgar, loud, common, dirty riffraff from the black belt, and resented and feared being equated with these people just because they happened to have some ancestors of the same race.[43] "We have too much unwarranted criticism to fight to be handicapped in this way," protested a Negro New Yorker in the conservative New York *Age*.[44] Even the best-established mulatto was terribly vulnerable, and it is understandable that he should vent his fears in anger at his poor, often very black cousins from the South. As Baker wrote, it was a tragedy to educate the man of mixed ancestry to high expectations, and "then lock him forever within the bars of color."[45]

Many of the migrants, of course, were as light in color as Washington's Four Hundred, and from the number of light-skinned people among them who were listed as leaders one can judge how important one's shade of color was at this period. People named in the Negro Year Book, in Kelly Miller's *Race Adjustment*, in *The Colored American Review*, and by DuBois in his Talented Tenth included very few black blacks. In the Who's Who in Colored America published by DuBois in 1916, of the 131 men and 8 women named, 124 men and all the women were of mixed ancestry.[46] The question comes to mind whether more full blacks would have made these leaders' lists if the compilers themselves had not been light-colored. Also, it is interesting and perhaps significant that Robert Abbott, the man who in large part engineered the migration, was one of the few really black men generally acknowledged as a leader. According to his biographer, Roi Ottley, Abbott had suffered from color discrimination among Negroes since childhood, and had been discouraged from becoming a lawyer by being told he was too dark to succeed in the Chicago courts; he was even rejected for the choir of Grace Presbyterian Church by the color-sensitive "Old Settlers" of the congregation, Chicago-born mulattoes.[47]

Although the influx of southern blacks created some bitter feelings within the race, the migration gave both light and darker

Negroes quite new social horizons. A new middle class, springing from the greater economic opportunities in the North, was less bound by the conservatism of the old elite and had more room for the black Negro. As for the mulatto, he found it much easier in the North to break through the "bars of color" and migrate into the white world. Around 1910, approximately 25,000 Negroes seem to have passed each year into the white community, most of them young men.[48] It would cause less question in the North than in the color-conscious South if one explained a slightly swarthy skin and dark eyes and hair by claiming to be Mexican, Cuban, Brazilian, Spanish, French, or Armenian. A loss of 25,000 per year out of an estimated 300,000 to 400,000 mulattoes is less than 10 per cent, but it adds up to 250,000 fewer people counted as Negroes from one decennial census to the next. The percentage loss remained essentially stable, probably because, although it was easier to "pass" in the North, the number of mulatto babies does not seem to have been increased much by the migration. As late as 1918, twenty-eight states legally forbade intermarriage, and in nearly all other states there were barriers that had quasi-legal force; as for permanent but extralegal unions, concubinage of black women by white men was infrequent in the North and a vanishing practice in the South in the twentieth century. Such increase as occurred in the mulatto population was believed to be chiefly the result of temporary irregular unions and secondarily of intermarriage between Negroes and Indians.[49] Exactly how much of the increase in the white population was occasioned by the entrance of mulattoes into that group is a question that cannot be answered.

The new elite that emerged as the migration went on consisted chiefly of self-made Negroes, black and light. They had left Booker T. Washington back in the South with their buckets; they were intent on moving upward and were not inhibited by the snobbish elitism of the Sons of New York, the Old Settlers, or the Four Hundred. The people who made their livings in business, banking, and real estate could not afford to separate themselves from the ghetto community on which they depended for support; they had to identify with lower-class people. Nor were old family and inherited wealth the values of other newly successful blacks, many of whom were artists and athletes. And the leaders who were the philosophers and organizers of new roles for black Americans rejected the old elite's doctrine of discreet advance through one's own efforts only, insisting rather on equality through legal and social reforms of the entire society.

Most of the emerging artistic elite were music and show people. The fruiting of black music in the migration period was so rich as to be almost unbelievable. A catalogue of leaders in the arts would have to start with the extraordinarily versatile James Weldon Johnson, who lived in many worlds: leader of the black bohemian group, lyricist and arranger of popular songs and spirituals, librettist for musical comedies, but also a United States diplomat in Venezuela and Nicaragua, a relative by marriage of the wealthy realtor John Nail, staff member of the NAACP, poet, essayist, novelist (*The Autobiography of an Ex-Colored Man*, published in 1912), and, later on, professor of creative literature at Fisk University. With all these varied accomplishments, Johnson was probably known best by the average black person for "Lift Every Voice and Sing," which he wrote with his brother J. Rosamond, composer and pianist, and which became the official song of the NAACP. Then there was W. C. Handy, perhaps greatest among black composers of the period, whose "Memphis Blues" was published in 1912 and "St. Louis Blues" in 1914; and Ferdinand Morton, whose "Jelly Roll Blues" arrangement came out in 1915. Bob Cole wrote many popular song hits with James Weldon Johnson, such as "When the Band Plays Ragtime," which are permanently fixed in the American repertory, as is "After You've Gone" by Henry Creamer and Turner Layton. Most of these black artists worked in several areas, like the popular comedy team of Flournoy Miller and Aubrey Lyles, who also wrote plays; Will Marion Cook, concert violinist and composer of serious orchestral music as well as musical comedies, which latter he also directed and produced; poet Paul Lawrence Dunbar, who wrote lyrics for a Cook musical comedy; and Bert Williams and Nash Walker, great favorites as vaudeville entertainers with both black and white audiences, who also collaborated in writing songs and musicals.[50]

The artistic energy of these years seemed unbounded. Among singers were the great Roland Hayes, who started with the Fisk Jubilee singers and who by 1917 gave a recital at Symphony Hall in Boston; and Marian Anderson, who was singing church music with Hayes in 1916. Then there was Sissieretta Jones, the concert singer who was called the "Black Patti," earlier mentioned as one of the performers who distributed the banned Chicago *Defender* to southern black audiences; and Harry Burleigh, singer, composer, and arranger, pupil and protégé of Anton Dvorak. It was Burleigh's arrangement of the spiritual "Deep River" that was woven by Dvorak into his "New World Symphony." The Hall Johnson Choir launched many of the great singers. The most famous of all, singer and actor Paul Robeson, was not widely known for his singing until after 1920; in the prewar years, however, he was a source of pride to blacks as a college football star.[51]

The women singers who interpreted jazz and blues were queens of the ghetto: Gertrude Melissa Nix Pridgett ("Ma") Rainey, Bessie Smith, Mamie Smith, Florence Mills, Ethel Waters, and, just after 1920, Josephine Baker. Most of them were very young and not yet known outside black music circles. Band leaders and instrumentalists, most of whom were also composers and arrangers, were ghetto kings, and probably at no other time has there been such an assemblage of "greats": Scott Joplin, Thomas Turpin, James Scott, Eubie Blake, King Oliver, Jelly Roll Morton, Louis Armstrong, Noble Sissle, James Europe, Ford Dabney, Tom Brymn, Will Tyers, and Will Vedery. They played every big city and some small ones from St. Louis east, with Chicago and New York the main stops, and jazz lovers flocked to hear them, both the "society music" of the orchestras that played the big roof gardens where whites went dancing and the classic jazz of the small bands and combos. In whatever other fields black artists might imitate white forms, in music they followed their own traditions, and white artists imitated them. A white music critic is said to have urged Jim Europe to play some Haydn and to urge black composers to write in the white classical style, to which Europe responded that "we colored people have our own music that is part of us."[52]

Another field in which a new elite emerged in this period was athletics. Achievement in sports was possibly more exciting to black people than achievement in music, because although the excellence of Negro music and entertainment had been acknowledged by whites since plantation days, black athletes, however good, had been prevented by segregation in sports competition from making a national reputation. Blacks in the North found discrimination in sports as in other endeavors, but since discrimination was not absolutely rigid, consistent, and required by law, a few outstanding people managed to crack through to fame.

Northern colleges had produced black athletes from time to time since about 1890, and many black leaders in various fields had gotten a good education through athletic scholarships. In the 1890s, William H. Lewis played football for Amherst and Harvard, and was named All-American center; in 1904 he was selected by Walter Camp for the coveted honor of a place on the All-Time All-American team. Lewis later became United States assistant attorney general under President Taft. Many northern colleges and universities had black players on their football teams —Rutgers, Brown, Colby, Tufts, Oberlin, Dartmouth, New York University, Michigan State, Northeastern, Northwestern, Vermont, Boston, Illinois, Iowa, Minnesota, Nebraska, and many others—and would probably have had even more except for race problems in intercollegiate competition; by "gentlemen's agreement," there could be no black players in the line when the team was playing a southern organization. Edwin B. Henderson, in one of the few books on blacks in sports, says that the black player had to accept being benched during such games "or withdraw from the team with the loss of his athletic scholarship."[53] Some great players accepted the terms. Fritz (more formally, Frederick Douglass) Pollard, halfback at Brown, in 1916 was named to the All-American team and played in the Rose Bowl game; later he went into professional football. Paul Robeson won letters four times at Rutgers, and made All-American in 1917 and 1918; Robeson at college was also a basketball player and debater, and member of Phi Beta Kappa; after graduation he paid his way through Columbia Law School by playing pro football, before making a career in acting and singing.[54]

One had to be a Robeson or a Ralph Bunche to get on a white college basketball team at that time; they were almost all segregated because of the prejudices of most white "conferences," and also because of the trouble involved on trains and in hotels when the team traveled, which latter must have plagued all teams in every sport. Bunche, at the University of California on an athletic scholarship, played in Pacific Conference games shortly after 1920, but he was the last black basketball player on a white college team for many years thereafter. Black collegiate track stars, on the other hand, were numerous, and some of them went on to Olympic teams. The first black athlete in the Olympics was George C. Poag, who placed in two events in 1904. He was followed by a string of great track men; by 1920 the Olympics had included John B. Taylor, Howard P. Drew, Sol Butler, Earl Johnson, and Harry Edwards. DeHart Hubbard and Ned Gourdin won first and second places in the running broad jump in the 1924 games.[55]

Professional football offered elite status to many former campus heroes who might otherwise have found themselves in unimportant, low-paid jobs. It cannot be overstressed how limited were suitable employment opportunities even for the most distinguished black people. Arthur Schomburg, whose collection of books, documents, and other materials became the nucleus of the Division of Negro Literature and History of the New York Public Library, is reported to have been a bank messenger for Bankers' Trust Company until 1932, when he was appointed curator of the collection he had given the city.[56] Pro football was an inviting field in which there was never much of a color line drawn, probably because the great player and manager Jim Thorpe, who was part American Indian, set a standard of absolute nondiscrimination.[57]

Professional baseball was another matter. There had been a few black players on white teams before 1900, but then a lily-white policy was established by both major and minor league teams, which lasted half a century.[58] With very few exceptions, black baseball players were restricted to their own all-black teams, although not because of complaints from white players, the St. Louis *Globe-Democrat* reported: ". . . the owners and not the players are the ones keeping the color bar in baseball," that newspaper said.[59] But John McGraw, manager of the New York Giants, is said to have knowingly signed on the light-skinned Negro, Charlie Grant, as a first baseman, representing him as an Indian chief. The trick worked until the team played in Chicago, Grant's hometown, where black fans packing the stands blew it by waving banners saying "Our Boy Charlie Grant." McGraw was forced by the league to let Grant go, but there were probably a few other black players who did pass in big league baseball as Cubans or whites.[60] By 1920, under the leadership of Rube Foster, once McGraw's pitching coach, black players began to form their own National and American leagues, and tried to duplicate the white league schedules and World Series. In postseason barnstorming games the black teams often played white league teams, and white players found out about black stars like pitcher Satchel Paige and shortstop John Henry Floyd. Sportswriters praised the black teams, commenting particularly on the swift base-running and whiplike throwing arms of outfielders.[61] On the road, especially in a southern town, life could be pretty miserable for the black teams. One player said, ". . . you don't eat. You can't get out of the bus. The secretary writes down all the stuff on a list . . . and then brings back the hamburgers and stuff."[62] But in cities like New York and Chicago the black teams were freer and very popular; in 1920 the two leading New York black teams played to a crowd of 16,-000 black and white fans at Ebbets Field. Players on the all-black American Giants and the Leland Giants of Chicago and on the Lincoln Giants and Bacharach Giants of New York were heroes to their black communities, important members of the new elite along with the campus athletic heroes and pro football stars and show business folk.[63]

The towering figure of the time, both personally and as a symbol of black supremacy, was fighter Jack Johnson, who probably more than any other one person influenced the tone of black-white relations from before 1910 until after 1915—a long while after, according to some observers.[64]

There had always been notable black fighters, as there had been notable black horse trainers and jockeys, because boxing and horse racing were old plantation sports in which one owner would pit his slaves or horses against those of a neighboring owner. Among the black fighter heroes before 1900 were Tom Molyneux, Bob Smith, Bob Travers, Jim Wharton, George Godfrey, Charles Hadley, Peter Jackson, George Dixon, and Andy Bowen. With few exceptions, blacks fought each other; where bouts were arranged between black and white fighters they were fought out of the United States, where the color line would not permit mixed fights. This rule held into the twentieth century, when outstanding black fighters like Joe Jeanette, Sam McVey, Sam Langford, and Harry Wills could not get matches with whites. Joe Gans, who held the lightweight title from 1901 to 1908, had to do most of his fighting on the road because New York City did not welcome black boxers. The white heavyweight champion from 1882, John L. Sullivan, avoided bouts with Godfrey and Hadley; Sullivan's successor, Jim Jeffries, refused to fight Joe Walcott although Walcott was entitled to a match, having beaten a man who had fought Jeffries to a draw.[65]

Jack Johnson, born in Galveston in 1878, fought his way up in the heavyweight ranks until he finally defeated the white champion, Tommy Burns, in 1908 in a bout in Australia. This victory made Jack Johnson heavyweight champion of the world, a situation intolerable to many—perhaps most—white Americans, the more especially because of Johnson's liaisons with white women. So Jim Jeffries, who had retired as undefeated heavyweight champion in 1906, was called back as the "white hope" who could put Johnson down. But on July 4, 1910, in a bout in Reno, Nevada, Johnson scored an easy knockout over Jeffries to become beyond any argument or technicality the world's heavyweight champion.[66]

This event apparently threw the country into a delirium of race hatred. Almost forty years after the Johnson-Jeffries fight a white sportswriter recalled: "Man alive, how I hated Jack Johnson in the summer of 1910. . . ."[67] Blacks were wild with exultation because their man had won while white spectators were yelling, "Kill the nigger!"[68] Within half an hour after word of Johnson's victory flashed over the wires, race violence broke out in many parts of the country. In Pittsburgh, blacks chased whites off streetcars. Three blacks were killed that night in Uvalde, Texas. A black constable was killed in Mounds, Illinois, when he tried to arrest some black men who were celebrating with guns. In Little Rock, Arkansas, a train conductor was shot during a fight between black and white passengers. In New York, a gang of whites roamed the streets terrorizing and beating blacks, and only police intervention prevented a lynching.[69]

The fever did not abate. Transportation of the fight pictures for commercial showing was prohibited. The District of Columbia banned film showings of the match on the ground that they might incite "race hatred." Two years after the match the New York State Boxing Commission prohibited bouts between black and white fighters.[70] Johnson's private life continued to scandalize white Americans. He ignored pleas by the black press for morality and moderation. "The world acclaims thee as a physical hero. Now live the life which no other pugilist ever lived, the life of a moral hero," said one paper, and another said, "Now that it is over, let Champion Johnson make good use of his money. . . ."[71] Champion Johnson, however, like other pugilists, lavished his money on big, fast cars and fast living. Roi Ottley calls him one of the "gaudy expressions" of his age, morally neither better nor worse than other boxers.[72] But Johnson did what was considered unforgivable in twice marrying white women. Immediately there was an outcry in northern states for laws forbidding interracial marriages, and a Georgia congressman demanded a Constitutional amendment prohibiting intermarriage, saying: "No brutality, no infamy, no degradation in all the years of southern slavery possessed such villainous character and such atrocious qualities as the provisions of laws . . . which allow the marriage of the negro Jack Johnson to a woman of Caucasian strain."[73]

After a flamboyant and sensational few years, Johnson was convicted of violation of the Mann Act, although there was no evidence of abduction of the white girl, Lucille Cameron, who had gone to live with him. Johnson was sentenced to jail for a year and a day, but escaped to Europe. In London, at the end of 1914, fight promoter Jack Curley arranged a bout between Johnson—still a fugitive—and the new "white hope," Jess Willard, to be fought in Havana, Cuba. Willard won that fight, on April 5, 1915, by a knockout, which Johnson always insisted he had agreed to in advance, the deal being that he would give the white world the satisfaction of being downed by a white champion in exchange for assurances that the Mann Act charges would be dropped and he could go home. The deal may indeed have been made, but it did not work out. Johnson returned to the States, gave himself up, and served his prison term.[74]

Johnson never ceased being the champion to black people, and was undoubtedly for many years the hero of his race, probably better known throughout the black community than Booker T. Washington and DuBois combined.[75] In the late 1920s, psychologists studying play activities of black children found that among two hundred activities the one outstandingly more popular with black boys than with white boys was boxing. From this the investigators drew some perhaps naïve conclusions; they deduced that black parents had a greater tolerance for boxing, that boxing was one of the few pursuits open to blacks, that it required little formal education or funds, and, chiefly, that it showed a drive to "compensatory reaction," being "an activity symbolizing mastery."[76] Nowhere did the scientists mention hero worship of Jack Johnson, or of the other powerful black boxers of the time—Harry Wills, Siki, Tiger Flower—who were the elite of the elite to powerless ghetto people. The enormous, gleeful pride in the black champion Johnson is rolled up in the demure statement attributed by the newspapers to his mother on an occasion when she saw a white beggar swathed in bandages, "Gracious me, if there isn't poor old Jeffries now. To look at him you wouldn't think he would refuse to shake hands with my boy."[77]

The Chicago *Defender* said in 1915: "Wouldn't it be a glorious thing if the Booker T. Washington faction, the DuBois faction, and the Monroe Trotter faction would get together on a common ground and fight unitedly for the things that they are now fighting singly for?"[78]

A great deal was heard in both the black press and the white press about black factionalism and about the inability of blacks to act jointly for social progress. But the criticism does not stand up under examination. First, there was no more black factionalism than white factionalism, but it was played up more, especially by whites whose purpose was to prove that blacks were incapable of organizing themselves. Second, the *Defender* and other voices were superficial in assuming that all black groups were fighting for the same things. They were definitely not. Booker T. Washington, in his prime around 1900, had indeed expressed the aspirations and goals of the overwhelming majority of blacks of the generation born during slavery: to make the white men their friends and patrons by faithful work and inoffensive behavior, and to gain what advantages they quietly could by proving themselves necessary to the white economy. "There was no question of Booker T. Washington's undisputed leadership of the ten million Negroes in America," DuBois wrote, "a leadership recognized gladly by the whites and conceded by most of the Negroes."[79] But the migration and the approach of war, bringing blacks an expansion of options in all areas of life and a taste of something like equality, opened other expectations and goals than there had been in 1900, and each one found a leader who believed his goal *the* goal, and his way *the* way to Negro advancement. To quote DuBois again, young blacks began to feel, " 'I don't give a damn what Booker Washington thinks. This is what I think, *and I have a right to think.*' "[80]

It is far more significant that black people no longer thought as a mass, that they had learned enough and done enough to separate and seek different paths to different places, that there was among blacks a conflict of hopes and goals, than that there was a conflict among leaders. The shifting of position of black leaders, the alliances they made and sometimes soon dissolved, their increasing or decreasing radicalism over a period of years have more significance as responses to new options and goals than as simple bickering. The proliferation of goals and leaders speaks very plainly of the social progress of black people.

Booker T. Washington and his "Tuskegee Machine," as DuBois dubbed the Washington faction, plus a pro-Washington press including such papers as the New York *Age*, the Washington *Colored American*, and the Indianapolis *Freeman*, plus powerful white supporters such as Andrew Carnegie, Julius Rosenwald, Carl Schurz, and Oswald Garrison Villard, kept the old conservative philosophy paramount until about 1910, although cracks had begun to appear soon after Washington's Atlanta Exposition address in 1895. John Hope, president of Atlanta University, had at once protested that "I regard it as cowardly and dishonest for any of our colored men to tell white people and colored people that we are not struggling for equality. . . ."[81] In 1901, outspoken criticism of Washington began to appear, especially in the Boston *Guardian*, founded that year by George Forbes and Monroe Trotter. DuBois's *The Souls of Black Folks*, published in 1903, bitterly protested against Washington's philosophy of adjustment and submission. Rather ironically, Washington by that time was quietly and covertly working against political discrimination, railroad Jim Crow, exploitation of tenant farmers, and other injustices. But Washington's way was to work anonymously through Emmett Scott, Robert Moton, the Afro-American Council, Kelly Miller, Archibald Grimke, and in some instances through white lawyers, so as not to risk losing the white support that kept Tuskegee Institute and other Washington projects solvent.[82] Trotter and DuBois were for a while drawn together by shared opposition to Washington's professed (not his secret) goals. Trotter in the *Guardian* attacked Washington editorially each week, so stridently and sometimes scurrilously that he lost many supporters. His emotionalism and lack of moderation finally alienated the intellectual and fastidious DuBois. But during the time when DuBois and Trotter were allies, the most important political development of that time for black people began to take shape: the National Association for the Advancement of Colored People.

The black leaders were painfully conscious of the strength that a unity of purpose could give them and had made a number of efforts to come together in a nonpartisan group. For a time, the Afro-American Council, headed by Bishop Alexander Walters from before 1900, seemed a possible vehicle; but in 1903 it was rocked by a fight for control between Bookerites and less conservative people, and Trotter later used it in launching a new organization, the Negro-American Political League.[83] Then, in 1904, Washington invited black leaders to form a common front in a Committee of Twelve, but this organization also turned quickly into a political arena for conservatives and progressives, and in 1905 DuBois resigned from the committee saying, "I propose to fight the battle to the last ditch." Trotter offered to help him, and so that alliance was formed.[84] That year, DuBois, Trotter, F. L. McGhee of St. Paul, and C. E. Bentley of Chicago set off the Niagara Movement at a leaders' meeting on the Canadian side of Niagara Falls; leaders came from all over the United States, but the gathering was noticeably short of Tuskegee people, naturally, because its purpose was to form an organization dedicated to manhood suffrage, equal civil rights and economic opportunities, and full access to all kinds of education. The second meeting of the group was held the following year, in August 1906, symbolically at Harper's Ferry; but within a year Trotter and DuBois became irreconcilably divided on matters of principle, and Trotter soon dropped out; the organization was weakened by division and by the loss of press support in Trotter's *Guardian*.[85]

Another effort at nonpartisan unification came in 1906, under the aegis of a white New Yorker, John E. Milholland, who felt called to lead a crusade for black rights; DuBois, Trotter, Grimke, and Kelly Miller attended the organizational meeting of this Constitutional League. But Milholland seemed to lack the tact and wisdom necessary to lead his crusade; Villard described him as "excitable at all times and sometimes goes off half-cocked."[86] Milholland's League was not to be the organ of unification.

All these calls and organizations and declarations of principles were dress rehearsals for the formation of the NAACP. The immediate impetus was a shocking race riot in Springfield, Ohio, in the summer of 1908. William English Walling, a white Southerner who had for some time been affiliated with Mary White Ovington and others working for black causes, was moved by the Springfield horror to call for an all-out campaign for black civil and political rights. The result was a meeting in February 1909 of black and white rights leaders who formed the National

Negro Conference.[87] Members of the Niagara Movement attended, along with such white progressives as Henry Moskowitz, Mary Ovington, Oswald Garrison Villard, Moorfield Storey, and John Milholland; Trotter was conspicuous by his absence. Out of this group, a biracial Committee of Forty formed a permanent administrative organization, and the following year the group took the name National Association for the Advancement of Colored People. All the officers were white except DuBois, who was named Director of Publications and Research, and thus editor of the NAACP organ, *The Crisis*. For a time it seemed that Trotter would make peace with DuBois and join the NAACP, but the temporary truce did not last.

As Trotter's National Equal Rights League splintered and floundered, the NAACP gathered strength. By 1914 it had 6,000 members in fifty branches; by 1916 the branches had increased to sixty-seven, with six of them in the South. In 1916, when Joel Spingarn, a white scholar who was chairman of the directors of the NAACP, called a meeting of black leaders at his home in Amenia, New York, unity seemed a lively possibility. Conservatives Emmett Scott and Fred Moore attended along with progressive leaders DuBois and John Hope and such centrists as Kelly Miller. Trotter was not there, but sent greetings. By then the NAACP's branch in Washington, D.C., had 1,164 members, and was keeping close watch over legislation touching on black rights; and DuBois had made *The Crisis* a most successful and exciting black publication. When the war ended, the NAACP had 300 branches, 155 of them in the South, with a total of 88,488 members of whom almost half were southern. The numbers of blacks who dared join an organization designed to achieve equality under the laws and in the courts is the most dramatic indicator of their social progress in the twenty years since 1900. And, although there were and continued to be differences of opinion among NAACP personnel, the survival and steadily increasing power of the organization is ample proof that where there was a common goal and agreement on the path to follow toward it, there could be unity among black leaders.[88]

The work of the other effective and permanent black organization, the Urban League, with migrants in the ghettos has already been touched on. The League stands beside the NAACP as an achievement in co-operation and organization, although less difficult of accomplishment because its goals were more tangible and less controversial than those of the NAACP. Still, the Urban League, too, was the culmination of a series of efforts to help black migrants, going back to the White Rose Industrial Association, the Association for the Protection of Negro Women, and the National League for the Protection of Colored Women. Then William L. Bulkley, a talented organizer, took in hand the improvement of industrial opportunities for urban blacks. Bulkley, born in rural South Carolina, was educated at Wesleyan University in Connecticut, studied in France and Germany, and took his doctorate at Syracuse University, New York—all to become a seventh-grade teacher in the New York City school system. By 1899 he was principal of a school in New York's Tenderloin district. Bulkley was moved to social action because, as he put it, his black students finished school only "to open doors, run bells or hustle hash"[89] for the rest of their lives. In 1906 Bulkley founded the Committee for Improving the Industrial Condition of the Negro in New York. The CIICN succeeded in prodding the Carpenters and Joiners Union into chartering a Negro local in New York, and it helped find work for plumbers, construction workers, painters, bricklayers, masons, and decorators; it was active in establishing night trade schools and in building model tenements. Also, it co-operated with other social service groups, as for instance in sending members to patrol the docks with workers of the National League for the Protection of Colored Women to prevent the exploitation of arriving women migrants.[90]

Even social welfare, however, was to some extent caught in the tug-of-war between conservative and progressive black leaders. Bulkley was a DuBois supporter, and it apparently irked Booker Washington that someone in that camp should infringe on his territory of training Negroes and getting them jobs. Washington allegedly sent his agents to CIICN meetings so they could report to him on Bulkley's activities.[91] In 1910, Mrs. William H. Baldwin, a wealthy white supporter of Washington's, called together a group of prominent blacks and whites and established the Committee on Urban Conditions among Negroes, whose purposes were very close to those of Bulkley's group. The following year, Bulkley's Committee merged with Mrs. Baldwin's group and with the National League for the Protection of Colored Women to become the National League on Urban Conditions among Negroes, popularly known as the Urban League. Sociologist George Haynes was selected as its first director.[92] The Urban League's motto, "Not Alms, but Opportunity," had been phrased only slightly differently by Bulkley in a speech in 1909: ". . . all we ask is opportunity. We do not beg for alms. . . ."[93] At that time, August Meier has said, the participation of wealthy and interested white people was apparently necessary to black-help organizations.[94] Both the Urban League and the NAACP were interracial in leadership at the start. They grew to be self-sufficient black organizations, in their different ways leading black people nearer to the social goals of equality in the economy and under the law.

Black Southerners were only too aware that, lacking the vote, they were doomed to remain at the bottom of American society, and one of the frequently mentioned reasons for going North was to feel a ballot in their hands. The migrants said they "voted with their feet." In politics in the South, Ray Stannard Baker said, the black man had always been an issue rather than an actor; even in Reconstruction times, when there were a few black legislators, "the Negro was in politics by virtue of the power of the North."[95] Prior to 1910 Kelly Miller had said, "The Negro is impotent. He makes his puny protest but the nation heeds it not."[96] This was a loss to all, William Pickens pointed out; if whites would heed the protest, "The blacks would gain voice, hope, a high sense of American justice, patriotism, civilization. And the whites would gain a sounder knowledge of the Negro's condition, needs, thoughts and aims, so that on bills affecting the interests of the Negro race the white majority would vote more wisely than it now votes."[97]

But this sound advice was ignored. There was no black man in the federal Congress from 1901, when Representative George White of North Carolina left, until 1929, when Oscar DePriest of Chicago was sworn in. A brief flareup of hope for southern

blacks occurred in 1915, when the Supreme Court struck down the "grandfather clause" by its decision in the case of Guinn *v.* the United States. Moorfield Storey, representing the NAACP, appeared as a friend of the court in this suit, which challenged the constitutionality of Oklahoma's voting law. The court decided that, while the Fifteenth Amendment does not specifically give blacks the right of suffrage, in operation its prohibition of racial discrimination would have that effect. Literacy tests, although not unconstitutional, were found by the Supreme Court to be so closely tied to the grandfather test that they, too, were stricken down.[98] In another case during the same Supreme Court term, the absurd argument was presented that although the right to vote might be protected by law, there was no law saying that all votes had to be counted; to this Justice Holmes retorted: "We regard it as equally unquestionable that the right to have one's vote counted is as open to protection by Congress as the right to put the ballot in the box."[99] Certainly it was a point won, to have erased the grandfather clauses from the statutes. But black men, with few exceptions, still could not vote in the South except when they were herded to the polls to vote "right" on a particular issue or candidate; the poll tax, property qualifications, illegal voting rules, or plain intimidation were as effectively disfranchising as any law.[100] And who was there to see to it, if a black man succeeded in voting, that his vote would be counted?

Northern blacks could vote and be counted. Many of them, as in other groups, did not bother to use the vote. As in other groups, many voted as they were told to by Republican or Democratic politicians—usually Republicans, because that is how the great majority of blacks voted. Some black votes were bought: $1.00 per vote seems to have been the standard price, and does not appear to have risen along with prices of other commodities. But black votes were no more purchasable for dollar bills and whiskey than white votes. In addition to and probably far outnumbering the dollar voters were the many blacks who voted according to their interests. By the beginning of the century, according to DuBois, blacks in Philadelphia already had their own political clubs, which delivered votes for local politicians who would do them favors, legitimate and otherwise. There was little

difference between black voters and white voters in turning out for politicians who would get them jobs or patronage. Republican politicians always faced the threat of black defection to the Democrats if they did not keep their promises; and as the black population increased to a point of controlling certain city wards, as in New York, the Democrats made a greater effort to annex black votes by whatever means. Educated and socially conscious blacks were appealed to by politicians with gifts for their churches, schools, and other worthy causes.[101]

Although a good many blacks voted in northern cities, the rewards were usually small and personal. In Pittsburgh, for example, although the black vote was frequently delivered as a bloc by a few shrewd black politicians, no candidate bothered to improve conditions for blacks. In Chicago, where astute black politicians held more appointive and elective offices than in other cities, and where DePriest began his long climb to Congress when he was elected alderman in 1915, the black community as a whole made no material gains, and no white politician rewarded the black vote by sponsoring major improvements in the ghetto. Even when the black vote was decisive in a Pittsburgh municipal campaign, neither the elected candidate nor the black politicians in his entourage did anything for the mass of Negroes. Still, says the Labor Department report on this Pittsburgh situation, blacks were very glad to have the vote even when they were merely used by politicians.[102] At least, they won the goodwill of politicians they helped, and might ask personal favors. As Mary Ovington wrote, ". . . the Negro learns that it is well to have a friend in court; that helplessness is the worst of all disabilities, worse than darkness of skin or poverty."[103]

As hope of any general gains through either of the major parties grew dimmer, a number of blacks, especially young blacks, in their disillusionment turned to parties of the left that pledged equality for all.[104] There could scarcely be more dramatic evidence of the chasm that had opened between those sophisticated, impatient, militant young blacks and the colored people they had left behind in the South, who would regard it as a dream come true just to be allowed to cast a vote for the party of Lincoln. DuBois, A. Philip Randolph, Chandler Owen, Cyril Briggs, and Hubert H. Harrison were among the leaders who variously saw

in socialism or Bolshevism or black nationalism a chance for blacks that the traditional parties showed no signs of granting.

A few more blacks achieved elective or appointive office through the major parties during and soon after the war period. New York City in 1917 elected Edward Austin Johnson, a migrant from North Carolina, to the state legislature, and in 1919 elected Charles H. Roberts a city alderman; more blacks were sent to the state legislature in the 1920s.[105] In the federal government, color barriers that will be discussed later prevented advancement in the civil service, but there were two important wartime appointments of blacks to minimize race friction during the national emergency, Emmett Scott in the War Department and George Haynes in the Labor Department. Although it was war rather than brotherly love that brought about these political advances, advances they were nevertheless.

In two decades, a social advance had occurred that a Mississippi or Alabama black sharecropper of 1900 could not have believed possible. The middle class had expanded far beyond the small, elite, brown enclaves the migrants found on arrival in northern cities. The working-class ghetto dwellers read the news or had it read to them,[106] and talked it over with their neighbors or fellow workmen; children of those laborers were going to schools which demanded that they attend and study, even if those demands were not always met. Blacks stood in line with whites at the plant gates and the polling places. New leaders scorned compromise and accommodation; nothing less than full, equal citizenship was to be accepted. There were even some who, disgusted by many broken promises of reform and improvement, turned to revolutionary ideologies, which vowed color-blindness; others began to feel strongly that nothing was ever to be expected of any white men, and that their future lay in their own black hands, and these people were ready and waiting when Marcus Garvey beckoned at the end of the war. Since it is true that the mass of black Americans had made great economic and social progress between 1900 and the war's end, one must see first what price was paid for this progress, and how the war convinced many blacks that the price was too high, before one can understand why black radicals and black nationalists cut themselves off from mainstream America.

CHAPTER 7

Counterattack: Racist Thought

His color had been the mark of en-
slavement and was taken to be also
the mark of inferiority; for prejudice
does not reason, or it would not be
prejudice.

William Pickens,
The New Negro

For man, whatever his race, is an animal that you unquestionably can de-
base to whatever level you please, if
you only have power, and if you then
begin early enough, and devote yourself persistently enough to the noble
and civilized task of proving him to
be debased.

Josiah Royce,
*Race Questions, Provincialism, and
Other American Problems*

A profound and passionate belief tells
much about the person who holds the

belief but it tells nothing concerning
the truth or falsity of the belief that is
held.

Edward B. Reuter,
The American Race Problem

Racist ideas appear always to have lurked in the minds of educated, influential white Americans; at points in United States history, these ideas have surfaced and won acceptance because,
apparently, they were responsive to national interests or problems of the time. And just as the national interest gives respectability to such learned theories, so that they are published and
approved, the theories in their turn give legitimacy to unbridled,
violent race hate among ordinary men.

In the first two decades of the century there were a number
of national causes that encouraged racism. The imperialist urge
had reached America, the hunger to annex territory, resources,
and markets that belonged to colored peoples; imperialism embraced any justification for acting as if our little brown brothers
were arrested children who must be controlled and protected.
At the same time, immigrants to the United States from central,
southern, and eastern Europe came in tremendous numbers, people not nearly so similar in culture to Americans as the earlier,
northern European immigrants. Their languages, personal habits,
dress, and customs struck Americans as outlandish and even re-
pulsive, and most of them had darkish coloring that reminded
white Americans unpleasantly of Negroes. Simultaneously, internal migration of large numbers of American blacks was produc-
ing grave situations in both the North to which they went and
the South from which they had come. The advances, economic
and social, made by the migrants aroused fears and angers, so
that the black became the target for racist darts of every shape
and kind. Also encouraging to racism was the prevailing economic doctrine of laissez-faire, a ruthless defense of the benefit
to the nation of permitting the strong to grow stronger without

restraints at the expense of the weak—and who was weaker than the poor Italian, the poor Russian Jew, and especially the poor black, who still showed the stigmata of slavery?

These political, economic, and social developments coincided with a flurry of activity and discovery in the sciences of biology and genetics, with the early years of the social sciences of anthropology and sociology, and with the birth of psychology. The tools of the young sciences, such as statistics and intelligence testing, were applied enthusiastically and sometimes recklessly;[1] findings in the social sciences were often bolstered by questionable analogies to the natural sciences, as in the assumption that races evolve in the same way as organisms. But however imperfect in logic and methodology, the conclusions of the new sciences, and of the history and literature they inspired, were greeted as the word of God.

The conclusions of practically all scientific thinking of the time, or at least of what was taught, published, and accepted, were the politically and socially expedient conclusions: that the white race was superior to the darker races; that the whiter (more Anglo-Saxon, Caucasian, Teutonic, to use the popular terms of the day) the more superior; and furthermore, that native-born Americans of Anglo-Saxon ancestry were the very best of the lot. Naturally, everyone claimed to be an Anglo-Saxon. As the wonderful satirist and humorist Peter Finley Dunne said:

I'm wan iv th' hottest Anglo-Saxons that iver come out iv Anglo-Saxony. . . . I tell ye, whin th' Clan an' the Sons iv Sweden an' th' Banana Club an' th' Circle Francaize an' th' Pollacky Benivolent Society an' th' Rooshian Sons of Dinnymite an' th' Benny Brith an' th' Coffee Clutch that Schwartzmeister r-runs an' th' Turnd'ye-mind an' th' Holland society an' th' Afro-Americans an' th' other Anglo-Saxons begin f'r to raise their Anglo-Saxon battle cry, it'll be all day with th' eight or nine people in th' wurruld that has th' misfortune iv not bein' brought up Anglo-Saxons.[2]

Most of the genteel, intellectual racists thought, as Woodrow Wilson had expressed it, that Negroes were "a host of dusky children untimely put out of school" by emancipation, and that they were unprepared for the responsibilities of citizenship.[3] And there was a man of science, Dr. W. M. Bevis, to back Wilson up. Bevis said that the ancestors of black Americans had only a few hundred years ago been "savages or cannibals" in Africa, and that, with Reconstruction, "citizenship with its novel privileges . . . was thrust upon the race finding it poorly prepared, intellectually, for adjustment to this new social order."[4] And how should it be dealt with, this allegedly childlike, primitive subculture within American society? Not by education, certainly, said Dr. William Lee Howard in an article in *The Ladies' Home Journal.* "Take him away from all cultural education," Howard prescribed. "Make it a penal offense to sell or give him alcohol or drugs. Make him the nation's ward, as are the self-respecting Indians."[5] It could perhaps be taken for granted that a governor of Alabama would believe Negro schools "were turning out thieves and vagrants in companies, battalions, and armies,"[6] but when a Columbia University sociologist, Howard Odum, agreed that educated Negroes were a force not for good but for evil, and that they practiced and condoned the vices that were bringing about race deterioration, his scholarly northern reputation gave these ideas weight and respectability.[7]

The United States Army must surely have been impressed by the concurrence in these opinions of one of its own doctors, R. W. Shufeldt, the more so because Shufeldt disclaimed any personal bias against blacks. In the Introduction to his 1915 book *America's Greatest Problem: The Negro,* Shufeldt said, "I have no prejudice whatever against the negro race on account of its color; the very thought of such a thing would be absurd." But this disclaimer is not convincing, since most of his statements are simply opinion, unsupported by fact; and a doubt creeps in about his color-blindness when he describes white America as being "still in the coils of the great black snake."[8] The Negro, Shufeldt believed, is absolutely without morals, "bestial by nature . . . revels in lewd conversation, in erotic practices and in unlawful pursuits";[9] worse still, he said, the Negro delights in encouraging the approaches of white men to his women, and the women themselves are not reluctant.[10] On the subject of a black charged with raping a white woman, Shufeldt had very definite suggestions; the suspect, after being identified, must be immediately tried, and if found guilty, his execution should take place not more than a few hours later.[11] As to the future of the blacks in America, Shufeldt entirely agreed with Dr. Howard, whose *Ladies' Home Journal* article he quoted, that the Negro should be made to understand "in emphatic terms that he cannot aspire to social equality with the white man";[12] Shufeldt's own expression of this idea was that any black who believed he would attain equality in the United States "is following a will-o'-the-wisp."[13] Certainly that was the belief of the United States Army, which Shufeldt served, as World War I would prove. It is obvious that Shufeldt regretted the end of slavery, from his statement that "instead of being slaves under control, they are free—free to pollute the entire country."[14] Mulattoes were no better, Shufeldt said: "I have found them equally superstitious, treacherous, mendacious, and unreliable."[15] Shufeldt was among those who believed the only possible solution was to deport blacks of all shades to some other country.[16] Whether this flagrant bigotry in Major Shufeldt of the U. S. Army Medical Corps helped to form or merely expressed Army thinking, there it was, on paper, a "scientific" analysis available for quotation when large numbers of blacks entered the military two years after the publication of Shufeldt's book.

The Army found another medical man it could quote, and did quote, on blacks, Dr. Frederick L. Hoffman of the Prudential Life Insurance Company. In 1896 Hoffman had published a book about Negro traits[17] that was being cited years later by a Major Willcox of the United States Army as proof that black soldiers were not qualified for artillery units because they could not learn the requisite skills, being both nonmechanical and unreliable.[18] In fact, Dr. Hoffman did not write this in so many words, although Willcox might well make the inference from what Hoffman did write. One of the most pernicious and popular characteristics of racist writing is that its lack of precision and documentation permits any inference or interpretation that suits

a particular situation or a particular reader's prejudices. Among
the many statements that Hoffman did make are: that the root
of the high disease incidence among blacks was an "immense
amount of immorality"; that Negroes had been much healthier,
more cheerful, more capable, and more moral when they were
slaves; that the black race is naturally inferior to the white, not
having the Aryan qualities requisite for success, and will soon
be extinguished; and that in the light of these handicaps, attempts to ameliorate the black condition by well-meaning whites
will bring only "a vast sum of evil consequences . . . as the natural result of misapplied energy and misdirected human effort."[19]
Dr. Hoffman, like Dr. Shufeldt, disclaimed racial prejudice, and
as clinching proof of the impartiality of his study pointed out
that he was "of foreign birth, a German,"[20] and thereby free of
native American biases. In fact, his opinions were not very different and no more scientifically sound than those of the American John Ambrose Price, who said: "I love the old South of the
days of my youth, the land of plenty, of blue blood, aristocracy,
and happy niggers";[21] but Hoffman's opinions were more influential because of his scientific credentials, which to Major
Willcox made him much more quotable.

Philosopher Josiah Royce, a cool, clean stream of reason in this
murky landscape, said that when race theorists use science to
support their own prejudices, "I begin to wonder whether a science which mainly devotes itself to proving that we ourselves
are the salt of the earth, is after all so exact as it claims to be."[22]

Nativism, which has been discussed in the context of labor
struggles, was one result of this "salt of the earth" science. Francis
Walker, president of the Massachusetts Institute of Technology
and a leading economist, deplored the cheap transportation that
was bringing hordes of the worst class of immigrant into the
United States, people who would undermine America by out-
breeding the native stock.[23] Fear of the fecundity of the new
immigrants was widespread, as was also the notion that all labor
strikes and radical ideologies were introduced by them; they
were also, paradoxically, held responsible for keeping wages

down and preventing the advance of labor. But all Nativists agreed that they were undesirable. Woodrow Wilson said that the new immigrants "are beaten men from beaten races; representing the worst failures in the struggle for existence. . . . They have none of the ideas and aptitudes which . . . belong to those who are descended from the tribes that met under the oak trees of old Germany to make laws and choose chieftains."[24] On such sentimental, salt-of-the-earth utterances was based what has been called the Anglo-Saxon myth. Emotions were fired by such theories as Walker's that the new immigrants would breed faster than the native stock, so that to admit them was to commit race suicide. Magazines published many articles on this subject, which became a national phobia; when Theodore Roosevelt was President he rejected with utmost vehemence all proposals for legalizing birth control, which would only, the Nativists were convinced, hurry the extinction of the superior, native-American stock.[25]

Scientific support for Nativism and the Anglo-Saxon myth was triumphantly produced from Darwin's evolutionary theories, which were unscientifically applied to prove that different races were at different levels on the evolutionary ladder.[26] Herbert Spencer was the outstanding intellectual proponent of this dubious metaphor likening biological to social evolution. He wrote a good deal on the quality of races, and his convictions on this subject led him to oppose marriage between individuals of "superior" and "inferior" races.[27] Racists took philosophical comfort from Spencer's thinking; laissez-faire economists and politicians, and also some practitioners of the new arts of sociology and psychology, leaned heavily on Spencer's theories. Natural selection and the survival of the fittest were acclaimed by rugged individualists as explanations of America's dramatic progress in its short history.[28] Yale economist and sociologist William Graham Sumner was probably the most prestigious disciple of Spencer and the Darwinian metaphor. His own contribution was the doctrine of social determinism, that is, the inexorable evolution of societies in line with unchangeable "folkways" over a period of time. Sumner called for a society left free to evolve in its own way, unfettered by tariffs, poor laws, labor regulations, or other restrictions imposed by government in an effort to change its pattern of "natural" growth.[29] Here was high-level support for the rugged individualists. The poor, according to Sumner, were unfit and should therefore be eliminated rather than helped: "The whole effort of nature is to get rid of such, to clear the world of them, and make room for better."[30] Darwin's "fittest" had turned into Sumner's "best." Here was full-fledged Social Darwinism—natural selection, survival of the fittest, and devil take the hindmost.

Scholars throughout the country acclaimed and taught Social Darwinism and its corollary, the Anglo-Saxon myth. Industrialists welcomed a "science" so applicable to their expansion and profit. John D. Rockefeller said in a Sunday-school speech: "The growth of a large business is merely a survival of the fittest. . . . This is not an evil tendency in business. It is merely the working-out of a law of nature and a law of God."[31] Darwin was no longer the anti-Christ even to the pious; and although monkey-theory might not be taught in the schools, it was inserted in the business bible. Politicians also seized upon Social Darwinism, adding it to other pretexts for taking charge of little brown brothers whose societies were said to be on a lower rung of the evolutionary ladder.

The leading proponents of Social Darwinism did not aim their shots at American blacks, but the bullets naturally ricocheted into their midst because they were the poorest of the poor, and were certainly not Anglo-Saxons. As the isms rained down from the high clouds seeded by Spencer and Sumner, it was the Negro who got wettest. Educator Thomas P. Bailey wrote an essay which Howard Odum included in his book on black traits, and this is his Social Darwinism: "The Caste of the Kin is the practice of the theory that blood is thicker than water; and the Sermon on the Mount can not invalidate God's own law of the Survival of the Fittest."[32] This idea that Christ was soft on social misfits would often be expressed. Bailey concluded that, if the races can't blend their blood—and science and instinct, he said, tell us that they cannot—then the only real basis for democracy and equality does not exist and cannot be created.[33] Bailey made those statements in 1910, when he was superintendent of schools in Memphis. By 1914 he was dean of the Department of Education at the University of Mississippi, and a book he published at that time leaves no doubt of how Social Darwinism could be turned directly against blacks; Bailey now used such phrases as "blood will tell," "the negro is inferior and will remain so," "this is a white man's country," "no social equality," "no political equality"; and, lest anyone be uncertain how to treat Negroes, Bailey prescribed that "in matters of civil rights and legal adjustments [justice, presumably] give the white man, as opposed to the colored man, the benefit of the doubt, and under no circumstances interfere with the prestige of the white race."[34] There seems little likelihood that young white teachers-to-be left Ole Miss without infection with their dean's racism.

The scribes and teachers of Social Darwinism were spreading the law of tooth and claw, the law of the jungle, a code that deified competition. Blacks saw the point all too clearly. Kelly Miller commented: "There is little room for the weak and helpless in a strenuous philosophy which glorifies the valiant man."[35] Exactly so, said Sumner; the poor, the weak, were unfit and would have to go if society was to move forward, because "a plan for nourishing the unfittest and yet advancing civilization, no man will ever find."[36] In Harvard psychologist G. Stanley Hall we hear echoes of Wilson's "host of dusky children" and Taft's "little brown brother." Hall viewed primitive races as arrested children, and thought they should be treated tenderly. But at the same time he opposed any aid to defective individuals—whoever was to determine that—lest we interfere with wholesome natural selection; and he recommended sterilization and segregation of the unfit. Sociologist Franklin Henry Giddings taught that "consciousness of kind" was the governing principle in social phenomena, and psychologist William McDougall strongly supported Sumner's theses that "legislation cannot make mores" and "stateways cannot change folkways." Even if the NAACP should succeed in getting legal protection of civil rights for blacks, these racist theories said plainly, social equality was a mirage of promised land that could never be reached. "A man may curse his fate because he is born of an inferior race," according to salt-of-the-earthling Sumner, but he will get no answer from heaven.[37]

An ugly, sick, but recognizable offspring of Social Darwinism went by the name Teutonism. Here racism blared shrilly what most Social Darwinists merely implied: Not only were Anglo-Saxons, or Teutons, best, but all others were filthy, disgusting, and depraved. Two Oxford University professors, Bishop William Stubbs and Edward A. Freeman, had enunciated the Teutonist doctrine in the late nineteenth century, tracing every good quality in English civilization back to some dubiously Teutonic forebears whose very barbarism was adorable in its openness and forthrightness, so unlike the craftiness of Celts and Latins. Stubbs contrasted the Teutons with "wretched Italians" and "horrid Poles"; he rejoiced that Jews were considering a return to Palestine, and wished the Irish would go off in search of "Scota, Pharaoh's daughter."[38] Discrimination against Jews and Chinese, Freeman declared, was "only the natural instinct of any decent nation to get rid of filthy strangers."[39] Lecturing in the United States, Freeman said "the best remedy for whatever is amiss in America would be if every Irishman should kill a negro and be hanged for it."[40] Although in a later lecture Freeman tried to pass this off as a joke, it does not seem to have been so; in a letter to a friend, he said of "the niggers who swarm here" that it would be "easier to believe they are big monkeys dressed up for a game" than that they were men. As for Negroes being allowed to hold office in the United States, Freeman confessed: "I feel a creep when I think that one of these great black apes may (in theory) be President. Surely treat your horse kindly; but don't make him consul."[41]

Another Englishman, Houston Stewart Chamberlain, was the Teutonist's Teutonist. A worshiper of the viciously anti-Semitic Richard Wagner and the husband of Wagner's daughter Eva, Chamberlain supported Germany in World War I, became a German citizen in 1916, and lived to cap his racist career by the friendship of a fellow Wagnerian, Adolf Hitler. In 1923, after their first meeting, Chamberlain wrote Hitler: "That in the hour of her deepest need Germany gives birth to a Hitler proves her vitality."[42] Chamberlain's *Foundations of the Nineteenth Century*, translated into English in 1913, was a hymn of praise to Teutonic supremacy. Jews were especially detestable to Chamberlain; Jesus, he said, was not a Jew but an Aryan Teuton, possessed of "the hardness of the heroic spirit" rather than the sickly humanitarianism of modern Christianity.[43]

The United States grew its own Teutonists. William F. Allen of the University of Wisconsin rewrote ancient history to clear the Germanic tribes of the sack of Rome, saying it was the Huns who had done that, "a Tartar race" from central Asia, "small, dark-hued, and hideous of feature."[44] Nicholas Murray Butler, president of Columbia University, credited the "extraordinary persistence of the Anglo-Saxon impulse" with bringing the United States into existence, an impulse that originated in "the Teutonic qualities and characteristics of the people so admirably described by Tacitus."[45] Among American scholars who rejected Teutonic superiority were Frederick Jackson Turner and Charles A. Beard; but Anglo-Saxonism and Teutonism were widely accepted, being flattering concepts to almost everyone except "th' eight or nine people in the wurruld that has th' misfortune iv not bein' brought up Anglo-Saxons."[46]

Concurrently with the obsession about Anglo-Saxon supremacy, the geneticists, biologists, and anthropologists were attempting scientific measurements of racial characteristics, which might indicate where on the evolutionary ladder the different races stood, according to the popular if misleading biological analogy. Color, hair texture, and physical features were all subjects of great interest; however, the men who studied them, with few exceptions, were too ready to embrace conclusions that served their own racial convictions.[47] For instance, the prognathous jaw, flat nose, massive cranium, long arms, and dark color found in some Negroes (it was naturally ignored that these traits were not common to all Negroes) were pointed to as evidence that black Africans were on a lower evolutionary step than whites, and nearer to the anthropoids; and a school of thought headed by Dr. R. B. Bean claimed that Negro brains were smaller, weighed less, and had less elaborate fissuring than white brains, and that this accounted for the deficiency of Negroes in such higher faculties as reason, self-control, and will power. But few people mentioned that certain physical features of whites—their body hairiness, thinner and paler lips—were more anthropoidal than the hairless bodies and thicker, redder lips of Negroes; and when Dr. Mall by more accurate and objective investigation proved that racial differences in brain size were not scientifically significant, and when other voices tried to say that in any case there was no proven correlation between brain size and mental capacity, these rebuttals were lost in the general applause for the "proofs" of white supremacy.[48] It was a nostrum for all aches and growing pains—immigration, the black migration, ghettos, labor exploitation, labor agitation, colonialization; it was a tonic that explained the vitality of the United States and its institutions, with special emphasis on rugged individualism and laissez-faire.[49]

Another and rather frightening offspring of the race "sciences" was called eugenics.[50] Like Teutonism, this bastard science was born in England at the right time to vindicate British mid-nineteenth-century empire building. Francis Galton, a cousin of Charles Darwin, founded and named the science of eugenics and invented its catch phrase, "nature, not nurture," by which he meant that a superior heritage could not be repressed by social or economic handicaps, nor could an inferior heritage be benefited by social or economic advantages. Convinced by perfectly reputable scientific investigation that acquired characteristics could not be inherited, Galton then enunciated some very dubious propositions about innate race differences that could not be affected by environment. He held that most Europeans were congenitally defective, whereas in England one found those superior individuals who were born to be "kings of men."[51] As for Africans, Galton declared them to be by heredity most inferior mentally, in many cases half-witted. Among his proofs, Galton offered the following: "It is seldom that we hear [in travel literature about Africa] of a white traveller meeting with a black chief whom he feels to be the better man."[52] British colonialism went forward, and Galton was knighted in 1909.

If a person's entire future was determined by his genes alone, the obvious next step was to control breeding as in botany or animal husbandry, to the end that only the most desirable individuals should carry forward the race. In fact, the American eugenicists based their work on the botanical researches of Luther Burbank and the theories of horse breeder W. E. D. Stokes. The ruling principle of eugenics, as laid down by Galton, was that the "vigorous classes," which tended to have too few children, must be encouraged to procreate, and the "incompetent, the ailing, and the desponding," which tended to have too many children, must be induced to have fewer.[53] Although most writers on eugenics were without scientific training, their ideas were widely discussed and accepted as of scientific value by the general public. Scientific dissection of the false claims of eugenics by anthropologists Franz Boas (as early as 1911) and Robert Lowie did not diminish popular enthusiasm; eugenics was still viable in 1937 when anthropologist Edward A. Hooton denounced it as little more than "a lay form of ancestor worship" clothed in "Ku Klux Klan regalia."[54] Eugenics stimulated interest in genealogy and heraldry. Even stanchly Republican Henry Cabot Lodge, sponsor of the Force Bill of 1890, deplored that democracy had submerged the lines of differentiation between men of different heritages, and suggested that "definition of a man's birth and ancestry has become more necessary. . . ."[55]

Since eugenics posited that native-born white Americans, especially those Anglo-Saxon by ancestry, were the best and fittest individuals and bearers of the best genes, it was, naturally, inimical to "new immigrants" and blacks. Stokes, in his book *The Right to Be Well Born, or, Horse Breeding in Relation to Eugenics,* made it crudely clear that Negroes were in his opinion inferior and therefore "eugenically undesirable."[56] By the eugenic principle, it was obvious that Negroes should be induced to have fewer children and should not be permitted to cross-breed with "superior" stocks, which they would adulterate. Some of the more radical eugenicists went so far as to propose total segregation and even sterilization of the "unfit." Eugenicists of the school of Charles B. Davenport warned of biological freaks that resulted from race mixtures, citing some very curious examples, as, that children of unions between big-bodied Scots and small-bodied South Italians would have large frames but small viscera incapable of serving the bodies that housed them.[57] Mulattoes were often cited as examples of the defectiveness of racial hybrids—except when they were pointed to by other schools of racism as superior members of their race because of their "white blood."[58]

The poor, the unfit, the new immigrants, labor organizers, as well as blacks, were all, to the rugged laissez-faire individualists, people who must be managed and controlled so they would not interfere with the free use of power by the fittest. Furthermore, those who opposed laissez-faire—the liberals, the Progressives—although deeply concerned about the poor workingman, were not often concerned about nor necessarily liberal about blacks. Liberal reformers stood for the political, economic, and social controls abhorred by the Social Darwinists and Social Determinists, but on the subject of race the reform group was little if any more egalitarian than the rugged individualists. Progressive Senator Albert Cummings of Iowa said of the race question: "I do not know whether it can ever be answered; at least, I have never heard an answer that satisfied my mind."[59] Farther south, where Progressivism flourished because of the exploitation of that area by railroads and other big business, most Progressives did know an answer: suppress the blacks. Liberal Thomas Nelson Page, who deplored the damage racism had done the South, nevertheless believed with the most convinced Teutonist that "this country is as 'fatally reserved for' the Anglo-Saxon race as it was when the Virginia Adventurers declared it to be so in their first report to Elizabeth."[60]

A number of liberals inclined toward racism because of their concern for the native white American worker and his need for protection against black and immigrant workers.[61] Professor John P. Commons of the University of Wisconsin, an outstanding Progressive economist, declared that Africa, being tropical, produced a race "indolent, improvident, and contented,"[62] men who were lacking in "the mechanical idea."[63] With true Progressive faith in education, however, Commons believed that Negroes could eventually learn good citizenship—but that until such time they should not be given the vote.[64] Professor E. A. Ross, a friend of Theodore Roosevelt and a good Progressive, was another champion of the native white American workingman; he was anti-immigration, and as for blacks, he wrote that "the energy and character" of America was "lowered by the presence in the

South of several millions of an inferior race."[65] Liberal sociologist Lester F. Ward, who called laissez-faire "a myth . . . surely to end in monopoly," believed that society improves through the struggle between an active, aggressive race and a passive, submitting race; he saw blacks as inferior people aware of their inferiority, and suggested that a black rapist was not motivated so much by lust as by an unconscious desire "to raise his race to a little higher level."[66] John Daniels, who wrote with exceptional liberalism and sympathy about blacks in Boston, explained with every confidence in his reasonableness that the Negro had always been treated as an inferior not because of his race or color but because he was indeed inferior (in health, stability, trustworthiness, thoroughness, morality, etc., etc.); race and color, Daniels explained, were sometimes mistaken for causes, but actually they were only peculiarities that made Negro inferiority conspicuous.[67]

If one were to encounter the following quotation unascribed, one might with good reason take it for the utterance of a Social Darwinist, a Teutonist, or a eugenicist: "Once aroused to murderous rage, the Negro does not stop with mere killing; he bruises and batters his victim out of all semblance to humanity. For the moment, under stress of passion, he seems to revert wholly to savagery."[68] It was written, in fact, by one of the blacks' best friends, the liberal, Progressive, muckraking Ray Stannard Baker in his ground-breaking exposure of discrimination, Jim Crow, race violence, and other sufferings of black Americans. With such racism in their friends, blacks did not need enemies.

A Christian socialist movement called the Social Gospel, started by liberal clergymen, was based on the tenet that every man has a duty to aid his brother for the over-all advancement of society and humanity.[69] The Social Gospellers, setting themselves in direct opposition to the Social Darwinists, championed the weak and poor Americans against exploitation by the rich and strong, and preached that all men could be brought by education to a condition of equality. One would expect blacks to benefit from such a doctrine; when it is examined closely, however, it is seen to promise help only to the white poor and weak. To the well-meaning Gospellers, apparently, Anglo-Saxons were a little more equal than others. Rev. Josiah Strong, an early leader of the movement, firmly advocated immigration restrictions, and his very influential book *Our Country* vibrated with race hostility. Although full of reforming zeal against "republican feudalism,"[70] as he called monopolistic big business, he abhorred "the infidel ribaldry of Robert Ingersoll, the socialistic theories of Karl Marx,"[71] and on race he was a plain bigot. White supremacist and nationalist as well as Social Gospeller, Strong trumpeted a clear call to arms for the imperialist Crusaders: "If I do not read amiss, this powerful race will move down upon Mexico, down upon Central and South America, out upon the islands of the sea, over upon Africa and beyond. And can anyone doubt that the result of this competition of races will be 'survival of the fittest'?"[72] It was destined, Strong declared, that mankind should be "Anglo-Saxonized"; so the reader is not surprised to find him speaking of "a snoring, disgusting Negro wench; an opium-eating, licentious Italian, et all" whom he had encountered in New York City.[73]

Other Social Gospellers, such as Ward, Washington Gladden, Lyman Abbott, George T. Herron, and Walter Rauschenbusch, were far less racist than Strong, but did not disavow him. Their racism was of the kind that simply takes as God-given that blacks are inferior to whites. Gladden, for instance, who thought blacks should have the opportunity for higher education, said it was wrong for a "superior" race to oppress an "inferior" one—thus tacitly accepting race labels. Herron and Rauschenbusch also believed in race differences, although they tended to assign Anglo-Saxon superiority to good fortune in leaders and institutions rather than to hereditary qualities.[74] Abbott did not champion Anglo-Saxon superiority, but he opposed the Force Bill on grounds that the South should be allowed to settle its own problem and that Negroes and the federal government should not go over the heads of white Southerners. Rauschenbusch was perhaps the most sensitive of the Gospellers to the plight of blacks, of which he said in 1914: "For years the problem of the two races in the South has seemed to me so tragic, so insoluble, that I have never yet ventured to discuss it in public."[75] He did go so far as to say that "no solution will satisfy the Christian

spirit of our United Nation which does not provide for the progressive awakening of hope and self-respect in the individual
Negro and the awakening of race pride and race ambition in all
Negro communities,"[76] but the Christian socialists took no effective steps toward these ends. As for Rauschenbusch's United
Nation, that could not become fact so long as a large body of
Americans was considered inferior or evil because of race, which
was the scientific dogma of the day. Social Gospellers hesitated
to put the Christian spirit before science. Progressives were re-
luctant to jeopardize their reform programs by incurring a pro-
Negro stigma. As DuBois sharply commented, "The nemesis of
every forward movement in the United States is the Negro
Question."[77]

Echoes of scientific and philosophical arguments concerning
inferiority and superiority of races, fitness and unfitness of peoples, were heard in every medium of human communication.
Talk of race differences and the generalizations of the day's isms
produced a tedious spate of lists of race traits. Shufeldt's catalogue of evils that he called black traits has already been discussed. John Daniels, a far less bigoted observer, nevertheless
drew up his own list and a pretty damning one; blacks, he asserted, were jealous of one another, dependent and servile (as a
result of slavery), lacking in race pride, not necessarily lazy but
hating monotonous and continued labor, not liars but unable to
stick to facts, unreliable, and unpunctual; however, they were
companionable, loving noise and laughter, warm-hearted, courte-
ous, droll, good-humored, musical by nature, although incapable of important accomplishment in music, and so on and on in
what added up to the black stereotype.[78] Mary Ovington, who
devoted much of her life to the welfare of blacks, also categor-
ized, although she saw chiefly good qualities: gentleness, loving-
ness, "some coarseness but little real brutality. Rarely does a
father or mother strike a child."[79] Blacks themselves fell into the
style of list-making, as for instance Rudolph Fisher: "Beneath
the jests, the avowed fear, the merriment, was a characteristic
irony, a typical disavowal of fact and repudiation of reality, a

marked racial tendency to make light of what was actually grave. . . ."[80] All these catalogues were equally faulty, of course, in calling racial traits what were culturally dictated qualities of certain individuals—and not necessarily actual qualities, either, but what appeared to be such to an untrained observer. Perhaps the most significant similarity in these lists, even when blacks were evaluating themselves, is that the characteristics in which blacks were said to be lacking were the very characteristics most respected by white American society—hard work, truthfulness, reliability, punctuality—and such good characteristics as blacks were said to possess were those least respected and most applicable to persons of inferior status, such as the gentle mammy, the droll clown, the court jester.

Racist books of a filthy and sadistic nature had long been popular. Just after the Civil War, the violent negrophobe Hinton R. Helper had published a prototype, *Nojoque,* in which white was a symbol of "life, health, beauty" and black of "ugliness, disease, and death."[81] It is an index of the respectability of negrophobia by the turn of the century that a comparable book by Charles Carroll, *The Negro a Beast, or, In the Image of God,* based on the thesis that blacks were beasts without souls, was brought out by a reputable publisher of religious books.[82] The Negro was either "Nojoque" or a big joke to white America, a beast to be lynched or a figure of fun on the stage or in amusement parks where signs urged white frolickers to "Hit the Coon and Get a Cigar."[83] It seems a long way from the philosophic ponderings of Herbert Spencer to a wooden ball thrown at a black head sticking through a hole in a curtain, but the path was straight. People who could not possibly read Spencer, Sumner, or McDougall nevertheless felt the ripples of the waves they sent out, because the works of erudite men patly fitted the prevailing social, political, and economic situation of the early twentieth century.[84]

The reputable academic historians, although far less vulgar on the subject of race than a Helper or a Carroll, were nevertheless influential in the spread of politely racist interpretations of history through the students they taught and launched into the outer world. From about 1900, studies of the Reconstruction began to appear in considerable number, most of them wholly in sympathy with the white southern view. In Woodrow Wilson's article on Reconstruction, Negroes were treated as "but children still" who were used by the unscrupulous carpetbaggers "as tools for their own selfish ends," and then "left to carry the discredit and reap the consequences of ruin when at last the whites who were real citizens got control again."[85] This view was shared by other historians, who argued that Reconstruction proved the Negro's sense of political and social order still so primitive that granting them equal citizenship was a grave error. Anti-Negro bias was easy to read in the works of the most respected historians, such as James Ford Rhodes and John W. Burgess, and especially William A. Dunning, who before World War I had broadcast his racist views through the students he had taught. The most eminent of these Dunning disciples, Ulrich B. Phillips and Walter L. Flemming, concentrated on the Reconstruction under the influence of Dunning's thesis: "The freedmen were not, and in the nature of the case could not for generations be, on the same social, moral, and intellectual plane with the whites."[86] Their general conclusion was that the carpetbaggers, the radical Republicans, and the Negroes, not the white Southerners—Wilson's "real citizens"—were to blame for the evils of Reconstruction and the perpetuation of antiblack feeling in the South. Flemming, for instance, saw the Ku Klux Klan as a valuable institution in that it "regulated the conduct of bad Negroes, punished criminals who were not punished by the States, looked after the activities and teachings of Northern teachers and preachers, dispersed hostile gatherings of Negroes, and ran out of the community the worst of the reconstruction officials," and also "kept the Negroes quiet and freed them to some extent from the influence of evil leaders."[87] None of these historians considered himself bigoted; Negro inferiority to them was simply a fact to be calmly accepted.[88]

Still more widespread was the influence of two popular writers of history, as they considered it, Theodore Lothrop Stoddard and Madison Grant. Stoddard was openly and vehemently antiblack and antibrown. His thesis, as set forth in his best-known work, *The Rising Tide of Color* (1920), was that the great Nordic race had been deteriorating since the late nineteenth century and that the black and brown peoples were becoming a threat that must be countered by a united white front, especially Nordic white. But Stoddard recognized that blacks were too valuable as a labor force to be exiled or extinguished, so he proposed that they be segregated in work camps, as Indians were segregated on reservations. Madison Grant's *The Passing of the Great Race* (1916) was probably the most widely read nonfiction racist work of the time; it went through three revisions within five years, and sold between 20,000 and 30,000 copies. Grant, a well-born and well-educated New Yorker, was concerned about race suicide as the new immigrants, with their high breeding rate, would eventually outnumber the old "Anglo-Saxon" native American stock with its lower birth rate. This would produce, according to Grant, "a race reverting to the more ancient, generalized, and lower type," unless immigration were barred to inferior races like the Alpine and the Mediterranean, which he carved out of the white people of central and southern Europe. Jews were particularly obnoxious to Grant, and he aimed his thrusts at them much more than at black or yellow people; but blacks could not fail to be hurt by a widely promulgated philosophy which held that the preservation of the superior race took precedence over the teachings of Christ and the constitutional guarantees of liberty.[89]

When the theories of the Social Darwinists were presented in a medium that could be understood even by illiterates who could not read Stoddard or Grant, to say nothing of Spencer and Sumner, the public thronged to be taught and titillated. The medium was that new and exciting one, the motion picture. The film was *The Birth of a Nation,* a sensationally and violently antiblack presentation of life in the South during the Civil War and Reconstruction. The admitted object of its author, Thomas Dixon, Jr., of Shelby, North Carolina, a onetime Baptist minister, was pure race propaganda. In Dixon's own words, his purpose was *"to revolutionize Northern sentiments by a presentation of history that would transform every man in my audience into a good Democrat! . . .* Every man who comes out of one of our theaters is a southern partizan for life—except the members of Villard's Inter-Marriage Society who go there to knock."[90]

The spreading of the southern Bourbon message through fiction had for many years been Dixon's vocation. In 1902 he published *The Leopard's Spots: A Romance of the White Man's Burden, 1865–1900;* this was followed in 1905 by *The Clansman: An Historical Romance of the Ku Klux Klan.* In them can clearly be read the racist ideas legitimized by such academic historians as Dunning and Flemming, but here shown in all their naked horror. Rev. Dixon's triptych of race hate was completed in 1907 with the publication of *The Traitor: A Story of the Fall of the Invisible Empire.*[91] *The Leopard's Spots* had been an instant best seller; the first edition of 15,000 copies quickly sold out, and the book soon became what was then called a "mob novel," selling several hundred thousand copies and brought out also in foreign editions.[92] Negroes were incensed. Kelly Miller protested to Dixon in an open letter of September 1905, to express the feelings of thousands of blacks about "the evil propagandism of race animosity" that Dixon was spreading as "the chief priest of those who worship at the shrine of race hatred and wrath."[93]

Although *The Clansman* may not have sold as many printed copies as *The Leopard's Spots,* it eventually had a much wider exposure. In 1906, a dramatized version of *The Clansman* was shown on the stage; a reviewer called it "as crude a melodrama as had ever slipped its anchor and drifted westward from Third Avenue."[94] When *The Clansman* played in Philadelphia, over black protests, 3,000 blacks marched and demonstrated in front of the theater, and city officials closed the production to prevent a riot. David W. Griffith, pioneer in movie making, became interested in Dixon's story. A Kentuckian and the son of a Confederate soldier, Griffith had already made a Civil War picture called *The Battle;* for the film version of Dixon's story, Griffith wrote an introductory section, a white Southerner's view of the Civil War, whose battle scenes were really the artistic triumph of the movie.[95] In 1915, movie houses were showing a frankly racist film called *The Nigger,* and it was probably to cash in on the market thus created that Griffith decided to release his version of the Dixon story, which by then was finished and waiting.

The Birth of a Nation, as the movie made from *The Clansman* was retitled, was shown in Los Angeles and San Francisco in February 1915, and was at once hailed by critics as an artistic and technical gem. Few critics were as discriminating as Vachel Lindsay, who, while sharing the general enthusiasm for Griffith's directorial genius, condemned those flaws in the script which derived from "the Reverend Thomas Dixon's poisonous hatred of the Negro."[96] In the normal course of events, the film before reaching eastern theaters would have to be viewed by the National Board of Censorship, a most respected private group whose decisions had practically the force of official censorship with film exhibitors. But this picture did not follow a normal course. Blacks in northern cities rose up in arms against its presentation. The NAACP said "a magnificent new art" had been employed in an "attempt to picture Negroes in the worst possible light."[97] Hoping to silence black protests and to block possible disapproval by the censorship group, in mid-February, immediately before the National Board was to view the film, Dixon arranged for two private showings of the film, first for President Wilson and his Cabinet and then for members of Congress and the Supreme Court. "Both showings were granted as favors to Dixon," Thomas Cripps says in his study of the film's career, "a former student of Wilson's at Johns Hopkins, with the stipulation that there be no publicity."[98]

According to Dixon, the President was enthusiastic about the picture, and called it "history written in lightning."[99] Also according to Dixon, Louisiana-born Chief Justice Edward White before the showing "leaned toward me [Dixon] and said in low tense tones: 'I was a member of the Klan, sir. . . . Through many a dark night, I walked my sentinel's beat through the ugliest streets of New Orleans with a rifle on my shoulder. . . . I'll be there!' "[100]

Despite vigorous efforts by the NAACP to achieve at least excision of the most offensive sequences in the film, the National Board of Censorship approved it by a vote of 15 to 8. It was advertised for a New York opening in March at the unprecedented price, for a movie, of $2.00 a ticket. NAACP officers tried for an injunction of the opening, but were denied; they urged Mayor

John P. Mitchel to ban the film as detrimental to public decency, but failed. Mitchel also refused their request for a license to parade in protest against the film. In another move, the NAACP sent to 500 newspapers copies of a review that had appeared in *The New Republic* calling the film "spiritual assassination" and asserting that it "degrades the censors that passed it and the white race that endures it."[101] DuBois complained bitterly that the film twisted emancipation into "an orgy of theft and degradation and wide rape of white women."[102] Booker T. Washington, equally horrified, believed that he acting alone could persuade Mayor Mitchel to order some of the worst scenes cut, where the NAACP had failed; the mayor indeed promised, but the cuts were not made.[103]

The Birth of a Nation continued to play to packed houses. D. W. Griffith welcomed the free publicity of NAACP protests, commenting: "The silly legal opposition . . . will make me a millionaire if they keep it up."[104] When the film was about to open in Boston, Mayor James Curley, who feared race violence and had for that reason banned movies of the Jess Willard-Jack Johnson fight, granted a hearing to protesting black groups; he agreed to cut a particularly lurid scene showing a black man chasing a white girl, and a few other offensive sex sequences. Monroe Trotter headed a delegation to protest the film to Massachusetts governor Walsh; Trotter had the backing of the Knights of Columbus, because of Klan persecution of Catholics, and some 1,500 to 2,000 blacks waited outside to hear the results of his interview with the governor. Walsh agreed to sign a new censorship law, but Mayor Curley, acting for Boston, abided by the decision of a censorship judge who found only the chase scene objectionable. The film, minus that one scene, opened in Boston in April. Negroes were barred from the theater, but two black men broke through the barrier and some violence ensued both inside the theater and on the streets around it. Trotter managed to secure a ticket but was arrested and fined, and blacks continued to be barred. A top-level meeting, including President Eliot of Harvard and William H. Lewis, recently relieved of his post as U.S. assistant attorney general, sought unsuccessfully to hammer out censorship legislation that would distinguish between art and propaganda and that would not violate the First Amendment. The Federation of Churches of Greater Boston condemned the film as "injurious to public morality."[105]

With this escalation of protest and criticism, Dixon broke his promise not to publicize the showings at the White House and before Congress, and released the news that many high government officials had seen the film and approved of it. Chief Justice White, infuriated at being quoted or misquoted, threatened to denounce the film if Dixon did not desist from using his name as a supporter. Wilson could not bring himself to declare publicly that he disapproved of the film, chiefly because that would seem to be capitulating to Monroe Trotter, who had once during a White House interview angered Wilson by what the President considered truculence and rudeness.[106] Despite the vigorous joint opposition of the NAACP and other black organizations, within a few months *The Birth of a Nation* could be seen in New York, Los Angeles, San Francisco, Boston, and practically every other city and town throughout the nation. It was, however, banned in Massachusetts exclusive of Boston, in Chicago and later throughout Illinois; and Cleveland's mayor, Newton D. Baker, another Johns Hopkins man who the following year was named by Wilson as Secretary of War, banned it from his city, although he failed in efforts to induce the governor to ban it altogether from Ohio.[107] Wherever the film was shown, however, it was a hit with its white audiences. The movies were a novelty, this one was a shocker, and the hate message of *The Clansman* was one for which white America had been prepared by all the racist thinking of the past twenty years.

The year 1915 brought not only Griffith's celluloid Klan but a rebirth of the Klan itself. According to one legend, that organization had originated at the end of the Civil War as a costume caper of some young southern blades, who dressed to call upon their lady loves in what they conceived to resemble the garb of knights of old, and who found, to their amusement, that their fantastically cloaked moonlit figures were scaring the wits out of ignorant rural Negroes.[108] During Reconstruction, the joke aspect was replaced by a more deadly purpose. Various groups of southern white men, calling themselves "Knights of the White

Camelia" and similar names, drawn together by the bitterness of defeat in the war, joined together to form the Ku Klux Klan. Bands of Klansmen roamed the countryside by night wrapped in their sheets, acting as vigilantes; now the terrorism was deliberate, and the vengeance of the knights against "trouble-making" blacks and their white supporters was swift and horrible. With the end of Reconstruction and the legalizing of Jim Crow and disfranchisement by new state constitutions, the Klan function was absorbed by legal officers and the vigilante activities gradually lapsed.

The Klan idea, however, was not dead. On October 16, 1915, surely not unrelated to the opening half a year earlier of the moving picture *The Birth of a Nation,* what is usually called a second Ku Klux Klan was organized in the South by William J. Simmons. Administratively, this organization may have been new, and its functions were certainly broader; but for over-all purpose and tactics, it seems still the same old Klan. The earlier Klansmen had had a single target, blacks; but in the half century that had elapsed by 1915, other elements had come upon the scene as polluters of the pure stream of white Protestant society: Jews, Catholics, and "new immigrants" of what the scientists, Nativists, and riffraff proclaimed to be inferior if not actually evil races. The reorganized Klan took for its broad objective the cleansing of America of all such impurities, including, of course, blacks of the new breed that Thomas Nelson Page so deplored.[109] In practice, that could mean any black the Klan chose. When the years after 1915 brought the black migration to a crescendo, there were Southerners who blamed the Klan for it. A Georgia farmer complained in the local paper that farmers feared losing their hands, housewives their cooks, and merchants their customers "if this foolishness is not stopped. . . . So in conclusion, in behalf of my community and other country communities, I feel it my duty to raise a warning voice against all such foolish ku-kluxism."[110] This could not have been a very popular or a very safe attitude, but it serves to show that the South was not a Klan monolith.

Warning voices were raised elsewhere, but they were feeble whimpers against the howls and snarls of the ravening haters. Black leaders spoke out: Kelly Miller, Archibald Grimke, Monroe Trotter, James Weldon Johnson, and always the exciting Du-Bois, especially through the medium of the NAACP *Crisis*. The New York *Post*, of which Oswald Garrison Villard was editor, the *Independent, New Republic, Cosmopolitan, McClure's, American, World's Work*, and a number of other white-edited publications provided a forum for muckraking exposures of black suffering from injustice, peonage, disfranchisement, and lynching. The roster of writers on these subjects includes many important names, such as Lincoln Steffens, Vachel Lindsay, Carl Sandburg, Theodore Dreiser, Carl Schurz, and Jacob Riis.[111] Ray Stannard Baker's book *Following the Color Line* and his magazine articles "The Negro Goes North" (1917) and "Gathering Clouds Along the Color Line" (1916); Mary Ovington's *Half a Man* (1911) and Herbert Seligmann's *The Negro Faces America* (1920) are some of the finest of the antiracist studies that appeared. The best of these social documents treated contemporary problems with illuminating objectivity, revealing causes of race tension that were either ignored or were concealed by the "common-sense myth" of Negro inferiority. Baker wrote in 1916: "A film play, called the 'Birth of a Nation,' excellent in many ways, which gives a picture of the Negro calculated to stir racial hatred, has been a real cause of irritation. The treatment of the Willard-Johnson prizefight at Havana by many newspapers, giving it the aspect of a racial struggle, served, as such minor things often do, to point and emphasize racial differences and animosities."[112] Seligmann, who was director of publicity for the NAACP, pointed out that urban race tension was "definitely subject to manipulation by political leaders and their allies in newspaper offices. . . . It is idle to talk about 'solving the race problem' when cheap and mendacious newspapers, making claims to utmost respectability, are purchasable by political factions and deprive Americans of the one essential to democracy—accurate information on matters of public concern."[113]

Through the arts and letters, many voices spoke against racism in one way or another. Louisianian George Washington Cable, in his novel *The Grandissimes*, written in the 1880s, attacked that cornerstone of southern propaganda, the myth of the happy slave, and roundly condemned the Black Codes.[114] Stephen

Crane and William Dean Howells dealt sympathetically with black woes. Mark Twain's clear-sighted wryness, and later, bitterness, about humanity in general gradually immunized him from infection with race prejudice: "All that I care to know is that a man is a human being, that is enough for me; he can't be any worse."[115] About the lynching of a Negro who was later found innocent of the charge against him, Twain wrote: ". . . there is no good reason why Southern gentlemen should worry themselves with useless regrets, so long as only an innocent 'nigger' is hanged, or roasted or knouted to death, now and then."[116] Winslow Homer and George Bellows used the graphic arts to express their egalitarian feelings. Southerners could not understand why Homer, working in Virginia, painted compassionate pictures of Negroes rather than portraits of pretty white girls.[117] Bellows' fight picture titled "Both Members of This Club," surely an antiracist pun on the phrase commonly used to introduce a bout between members of the same athletic organization, shows audience approval as a black boxer lunges and forces his white opponent to his knees. But how could printed words and still pictures compete with Griffith's mob movements and Dixon's hate acted out by live people?

From the fields of philosophy and science a few logical voices had always tried to cool race passion, but who heard them above the clamor of the Teutonists and eugenicists? Before the Civil War, the English reformer John Stuart Mill had enunciated the logical slovenliness of racism in a way that should have given pause, but did not, to Sumner and Dunning and Grant: "Of all vulgar modes of escaping from the consideration of the effect of social and moral influences on the human mind, the most vulgar is that of attributing the diversities of conduct and character to inherent natural differences."[118] Fifty years later, Josiah Royce at Harvard was saying much the same thing about assertions concerning "the permanent, the hereditary, the unchangeable mental characteristics" in races. Said Royce, "The souls of men, then, if viewed apart from the influences of culture, if viewed as they were in primitive times, are by no means as easy to classify as the wooly-haired and the straight-haired races at first appear to be."[119] Primitive men everywhere and of all races, Royce said,

share the same moral defects and virtues; superstitiousness, savagery, mental sloth and dullness, sensuousness, and cruelty "are
simply the common evils, traits to which our own ancestors were
very long ago a prey. . . ."[120] He answered the Anglo-Saxonists
and Teutonists with the argument that Germanic peoples were
not different from other races but more fortunate; they had met
civilization, in the shape of Rome, under favorable conditions,
in that they as a people were never enslaved, but they could
have been exterminated without ever becoming civilized if
Caesar had debased or slaughtered them, as the man with
power can always do. Instead, Royce said, Rome gave the Germanic peoples an opportunity to learn, to become equals. "Let
their descendants not boast unduly until they, too, have given
other races . . . some equal opportunity to show of what sort of
manhood they are capable,"[121] Royce wrote. Our so-called
race problems, he believed, spring from our own hates; and he
added, in a thoroughly existential syllogism, that if you train a
man to give names to his antipathies, and then teach him to regard them as sacred because they have names, you end up
with race hatred. How can blacks and whites best learn to live
with least friction and most co-operation? Surely not by "keeping
the Negro in his place" as an inferior, Royce believed, which was
an irritant to both blacks and whites, but by giving him every
opportunity to become superior.[122]

The anthropologists' fight against racism has been mentioned
in passing, but their importance in opposing the scientific vendors
of white supremacy must not be scanted. Major anthropologists
from the beginning rejected theories of inherent racial traits of
mind and temperament. In England, Edward Burnett Tylor had
produced the seminal work on cultural anthropology, *Primitive
Culture*, in 1871. Shortly after 1900, anthropologists were attacking racial theories with vigor, armed with new techniques. The
chief antagonist of the Social Darwinists and their brood was
Franz Boas of Columbia. In a magazine article as early as
1907, entitled "The Anthropological Position of the Negro," Boas
by the application of exact measurement and of statistical methods exploded Bean's theory of differences between the brains,
and consequently the traits, of blacks and whites.[123] Boas' re-

search showed that the brains of the vast majority of people, of whatever race or color, were in the same, average size-range.[124] Also, Boas pointed out that a true assessment of Negro character and abilities could not be arrived at without taking into account the great cultural achievements of Negroes in Africa, where they had been free to develop without the economic, social, and emotional shackles that bound American blacks. In all his later major works, from *The Mind of Primitive Man* in 1911, Boas disproved any correlation between mental/emotional traits and physical traits such as hair type or skin color. In a scornful review of Stoddard's *Rising Tide of Color*, Boas said: "An author . . . who considers civilization as the result of 'the creative urge of a superior germplasm,' who refuses to recognize that civilization is the outcome of historical conditions that act favorably on one race at one time, and unfavorably on other occasions . . . must be led to the abject fear of an equal development of all the members of mankind, without, however, being able to give any kind of convincing proof of the correctness of his theories."[125] At that time, only the few not caught in the rising tide of racism received Boas' message, but he, his colleagues, associates, and pupils carried it forward through the 1920s and beyond, into a more receptive era. Robert Lowie, Clark Wissler, Edward Sapir, Ruth Benedict, Otto Klineberg, Zora Neale Hurston, and, most prominent in the mind of America, Margaret Mead, carried along Boas' passionate devotion to truth and his clear-sighted exposure of the common-sense myths, false analogies, unsupportable generalizations, and self-serving charades that passed for a science and literature of race in the first twenty years of the century.[126]

CHAPTER 8

Prejudice in Action

A Confession of Prejudice

I am Prejudice—supreme monarch of the South, with vassal tributaries in the North and West. . . .

I have murdered Negroes without cause, hanged them without provocation—I have raped, robbed, maligned, segregated a defenseless people, and neither pulpit, press, nor President has disturbed my exalted peace of mind. . . .

The rope, torch, and shotgun are the sacred symbols of my majesty and power, and my will is inforced from Boston to Los Angeles, from Seattle to Miami—I am not a stranger at the Capitol! . . .

I, alone, know how to keep him blind, poor, and degraded, for I recognize none of his distinctions, I acknowledge none of his merits, I ignore all of his "progress." . . .

Poem by a Negro Soldier,
in *The Challenge*, September 1919

It is difficult to reconcile the increasing oppression of black Americans with an era in which the country's political leaders dedicated their efforts to reform of many kinds: to a more equable distribution of wealth and power through government regulation of business, to the exposure of corruption and injustice, and to the relief of social and economic distress. These were sincere objectives of the Progressives, whose philosophy was dominant in politics from 1900 to 1920. But the Progressive movement was not radical, and its leaders, men like Theodore Roosevelt and Woodrow Wilson, can certainly not be described as revolutionary. The object of progressivism was not to overturn existing American institutions, but through reform to continue the forward drive of the country toward accepted capitalistic goals. It was distinctly not a workers' movement; it was interested in harnessing labor as well as big business. It was not a people's party, although many of the reforms that had been striven for by the Populists became law ten to twenty or more years later under Progressive sponsorship, such as government regulation of railroads and other industries, direct election of senators, and shorter hours under better conditions for the workingman. Progressivism, modern scholarship points out, was essentially conservative, more interested in protecting the position of the outstanding man in society than in improving the condition of the masses. The typical Progressive, at least in the North, was urban, middle- or upper-class, often the scion of an aristocratic family, educated at an Ivy League college or an excellent state university, and conservative in his general philosophy. William Allen White perhaps oversimplified in characterizing progressivism as simply populism that "had shaved its whiskers, washed its shirt, put on a derby and moved up into the middle class. . . ."[1]

Blacks had made out better with the bewhiskered, unwashed Populists—at least in the early years, when black support was welcomed—than with the Progressives, who all too often regarded the black man as only an embarrassment. An editorial in the Progressive magazine the *Independent* made a tongue-in-cheek comment reminiscent of DuBois's lament that every forward movement in the United States was blocked by the race question: "It is provoking," the *Independent* editorialized, "that whatever we want to do the Negro should be everlastingly putting himself in the way to bother us. In the most unexpected ways and places he bobs up, stumbles in where he is not wanted and sets agley the wisest plans of statesmen. One has to look out for him always. If some new scheme of public reform is proposed, the first thought is *'Cherchez le negre'*."[2]

However sympathetic individual Progressives like Ray Stannard Baker and Mary Ovington might be toward Negroes, the Progressive party did not intend to dilute its power or endanger its national programs to embrace the unpopular black cause. Southern Progressives included some of the most outspoken racists, men like Vardaman and Hoke Smith; and few northern Progressives repudiated the racist thinking of the day, at least, the subtler varieties.[3] But it seemed of particular significance to blacks that United States presidents between 1900 and 1920, a period of rising power of the presidency, subscribed to the Progressive philosophy and programs. In spite of the desertion of the Negroes by the Republican Party before 1900, the election of Theodore Roosevelt was regarded by most blacks as promising to their cause. A northern liberal who had praised black troops for their help to the Rough Riders in taking San Juan Hill appealed to black voters, even though they had been ignored or sold out by other Republicans from Hayes through McKinley. But Roosevelt when he took office in 1901 announced that he would "continue absolutely unbroken" the policies of McKinley and the Republican Party.[4]

Roosevelt's business was politics; while certainly not a Negrohater, his actions and statements about blacks seem more consistent with political expediency than with any deep-rooted race egalitarianism. He was quite willing to court black support through Booker T. Washington, but his opinion of most black Republicans was that they were people "who make not the slightest effort to get any popular votes, and who are concerned purely in getting Federal offices and sending to the national convention delegates whose venality make them a menace to the whole party."[5] As a Northerner, Roosevelt was free of southern taboos about calling a black man "Mister," or shaking his hand, or sitting at table with him; but he nevertheless felt, as he wrote to his friend Owen Wister, who idealized in *The Virginian* and other fiction the blond, blue-eyed Anglo-American: "I entirely agree with you that as a race and in the mass they are altogether inferior to the whites."[6]

In New York politics Roosevelt had indeed championed black rights, and as New York's governor had appointed a few blacks to minor offices. In his early years as President, he reappointed Dr. William Crum, a black man, as collector of Charleston, over strong party opposition, and made some other black appointments; and he reinstated Mrs. Minnie Cox, postmistress of Indianola, Mississippi, who had been forced to resign by an outraged citizenry spurred on by Vardaman's taunt that they were "tolerating a negro wench as postmaster." Most dramatically of all, Roosevelt invited Booker T. Washington to dinner at the White House. These gestures of friendliness were cherished far beyond their significance by black people. The Negro appointments, on which Roosevelt sought Washington's advice, were apparently calculated to capture the black vote and thus to weaken the lily-white Republican faction led by Mark Hanna, a potential rival of Roosevelt's in the upcoming 1904 election. As for the Indianola incident, Kelly Miller pointed out that it ended with the appointment of a white postmaster when Mrs. Cox resigned in fear of her life. And Booker T. Washington was never again asked to take dinner at the White House.[7]

That meal of the Roosevelt family with Washington raised such an outcry in the South that no man who hoped to be re-elected President could ignore his political error. Roosevelt was accused of turning the White House into a "nigger restaurant"; he was said to have committed "the most damnable outrage," "a crime equal to treason," "a crime against civilization, and his nigger guest has done his race a wrong which cannot soon be erased." One Southerner wrote that "no southern gentleman would sit at a table with him [Roosevelt] under any consideration whatsoever," and a Memphis paper said "no Southern woman with proper self respect would now accept an invitation to the White House." When a northern newspaper editor deplored these venomous attacks, the Memphis *Commercial Appeal* answered: "Let him [the Negro] take the editor's daughter to the opera. Let him be the editor's son in law. Why didn't the editor invite the negro from the dining room into the marriage chamber? Let the editor select Booker Washington as god father for his clay-colored grandchild." When Roosevelt canceled a dinner invitation to Senator Ben Tillman because Tillman had committed the offense of engaging in fisticuffs on the Senate floor, the senator from South Carolina retorted that he never expected to eat at the White House while Roosevelt was in office; and Vardaman labeled Roosevelt "the coonflavored miscegenationist in the White House." North Carolina-born Josephus Daniels, who later became Wilson's Secretary of the Navy, commented more urbanely that the dinner with Washington "was not a precedent that will encourage Southern men to join hands with Mr. Roosevelt."[8]

Although Roosevelt blustered that he would invite whom he wished to dine with him, he never repeated his mistake. He tried to pass off the incident as something done on impulse—an impromptu invitation to stay to lunch because Washington happened to be at the White House at noon[9]—but the meal was almost certainly dinner, not lunch, and the invitation does not appear to have been made on the spur of the moment. However, Roosevelt admitted to Owen Wister that the invitation "had not been politically expedient"; he told historian James Ford Rhodes that it had been a mistake; and he explained to Henry Cabot Lodge that he had invited Washington as "a matter of course" but had not considered the political effects.[10] Apparently he did consider them more carefully in future, and, although there is no reason to doubt Roosevelt's statement that he wanted deserving blacks to have the chance for "a little reward, a little respect,"[11] he apparently wanted even more to be re-elected and to carry onward his trust-busting and other Progressive reforms. He did beat out Mark Hanna's conservative faction, and in 1904 won a second term.

During the second administration an incident occurred which shook the black community and its faith in Roosevelt and Republicanism, and which was called by Virginia's leading Negro newspaper the "monumental blunder" of Roosevelt's time in office.[12] In the summer of 1906, three companies of the 25th Infantry Regiment, one of the four black regiments in the U. S.

Army, arrived at their new station at Fort Brown near Brownsville, Texas.[13] Brownsville was unhappy about the proximity of the black troops, and several racial incidents occurred. Then a white woman charged that a black soldier had attempted to rape her. The following night, firing took place near the town and a white civilian was killed. It was claimed that black soldiers had shot up the town, but an immediate check by the post commander showed all his men in camp except for two who were in town by permission; furthermore, an immediate inspection found all rifles to be clean and not recently fired. The next day, however, the mayor of Brownsville produced empty government-issue rifle shells alleged to have been found at the scene of the shooting. The inspector general of the Army ordered an investigation, which, despite testimony that the shells were faulty rejects stolen from the camp and deliberately planted where they were "discovered," convinced him that some of the soldiers had been responsible for the shooting. But he could not get anyone to identify them. Perhaps the guilty were being shielded by the innocent, the inspector general reported, although, he added, he could find no evidence of this.

President Roosevelt, however, was convinced that some men were guilty and became infuriated by the silence of the other men when asked to name them; therefore, although there had been no trial, the President signed an executive order which was carried out by Secretary of War Taft, discharging "without honor" every man in the three companies. Roosevelt called the incident "one of horrible atrocity . . . unparalleled for infamy in the annals of the United States Army,"[14] although this would have been hyperbole even if there were proof that what was alleged to have occurred had indeed occurred. Senator Joseph B. Foraker of Ohio, anti-Progressive political opponent of Roosevelt, made an investigation of his own which led to the conclusion that the incident had been engineered by the people of Brownsville in order to get the soldiers removed; but Roosevelt would not budge farther than to say that any man who could prove his innocence would be reinstated—a flat reversal of the basic concept of American jurisprudence that a man is presumed innocent until proven guilty, the proof resting on the prosecution.

The election campaign of 1908 brought to light that Senator Foraker had for years been in the pay of the Standard Oil Company. This scandal was another severe blow to blacks still stunned by the Brownsville injustice, because many black people regarded Foraker as a hero come to right their wrongs.[15] The Republican candidate, hand-picked by Roosevelt to succeed him, was his Secretary of War, William Howard Taft. Black voters by then were disenchanted with both Roosevelt and Taft, especially since Brownsville, but they were certainly not enchanted with the thought of voting for a Democratic candidate, even though it was William Jennings Bryan, no Bourbon. Taft may have been "fat, genial, and mediocre" and his policies toward blacks may have been "reactionary," as DuBois said in after years,[16] but Booker T. Washington supported Taft and the Republican Party in preference to Bryan, who, Washington said, might agonize over oppressed Filipinos but was willing to let American Negroes remain disfranchised in the South rather than risk a recurrence of carpetbag government.[17] It is not clear what better alternative Washington thought was offered by Taft, who in 1908 said that Negroes were "political children, not having the mental stature of manhood,"[18] and whose inaugural address included the promise that he would make no appointments that would meet local—meaning southern—opposition. Blacks correctly interpreted this as preface to a decline in the number of Negro office-holders.

Incoming President Taft was constitutionally a conservative, and although at the beginning of his term he pressed forward Roosevelt's Progressive programs, within a couple of years it became apparent that Taft was philosophically opposed to change, particularly if the change was urged by political pressure from the lower ranks.[19] Negro protests and demands, therefore, left him cool; he earned the hearty dislike of black people. By 1910, bitter opposition to President Taft had arisen within his own party, at least in its Progressive wing, and, due to the schism in the Republican ranks, Democratic candidates made a great comeback that year, both in Congress and in the state houses of many traditionally Republican states.[20] As the presidential election of 1912 neared, Roosevelt broke permanently with his old associate

Taft and formed the Progressive, or Bull Moose, party, a third party whose candidate Roosevelt would surely be.

Negro voters were in a quandary. Even loyal Republican papers attacked Taft for his indifference to blacks and his devotion to property rather than human rights. Black independents who had voted for Bryan in 1908 were reluctant to support Woodrow Wilson, a Southerner as well as a Democrat, and black Republicans castigated Wilson for treating Negroes as "foreigners and outcasts" while he was governor of New Jersey.[21] As for the third-party candidate, Roosevelt, although he was the only President to have invited a black man to dinner, he could not live down his reputation as the "Brownsville lyncher." Monroe Trotter used the *Guardian* to oppose Roosevelt, telling readers that in his second term TR had gone over to the South; and when Trotter's Negro Political League could not be brought solidly against Roosevelt, Trotter formed the Massachusetts Anti-Roosevelt Committee. But the opposition of militant blacks such as Trotter to any candidate with ties to the Republican party was viewed by many other blacks as being at least as much anti-Booker T. Washington as anti-Taft or anti-Roosevelt. As for Washington, although he was far too sophisticated to expect race support from either Taft or Roosevelt, Republicans had supported him personally and his Tuskegee Institute, and he remained faithful to the party. Although he discreetly refrained from attacking Wilson, his friend T. Thomas Fortune, editor of the New York *Age*, warned through his influential paper that lynching and violence would ensue if Wilson were elected, and expressed disbelief that any "self-respecting colored man" would vote for him.[22]

DuBois saw the political tangle as an opportunity to wring some concessions from Roosevelt, whose Progressive program seemed the least damaging to blacks, in exchange for the Negro vote, which might very well swing a close, three-way contest. According to an analysis by Andrew B. Humphrey, a black voter of Colorado, 600,000 black voters could command enough electoral votes in 22 states to give their chosen candidate 327 electoral votes, far more than the 266 that would mean victory. From these statistics emerged the appealing idea that blacks held the balance of power in the upcoming election. The Chicago *Defender* and the *Crisis* hailed this prospect with excitement, unrealistic as it was to believe that a monolithic vote could be expected of any ethnic or racial group.[23]

DuBois and the NAACP believed that blacks could demand a high price for their balance-of-power vote. In the summer of 1912, DuBois wrote and Spingarn presented to Roosevelt a declaration that they hoped would be adopted as a platform plank by the Bull Moose convention. "The Progressive Party recognizes that distinctions of race or class in political life have no place in a democracy," the statement began, and it went on to say that the Progressives therefore demanded an end of laws that disfranchised or otherwise discriminated against blacks. What followed was humiliating. Roosevelt and the Progressives not only rejected DuBois's plank, but Roosevelt told Spingarn and two accompanying NAACP directors, Jane Addams and Henry Moskowitz, that DuBois was a dangerous man.[24] Then, at the convention, Roosevelt refused to let the black delegates from southern states be seated, claiming that they were mostly men of bad character and acting simply for personal gain. The political reason for not seating them, it was apparent, was that black southern delegates could deliver too few votes, in Roosevelt's opinion, to balance the risk of antagonizing white southern voters. And then, to overflow the cup of black bitterness, after Roosevelt was nominated the convention joined in singing "John Brown's Body." After the Progressive convention, there was no further effective black support for Roosevelt. Black leaders began, however reluctantly, to turn toward Wilson.[25]

In the middle of July 1912, Wilson held a meeting with Trotter and another militant leader, J. Milton Waldron. Trotter and Waldron came away with a very pleasant impression of Wilson, and the conviction that they had his pledge to assure equal rights for black people in exchange for their votes. This conviction they publicized. But when, soon after, Oswald Garrison Villard sought to get a statement on blacks from the Democratic candidate, Wilson told him that Waldron and Trotter had misinterpreted him; that he had promised them very little; that he could do nothing about lynching, which was not a federal matter; and, furthermore, that he did not believe the Negro vote was crucial for his election. Villard persisted in trying to get some commitment from Wilson that would rally black support, but Wilson refused to sign a very moderate statement drafted by DuBois, which carefully pointed out that the Democratic platform was "without special promise or discrimination of any kind."[26] However, Wilson may have changed his mind about the importance of the black vote, because, a month before the election, he authorized Bishop Alexander Walters to let Negroes know of his earnest wish that "justice be done them in every matter, and not mere grudging justice, but justice executed with liberality and cordial good feeling," and to say that if he became President, Negroes could count on him for "absolute fair dealing" and for help in "advancing the interests of their race in the United States."[27] Although this promise seemed to DuBois "disconcertingly vague," he nevertheless believed it was better to elect Wilson "and prove once and for all if the Democratic Party dares to be democratic when it comes to black men."[28] The November *Crisis* came out with that rather lukewarm endorsement of Wilson. Bishop Walters was more enthusiastic, and stumped for Wilson in the big industrial cities.[29]

It has been estimated that between 40 and 60 per cent of the black electorate voted for Wilson. But Wilson had apparently been right in saying he did not need the black vote, because he won by a popular plurality of more than 2,000,000 and an electoral vote of 435 to 88 over Roosevelt, Taft trailing with only 8 electoral votes. Although the black vote was negligible in the South, Wilson won a popular majority in every southern and border state except West Virginia.[30]

Wilson's election was generally acclaimed by blacks, although in fact his New Freedom program did not mean freedom for them; it was the old Progressive program of restoring free competition in business and assuring the outstanding man freedom to develop his individual energies. To Wilson, the thought of federal legislation favoring farmers or labor—or blacks—was as repugnant as legislation favoring trusts and monopolies.[31] Blacks who hadn't supported Wilson took a wry satisfaction in his election, if only because he had beaten the "Brownsville lyncher." Militants who had supported Wilson were overjoyed, both because he represented a victory over the old conservative Washington leadership and because many of them believed, with Monroe Trotter, that Wilson was a "second Abraham Lincoln."[32] Even Booker T. Washington asserted, when Wilson took office, that "Mr. Wilson is in favor of the things which tend toward the uplift, improvement, and advancement of my people, and at his hands we have nothing to fear."[33]

Not everyone, however, joined the jubilee. Rayford Logan, a high school student at the time, recalls some blacks who were alarmed at the numbers of southern, Bible-belt Democrats who rode Wilson's coattails into Congress, some of whom were said to be publicly declaring that they were in Washington to "fight niggers and liquor."[34] But for most, the awakening took a little time. Francis J. Grimke, a few weeks after the election, wrote to tell Wilson of his confidence that, with a man of such "known Christian character at the head of affairs," no citizen of any race need have any reasonable grounds for fear or complaint.[35] But Dr. Charles B. Privus was not so sure, and wrote to Grimke: "Will it [the Democratic victory] develop a Moses to lead the oppressed of our country out of bondage, free it from persecution and abuse? . . . Or will it relegate, banish from its ranks the Tillmans, Vardamans, Smiths, and Williams? . . . I cannot be thankful for that which I do not know. . . ."[36]

By the following autumn, blacks knew. Less than a year after Wilson's election, the Cleveland *Gazette* said: "When it comes to this race of ours, the writer can remember distinctly what a disappointment were Presidents Garfield, Arthur, Harrison, McKinley, Roosevelt, Taft and even Cleveland; but little less than these, President Woodrow Wilson has already proved himself to be."[37] And about the same time the very disillusioned Grimke wrote to Wilson vigorously protesting "the disposition, under your Administration, to segregate colored people in the various departments of the Government. To do so is undemocratic, is un-American, is un-Christian. . . ."[38]

Before 1900, and into the next decade, blacks had had a pretty good chance of employment in the federal government, at least on low-paid levels. In 1891, for example, before Cleveland's second administration, of 23,144 federal workers in Washington nearly 2,400 were blacks. There were also a number of black postmasters throughout the country, mostly in small towns and mostly low-paid, as low as $25 a month in rural areas. This substantial amount of patronage was a sign of the good relationship of Booker T. Washington with the Republican party. But soon burgeoning racism took its toll in politics as elsewhere. Southern whites began to balk at having black postmasters; the postmistress of Indianola was hounded out of her job not for her trifling salary but because she was black.[39]

During the administrations of Roosevelt and Taft there existed a certain amount of segregation of black federal workers in Washington, although in no consistent pattern. In 1904 a "Jim Crow corner" appeared in the Bureau of Printing and Engraving of the Treasury Department, and at about that time in the Pensions and Records Division of the War Department black clerks were segregated into a "Negro colony" in one corner of the building. Within five years, separate locker, washroom, and eating facilities were customary in the Treasury and Interior departments. Lunch rooms in various federal buildings refused to serve blacks, turning away men of the stature of Lewis H. Douglass, son of Frederick Douglass, and Judge Robert H. Terrell. By 1910 segregated eating areas had spread to the Census Bureau and the dining room for White House employees. But still segregation of black federal workers was spotty, and had no official endorsement in Washington or elsewhere. For example, black and white postal workers on long-distance runs slept in the same railroad cars and depot accommodations, although white workers were beginning to complain.[40]

Early in Wilson's first term, segregation became formalized in the federal Civil Service. The underlying thrust, there seems little doubt, lay in the philosophy of white supremacy spread by the scientists, intellectuals, and popular writers whose theories and works have been examined. There is also little doubt that, as Wilson's biographer Arthur Link pointed out, the President carried into the White House certain ideas, values, and traditions of the South where he was born and reared—from his fondness for rice and fried chicken to his upper-class southern attitude of patronizing affection for blacks, and his conviction that the black man should remain segregated and not aspire toward social equality with whites.[41] But Wilson had other characteristics that made him inactive in helping blacks or in preventing their injury. He was intellectual, an academic, and a statesman, a man of mind far more than of heart. As another biographer, John Norton Blum, has expressed it: "Searching for the first principles of persuasion, hoping to discover grand rules for governing groups of men, Wilson had little interest in the petty problems of individuals."[42] The whole racial question was outside the sphere of Wilson's concerns, and he was quite willing to drift along with the racist thinking given respectability by so many of his fellow academics. He never, for example, used his influence to discourage then current efforts to segregate streetcars and outlaw interracial marriages in the District of Columbia.[43]

Wilson did occasionally suffer a twinge of conscience about blacks, it seems, and is reported to have told Villard: "I say it with shame and humiliation, but I have thought about this thing [the race problem] for twenty years and I see no way out."[44] If he had honestly seen no way out, a natural reaction might have been regret or frustration, but he would have had no cause for shame; shame would more likely be produced by seeing the way out but choosing not to pursue it, because it ran counter to his prejudices, or would take up energy he needed for other purposes, or would offend and antagonize men whose help he needed to achieve his Progressive aims.

It is less significant, probably, that Wilson was born in Virginia—he had been working in the North for about twenty-five years[45]—than that his closest associates in government were Southerners. Five men of Wilson's first Cabinet came from the South: Secretary of the Treasury William Gibbs McAdoo of Georgia, who in 1914 married Wilson's daughter; Postmaster General Albert S. Burleson of Texas, of all government heads the one with most patronage to dispense; Secretary of the Navy Josephus Daniels of North Carolina; Secretary of Agriculture David

F. Houston of North Carolina; and Attorney General James C. McReynolds of Kentucky.[46] In addition, Wilson's closest White House aide and personal friend was Colonel Edward M. House of Texas. In the Senate, more than half the Democratic majority were Southerners, and in the House, more than 40 per cent; the majority leaders of both houses were from the South.[47]

Among the most influential of the southern Progressives were men whom blacks had good reason to hate and fear: Vardaman, Williams, Blease, Tillman, Daniels, Smith, Bilbo, Charles B. Aycock, and Carter Glass, all of whom, as legislators and/or governors in their home states, had oppressed and cheated black taxpayers. Yet in their opposition to political bossism and machines, to giant corporations and railroads, insurance companies and trusts; in their support of direct primaries, initiative and referendum, corrupt-practices acts and antilobby acts, and of legislation to protect miners, factory workers, child labor, and the consumer, they were long-time, active Progressives. But "consciousness of kind" was basic to their philosophy, and be damned to other kinds. During Wilson's campaign, Daniels editorialized in his North Carolina newspaper that the South would never feel secure until the North and West adopted disfranchisement and social segregation of blacks.[48] Vardaman declared, "We would be justified in slaughtering every Ethiop on the earth to preserve unsullied the honor of one Caucasian home,"[49] and his poorwhite constituents chanted, "We are the low-brows, we are the rednecks, rah for Vardaman!"[50] Tom Watson declared that the Negro simply had "no comprehension of virtue, honesty, truth, gratitude and principle," and that it was necessary "to lynch him occasionally, and flog him now and then, to keep him from blaspheming the Almighty by his conduct, on account of his color and smell."[51] Demagogues, armed with down-home quips and tobacco juice, vied to "outnigger" the opposition with their redneck and woolhat constituents.[52] Yet, within the limited political sense, they might be good Progressives. As William Miller has assessed progressivism, "The movement, being pragmatic, subscribed to no transcendent principle of morality that required an examination of conscience regarding the general tendency to brand the Negro as inferior."[53] There were also plenty of north-

ern Progressives who viewed Negroes much as they did the colonial Filipinos, as inferiors who, only if firmly supervised, could
hope to achieve to the utmost of their limited capabilities.[54]

At state and local levels Progressive reforms did bring blacks
some tangential benefits: agricultural and mechanical education
in Mississippi, for example, and urban improvements in Mayor
Ed Crump's Memphis.[55] At the national level, however, with
which the President was concerned, the benefits of progressivism
for blacks were so remote as to be impalpable. Wilson's first-term
domestic accomplishments were considerable: lower tariffs, reorganized currency and banking systems, and stronger antitrust
legislation. But in the area of social reform, where blacks could
be beneficiaries, Wilson was less effective. The Smith-Lever Act
for federal aid to agricultural education, as it stood when introduced in January 1914, would have helped the black southern
farmers and their children; but when it finally became law some
months later, as amended by southern Progressives (despite bitter protests from the NAACP), it placed the administration of
aid funds in the hands of the state legislatures, thus effectively
cheating blacks of a fair share in this Progressive program.[56]

Within the framework of southern power, it was almost inevitable that blacks would soon have no place in government.
An NAACP official noted early in 1913: "Segregation is no new
thing in Washington, and the present administration cannot be
said to have inaugurated it. . . . The past few months of Democratic control, however, have given segregation impetus and have
been marked by more than a beginning of systematic enforcement."[57] Pressures for segregation began immediately after Wilson assumed office. Early in April 1913, white postal clerks
protested to Postmaster Burleson about nonsegregated sleeping
and toilet facilities on mail coaches. Burleson, within a week,
brought the matter up at a Cabinet meeting. According to Secretary Daniels' notes on these meetings, Burleson recommended
segregation in all federal departments and claimed that Bishop
Walters approved of this measure. Wilson responded vaguely
that he had made no promises to the Negroes, but that he didn't
wish them to have fewer federal jobs than they now had, and
hoped the issue could be solved with the least possible friction.

Burleson remarked that segregation would actually be a good thing for the Negroes, because it would protect them from white hostility; and he raised the scare issue that Negro males and white females sometimes worked together in his department. Wilson told Burleson to do as he thought best in the least offensive way.[58]

Supported by an executive order signed by President Wilson, Burleson segregated blacks in the Post Office Department; McAdoo and Daniels quickly followed suit in Treasury and Navy, respectively. Blacks in their departments were assigned to separate working, eating, and toilet facilities. Mrs. Ellen Wilson, the President's Georgia-born wife, is believed to have played some part in this racial separation. In April she visited the Bureau of Printing and Engraving and found black and white women working and eating together; shortly after her visit, blacks were assigned a separate section of the lunch room.[59]

The three departments of Treasury, Post Office, and Navy employed more than half the 19,000 blacks in the federal Civil Service in 1912. With increasing pressure from Southerners in Congress and from a white-supremacy group in Washington calling itself the National Fair Play Association, every part of the federal service had soon instituted segregation.[60] Ray Stannard Baker in his sympathetic biography of his friend Woodrow Wilson insisted that the President was concerned about race relations, and Link pointed out that Wilson consistently avoided the cruder forms of racism; nevertheless, Wilson gave his approval to discrimination in the government, and many times echoed Burleson's self-serving argument that segregation was really in the best interests of blacks.[61] He very possibly was unaware that black employees who resisted segregation were discharged; that white southern postmasters could fire black workers at will; that the Civil Service Commission demoted a black mail supervisor in North Carolina simply because it was found intolerable by some white citizens that a black should be in charge of whites; and that in Georgia the collector of Internal Revenue announced "there are no Government positions for Negroes in the South."[62] Such obscure events would not come to the attention of a President, probably, so one cannot censure Wilson for taking no action on them. But he did have an opportunity to create a watchdog body that might have brought such inequities into the open, and he rejected it.

In May 1913, Villard as secretary of the NAACP met with Wilson and proposed a National Race Commission for the purpose of making a "non-partisan, scientific study of the status of the Negro with particular reference to his economic situation."[63] Wilson indicated interest, and, Villard reported, was ready to appoint such a commission "when it became clear that his relations with the Senate and the House would permit it."[64] Villard went abroad for a short time, and, on his return in July, found an NAACP horrified by the rapid spread of segregation in the federal service. Villard remonstrated with Wilson, saying that blacks had thought the "New Freedom" would include them, that they were desperately disappointed, and that he personally, as one who had urged blacks to vote Democratic, was greatly embarrassed. Wilson replied that segregation in government departments had the approval of "influential Negroes" who agreed with him that it would reduce friction and give blacks more security in their jobs and more chances for promotion.[65] Perhaps he had in mind as a model an all-Negro section that McAdoo had established in the Treasury, which was to be headed, if Congress would approve Wilson's appointee, by a black man, Adam E. Patterson.

But Wilson's answer did not appease Villard, who pursued the Race Commission idea through the summer, with the President at first postponing a decision and finally, in late August, admitting that he had to reject the plan because to bring up the race issue at that time would be a political blunder. He himself was shocked, he told Villard, to find himself utterly blocked by the sentiments of senators, and not only southern senators. Villard persisted, telling Wilson that blacks were so incensed by events that they scorned and spurned the Wilson supporters in their midst. Wilson repeated that his hands were tied: "What I would do if I could act alone you already know, but what I am trying to do must be done, if at all, through the cooperation of those with whom I am associated in the government."[66] In October Villard again saw Wilson, and got the same answer except that

Wilson no longer insisted that blacks favored segregation—indeed, they were most bitterly protesting it, as he must have known;[67] it was in this interview that Wilson expressed shame that he "could see no way out" of the race problem,[68] and he asked Villard to try to keep the segregation issue at "a just and cool equipoise" until the time was right to make changes, because "a bitter agitation" would render those changes impossible of achievement.[69]

But white Southerners did not keep the race issue at "a just and cool equipoise." Such a furor was raised when Wilson nominated Patterson for register of the Treasury that it became clear the Senate would never approve him. Thomas Dixon was among those who protested to Wilson about the unthinkable prospect of a black man bossing white girls. But Dixon was under a misapprehension. Vainly Wilson tried to explain to his southern critics: "I do not think you know what is going on down here. . . . We are trying—and by degrees succeeding [in]—a plan of concentration which will put them [blacks] together and will not in any one bureau mix the two races. This change has already practically been effected in the bureau in which I proposed the appointment of Patterson."[70] This does not sound like the same man who promised Villard changes if only Negroes would be patient. Wilson's doublespeak is easier to understand in the light of a threatening statement from Vardaman that the defeat of the Patterson appointment "is of more importance than the tariff bill and the enactment of currency legislation."[71] To Wilson, the latter were much more important than the Patterson appointment. Finally Patterson withdrew his name—drawing the wrath of DuBois and other militants—and a Choctaw Indian got the job of register.

Monroe Trotter, meanwhile, had also been working to persuade Wilson to stop segregation in government. The month Wilson took office, Trotter had written introducing himself to the President as the son of the recorder of deeds in the District of Columbia in Cleveland's administration, and offering to advise on Negro affairs. When systematic segregation began to emerge in government departments, Trotter was among those who pleaded with Wilson to intervene. By November, even Bishop

Walters was losing faith in Wilson and the Democrats. Trotter led a delegation from the National Independent Political League to present Wilson with a 20,000-name petition to end segregation. Wilson heard the delegation politely and promised to give the matter his attention. Trotter wrote him reminders, but Wilson remained silent.[72] A year later, in November 1914, Trotter again headed an NIPL delegation to the White House. Trotter had been put off for twelve whole months, and he was not a man noted for patience or an equable disposition; Wilson, grieving over the recent death of his wife, was not in a receptive frame of mind. After a few polite opening remarks, Wilson again took the patronizing line that segregation was not a handicap but a benefit to blacks, and Trotter indignantly countered that blacks were not "dependent wards of the nation" but "full-fledged American citizens, absolutely equal with all others," and pointed out that blacks and whites had worked together in government offices without friction for the past fifty years.[73] At this Wilson got angry and said Trotter's attitude with its "background of passion" was offensive; and he told the rest of the delegation to elect a new leader if they wanted to talk with him again. Trotter stood his ground, informing Wilson that blacks who had voted for him were now reviled as race traitors. Then the President really lost his temper (as he later privately admitted), said Trotter's remark was political blackmail and he would do as he saw fit, and ordered Trotter out of his office.[74]

This meeting was widely covered in the newspapers, with most of the white press (outside the South) condemning the President, and much of the black press, even DuBois in the *Crisis*, praising Trotter's behavior. Some white benefactors of Negro causes, including Rosenwald and Albert E. Pillsbury, deplored Trotter's "rudeness" and called him a notoriety seeker—but these were conservatives whose model of a black man was Booker T. Washington. More liberal whites in Boston attended a protest meeting and called Wilson's policy toward blacks the "new oppression in Washington." Southern papers called Trotter a "darky" who tried to "sass" the President, "not a Booker T. Washington type of colored man . . . merely a nigger."[75]

Organized agitation against Wilson's attitudes and actions was

led by the NAACP, aided by Villard's *Nation* and the liberal
New York *Post*. Everywhere except in the South, humanitarians,
social workers, clergymen, and liberal editors and political leaders responded to the NAACP's plea to denounce segregation in
government. Frank Cobb of the New York *World*, a good friend
of Wilson, said the President "ought to have set his heel upon
this presumptuous Jim Crow government the moment it was
established."[76] The President's insistence that segregation was
good for blacks was called in a Massachusetts paper a "distress-
ing and sinister development."[77]

Link wrote that the volume and sharpness of criticism, while
it did not put a stop to segregation, did check its advance. But
there was not very much farther for it to go. Of the thirty or so
blacks who held federal offices of any importance when Wilson
became President, only eight were left in 1916. William H. Lewis,
who as assistant attorney general had the highest office ever
held by a black man, in 1913 was told his job was at an end.
Lewis's office had dealt mainly with Indian affairs, and Attorney
General McReynolds announced that since the work was finished,
Lewis would have to go; but a few weeks later, McReynolds
hired a new assistant, a white man. Even traditional Negro posts
were lost, such as register of the Treasury, recorder of deeds,
and collector of customs in the District of Columbia, and minister to Haiti. By 1916 only one black man held an appointive
job in the District, Municipal Judge Robert Terrell.[78] Here, as
Baker pointed out, Wilson did oppose the will of southern Progressives like Hoke Smith of Georgia. As Wilson explained the
affair to Senator John Sharp Williams of Mississippi, another pro-
tester, "I assure you that I could not avoid the nomination of
Terrell. In the first place, there is every reason to believe that
he has not only performed his duties excellently, but that he has
been the best judge of his rank in the District. . . ." In keeping
him, Wilson continued, he was honoring a campaign promise
to some "very straight-forward and honorable" black supporters
not to let blacks suffer any greater political disadvantage than
they had under previous Democratic administrations.[79] But
clearly he was not going to give them any greater advantages,
either; and since the last Democratic President had been Cleve-

land, under whom blacks had been reduced to their deplorable condition at the beginning of the century, a maintenance of the Cleveland status quo was not much of a promise. Except for Terrell, Wilson never opposed the wishes of his southern supporters. His only other appointment of a black to any senior position was that of James L. Curtis as minister to Liberia in 1915, and that nomination went through unchallenged because the job was considered degrading for a white man; indeed, Senator Williams had objected on that ground to Wilson's appointment of a white man as minister to Haiti.[80]

It is impossible to find any improvement in race relations, in government or outside it, during Wilson's first administration. By 1914, all applicants for federal Civil Service were requested to submit a photograph.[81] Early that year, southern Congressmen introduced two bills aiming at legal segregation of all federal workers.[82] An anti-immigration bill introduced by Senator John Burnett of Alabama, as amended by Senator James Reed of Missouri with the support of Senator Williams and other southern senators, would have banned forever entry into the United States of "all members of the African or black race"; but the amendment was killed by liberal opposition.[83] A woman suffrage bill of 1914 also aroused southern opposition because it would give black women as well as white women the vote—and then, as a Boston newspaper wryly commented, the South would have to think up "grandmother clauses"; Vardaman and Williams offered to support the bill in exchange for the repeal of the Fifteenth Amendment![84] In 1915 a bill was proposed in Congress to segregate streetcars in the District of Columbia, and another to bar interracial marriages there. Neither bill passed, but the mere proposal to legalize Jim Crow in the federal city alarmed Kelly Miller, Archibald Grimke, and other black leaders.[85]

Through all this flurry of racist legislative attempts, the President remained silent. Grimke said Wilson spat in the faces of ten million Negroes;[86] Booker T. Washington told Wilson he had "never seen the colored people so discouraged and bitter as they are at the present time."[87] DuBois said "effective guns" in black hands might be the only way to stop lynching, and that murder "may be necessary" to achieve Negro freedom.[88] But Wilson was looking forward to a second term and needed all possible southern support. By keeping silent, by voicing no criticism of such slurs on black people as *The Birth of a Nation,* by permitting segregation in government to go unchecked, he pursued a southern strategy that worked. He won his second term, although by the uncomfortably small margin of just over half a million votes. Had the black vote four years earlier been more important than Wilson realized?

The war in Europe was threatening to draw in the United States, although most Americans were firmly opposed to involvement. "He kept us out of war!" was a Wilson campaign slogan in 1916. But scarcely was Wilson re-established in the White House when the threats of unrestricted German submarine warfare and of aggression by Japan and Mexico drove him to the reluctant decision that neutrality was no longer possible.[89] The support of Congress for an unpopular war had somehow to be won. Again the southern strategy paid off. According to the New York *Times,* when Wilson, in his war address to Congress in April 1917, declared that "the world must be made safe for democracy," the first legislator to applaud that famous phrase "gravely, emphatically," was Senator John Sharp Williams; "and," the *Times* report continued, "in a moment the fact that this was the key word in our war . . . dawned on the others. . . ."[90] Wilson was thus assured of vital southern support in the war. The cost? An official of the NAACP said, "The effect [of segregation] is startling, those segregated are regarded as a people apart, almost as lepers."[91] A comment by Kelly Miller matched or surpassed Wilson's phrase, although it never became as famous: "He believed in democracy for humanity but not for Mississippi."[92]

Throughout Wilson's first term fifty to sixty blacks each year found equipoise at the end of a rope, almost all of them in the South; and during the war for democracy and the year after, the numbers increased. The NAACP, Trotter, the more moderate Kelly Miller, practically the entire black leadership begged Wilson to do something about this shameful situation. Villard had reported that Wilson, after his nomination in 1912, had promised to speak out against lynching,[93] but by 1916 Wilson had still not broken silence on the subject. In that year Ray Stannard Baker wrote that lynchings were on the increase, that now Negroes were "lynched for all sorts of crimes and offenses, sometimes of the most trivial character," and that often "wholly innocent Negroes have been lynched."[94] William Pickens wrote that same year: "No law and no executive can do away with such evils until . . . civilizing influences have done their work; but a good law and a strong executive are powerful elements behind this evolutionary process."[95] This was surely directed at Wilson and the Congress, but they made no move. In July 1918 Wilson's Secretary of War, Newton D. Baker, who as mayor of Cleveland had had experience with the black community, suggested to Wilson that, to calm Negro unrest resulting from an upsurge of lynchings, the President should urge upon the governor of one of the notorious lynch states the prosecution of lynch leaders.[96] The President went only so far as to issue a statement later that month that anyone involved in a lynching was "no true son of this great democracy, but its betrayer," because he has "adopted the standards of the enemies of his country, whom he affects to despise."[97]

The NAACP lobbied vigorously for a bill first introduced in Congress in 1919 by Representative Leonidas Dyer of the East St. Louis area of Illinois, which would have made mob murder or failure to protect prisoners a federal offense. The bill was defeated; and when it was reintroduced in 1921, it passed the House but failed in the Senate.[98] One important outcome, however, of the long, losing fight for the antilynch bill was the NAACP-sponsored study called "Thirty Years of Lynching, 1889–1918." It revealed, among other astonishing facts, that more people had been lynched than legally executed during that period, and that fewer than one out of six lynch victims were accused of sexual crimes. The report of the study was launched at an NAACP antilynch convention in 1919, which was attended by delegates from twenty-five states. The organization by then had 88,500 members in 300 branches, half of which were in the South. Among those who attended the convention were a former governor of Alabama and another white Southerner who belonged to the

Mississippi Welfare League.[99] But such signs of progress were illusory. Discouragingly little was accomplished in the way of curbing lynching. The horrors continued unchecked by executive influence or legislative action, undoubtedly encouraged by the President's approval, or at least acceptance, of segregation and discrimination in government.

In a situation where Negroes were regarded practically as lepers, very little excuse needed be given for perpetrating outrages upon them. Herbert Seligmann noted in 1920: "The penalty for the social and political disabilities imposed upon the Negro has been that he is constantly in the minds of white people. From contempt, with its admixture of self-reproach, to hostility is a short step and an easy one. Hence the apprehension with which the white South looked upon the induction of Negroes into the army; hence, in the past, the quick resort to the rope, the pistol, the torch. That the South is a 'white man's country' is a dogma affirmed in practice not only oratorically and by editors, but with bullets and whip."[100]

Contempt and apprehension were demonstrated in the Wilson years by tightened segregation and discrimination not only in government but in housing, industry, and in the use of recreational and other public facilities. Ray Stannard Baker observed increasing white hostility as a reaction to the expanding wealth, self-confidence, and aspirations of blacks. Increasing hostility led to increasingly horrid outrages. Burning, beating to death, and hacking to pieces were not uncommon methods of lynch mobs. Walter White, who became NAACP secretary in 1918, reported that the increase of automobiles in the South brought into vogue a new kind of lynching—tying the victim to a car and dragging him until he was dead. Whatever crime the victim might be charged with, his real offense was in getting ahead a little, because the real purpose of lynching was to "keep the Negro down," to "show the Negro his place."[101]

And what if the black man, who was beginning to have quite a new concept of himself because of his advances, dared challenge the dogma of white supremacy, the "color psychosis" of the South, as Seligmann called it, which pervaded science, philosophy, fiction, films, and government, and was therefore influencing the racial attitudes of the whole country? What happened when he refused to stay down, to remain in his place; when the white society around him encouraged vice and corruption; when white men expressed their fears and hate by physical brutality? Under such circumstances, what happened often was a race riot—a violent confrontation between racial groups, caused by accumulated tensions and often precipitated by a beating or lynching, in which black people show signs of organized resistance to mob action. In short, race hate is expressed in lynchings and beatings "until the spirit of the Negro begins to change and he buys arms to defend himself," as Seligmann said.[102]

One theme pervading almost every serious racial clash was the flagrant disregard for law on the part of law-enforcement bodies. Sometimes, as in a New York City riot in 1900, policemen openly led mobs in seizing and beating Negroes. A less visible but more pernicious theme was corruption in politics, crooked politicians paid off by saloon, gambling, and prostitution interests to let vice flourish in the Negro sections of cities. Corruption prevailed in towns and cities that were the scenes of racial clashes, from Greensburg, Indiana, where in 1906 blacks were chased out of town after an alleged assault on a white woman by a half-witted black man, to the much more serious riot of 1917 in East St. Louis. Where there were vice and crime in the black slums—and it was profitable to politicians that there should be—white people generalized that all blacks were vicious and criminal, which served as an excuse for mob action against the whole black community, not just the lawless element. This pattern was particularly prevalent in the southern "Bible belt," where Progressive politicians had long found that crusades against liquor and red-light sin won them votes. The remark of southern Democrats who came to Washington with Wilson, that they were there to "fight niggers and liquor," makes it clear that they classed "the law-abiding, thrifty, industrious and intelligent Negroes indiscriminately with the lawless and undesirable," as George Haynes wrote.[103]

Contributing to this characterization of the entire black com-

munity as vicious was the sensational publicity given by the
newspapers to crimes committed by Negroes. "The newspapers
play upon these with flaring headlines and minute descriptions
suggestive of racial turpitude and criminal tendencies," Haynes
said.[104] Atlanta, Georgia, in 1906 had been heated to riot tem-
perature by a production of Dixon's play *The Clansman;* newspapers cashed in on the outraged white feelings engendered by
the play by featuring exaggerated stories of alleged Negro crimes,
luridly headlined. Probably an underlying reason for racial tension in Atlanta that year was a long and bitter gubernatorial
campaign, with the black vote a major issue; Hoke Smith, who
ran foursquare on a Negro disfranchisement platform, won an
overwhelming victory. But without sensationalism in the press,
feelings might gradually have simmered down after the election,
and the worst southern race riot in the first decade of the century
might have been avoided. The papers kept public opinion at the
boil with exaggerated stories of black attacks on or rapes of
white women, until a hysterical white mob rampaged through
Atlanta and its Brownsville suburb, to which the riot spread. The
toll when the riot finally subsided was about 70 wounded, some
of these permanently disfigured or disabled, and 2 whites and
10 blacks dead. Many law-abiding blacks fled Atlanta. Factories
were closed, transportation was crippled, and the city was virtually paralyzed for weeks.[105]

A riot of 1908 in Springfield, Illinois, the Emancipator's birthplace, had all the characteristic components of riots anywhere
in the country plus the additional one that was believed present
in most race riots in the North: industrial competition between
blacks and whites, especially white immigrant laborers.[106] Perhaps these riots were underpinned by racial competition and
animosity, but, as an anonymous reporter of the Springfield riot
observed: "No mob, or mob violence can disturb a community
unless there exists behind the immediate causes of the outbreak a
wrong state of affairs, vicious conditions, as complex as society
itself, of which it is the inevitable outcome. . . . The seeds of
violence were sown, not when the first Negroes came to Springfield, but when municipal rottenness fertilized the lower strata
of society."[107] Votes were systematically bought and sold, a

gambling ring dominated the city government, and lawbreakers kept out of jail either by votes or money. These illegal practices had for years fostered a lawless class among both blacks and whites. It is essential to view the details of the riot against this sordid background to understand how a homicide and rape, allegedly committed at two different times by two different black men, could touch off a spree of mob violence during which two Negroes and five whites were killed, a child died of exposure, at least one hundred persons were wounded, forty black families watched their homes burned, two thousand black people were driven out of the city, property worth $120,000 was destroyed, and almost four thousand troops of the National Guard were called up at an expense to the state of $200,000—almost as many Guardsmen as there were Negroes in Springfield.[108] Furthermore, "Springfield had no shame" for these dreadful and terrifying occurrences, wrote William English Walling, the social reformer who had gone to Springfield to report the riot for the *Independent;* he said, "She stood for the action of the mob."[109] Walling said the masses of the people were the culprits, not the leading citizens; but many of the latter, according to a Springfield newspaper, considered the outbreak inevitable in the light of "existing conditions"—by which they meant not municipal corruption but "the Negroes' own misconduct, general inferiority or unfitness for free institutions. . . ."[110] A few newspapers in the state pointed out that bad government was the villain, but others blamed either the blacks or the "foreign population of Polaks and Italians . . . the ignorant foreigners from the coal mines,"[111] thus echoing the nativist, anti-immigrant sentiments of the day. No one blamed the "leading citizens," although there seems no good reason for exonerating them, considering that they, not the blacks nor the ignorant foreigners, were the people with the power to clean up the government and morals of their city, had they wished.

Southerners who had sarcastically predicted that the migration of blacks to northern cities would teach the North a thing or two were quite smug about the Springfield riot. Vardaman took the occasion to comment in the Senate that "God Almighty never intended that the negro should share with the white man in the

government of this country. . . . It matters not what I may say
or others may think, it matters not what constitutions may contain or statutes provide, wherever the negro is in sufficient numbers to imperil the white man's civilization or question the white
man's supremacy the white man is going to find some way around
the difficulty. The feeling against the negro in Illinois when he
gets in the white man's way is quite as strong, more bitter, less
regardful of the negro's feelings and conditions than it is in Mississippi."[112] What more perfect opportunity than a riot in Lincoln's birthplace to rub it in that Northerners didn't believe in
racial equality any more than Southerners, and basically didn't
even like Negroes, as it was claimed Southerners did who were
accustomed to living at close quarters with them.

Springfield remained unrepentant, and the riot was quickly
forgotten except by the blacks who had suffered in it and by a
group of militants, both blacks and whites, who moved ahead on
the impetus of the Springfield violence to found an organization
dedicated to the cause of equal rights for Negroes. The earlier
Niagara Movement had faltered because of personal and policy
differences, but Walling's cry of indignation after Springfield re-
kindled hope in the social activists. "If these outrages had happened thirty years ago," wrote Walling, himself a Southerner,
"when the memories of Lincoln, Garrison and Wendell Phillips
were still fresh, what would not have happened in the North?
Is there any doubt that the whole country would have been
aflame . . . ?"[113] Some did catch fire. A call was issued for a
conference dramatically set in Springfield itself on the one-
hundredth anniversary of Lincoln's birth, six months after the
riot. The NAACP, which evolved from the Springfield meeting,
grew stronger and more effective over the years, and was the
backbone of organized opposition to the racism of Wilson's administration.[114]

Three months after Wilson won the applause of the Senate
by pledging a world made safe for democracy, the worst race
riot of the century so far occurred in East St. Louis, Illinois. Both
whites and blacks had guns. Days and nights of violence ended
with eight whites and at least thirty-nine blacks dead, over a
hundred blacks shot or mangled into helplessness, and perhaps

six thousand blacks left homeless by the burning of the black neighborhood.[115]

East St. Louis, a city of about 75,000, situated across the Mississippi River from St. Louis, was noted for huge industrial plants, including chemicals, aluminum, slaughtering, and meat-packing. The whole city in 1917 was an industrial slum, described by one social worker as "a satellite city . . . not a city of homes in the American acceptance of that term." It was outstandingly a city of the vermin-infested, filthy, furnished ghetto rooms, the beds rented by day and by night, the squalor and vice and lack of municipal services. The city government was totally corrupt. The great companies controlled the city's politics and politicians. The police force—in 1917, thirty-six patrolmen and sixteen plain-clothesmen, six of the latter being black—was poorly paid and inefficient; and despite the vast wealth that flowed into and out of East St. Louis, the city depended chiefly on the proceeds of saloon licences for what government it provided. At the time of the July riots, there were 376 saloons in East St. Louis; gambling houses, whorehouses, and dives of every kind operated openly. In this rotten corruption, as with other crookedly run cities, lay the seeds of violence. There was, to be sure, a degree of race friction among laborers, mostly blacks and immigrant whites, plus some native whites from Tennessee, Kentucky, and other southern states; still, peace might have been maintained if the inhabitants of the city had had any reason to respect their government and law-enforcement officers. Also, there was explosive potential in the crowding of the black population into a ghetto too small to hold them in any kind of decency or comfort; the Negro population about doubled from 1910 to 1917, when it numbered 10,600, and whites whose neighborhoods were being encroached on feared further migration of southern blacks.[116]

The white immigrant workers who lived on the fringes of the black ghetto had had no previous experience with blacks, nor had the southern blacks had any experience of European immigrants; suddenly to be thrown together in a crowded, dreary, drinking, whoring city and at the plant gates looking for jobs fed all the racial prejudices and antipathies of both blacks and whites.[117] Furthermore, as Charles Johnson pointed out, Negroes who in the South had through custom and caution restrained hostile impulses, after migrating North were quick to resent discrimination and insults, and to retaliate.[118]

Labor relations need not have further strained race relations. Cutthroat competition was not generally necessary in East St. Louis, because the war was creating more jobs for both skilled and unskilled workers than there were men to fill them. However, although black migrants were not snatching jobs away from whites, labor organizers encouraged white workers to believe that they were, in order to induce the white workers to join the unions for protection, which would in turn increase the power of the unions. Further complicating the situation, it seems pretty certain that employers sometimes gave job preference to blacks, because they were not nor were they likely to become union men. Worst of all for any sort of racial harmony, employers in some cases did bring in blacks as strikebreakers, and union men instigated by union leaders came to think of all blacks as strikebreakers who weakened the unions.[119] But so few blacks were in the skilled levels of labor, where unions were strongest, that it is an error, as the Department of Labor pointed out, to view the East St. Louis riot as a struggle between organized and unorganized labor; rather it was, at least in its economic component, a struggle "between the white and black unorganized workers crowding for a place on the lowest rung of the industrial ladder."[120] Unions were trying to organize that level, but had not yet made much headway; and, the Labor Department said, on that level there was a temporary surplus of labor in 1916 and 1917 as great numbers of black migrants were passing through East St. Louis headed for places farther off. But these were transients, and it is misleading to generalize a temporary situation of a particular time and place as a labor war between races.

That was the situation in East St. Louis in 1917, and it was, as the *Crisis* pointed out, used divisively by unions and employers: "Instead of his [the Negro's] cause being the cause of the working class at large, the two became separated and pitted against each other. . . ."[121] Tensions kept building up as more and more blacks arrived. In 1916–17, about 2,400 blacks migrated to East St. Louis.[122] Some of them were brought in by industries to relieve severe strikes of 1916. Others were encouraged to come by Republican politicians to strengthen their party in southern Illinois for the 1916 election;[123] by 1916 it was a pretty safe bet that few blacks anywhere would vote for Wilson or the Democratic Party, which may explain in part Wilson's narrow margin of victory.

For all these reasons, when violence broke out in the lawless city of East St. Louis, it was so terrible that a congressional investigation was later made into its causes, details, and handling by the authorities. When Colonel S. O. Tripp, the ineffective commander of the militia, finished his testimony before the congressional committee, Representative Raker of California is said to have exclaimed: "What chance on earth has a poor, innocent Negro in a place like this?"[124]

There were numerous industrial cities outside the South where a Negro had no better chance than in East St. Louis. Racial violence flared in 1917 wherever large numbers of blacks entered a new area. Pittsburgh, Philadelphia, and Weehawken, New Jersey, were the scenes of more or less serious racial conflicts. Chester, Pennsylvania, suffered a severe race riot less than a month after East St. Louis, which the Chester police chief ascribed to "the presence of riff-raff of both races from the South and to the organized activity of a gang of local roughs."[125] Some of them were black roughs, who ganged up on newly arrived black migrants and took away their pay. A corrupt political machine and a lax police force let violence go unchecked; it was said that city leaders allied themselves with the liquor interests, which delivered the 30 per cent black vote in Chester.[126] But it was white roughs who started the riot on July 31, claiming as their motive vengeance for the stabbing of a white man. They went after all Negroes, the law-abiding and the lawless, dragging them off streetcars and chasing them through the streets. At least eighty blacks were severely beaten.

A few months later, on Thanksgiving Day 1917, the town of Homestead, Pennsylvania, had a riot of much the same nature. The Labor Department summed up, in reporting the riot: "Undoubtedly similar and even more serious outbreaks of violence may be expected where there does not exist effective police control of the vicious elements of both groups. However, casual work, indecent housing conditions, and drinking and gambling in leisure time are steadily creating viciousness. Disease, crime, and race friction are perhaps inevitable in those communities to which the Negroes have come in considerable numbers, and which are making no provision for the selection and supervision of colored workers, the regulation of housing and lodging, and the creation of wholesome recreation facilities."[127]

To protest the East St. Louis nightmare of shootings, burnings, and hangings, about 15,000 New York City blacks paraded silently down Fifth Avenue. Kelly Miller addressed an open letter to President Wilson appealing for a moral crusade as well as federal legislation against mob law and lynching. "The white people of this country are not good enough to govern the Negro," Miller said; and, "The vainglorious boast of Anglo-Saxon superiority will no longer avail to justify these outrages." As for making the world safe for democracy, Miller declared: "If democracy cannot control lawlessness then democracy must be pronounced a failure." Lynching and race riots, he said, were "but the outgrowth of the disfavor and despite in which the race is held by public opinion," and nothing could stop race violence short of federal intervention. True, race issues had always been considered matters for local and state control, but there was little comfort for the black man, Miller said, "when he is beaten and bruised and burned in all parts of the nation and flees to the national government for asylum, to be denied relief on the ground of doubtful jurisdiction." At least for the duration of the war, Miller shrewdly pointed out, the President could ask Congress for emergency powers to stop lawlessness and violence against the Negro. After all, Negroes had always given their blood to their country, "from Boston Commons to Carrizal." And Miller asked the question that expressed the sum of black anxiety and hope in the first few months of the war: "The Negro, Mr. President, in this emergency, will stand by you and the nation. Will you and the nation stand by the Negro?"[128]

CHAPTER 9

In the Great War for Democracy

> This war is an End, and, also, a Beginning. Never again will darker people of the world occupy just the place they have before.
>
> W. E. B. DuBois

> Men of darker hue have no rights which white men are bound to respect. And it is this narrow, contracted, contemptible undemocratic idea of democracy that we have been fighting to make the world safe for, if we have been fighting to make it safe for democracy at all.
>
> Rev. Francis J. Grimke

The approach of war had already changed the place occupied by black Americans through increased job opportunities, and those opportunities had drawn hundreds of thousands of them North, where social as well as economic advance beckoned although violence was likely to punctuate progress. When America entered the war, many black men found the prospect of military service exciting because, in the words of one black teacher, "when we have proved ourselves men, worthy to work and fight and die for our country, a grateful nation may gladly give us the recognition of real men, and the rights and privileges of true and loyal citizens of these United States."[1]

The service of blacks in earlier wars had not accomplished this goal, and they had served in American wars from colonial times. Perhaps 10,000 had been in the Revolutionary War, and by the end of the Civil War some 180,000 blacks had been mustered into the Union Army, but blacks with guns had always been considered a problem by the military. George Washington in 1775 decided against accepting black soldiers, although this policy was changed later partly to counter British urgings to the slave population to revolt; black soldiers fought side by side with whites in that war and in the War of 1812. In the Civil War the Union Army had grappled with the question of black soldiers for two years before deciding to admit them and form them into segregated units up to corps size, with a few black officers; in general, their service was commended. There had also always been blacks in the Navy, and up to the twentieth century their best opportunities lay in that branch. There were 29,000 black sailors in the Civil War, forming 25 per cent of the entire Union Navy, and 2,000 in the Spanish-American War; these were fighting sailors, to whom all ratings were open. But after 1900, Negroes were used in the Navy almost exclusively as messmen and other menials, and in World War I there were only 5,300 blacks in a naval force of 435,400 men, or slightly more than 1 per cent.[2]

There had been, since the Reconstruction Act of 1866, four regiments of black Regulars in the United States Army: the 24th and 25th Infantry, and the 9th and 10th Cavalry. Some of their officers were white West Point graduates on their first assignment to duty; some junior officers and the noncoms were black, and the very few black West Point graduates were also assigned to these regiments. Most of the time the black Regulars were kept busy fighting Indians in the Southwest and patrolling the Mexican border, but their proudest service was in Cuba during the Spanish-American War, where they took part in the siege of Santiago and supported Teddy Roosevelt's Rough Riders in the charge of San Juan Hill. Later they fought well in the Philippine insurrection. Although the 10th Cavalry ran into trouble in Mexico fighting Pancho Villa's forces in 1916,[3] on the whole the black troops had the reputation of being tough, efficient, and brave, and places in the regiments were eagerly sought by young black men. Roosevelt said of the black soldiers in Cuba, "No troops could behave better than the colored soldiers,"[4] and ten years after the campaign he reminisced that "my own men, who were probably two thirds Southerners and Southwesterners, used to say, 'The 9th and 10th Cavalry are good enough to drink out of our canteens.'"[5] The man who as President created such a furor by breaking bread with Booker T. Washington could appreciate what a great tribute this condescension was intended to be.

With the gradual encroachment of racism and Jim Crow on American thought and life, black soldiers came to seem less and less desirable. The first serious racial clash in which they had been involved was at Brownsville. The next one, much more serious, erupted ten years later, also in Texas, this time at Houston, where a battalion of the 24th Infantry was stationed.[6] Jim Crow regulations in Houston had been dusted off in anticipation of the liberties that might be taken by the independent, self-confident, and not necessarily southern blacks of the regiment. The soldiers resented and resisted Jim Crow restrictions; troops whose brothers-in-arms had been judged worthy to use the Rough Riders' canteens refused to drink from water barrels assigned to black laborers. The police beat and arrested them when they resisted insults and discrimination. Matters grew steadily worse between town and camp, until on the night of August 23, 1917, less than two months after the terrible East St. Louis riot, racial violence exploded in Houston, bringing death to two black soldiers and seventeen white men. Exactly what happened was never established; white accounts were inconsistent, and the black soldiers would not talk. At a court-martial held early in December, thirteen soldiers were sentenced to death and summarily hanged a few days later, several months before their cases reached the judge advocate general for review; the same court sentenced forty-one soldiers to life imprisonment and four to shorter terms, and acquitted five. In later trials fifteen more soldiers were sentenced to death, twelve more to life imprisonment, and twenty-four to jail terms of two to fifteen years. But the citizens of Houston were not assuaged even by these harsh and legally questionable punishments; they insisted that the soldiers had meant to massacre every white man, woman, and child in the city, and demanded that the "mutineers" be tried on murder charges in Texas courts.[7]

If facts are obscure, causes are not. A War Department investigator said the trouble occurred because some of the soldiers "resolved to assert what they believed to be their rights as American citizens and United States soldiers."[8] A year after the riot, Secretary of War Baker reported to the President that the source of the trouble was the "enforcement of so-called Jim Crow laws. . . . There were some instances of assaults committed upon colored soldiers by Houston policemen and, generally, verbal disputes and clashes were of frequent occurrence."[9] Then, on August 23, after a raid on a crap game, a policeman arrested a black soldier "with perhaps unnecessary violence,"[10] Baker reported, and in a quarrel later that day with a policeman, a black corporal was shot at, hit over the head with a revolver, and arrested.[11]

Black Americans everywhere were stunned by the Houston trials and sentences, and especially by the summary hanging of the thirteen, who were regarded as martyrs. A "formidable petition," as Baker called it, urging commutation of sentence for the others, was presented by black citizens to the President. Baker's investigation convinced him that six more soldiers deserved the death sentence, but he recommended that the other ten death sentences be commuted, and that the President explain this was being done not because the trials were unjust but in recognition of the fidelity and valiant military service of Negroes and in the hope that never again would the United States Army be so disgraced. Wilson followed Baker's recommendation. Six, not sixteen, more soldiers were hanged; the rest remained in prison.[12]

After Houston, white Southerners declared that they would never again tolerate armed blacks stationed among them. This caught the War Department and the Army in a trap from which there appeared to be no exit. The first draft call was due in a few weeks. The military had decided that blacks as well as whites must be drafted and that southern camps, where temperate weather permitted year-round training of draftees, were absolutely necessary. It looked as if the South would not tolerate black draftees, but the Army needed them; furthermore, the black community was incensed by injustices at East St. Louis and Houston, and treatment that might further disaffect them must be avoided.[13]

For years black American citizens had sought more opportunities to serve in the military, and had been brushed off by the War Department and the Army. In 1895, Senator Joseph M. Carey of Wisconsin sponsored the application for a commission of a black civilian. This had evidently caused a small flurry in the War Department. The reply, edited from a draft with a rather lengthy legal explanation of why such a commission was not possible, said pithily that there was no vacancy then, or likely to occur in the future, for the applicant, adding carefully: "The laws make no distinction between white and colored applicants or white and colored regiments."[14] In 1907, when Emmett Scott requested that black units of field artillery and coast artillery be created, a negative report was made by a Major Willcox, quoting Dr. Frederick Hoffman's *Race Traits and Tendencies of the American Negro*, and concluding that there were just too few blacks capable of learning high-level skills, and that blacks were for the most part unreliable and nonmechanical. "It is surely not by way of discredit to the negro race," Major Willcox wrote, "that we assert it to be inferior to the white race in intelligence and mental ability. This fact is now recognized."[15] Further, Willcox cited the recent Brownsville trouble as an additional reason for denying Scott's request, pointing out the potential dangers "when these [black] companies are stationed in the South."[16] Whether or not the Army really believed blacks incapable of learning rather simple mechanical operations, the thesis had always provided a convenient lever for prying blacks out of combat units and dumping them into labor units, as for example in 1913, when the adjutant general asked to have as many as possible of the black cavalry recruits transferred to the Quartermaster Corps to be teamsters and packers.[17] The book that Army doctor R. W.

Shufeldt published in 1915, *America's Greatest Problem: The Negro*, would have provided the military with any further desired "scientific" proof in support of restricting Negroes to menial work, for to Shufeldt, as mentioned earlier, all people of any shade of black were equally "superstitious, treacherous, mendacious, and unreliable."[18] Small wonder, then, that a bill was introduced the year Shufeldt's book appeared which would have prohibited the appointment of any black man to commissioned or noncommissioned rank in the Army or Navy;[19] or that a request by blacks in 1916 for the creation of four new black regiments as part of the Army expansion was denied;[20] or that Mississippi's Senator Williams in April 1917 passed on to the Secretary of War the recommendation of a constituent "concerning the organization of an army of negroes to cultivate unused lands."[21]

With United States entry into the war, the War Department was besieged with letters asking for a place for black men in the Army.[22] Villard, for the NAACP, pointed out that it would be easier to enlist black soldiers than white because blacks had so few opportunities, "and there can be no question as to their being magnificent military material."[23] A letter from a black former National Guard captain pleaded for a "Place in the Sun" for young colored men by the formation of more black units and the use of educated black men to staff them.[24] A black organizer for the United Mine Workers wrote that blacks feared the War Department did not want them and longed for a word of reassurance.[25]

But black people were no more unanimous in their desire to "do their bit" than white people. Many blacks were too angry about Houston to see why they should rush to the colors. Archibald Grimke wrote a bitter poem about the Houston soldiers:

> What did she do, she who put that uniform on them,
> And bade them to do and die if needs be for her?
> Did she raise an arm to protect them? . . .
> Did she do anything in defense of her black soldiers?
> She did nothing.[26]

Socialist Hubert Harrison in 1917 founded the antiwar Afro-American Liberty League, and Marcus Garvey addressed its first rally. A black newspaper in Virginia was barred from the mails for urging blacks not to volunteer. Black people who knew of Belgium's brutality in the Congo were not much incensed by German atrocities in Belgium, and they felt that British imperial rule in Africa was no less savage than Germany's.[27] Trotter wrote, "We believe in democracy" but "we hold that this nation should enter the lists with clean hands. . . ." Although many blacks favored the cause of France, that was chiefly because they believed the French had been more liberal toward colored peoples; they had no particular animus against the Kaiser. If they had had any idea of the virulence of the Kaiser's "color psychosis" they might have felt differently.[28]

Still, it is probable that the majority of black people supported the war, although in different ways and degrees. At a black leaders' conference representing such diverse elements as Du-Bois, Moton, Terrell, Archibald Grimke, and Robert Abbott, some mildly patriotic resolutions were passed promising the loyalty of the black man in the war and asking only "for the minimum of consideration which will enable him to be an efficient fighter for VICTORY."[29] Trotter, who did not attend the conference, was willing to co-operate in the war effort, but hoped to gain in exchange legislation against lynching and discrimination in federal jobs and providing for integration in the armed forces.[30]

In the murky war atmosphere of xenophobia and suspected loyalties, it was wise to show patriotism in any way one could, and one way was to buy Liberty Bonds and War Savings Stamps. Negro civilians are said to have bought $250,000 worth. Some blacks, like some whites, bought cynically, for business or professional reasons rather than for patriotism. Other black people, particularly in the South, are said to have bought enthusiastically because it was the first time they had ever been asked to join in a common American effort.[31] Some of the most militant blacks were keenest to show their loyalty. Robert Abbott did it by buying $12,000 worth of bonds, "to substantiate my sincere feelings for the great cause of democracy."[32] DuBois did his part by an editorial in the *Crisis* headed "Close Ranks," calling on black people to "forget our special grievances and close our ranks shoulder to shoulder with our own white fellow citizens,"[33] and by asking blacks to co-operate in bond buying, food saving, and so on, because "when men fight together and work together and save together, this foolishness of race prejudice disappears."[34]

While DuBois was urging pure patriotism with no quid pro quos, and thus drawing down Monroe Trotter's wrath as "a rank quitter of the fight for our rights,"[35] he was under suspicion by the government of collaborating with the Japanese or the Mexicans or both against the interests of the United States. For years there had been rumors that blacks were hatching revolts or other plots with Mexicans, especially with the insurgent leader Pancho Villa, whom Wilson had for a time backed but whom he deserted in 1915 to support Venustiano Carranza for President of Mexico. As early as 1895 the emigration of a few southern Negroes to Wapimo, Mexico, had caused much excitement and fear in government, but the blacks were not welcomed in Mexico and had soon returned to their home states.[36] In 1910, a white American who had lived for about ten years in China and Japan reported that Japanese propaganda was being spread among American Negroes; an Army general commented about this report that six months earlier he would not have believed it, but that now the statements "are born out in such detail, even to the very name of one of the chief characters: Du Boise or Dubose" that the report no longer seemed exaggerated.[37] Along with the general's letter in its repository in the National Archives is a clipping from the New York *Sun* of August 7, 1910, describing a convention of Trotter's National Independent Political League. The article reported the League's denunciation of Brownsville, and its demand for an antilynch law, an end to disfranchisement, and other such "radical" reforms; it also gave a list of the delegates attending, in which the name "Prof. W. E. B. DuBois of Atlanta, Ga." had been underlined by someone, possibly the general.[38] In the context of the report and of the general's comments on it, presumably black demands for justice and equal rights were believed inspired or encouraged by Japanese propaganda.

Fears of a Japanese-Mexican alliance kept increasing. The Kaiser believed that 10,000 Japanese soldiers were training in Mexico and would co-operate with the Mexicans in a war on the United States, and it suited the purposes of German propaganda to put out rumors of this kind in the hope of keeping the United States Army stationed on its own borders. In 1911 the Army mobilized 20,000 troops on the Mexican border in response to such rumors. The Japanese had long been feared in California, and now the Kaiser's term "Yellow Peril" was heard throughout the country.[39] In 1916 the Secretary of War reported to the Adjutant General a letter alleged to have come from certain Japanese in California offering to help Mexico in case of war between that country and the United States.[40]

As for black sympathy with Mexico, there is evidence that at least after the war some of the most militant black people did regard that country as offering better opportunity and more freedom than the United States.[41] However, rumors had been current for years before the war of dealings between Mexicans and the black Regulars stationed on the border. Most dramatic, probably, was a rumor, which the Chicago *Defender* investigated in 1916, to the effect that Pancho Villa himself was a Negro; that he was, in fact, Henry O. Flipper, the first black West Point graduate (class of 1877), and formerly a lieutenant in the black Regulars. Abbott got information, however, which convinced him that Flipper could not be Villa because Flipper was actually working in the States as a porter, so the *Defender* dropped the matter. Perhaps Flipper was a porter in 1916, but the story is not that simple. He had been discharged from the Army after a court-martial found him guilty of mishandling, though not of embezzling, some Army moneys. He next appeared, according to the official West Point biographical register, as a special agent of the Department of Justice in the 1890s, and was described as a specialist in Mexican land laws. He was still a special Justice Department agent in 1901, and then an engineer in Mexico, and was reported at that time to be a member of the National Geographical Society and the Southwest Society and to have translated many Mexican codes into English.[42] Perhaps Flipper was sent to Mexico by the Justice Department to keep an eye on Mexican insurgents and on Japanese activities, or perhaps he found opportunities in Mexico that he did not have in the States; in any case, it is interesting that the Justice Department employed in Mexico a court-martialed black officer. It is also interesting (if the *Defender's* information was correct) that a man of Flipper's education, knowledge, experience, professional standing, and reliability—presumably the Justice Department thought him reliable enough to employ him in a sensitive area—that such a man, who happened to be black, could do no better in the United States than a porter's job. There is no good reason to doubt this; it is simply an unusually dramatic example of a national tragedy, the persistent misuse of capable black people, while little major willcoxes explained that no insult was intended by saying blacks were just stupid.

A still more dramatic example is the misuse of the most highly qualified and highest-ranking black officer in the United States Army, Colonel Charles Young, at a time when experienced officers were desperately needed. Young had been the third black West Point graduate, class of 1889, and was the only one still in the Army in 1917.[43] For an understanding of what followed, it must be remembered that most officers in black regiments were white, and also that the black regiments provided the only berths for the very few black officers. Upon graduation in September 1889, Young requested assignment to the 10th Cavalry. He was so appointed, but as an "additional" second lieutenant, there being no opening at the time for a permanent commission in that regiment. A few weeks later, Young learned that he had been transferred to the 25th Infantry. Young protested this change, as he was to protest other decisions when he felt them arbitrary or unjust, saying that he had already at great expense bought his cavalry uniform and gear, that he liked horses, and that he would rather wait for an opening in the 10th Cavalry; the Adjutant General answered that as soon as there was a cavalry opening Young's request for transfer would be considered. Before the end of October a suitable opening occurred in the 9th Cavalry, in which another black lieutenant, West Point graduate John Alexander, was serving. Young was offered the spot and accepted it at once.[44] But in January 1890, the acting commander of the 9th

Cavalry, Major Guy V. Henry, protested to the Adjutant General that Young was one colored officer too many, and that white officers would not apply for assignment to the regiment if he stayed; perhaps Young had been sent to the 9th in the misguided thought that he would be company for Lieutenant John Alexander, Major Henry added, but in fact "Lt. Alexander objects to Lt. Young's assignment, as keeping them together gives no breadth to their efforts to advance their race," and he adduced as an additional reason for transferring Young from the 9th to the 10th that it would be "for the benefit of the colored race. . . ."[45] Major Henry's request was denied for reasons set forth bluntly in an internal War Department memo: "It will be remembered that Young was first assigned as an *additional* in the 10th Cavy; that when in that position he was liable (as the Senior Cavy additional) to have a vacancy fall to him in a *white* reg^t at any moment; that to avoid this he was appt^d to a vacancy in the 25th Inf. (the Secty having decided he should be in a colored reg^t), and that, as Young had purchased a *Cavalry* uniform, and wanted Cavalry, he was transferred to the first vacancy in a colored Cavy reg^t, which happened to be *the 9th*. . . ."[46]

Young's first efficiency reports in the 9th Regiment, in 1890, contained severe complaints from a Colonel Tilford about Young's lack of experience and "indifference" and carelessness in his regard to duties. Young answered these charges by saying that any failure of his was unintentional and due to lack of practice, "as I would scorn to draw pay as an officer knowing that I had wilfully neglected my duty as one."[47] An efficiency report of December 1891, signed by a different commanding officer, Colonel James Biddle, was quite different. Either Young had improved greatly, or Biddle was a fairer judge: "Remarks: I saw this officer for 2 days. . . . He made but one mistake, I think from a misconception of the orders. . . . He was neat . . . his bearing was gentlemanly, and he was highly spoken of by the officers."[48] Even Colonel Tilford had found no fault with Young's conduct, habits, or care of his men.

Young served with his regiment at various posts until the end of 1911, when, now a major, he was detailed to the State Department to be sent as an adviser (although designated Military Attaché) to Liberia, to help the Liberian Government use a United States loan of $1,700,000 "in reorganizing and bringing under discipline an armed force of Liberians"—or, in nondiplomatic terms, to keep the Liberian Government and Army from collapsing before a popular insurrection, which would have been inimical to United States' interests. At the urging of Booker T. Washington that he could benefit the race, Young accepted the post. His assignment, it seems, included engaging in combat with the rebels—questionable employment for a State Department adviser—and he distinguished himself for bravery in rescuing a surrounded force of Liberians. In 1913 Young came down with a malignant malaria, commonly called "blackwater fever," and was relieved finally in 1915, to return to the States with kudos from Liberian officials for his services. He went back to his regiment, which was now the 10th Cavalry.[49]

Later that year, one Walter D. Denegre of New Orleans relayed to the War Department the distress of his ward, Second Lieutenant John Kennard of the 10th Cavalry, at being under the command of a black officer, Major Charles Young, and asked if something could not be done about this. The Chief of Staff replied that Kennard had got to take the same chance as other officers of the 10th Cavalry—which perhaps reflects Young's reputation for being a rather stern disciplinarian. However, although the Chief of Staff here defended Young as he probably would have any white officer of field rank against complaint from a second lieutenant, something does seem to have been done for Kennard. By 1917 Kennard (promoted first lieutenant) was accepted at aviation school, but soon flunked out; and when he returned to a regiment, it was not the 10th.[50]

In 1916 Young with his 10th Cavalry served as part of General John J. Pershing's forces in a punitive border expedition against Pancho Villa. Fighting was severe, and the regiment lost twenty-two men. Young must have performed well, because Pershing recommended him to command militia.[51] When America entered the war the following year, Colonel Young, then stationed with his regiment at Fort Huachuca, Arizona, was very eager for a command that would take him to France. There was to be a black draft, and it seemed perfectly reasonable to Young and to the whole black community that a high-ranking black West Pointer with an excellent record should occupy a position of command. But the politics of race then and there changed Young's future.

On July 25, 1917, President Wilson communicated to Secretary Baker a problem with which he had just been confronted by Senator John Sharp Williams of Mississippi. Williams had written him, Wilson told Baker, about First Lieutenant Albert B. Dockery of the 10th Cavalry, a Southerner, who "finds it not only distasteful but practically impossible to serve under a colored commander"; if Dockery remained under Colonel Young's command, the President said, it was hinted he might commit some "serious and perhaps even tragical insubordination," so could Baker arrange to have Dockery transferred?[52] Baker's immediate reaction was an irritated memo to Chief of Staff Tasker Bliss that Dockery "should either do his duty or resign." But he was in duty bound to add the President's question, "Is there anything we can do about it—?"[53] The answer was "there is nothing further to be done than the action that has been taken."[54] That action seems to be what Baker referred to in a letter of the next day, June 26, to Wilson. In it he told Wilson that there had been other complaints like Dockery's, and that to relieve the situation he was assigning Young "in connection with the training of colored officers for the new Army at Des Moines, Iowa. It seems likely that I will be able to tide over the difficulty in that way for at least a while."[55] But there was also a long-range plan. Baker's letter continued:

> In the meantime, Colonel Young, who is a West Point graduate and was for many years our attaché in Liberia and Hayti, is now definitely returned to the United States, but apparently is not in perfectly good health, and for the next two or three weeks he will be at the Letterman General Hospital in San Francisco under observation to determine whether his physical condition is sufficiently good to justify his return to active

service. There does not seem to be any present likelihood of his early return to the 10th Cavalry so that the
situation may not develop to which you refer.[56]

On June 29, Wilson conveyed that news to Senator Williams:

I have conferred with the Secretary of War about the
case of Captain Dockery,[57] and I believe that the
Lieutenant Colonel referred to will not in fact have
command because he is in ill health and likely when
he gets better himself to be transferred to some other
service.[58]

What is difficult to understand is how, *three days* after Baker
wrote the President that Young would be in the hospital under
observation for *two or three weeks* to determine his state of
health, Wilson could inform Senator Williams that he "*will not
in fact have command because he is in ill health*" [my italics].
The reasonable, if ugly, inference is that the President of the
United States, the Secretary of War, the General Staff, and the
staff of Letterman General Hospital conspired to relieve Colonel
Young of his command. Such chicanery would not have been
congenial to high-minded Wilson nor to generally fair Baker, so
they must have been really chagrined when on June 30 Williams
answered the President insolently that the action taken was not
satisfactory; Dockery wanted out of the 10th entirely. "You seem
to have forgotten," Williams wrote, "that it is a negro regiment
as well as a negro colonel."[59] Wilson, with some embarrassment,
passed this letter on to Baker. On July 7 Baker answered the
President that Young had already been "ordered before a retir-
ing board on the report of the surgeons that he was incapacitated
for duty by reason of Bright's Disease."[60] He would be sent to
Ohio to serve with the colored militia there, Baker said—evidently
the plan to assign him to the black OTC at Des Moines had fallen
through very quickly—and his replacement in the 10th Regiment

as well as all its other officers would be white, which should settle the Dockery matter.[61]

Young fought his retirement in every way he could without
embarrassing the service to which he was devoted. To prove his
physical fitness he rode on horseback from Chilicothe, Ohio, to
Washington, D. C. His personal physician testified that Young's
blood pressure was not abnormal for a man his age, which was
forty-nine.[62] In a letter to the Pittsburgh *Courier*, reprinted in
the *Crisis*, Young admitted to some elevation of blood pressure,
which he attributed to his work in the tropics, but insisted that he
was not then and never had been sick from it. He said he believed his retirement a mistake, but felt certain the Army doctors
had been "sincere and perfectly honest and upright in their
dealings," and pleaded that it not be made a race issue at a time
when the Administration had so many problems.[63] There may be
some doubt about Young's blood pressure; there seems no
doubt that the President yielded to political pressure from a leading southern Progressive, the first to applaud Wilson's battle cry
to Congress, and that the President participated in at least some
degree of conspiracy to deprive a citizen of his constitutional
rights.

For Young the problem was that he had no work. The Ohio
militia to which he had been assigned was mustered into the federal service, leaving him jobless.[64] He was offered a post in the
War Department assisting Emmett Scott, who had been named
the department's adviser on Negro affairs, but he declined.[65] He
wanted a command. The president of Wilberforce University,
where Young had taught military science, wrote to Baker asking
that Young be put in command of a regiment of black drafted
men, as the black community had counted on. Baker's response
was that service in Europe was most exacting, and that only officers in top physical condition could cope with the hardships;
furthermore, it was contrary to War Department policy to assign
to duty any officer who was in any way disqualified.[66] Still Young
persisted. In April 1918 he was again petitioning the War Department for work, now desperately suggesting that his retirement
might have been caused by a verbal error in reporting the recommendation of the retirement board, so that the words "active

duty" had been substituted for "active service." He was assured
that there had been no such error, and that he had been found
physically unfit for "active service."[67]

Still Young could have been given useful work to do, but he
was not. After spending the war period in wasteful assignments
to various camps, in November 1919 Young was reactivated so
that he could be sent back to Liberia for the kind of work he had
done before. If indeed Young was not fit for active duty, surely
it was at the least unwise to send him back to the tropics, where
he had been so ill. He suffered a recurrence of malignant malaria
and died in January 1922. He was given a fine send-off, with a
speech by Assistant Secretary of the Navy Franklin D. Roosevelt
and burial in Arlington National Cemetery.[68] But this was cheap
reparation to a conscientious soldier, to the black people whose
wartime service he could have so inspired, and, indeed, to the
country that had just fought a war to make the world safe. . . .

A short time after America went to war there were 14 officer-
training camps operating, but, despite Secretary Baker's insistence
that there would be no racial discrimination in the Army, not
one of them was open to blacks.[69] Joel Spingarn and James Weldon Johnson, acting for the NAACP, therefore proposed to Baker
a separate OTC for blacks. Baker thought it might be feasible
if enough candidates could be found. Spingarn at once presented
a list of 350 eligibles, and through the efforts of the Central Committee of Negro College men, organized at Howard University,
1,500 qualified applicants were found.[70] When the War Department announced the age qualification for black officer candidates
as between twenty-five and forty, many of the 1,500 college men
were disqualified by their youth, and a new drive was made to
find eligibles.[71] At last the Des Moines, Iowa, black OTC was
authorized, opening in July 1917 with 1,250 officer candidates for
a regulation ninety-day training period under the command of
General Charles C. Ballou.[72] Considering the many problems
surrounding the establishment and career of Des Moines,
Spingarn seems to have been justified in saying: "The army offi-

cers want the camp to fail. The last thing they want is to help colored men to become commissioned officers."[73]

A probe of official documents reveals that authorization of the black OTC was a result more of political than of military considerations. There were going to be two black combat divisions and many labor and service battalions, which the Army would much have preferred to staff with all white officers, but it was feared that perhaps dangerous dissatisfaction would spring up in the black community if they were not allowed to contribute any officers, only privates and noncoms. The Army therefore agreed to the black OTC, reluctantly and with the reservations that no more than 2 per cent of officer candidates should be black men (although 13 per cent or more of draftees were to be black); that few of these black officers should be given assignments (in the event, less than half the number of black officer candidates); that these few should be washed out as quickly as they could be charged with incompetence; and that there should in any case be no black officers of field rank—major or above.[74]

One thousand of those who went to Fort Des Moines were civilians, and the rest were from the four regiments of black Regulars, many of them noncoms. Morale at the camp was shaken by the riots at East St. Louis and Houston, which took place during the course. General Ballou and white West Point instructors set high standards and worked the candidates hard in exclusively infantry subjects. In free time, the students gave public drill exhibitions and concerts, and the local citizenry in general found their conduct exemplary. The shock to the students was all the greater, things having gone so well, when suddenly, a few days before the end of the 90-day course, it was announced without explanation that graduation would be postponed until October 15. The reason behind this was that the black draft call had been postponed from September until October 3, and the reason for that was that the War Department did not know where to send blacks once they were drafted (especially in the light of the Houston trouble), nor did there exist the separate facilities, attached to white training camps, which would be necessary for the segregated black troops; it would take months to prepare for black troops.[75] That being the case, "graduates [of Des Moines] will probably not be needed prior to that date, and meanwhile a further study can be made as to best disposition of these men,"[76] say the records of the War Department. For two reasons, this was considered by the Army a better solution than to graduate the Des Moines students at the promised date and then put them on inactive duty in the Officers' Reserve Corps: first, because many of them were overage in grade for ORC,[77] and second, because they would feel discriminated against and "would immediately use all the 'influence' they could bring to bear on the War Department to have themselves put on active duty, and pay status, as has been done with graduates commissioned from white OTC."[78] This thrifty thinking could not be revealed, naturally, to the black officer candidates. Instead, the 622 who were recommended for commissions were simply kept on for extra study, with the humiliating implication that they needed more instruction than white officer candidates, until plans for their utilization were more or less firm; the 316 who were not recommended were allowed to go home.[79]

In June, a second black OTC at another location had been under consideration,[80] but in October the Chief of Staff recommended that "another Training Camp for colored troops [sic] shall not be held at this time," either at Des Moines or elsewhere. Graduation at Des Moines was set for October 15, after which groups of the commissioned graduates were to report to various Army camps among which the black draft was to be distributed, the farthest south being Camp Meade in Maryland. Camp Des Moines was closed, and the War Department announced that black candidates in future would attend regular OTCs. No large number ever did.[81]

Artillery officer candidates were an exception. They had to attend regular artillery schools because no instruction had been given at Des Moines in any branch except infantry. These men had a particularly bad time, shifted from camp to camp, separately housed and messed, insulted by the camp commander and other officers, and at the end of the course, if they stuck it out, likely to find themselves commissioned only for battery service, a lowly, dangerous, and fatiguing duty.[82] The Army had been convinced for a long time, it will be remembered, that blacks were incapable of such responsible and technical work as artillery; still, some of the black graduate artillery officers were sent overseas with their artillery regiments, because, if they had been transferred to labor battalions as many Army officers would have preferred, they might have earned promotions and might thus outrank some of the white officers in the battalions. The fear of blacks rising to a position of command over whites lay behind much racial discrimination. The Army did not even want blacks and whites of equal rank in any one unit, and thus in a competitive situation; this was the reason for many of the transfers of black officers from unit to unit, although the excuse given was that they were inefficient.[83] The problems that sprang from these initial experiences with training and assigning black artillery officers persuaded Army authorities not to commission any more of them, although the reason alleged was that very few black men "have the mental qualifications to come up to the standards of efficiency of the Field Artillery officers."[84] The battle performance of black artillery officers proved the charge wholly unjustified, although an official report acknowledged that they had been poorly trained.[85]

Complaints came from many divergent quarters, from Du-Bois to Ballou, that black officer candidates were not as good as they might have been. They were not, in many cases, the fittest young men available, nor the best-educated.[86] Ballou said the War Department did not fulfill Baker's intention of training good officers for the black draft division: "For the parts of the machine requiring the finest steel, pot metal was provided."[87] Two black officers complained that the highest commissions went to ignorant Regulars who had given satisfaction as privates and noncoms, to passive Hampton Institute men, and to men with political pull, to ensure that the black division would fail. The case of one of the very few black majors, reported in 1917 by Robert Moton to Emmett Scott, seems to bear out this accusation; this man, who had been a messenger in the Adjutant General's office, was a notorious toady to white officers, weakly accepting whatever they said and did "whether humiliating, and embarrassing or not," Moton said, and thus making himself so disliked by the men under him that white officers could point to their hostility as proof of the Army's conviction that black soldiers did not want black officers.[88]

Perhaps it was only the toady, the weakling, who could survive unhurt the humiliations heaped upon black officers both Stateside and, later, abroad. The matter of the salute was a constant irritant. A congressman from South Carolina informed Secretary Baker that having to salute a Negro made young southern whites "do violence and treason to the principles which are the very foundation of southern social safety, and offend the women who gave them life," and that insistence on the salute would cause trouble.[89] This is how one camp commander is quoted as having tried to assuage his young white officers: "I met some junior officers who said they were not keen on saluting Negro officers. They would not feel that way if they understood the spirit of the salute. If one of them came from a town where there was an old Negro character, one of those old fellows who do odd jobs and is known to everybody, he'd at least nod his head and say, 'Howdy, uncle.' Now suppose through some freak of nature this old Negro should be transplanted into an officer's uniform; the salute would be merely saying to him, 'Howdy, uncle,' in a military way."[90] A black first lieutenant in a draft regiment bitterly recalled in later years the segregation and insults in the Army: "The hate and scorn heaped upon us Negro officers by our Americans . . . convinced me that there was no sense in dying for a world ruled by them. Our battleground was not in France, it was in America."[91] Professor Rayford Logan, who had been a first lieutenant in a World War I black regiment, expressed equally bitter memories of the crowding in segregated barracks, of the separate seating at mess and entertainments; twenty-two-year-old Lieutenant Logan, fresh from the free atmosphere of Williams College in Massachusetts, was so insulted and humiliated that he tried to be discharged in France at the war's end rather than return home.[92]

There must have been some northern white officers who ignored or perhaps even enjoyed the continual abasement of black officers, but the policy of "keeping the Negro in his place" was established by southern officers, of whom there were many in the black draft units because they were believed by the Army to know "how to handle blacks." The deliberate degradation of black officers made it almost impossible for them to develop the self-confidence an officer must possess in order to lead troops, or to inspire the kind of trust that would make troops follow. When trouble came, in battle, where firm command and instant obedience were vital, that was the major reason for it. Considering all the disadvantages under which black officers labored, and the continual efforts of efficiency boards to discredit them, it is amazing how many of them survived—650 combatant and 418 noncombatant black officers as of August 1918[93]—and how little trouble did occur in battle.

Of the 100,000 black men who served overseas, more than 30,000 were originally slated for combat; the others, all drafted men, were to be Army laborers.[94] The laborers would have numbered an additional 25,000 or so, if the wishes of the War Plans Division had prevailed. General Lytle Brown wrote the Chief of Staff: "It is believed that organizations contemplating their [Negroes'] service as laborers and of a noncombatant nature would be best. However, on the other hand, they desire combat service and public sentiment, to a certain extent, demands their organization."[95] So the disposition of the black draft, like the question of black officers, was dictated by political expediency.

About 25,000 of the best-qualified draftees were organized into the 92d Infantry Division, a full division with the prescribed artillery, engineers, hospital and ambulance, and other supporting units. Commanding this large organization of black men and a number of black officers was General Ballou, in the spot that black people had hoped Colonel Charles Young would occupy. One other regiment of combat troops was carved out of the draft to fill out the four regiments which would be the total complement of what was called a "provisional" division (as against a full division), the 93d Infantry. In that division, the drafted men were formed into the 371st Regiment; the other three regiments were organized almost entirely (except for a few from the draft in the 372d) from the sizable black National Guard companies of New York and Illinois and the smaller companies of Washington, D.C.,

Tennessee, Ohio, Massachusetts, Maryland, and Connecticut. The
Guard companies came to a total of between 5,100 and 5,600,
with 175 officers, of whom 125 were black.[96] When they were
combined to make the 93d Division, white officers were added
and gradually black officers were dropped; practically all would
have been dropped but for the opposition of Secretary Baker.

To recapitulate, what had delayed the graduation of the Des
Moines officer candidates was a delay in calling up the black
draft; and what had caused that delay was uncertainty in the
War Department as to how to use black draftees and where to
train them, once they were drafted. The South protested vehemently that it wanted none of them in southern camps, no more
Houston riots. The President was warned not to have any black
troops sent to South Carolina for training, because "the enemies of
Administration . . . would want no bigger club. It would be almost fatal."[97] This information Wilson passed along to Baker
with a note: "Dear Baker: I would very much fear the results of
this (if it is true) because of [Governor Coleman] Blease and
the passions he would rejoice to raise. W. W."[98]

And indeed, the 369th Infantry, 93d Division, then still called
the 15th New York National Guard and headed by socially prominent white New Yorkers, found Spartanburg, South Carolina,
geared for trouble when it arrived at Camp Wadsworth about six
weeks after the Houston riot. Although the officers of the regiment defended the behavior of their men, within two weeks an
alarmed War Department snatched the 369th out of Spartanburg
and as quickly as possible shipped it abroad, making this the first
black combat unit to arrive in France. The 370th Regiment (the
8th Illinois National Guard) was sent to train at Camp Logan, the
Houston trouble spot itself, which does not seem to have been
very wise. There were, of course, racial incidents in the tense
city, and although no major clash occurred, the 370th was
quickly prepared for embarkation and removed from Logan with
dispatch. Doubtless one way in which the 370th offended was in
having a full complement of black officers, from Colonel Franklin
A. Dennison down, which outraged Southerners. The 372d Regiment was also sent South, to Camp Stuart, Virginia; the very
rigid discipline of its white southern colonel, Glendie B. Young,

seems to have made this regiment less objectionable to Southerners than the 369th and 370th, but that same rigid discipline brought the morale of the regiment extremely low. In the fourth regiment of the division, the draft 371st, most officers were white and southern. DuBois described them as "arrogant and overbearing men," who were said to be inexperienced, insecure, and not happy about commanding black troops. But the 371st shaped up well physically, after about two thirds of the original 3,380 had been weeded out as unfit.[99] Like the 372d, the 371st had little trouble with local whites. Writer Lawrence Stallings observed: "The different attitude [of white Southerners] toward Negroes still under white masters was one for psychologists, not soldiers, to ponder."[100] His observation would explain why the New York and Illinois Guard regiments were the ones to have most trouble, or, at least, threatened trouble, because they were the ones with most men who were their own masters, many of them middle-class and educated people.[101]

Nevertheless, perhaps overcautiously, the Army split up the draft 92d Division among more than half a dozen camps in the North, with the result that men and officers in the same regiment sailed for France without any previous common experience. No other full division in the Army had been so fragmented throughout training. This circumstance was a particular hardship on the black officers, many of them newly commissioned Des Moines graduates, who had no opportunity for building relationships with the men they were to command. In addition, DuBois claimed, the black officers assigned to the 92d were not the best available, and the War Department refused to transfer to the division well-trained personnel, without which it was bound to be a failure; and DuBois asked, "Is it possible that persons in the War Department wish this division to be a failure?"[102] Nor were the white officers of the division the best available material; they were assigned not for merit but because they were "surplus" National Guard officers, especially if they were Southerners who had had previous experience with Negroes.[103]

Racial friction in the division was chiefly internal, between the white officers and the black officers and men, or between members of the black division and the white soldiers who occupied the main section of each camp. But at Funston, in Kansas, which was divisional headquarters, trouble was not restricted to camp. At and about that camp, racial feelings were always ready to burst forth in violence. After an alarming incident in the nearby town of Manhattan, when a black sergeant tried to buy admission to a theater and was refused (in violation of Kansas law), General Ballou stepped in firmly. He issued, simultaneously, orders to investigate the action of the theater owner and an order to his men known as Bulletin No. 35, chewing out the sergeant for provoking the incident.[104] Bulletin No. 35 won among blacks an undeserved reputation as the epitome of Army discrimination. There are, in fact, expressions of discrimination a thousand times worse than Ballou's Bulletin No. 35, but they have reposed quietly in War Department archives, whereas Ballou's bulletin was published and circulated by its tactless, self-righteous author. Ballou began mildly enough, saying that the sergeant "is strictly within his legal rights in this matter, and the theater manager is legally wrong." But, he continued, "the Sergeant is guilty of the *greater* wrong in doing anything, no matter how *legally* correct, that will provoke racial animosity." And further, "The Division Commander repeats that the success of the Division, with all that that success implies, is dependent upon the good will of the public. That public is nine-tenths white. White men made the Division, and they can break it just as easily if it becomes a trouble maker."[105]

The camp seethed with anger, the NAACP protested, but Ballou blundered onward in an address to his men saying, "I simply *will not* tolerate having the success of this camp, with all that that success means to your race, ruined by the acts of a selfish and conceited handful of men" whose ambition and pride "have entirely obscured the great issue of demonstrating physical, mental and moral fitness for the responsibilities of commanders and leaders of men."[106] Whether Ballou was well-meaning and rigid, or arrogant and racist, as his division believed, he then and there lost the respect of the 92d, and severely damaged its effectiveness as a fighting organization.

The two combat divisions, although they were the pride of the black community, represented only a small proportion of black troops. The others were the great bulk of the black draft, and that included practically every man of draft age who could meet the minimal Army criteria for mental and physical adequacy.

One of the documents in the archives that makes Bulletin No. 35 read like a love letter is a long memorandum prepared by Colonel E. D. Anderson, Chairman of the Operations Branch of the General Staff, headed "Disposal of the Colored Drafted Men."[107] Only a small part of the black draft—"the cream"— Anderson wrote, was capable of combat; the rest were of the "ignorant illiterate day laborer class" without the "physical stamina to withstand the hardships and exposure of hard field service. . . ." Anderson recommended that these men be organized into fifty reserve labor battalions, employed at useful labor in the States ("there is no great amount of training required"), and picked for physical fitness just before sailing because about half of them would be found to have venereal diseases. The unfit would be kept busy at useful work in the States "instead of laying around camps accomplishing nothing of value, getting sicker and in trouble generally," and perhaps meanwhile the doctors could cure them. General Pershing had been complaining of "colored stevedore troops arriving [in France] with tuberculosis, old fractures, extreme flat feet, hernia, venerial [sic] disease," Anderson said, and asked that such men not be sent to him. Anderson cited figures showing that of 3,604 black drafted men examined at a port of embarkation, 1,559, or 43.25 per cent, were found physically "ineffective." But, Anderson said, "it would be no use to exempt such men from the draft"—that is, the colored draft. "Such exempted men would be replaced by others of a similar kind and the draft boards would run through the colored race in the United States and exempt a large part of them. In these days of conservation," Anderson judiciously pointed out, "when every rag and bone and tin can is saved, human beings cannot be wasted. These colored men have to be inducted into the service by draft in their turn and put right to work at useful work. . . ." A battalion or company of them could be placed in each cantonment or camp to keep the roads passable, unload supplies, cut wood, and so forth, freeing the white men in the camps for un-interrupted combat instruction. Separate quarters would have to be built for the black battalions, but they could live in tent camps until the cold weather (Anderson's memo was dated May 16, 1918). The labor battalions should be staffed with white officers and noncoms "unfitted for service overseas." There was no need to worry about sectional race prejudices in assigning labor battalions to camps: "These camps are mainly situated in the southern states. . . . Each southern state had negroes in blue overalls working throughout the state with a pick and shovel. When these colored men are drafted they are put in blue overalls (fatigue clothes) and continue to do work with a pick and shovel in the same state where they were previously working.[108] If it is assumed that trouble will occur between whites and colored, that encourages it to occur, but if negroes are sent where they are needed and the possibility of trouble ignored there is not much probability of trouble occurring." (Nevertheless, the War Department took the extra precaution in case of racial clashes of maintaining a "safe ratio" at any camp where blacks were stationed, that ratio having been set at two whites to one black.[109])

The detail in which Anderson's long memorandum set forth plans for using the black draft for labor makes all the more conspicuous the vagueness of his recommendation of an avenue of escape for black draftees of higher capabilities by transfer to a combat training company, which each labor battalion was to include; as to the mechanics of such transfers, Anderson said only: "It will not be attempted to go into the minute details of just how the men are to be transferred from the three straight labor companies of the reserve labor battalion to the training company and from the training company to combatant troops. These are details easy to arrange if the general policy is approved."[110] In fact, the opposite of this procedure was much more general, with individual commanders frequently trying to convert black combat troops or the ambiguous depot brigades and pioneer infantry into strictly labor troops. By the end of the war, 80 per cent of black troops were at labor duties, and only 20 per cent ever saw combat, contrary to Baker's pledge to DuBois by which about 65 per cent would have been labor troops and 35 per cent combat troops.[111]

A look at draft figures shows the rag-and-bone-and-tin-can school of thought at work. Of all men in the first draft call, 51.65 per cent of blacks were put in Class I—immediately available— but only 32.53 per cent of whites; of Class I blacks, 36 per cent were inducted, but of Class I whites only 24 per cent. About 22 per cent of all draftees taken into the service at that time were black, although blacks formed only about 10.5 per cent of the total population. White men with the kinds of handicaps described by Anderson and deplored by Pershing were exempted from the draft or put in the last category for call-up. The extremely low standard set for black draftees explains why Army doctors found, on the basis of sick reports, that there was almost 20 per cent more sickness among black troops than among white troops. The figure would doubtless have been still higher if officers had not made it so difficult for blacks to report sick, but there was such a general conviction among white officers that blacks were natural malingerers that many very sick men were denied medical attention. Considering the rag-and-bone-and-tin-can criterion for black draftees, the finding of psychologists that whereas the average mental age (IQ) of white draftees was 13.15, that of black draftees was 10.1, seemed reasonable. The Army Alpha and Beta tests on which these findings were based have long been discredited as scientific measurements, but this did not prevent military authorities from exploiting the IQ figures as a reason for keeping the Negro in an inferior position.[112]

In October 1917, when blacks were drafted, the Chief of Staff ordered the establishment of stevedore and labor units to employ about 70 per cent of colored servicemen, but he cautioned that the plan should be kept confidential.[113] The black labor companies and battalions formed under this and later orders were staffed with white Army officers rejected for overseas service, who were more overseers than officers, and with white noncoms, except for a few black corporals. Even these few corporals were resented. Lieutenant Colonel U. S. Grant protested, "Everyone who has handled colored battalions knows that the gang bosses must be white if any work is to be done."[114] General Lytle

Brown assured the Chief of Staff that this was indeed so. "These labor companies are expected to work," General Brown said.[115]

Work they did, throughout the war, often under inhumanly cruel conditions of housing and feeding, deprived of medical care, physically abused by their overseer-officers, and only occasionally receiving the training and schooling they were supposed to get and that white labor troops did get. In France, the black labor battalions—later renamed the Services of Supply (SOS) at the suggestion of General Pershing, who thought that title carried more dignity and sounded less like a penal institution than "labor battalions"—performed prodigious work feats. Stevedores unloaded 5,000 tons of material in a day, took off a ship's entire cargo of coal in eighteen hours, and unloaded 62,000 tons of flour in six days; a labor battalion cut 40,000 cubic meters of wood in 108 days.[116] Hundreds of examples of such herculean labors could be cited. Leisure time was scanty, and when there was any, the men could not get passes; if they had got them there was almost no place to go, because neither they nor, in most cases, black combat troops were permitted to mingle with French civilians,[117] and the service organizations provided very little for them in the way of recreation. The YMCA, a haven for white servicemen, was strictly segregated, and only occasionally was a leaky hut or tent provided for black troops. It was not until the end of the war, when black labor troops grew dangerously restive doing the horrid task of reburying the war dead in the American cemetery at Romagne, that the YMCA agreed to send a few black women to staff Y facilities in France in the hope that they could tranquilize the nervous, rebellious black gravediggers.[118]

The military were generous in praising the performance of black laborers in uniform. General Frederick Palmer said "the powers of darkness came to the rescue" when French stevedores proved unequal to handling the vast cargoes brought by American ships.[119] The records contain some complaints that the black laborers were lazy, but many more tributes to "smiling darkeys," "cheerful black boys," and "the lilt of darky voices" as the SOS or pioneers performed some heroic and often dangerous task. As in civilian life, almost everyone was willing to give the "good"

Negro his due as an unskilled laborer, commonly considered his proper job.[120]

Combat was not considered the Negro's proper job, and praise of black fighting troops is harder to find—except, interestingly enough, in unit histories by white field officers who lived and fought alongside their troops. But General Pershing was delighted to have the 93d Division shipped out to France as early as it was,[121] because he had promised the French Army four American regiments, and these were four he felt he could spare. The French drew no color line and were happy to get the black regiments. When Colonel William Hayward of the 369th told a French colonel that his men felt like foundlings dumped on the doorstep of the French, the French officer replied, "Welcome leetle black babbie!"[122] Although the black soldiers thoroughly enjoyed the brotherly attitude of the French, the transfer presented many problems: different language and customs, different rations and uniforms, and especially different weapons from those they had trained with. However, if the French had not taken these regiments, the regiments would almost certainly have been absorbed into the pioneer infantry, which was virtually indistinguishable in function from the SOS.[123]

With only the sketchiest additional training, the various regiments of the division were thrown into action beginning in mid-April 1918, fighting in major operations from then until the Armistice, and earning a good deal of praise from their own officers, in most cases, and from the French. As early as May, Sergeant Henry Johnson and Private Needham Roberts of the 369th provided Americans with two bona fide black heroes; for their courage in routing a German patrol and killing many of the enemy, they were awarded the Croix de Guerre, the first in the war to be won by Americans, as their commanding officer boasted. By the end of the war the 93d was loaded with honors. The 369th Regiment as a unit and about 170 individuals of the regiment won the Croix de Guerre; the other regiments collected their share of medals, with the 371st, the draft organization, doing as well as or better than the three National Guard regiments.[124]

The 369th was probably the most fortunate regiment of the division, both for the strong support of its commanding officers, and for the fame won by the regimental band, led by Lieutenant (later Captain) James Reese Europe, which became known throughout the service and which popularized American jazz in France. Morale in the regiment was excellent, which was particularly important because, according to its commander, the 369th was under fire for 191 days, longer than any other regiment in the American Army.[125]

Unfortunately, the black officers of the regiment did not last to enjoy their share of the glory and honors of the 369th, because all five who started out with the regiment were transferred elsewhere during the course of the war.[126] The other regiments that had black officers went through the same experience. The 370th began to lose its black officers as soon as it docked in France. Colonel Dennison was replaced by a white commanding officer, Colonel T. A. Roberts, who won the bitter hatred of the troops by getting rid of other black officers whom he considered weak. After some hard action in the summer of 1918, in which the 370th gave an excellent account of itself, the regiment ran into trouble in a confused engagement in the last offensive of the war, in which elements seem to have lost their way and perhaps overshot their objectives. For this the blame was put by the Army inspector on the inefficiency of some black officers, although Colonel Roberts, thought by the men to be rankly racist, was not so censorious; and two black officers of the 370th, Duncan and Patton, were singled out for praise by the commander of the French division to which the regiment was attached, so obviously not all black officers were at fault.[127] The 372d, which was the other National Guard regiment, lost almost all its black officers by action of an efficiency board convened at the request of its commanding officer. The result was a sharp drop in the regiment's morale, and a buildup of tension to such a degree that white officers were ordered to go armed at all times; one of them shot a black soldier. This situation developed, unfortunately, at a time when the regiment was to have been brought to peak form for the Meuse-Argonne offensive, and probably, therefore, contributed to the extremely heavy casualties suffered by the 372d during a brief exposure to fire in late September—although, it is interesting to note, a white lieutenant said the casualties occurred because the troops refused to retreat or surrender.[128] The 371st Regiment, formed from the draft, had no black officers from the start and so lost none. With no competition on the officer level, white officers were rather generous in praising the work of the troops. Lieutenant Allen G. Thurman wrote home concerning his men of the 371st in the Meuse-Argonne attack: "You will have to hand it to these coons as they certainly did some fight-ing." Furthermore, he said, those men withstood constant shelling days and nights on end, in foul weather, without shelter or food; but "our men waded right into them [the enemy] from the start and they didn't seem to want to be bothered with prisoners."[129] A major said, "I'd take my chance of going anywhere with these black soldiers at my back."[130]

It was clear, however, that the brave soldiers were "coons" and that "anywhere" was restricted to battlefields. Socially, the color line never wavered. The regimental intelligence officer of the 371st issued a dispatch urgently requesting French civil authori-ties to see that their people avoided "undue social mixing" with the black troops, because such behavior would establish expec-tations that could cause a dangerous situation when the troops returned home.[131]

The 92d Division did not have the luck to be assigned to the French. The command troubles that had so plagued the division stateside made the trip overseas with it, and, in fact, took on a new dimension in France. General Ballou could do nothing right in the eyes of General Robert Bullard, who during the latter part of the war was given command of the American Second Army, of which the 92d was part. Bullard's own words show him for an uncompromising white supremacist and black detractor, as was also Ballou's chief of staff, Colonel Allen J. Greer, who reported to Senator Kenneth McKellar of Tennessee, and later to the Army War College, how cowardly and ineffective blacks were, especially black officers.[132] It is significant that the name appearing at the bottom of Bulletin No. 35 is that of Allen J.

Greer, although he says it was written by command of Major General Ballou. As for Bullard, he wrote in his war diary: "Poor Negroes! they are hopelessly inferior."[133] But his fire was really aimed at Ballou, who in Bullard's opinion was largely responsible for the alleged failure of the 92d Division: "I'm inclined to think he [Ballou] will have to be S.O.S.'ed and I'll have to get this done."[134] (By "S.O.S.'ed" he presumably meant transferred to that much less prestigious arm of the service.) Ballou, for his part, felt such men as Bullard and Greer were "rabidly hostile to the idea of a colored officer," and "will never give the negro the square deal that is his just due."[135]

In September, soon after the 92d Division had had its first taste of the miseries of trench warfare and suffered its first casualties, the War College issued a new table of organization for the division that should have satisfied those who could not endure the idea of black officers. By the new table, all positions in the division that were slated for majors or colonels, and about half the captains' positions, were designated for white officers only. This effectively prevented black officers from rising above the rank of captain and made it impossible for more than a few to go so far. In practice, it limited all but a very small number of black officers to the rank of lieutenant, there being no jobs into which they might be promoted no matter how competent they were. The table further specified that "colored officers who are incompetent will not be retained," but no such rule was applied to the incompetent white officers of whom Ballou complained. Black officers were continually being dropped or transferred, so that the 92d, which had started out with 82 per cent black officers, ended the war with only 58 per cent. In short, by running as hard as he could, the best the black officer could do was stay in place. By extension, the black noncom could not win promotion to lieutenant because no vacancies would occur.[136]

If anything more were needed to break down morale in the division, the steadily tightening isolation of the men from any social contact with the French people finished the job. Strictures against treating blacks as equals were circulated wherever the 92d went. White officers told French civilians that all blacks were lazy, dirty, liars; Rayford Logan recalls that when he would take his men to bathe in a little swimming hole, French people would gather around to watch them, because, Logan learned, they had been told all Negroes had tails and wanted to see this sight.[137] The French were warned of Negro lust and bestiality. Rape was alleged to occur frequently, and was adduced as an excuse for ever-increasing oppression, with hourly attendance checks on the troops and prohibition of virtually all passes. There is a suspicious inconsistency in reports on the incidence of rape. Bullard in late summer 1918 said there had been fifteen cases; Greer wrote McKellar that there had been thirty cases, and that not only did the black officers fail to control their men but were themselves "engaged largely in the pursuit of French women. . . ."[138] More reliable military records indicate that only one man was convicted of rape and five of attempted rape during all six months that the 92d served in France; and that the one rape conviction was in a unit commanded by white company officers. Considering the psychotic dread of sex relations between black men and white women, charges of rape were the surest way to hang the black man, literally or figuratively. The men were told that General Pershing would send the division back to the States or use it for labor "if efforts to prevent rape were not taken more seriously."[139]

Considering the hardships of those oppressed and vilified men, not only in the 92d but throughout the black troops, it is astonishing how few of them deserted. Some of the German propaganda leaflets were aimed directly and cogently at black troops, asking them what they were fighting for, since they did not enjoy freedom, democracy, or opportunity at home, but rather were the victims of lynching and every sort of injustice; don't be cannon fodder, the leaflets urged, but come over to the German lines, where you will find friends who will like you, respect you, and help you.[140] Tempting as the leaflets must have seemed, especially to men under fire in trenches knee-deep with mud, there seems to have been no significant number of desertions. Sometimes there were hundreds missing after a battle, but almost all, it turned out, were wounded or had lost their own units and attached themselves to some other.[141]

For those seeking finally and totally to discredit blacks as combat soldiers and officers, an opportunity presented itself in the last battle operation of the 92d Division, the Argonne offensive of late September 1918. Only one regiment, the 368th, which went in first while the other three were held in reserve, became seriously disoriented and disorganized—in fact, only the 2d Battalion of the regiment. But the alleged failure of that one battalion of one regiment was later generalized to include the entire division, and beyond the division, all black combat troops and officers.

Through the reports of officers emerge flashes of a bitter five-day battle, beginning September 25,[142] under shattering enemy machine-gun fire, over wooded, broken terrain held for years by the Germans and fortified heavily with barbed-wire entanglements, with only sporadic support from the French artillery, the artillery of the 92d having been detached and assigned to other units. The planned role of the 368th was as a liaison unit between French soldiers on its left and the 77th Division on its right, and not, apparently, as an assault unit prepared to encounter heavy enemy opposition. The men had not been given the necessary heavy-duty wirecutters, signal flares, and grenade launchers, and had not been supplied with maps. Communications with the forces to the left and the right were almost immediately lost and never re-established. Through days and nights under heavy fire, companies and platoons were ordered to advance or withdraw according to no concerted plan; headquarters was left far in the rear. The 2d Battalion particularly was unable to locate its commanding officer, Major Max Elser, for orders; some of the men turned back, probably on an order to retreat, although they were later accused of cowardice and panic. Somehow, through the chaos, parts of the regiment managed to break through to a relatively safe area behind the German lines and to establish contact with each other. After five days of fighting, the 368th was pulled out, in disgrace. A number of black officers were immediately relieved, and many were later subjected to court-martial. Some reputation might have been retrieved in subsequent actions, General Ballou believed, "had there not been too much eagerness to get the negroes out while the credit was *bad*, as many preferred it should remain."[143] From that time through World War

II and after, the alleged failure of the 92d Division was cited over and over again in proof that black men ought never be used as combat troops, particularly not under the command of black officers.[144]

To an unprejudiced mind, any failure of the 368th Regiment seems amply accounted for by the physical handicaps under which it operated. In any case, its failure was no more serious than, for example, that of the white 7th Division, to whose aid a battalion of the 367th Regiment was sent when it was pinned down by enemy fire.[145] As for the unfortunate 2d Battalion, it labored under the additional and devastating handicap that its commander, Major Elser, suffered an emotional or nervous collapse at the very outset of the battle. Records and statements totally support the complaints of black officers that they received vague and conflicting orders to advance and withdraw, and that couriers they sent could not locate Major Elser for clarification; a statement by Major Elser reveals that he did indeed, at one point, order a withdrawal, without being specific as to how far back the troops were to go. Black officers of the battalion said Elser was a case of "battle fatigue," and a black doctor reported that Elser afterward was hospitalized for psychoneurosis. Adding weight is the statement of Elser's commanding officer, Colonel Brown, that on September 28—when the battle situation was at its worst—he decided to relieve Elser because of "physical exhaustion." Weightiest of all is Major Elser's own admission that he was a mental and physical wreck during the battle.[146] Yet no one in authority came forward and said Elser had defaulted because he cracked under the strain of battle, and that what his battalion had suffered was misfortune, not failure. It is difficult if not impossible to believe that, had a white battalion suffered a leadership collapse while under fire, the troops, noncoms, and officers would have been pilloried to save the reputation of one sick major.

Somehow, although many recommendations for decorations were denied, twenty-one members of the 92d Division received the Distinguished Service Cross; the 367th, which called itself the Buffalo regiment, was awarded a unit Croix de Guerre. Black officers and noncoms of the field artillery, that branch long held too technical for Negroes, won special praise; no efficiency boards sat in those regiments, and they were exceptional also in that lieutenants were promoted and noncoms moved up to fill the resulting vacancies.[147] Perhaps if the 92d had been lucky enough to be detached to the French the honors would have equaled those amassed by the 93d.

The military for some reason respects high casualty figures as an index of performance, and an additional cause of dissatisfaction with the black soldiers was that they were thought not to have lost the appropriate amount of blood. The 92d Division, in action for only the last three months of the war, lost 185 killed, 1,495 wounded, and 17 captured. The 93d, parts of which had seen action for up to four months longer, had 574 killed, 2,009 wounded, and four captured.[148] These are War Department figures; other sources differ, from slightly to grossly. Colonel Hamilton Fish, commanding officer of the 371st Infantry Regiment during the war, claimed that the combined casualties of the 369th, 370th, and 371st regiments represented a greater proportion of the personnel of those regiments than could be claimed by any other American organization except the 1st and 2d divisions.[149]

Black soldiers were not permitted to march in the Allied victory parade in Paris, nor were they depicted in the heroic war mural, Le Pantheon de la Guerre, although black colonial troops of the Allied nations were represented in both. The Army's plan for black troops after the war was to keep them under tight control and ship them home as rapidly as possible. Deprived of leaves or of any chance to blow off steam and celebrate the war's end, the men were sullen and rebellious. Robert Moton was sent out by the War Department to make soothing speeches to the black troops, and to adjure them to be well-behaved when they got home. Rayford Logan, then Lieutenant Logan, recalls his efforts to prevent racial violence at the port city of Brest, crammed with restive troops awaiting sailing orders. Combat soldiers were the first to be gotten off French soil. By mid-February 1919, the 369th was proudly stepping up Fifth Avenue and into

Harlem, to the cheers of throngs of New Yorkers and the music of the regimental band. Black citizens turned out to watch their soldiers marching home in Chicago, Cincinnati, Des Moines, Cleveland, Columbus, Kansas City, and other northern urban centers in which black communities had grown up because of the migrations of the first two decades of the century.[150]

In demography, geography, psychology, and training for the demands of modern industrial society, black people had undergone vast changes in those decades, especially during the war years. A country that could have openheartedly welcomed progress by a large body of its citizens, who happened to be black, could have benefited greatly by it. But black progress was undesirable to many whites throughout America and intolerable to some, especially in the South. Before the black soldiers went overseas, a white speaker had told a group of them in New Orleans: "You niggers are wondering how you are going to be treated after the war. Well, I'll tell you, you are going to be treated exactly like you were before the war; this is a white man's country and we expect to rule it."[151] He was a good prophet. America got right down to the job of wiping out any foreign notions of equality the black troops might have picked up in France.

CHAPTER 10

Home to White America

We *return.*
We *return from fighting.*
We *return fighting.*

Make way for Democracy! We saved
it in France, and by the Great Je-
hovah, we will save it in the United
States of America, or know the reason
why.

W. E. B. DuBois,
editorial in the *Crisis,*
May 1919

It must be entered on the plus side of that horrible war that
for a year or two black people enjoyed a status nearer parity
with whites than at any time since Reconstruction. When the
nation needed its full manpower, it grudgingly bartered to blacks
some rights and privileges in exchange for their co-operation.
Blacks had been included in the draft and had been trained as
officers; some black troops had been given guns and had served
in combat. Also, to satisfy pressure from black newspaper publishers, a black newsman, Ralph W. Tyler, had become the first
accredited Negro war correspondent, and he sent back word of
the black soldiers to a rapidly expanding black press. In 1919
a dozen black papers had circulations of 20,000 or more, and
there were scores with smaller circulations; the war boom pushed

the *Defender's* circulation to 150,000, that of the *Crisis* to 100,000, and in addition there were half a dozen black magazines with significant circulations.[1]

Back in Washington, blacks had gained a special assistant on Negro affairs in the War Department, Emmett Scott, and a Bureau of Negro Economics, headed by George Haynes, in the Department of Labor. During Haynes's brief tenure the exceedingly valuable study of black migration in 1916 and 1917, often quoted in this work, was published, but in 1920 the bureau "was permitted to go out of existence for lack of appropriations of funds to carry on its valuable and useful work,"[2] Seligmann said. Perhaps it was allowed to die because Haynes, a capable social scientist and one of the founders of the Urban League, posed the threat of publicizing black conditions as they actually were. The War Department job, on the other hand, is still on the books, and the special assistant's chair is still warmed, quite likely because Emmett Scott's Tuskegee philosophy kept matters at a "cool equipoise" and posed no threat at all.[3]

When the black troops came home, it was with the heightened expectations of men who had served their country well. Kelly Miller observed that "no one now expects the Negro soldiers of the World War to revert with satisfaction to the status they occupied before the war for the emancipation of mankind."[4] The southern reaction to any notion of increased status for blacks was instantaneously, uncompromisingly negative. If wearing the uniform gave blacks ideas of social and political equality, the best thing was to get them out of uniform quickly as possible. Although legally they were permitted to wear the uniform for ninety days after discharge, there were reports of black soldiers stripped of their uniforms as they got off trains at southern railroad stations. Soldiers in uniform were beaten and driven out of town in many parts of the South, the NAACP found.[5] Officers fared particularly badly. "Back in the United States," wrote Charles Houston, "whites scorned us despite the fact we were U. S. Army officers, wearing obvious overseas chevrons on our sleeves."[6] In the South, much the wisest course was to discard the uniform immediately; a black officer seemed an irresistible target for insults, jostlings, and beatings. The treatment of black veterans so angered the black community that the NAACP demanded a congressional investigation, but none was made.[7] Black people on all levels of society felt threatened, Seligmann wrote, "by the reports given currency by politicians like Vardaman, that 'Frenchwomen-ruined-niggers' were coming back to this country from France to make trouble and to disturb the supremacy of the white race," and even the most substantial Negroes, who customarily did not get involved in violent protests, had to consider fighting for their manhood "not with the ballot, but with the gun."[8]

Black soldiers and officers who wanted to re-enlist found that choice closed to them, however good their military records might be, by a secret order of the War Department. Even the four Regular black regiments gradually withered away, and personnel were reduced from their former role as fighting soldiers to the level of menials for white regiments.[9]

Veterans' organizations should have defended the rights of black servicemen, but in fact were practically closed to them. The American Legion gave local option to its state branches, allowing them to reject blacks entirely or let them establish their own segregated posts. Black posts, however, were not permitted delegates to state and national conventions, nor were they allowed to hold any office above the local post level, and consequently did not share in the power and patronage of the Legion. The Legion and other veterans' organizations justified their Jim Crow posts with the threadbare excuse that "Negroes wanted it that way."[10]

Black Americans, especially those just returned from the horrors and miseries of the war, began to pour out their bitterness in the black press. Veterans contrasted their treatment by the French, who had taken them into their homes and lives as equals, with the ruthless discrimination and hostility in the United States. French women did not scream rape every time they met a black man; in fact, an estimated 1,000 to 2,000 marriages had taken place between French women and black American soldiers. French men had treated the black soldiers as men, and were astonished by American color prejudice. William N. Colson, a young former lieutenant in the 367th Infantry Regiment, 92d Division, who wrote a number of such articles for both black and white publications, was particularly articulate and angry. An article written by Colson and A. B. Nutt, also formerly of the 367th, blamed the shortcomings of the 92d Division on poorly chosen officers, both black and white, and on poor training, lack of organization, consistent discrimination, and destruction of morale.[11] In an article on patriotism, Colson said black soldiers had scoffed at the concept that the war was being fought to make the world safe for democracy; in battle, southern blacks had whipped themselves to fury by pretending that the German Huns before them were "the Huns of America, the convict leasers, the slave drivers, their domineering white American officers, the lynchers, their oppressors, instead of the Boches."[12] The black troops had decided, Colson said, that "their next war for 'democracy' would be in the land of The Star-Spangled Banner."[13] For such writing, Colson was marked by the Department of Justice as a dangerous radical, but he was merely expressing the indignation of many, many black soldiers who had, for the first time, seen white Americans from the perspective of a distant land—and with guns in their hands.

The war had been the first opportunity, for almost all American blacks, to see something of other black people. They observed, and sent the word back home, that the black colonial troops of France were treated far better than black American troops. Tales of fighting Sudanese, Senegalese, and West Indians, of their different languages and customs, of their gallantry and recklessness in battle, of their high-ranking officers, appeared in both black and white publications, opening to American blacks a thrilling view of people of their own color, people who came from the lands of their own ancestors. A spiritual bond with other black people was not at all new, but the war broadened and deepened it, and brought home to many black Americans a conviction that blacks must band together to end their exploitation by whites.[14]

A world safe for democracy, self-determination of peoples, the rights of small nations—all the idealistic aims expressed by the Allies during the war and presumably to be implemented at the

Versailles Peace Conference—gave blacks reason to hope that they might be guaranteed some rights in the postwar world. A number of black leaders and organizations tried to present these hopes at the peace talks. DuBois, who had been active in the Pan-Africa movement since its first congress in London in 1900, went to Paris with Joel Spingarn to represent the NAACP at a Pan-African conference that was to include African and West Indian delegates. The conference demanded a pledge in the Versailles Treaty guaranteeing political, social, and economic equality for black people, violators to be subject to League of Nations sanctions. The International League of Darker Peoples was formed in the United States for the purpose of organizing all black delegates to the Peace Conference so that a unified demand for black rights might be made. Monroe Trotter, who had just organized the National Race Congress for the same purpose, sought accreditation to the Peace Conference as a delegate of the National Equal Rights League, but the State Department refused him a passport. He managed to get seaman's papers as "William Trotter," worked his way overseas as a second cook, and sneaked ashore at Le Havre in May 1919, but his NERL petition was rebuffed by Americans at the Peace Conference. The indomitable Trotter was scarcely back in the States, however, when he appeared with other black spokesmen before the Senate Foreign Relations Committee at its hearings on ratification of the Versailles Treaty, demanding the insertion of a clause guaranteeing racial justice. John Milholland observed that "the Republican members followed the presentation very closely," but there the matter ended.[15]

Still, something had been accomplished by black effort. Trotter had spread the story of American race relations through the Paris press during his brief stay in France. Successive Pan-African Congresses met, with Rayford Logan, who lived in France for a time after the war, serving as secretary-interpreter until 1924. Logan was one of a small community of black Americans living in Paris at that time, mostly artists, scholars, musicians, and entertainers, some earning a living as doormen, dishwashers, or bouncers in nightclubs. When Langston Hughes arrived broke in Paris in the early 1920s, Logan got him a job as dishwasher at a nightclub. The status of the black man had not greatly changed through the war, either in Paris or New York, where he was usually either an entertainer or a menial, regardless of his abilities. But the world had been exposed to black Americans, and they had been exposed to the world. It was one of the distinguishing characteristics of what was called the "New Negro."[16]

Attorney General A. Mitchell Palmer, off on a postwar binge of witch-hunting unmatched until the McCarthy period, regarded any expression of "new" black thought as "dressing for the . . . salad" of political radicalism, and therefore gathered many expressions of "New Negro" kind in a cautionary publication of the Justice Department.

An article quoted from the *Crusader,* for example, declared that Negroes, especially American Negroes, were superior to the whites among whom they lived in character, manners, and looks, and that they must shake off the false doctrine, "instilled into them for centuries . . . that that only is beautiful which is white. . . ."[17] A Cleveland newspaper said that white Southerners were, in fact, "basely immoral" brutes, "monumental liars," "men who spared neither their own white nor colored women."[18] The *Messenger* commented on mob violence: "New Negroes are determined to make their dying a costly investment for all concerned. . . . it is the white man's own Bible that says: 'Those who live by the sword shall perish by the sword' and, since white men believe in force, Negroes, who have mimicked them for nearly three centuries, must copy them in this respect. . . . The new Negro has arrived with stiffened backbone, dauntless manhood, defiant eye, steady hand, and a will of iron."[19] The Attorney General characterized this editorial as "insolently offensive" and typically Negro in its "emotional abandon."[20] Colson in an article on patriotism and the Negro said that "the teaching of patriotism the world over has usually been a mass of silly and mendacious fact" and that in the 92d Division "the disillusioned, the new Negro and his new patriotism . . . asked without hesitation the reason for their fighting in the war."[21] Poems such as Claude McKay's *If We Must Die,* Carita Owens Collins' *This Must Not Be,* and many others such as *The Mob Victim, A Confession of Prejudice,* and *An Oath,* breathed fire against those who persecuted and lynched blacks. The last lines of a poem signed "Razafkeriefo" spoke for the black veteran:

> For by the blood you've spilled in France
> You must and will be free,
> So from now on let us advance
> With this: Don't tread on me![22]

The New Negro who so irritated Attorney General Palmer did not request, he demanded equality, and even the President was attacked in the black press for acquiescing in the southern treatment of Negroes.[23] A Chicago paper hailed the death of "Pitchfork Ben" Tillman as the "most glorious event in Negro history," and it adjured death in his next journey to take Blease, Smith, Vardaman, Bilbo, and the other southern racist politicians.[24] The Old Negro was damned for his "lick-spittle" acceptance of lynching, but it was predicted that he would soon be an extinct species;[25] the death of Booker T. Washington about five years earlier was called an event that had saved the black people from "five years under ether."[26] The New Negro would practice "race first" in "a world of wolves"; he knew, and whites were discovering, that "the black man is a power of great potentiality upon whom consciousness of his own strength is about to dawn—a veritable giant awaking out of sleep."[27]

There had always been some blacks who spoke up about race pride and resentment of injustices, but the volume and intensity of these examples garnered by Attorney General Palmer, all published in the first postwar year, showed plainly that there was indeed a New Negro, or, in Alain Locke's concept, a real black man instead of a black myth, who had been awakened by the war to a realization of his beauty and power.

The New Negro shared with his former self a need to eat that was hard to satisfy in the slowed-down economy of the postwar years. Some southern black farmers were perhaps better off financially at that time than those who had migrated to industrial cities, because the war had boomed cotton prices; many of them used their money to pay off debts and buy land of their own. This alarmed the white South, whose economy was dependent on the crop lien and tenant system, and it has been suggested that severe postwar measures against blacks in the South were desperate efforts to keep them in line as laborers and tenants rather than as free farmers. But the net gains in land-owning for southern black farmers were actually too small to disrupt the system; statistically, indeed, they show a loss, going from about 75 per cent tenants (out of the entire black farm population) in 1910 to slightly over 76 per cent in 1920.[28]

In other parts of the country, blacks probably fared worse. White workers returned to their jobs, industrial activity abruptly dropped, and black workers found themselves pushed out of jobs they had held during the war, especially the better jobs. There was no returning to the old "Negro jobs" such as barbering, because these had ceased to be a black monopoly; and it was much harder than before the war for a black to get work as a postman or policeman. Many black women had to go back to domestic work to help feed their families; many black men returned to domestic or personal service. In the winter of 1920–21, thousands of workers, black and white, were out of work in Chicago, Detroit, and other industrial cities. Wartime and postwar inflation had driven consumer price indexes sky high: in the period 1917–20, food rose from 49.1 to 70.8, rent from 56.3 to 72.9, and clothing from 45.9 to 98.[29]

The vast majority of black workers did not belong to unions, so they lacked the protection available to organized labor. The Urban League held unions entirely to blame, pointing out that black workers were ready enough to organize in fields where they had a monopoly or were so strong that an effort had been made to unionize them, such as the mine workers and Pullman porters. The blame lay entirely with the AF of L, insisted the Urban League, partly because it was still structurally a horizontal, craft-union federation and thus inadequate for both black and white workers in automobile manufacturing and other highly mechanized industries, which required vertical organization, from top to bottom.[30] Especially was it inadequate for black workers, because although the national organization denied any color barriers, there was no doubt that the locals were Jim Crow. Despite Urban League protestations to the contrary, some investigators found a certain apathy among blacks toward the labor movement. Conservative, upper-class black people discouraged the association of black workers with a movement which, to conservatives, smacked of economic radicalism; and the black workers were not eager to expose themselves voluntarily to a Jim Crow situation when they could avoid it simply by not joining a union. The New Negro, in sum, was not in any significant number either drawn toward or embraced by labor unions. In the slack postwar years, job competition between blacks and whites, between union and nonunion men, was a constant irritant that might flare into demonstrations of race hostility.[31]

Black businessmen did not do well in the postwar years, either. By 1920 there were about 50,000 to 60,000 black businesses employing about 70,000 people, but at least half these businesses went under in the next ten years; of eighty-eight black-owned banks begun since 1900, only forty survived the postwar decade.[32] Black leaders as disparate as Washington and DuBois had recognized the necessity of black businesses for providing the black community with jobs and capital on which to draw. But, for reasons discussed earlier, "buy black" simply could not work well enough, and the wartime earnings of black workers went almost entirely into the tills and vaults of white businessmen. Rudolph Fisher in his 1928 novel *The Walls of Jericho* had a character complain that blacks had no solid, middle-level business class, "nothing but the extremes—bootblacks on one end and doctors on the other. . . . Everybody wants to quit waiting table and start writing prescriptions right away."[33] Lack of a business class is probably one reason why, after the war, home ownership in Chicago was lower among blacks than in any other racial or ethnic group. But a much more compelling reason for black families not to buy homes in Chicago was the danger in it. Between July 1917 and March 1921, fifty-eight Negro homes in that city were bombed, resulting in two dead, several injured, and $100,000 in property damage.[34]

Dr. Henry Pratt Fairchild, a sociologist of the postwar period, wrote as follows:

> Of course, the [race] feeling itself is not inherited; no feeling is. But it is wholly probable that the neural connections which cause a certain feeling to arise in response to a given stimulus are inherited. . . . As a practical matter it does not make much difference whether race feeling is innate or acquired.[35]

As a practical matter, it did not make much difference to black residents of mostly white Vincennes Avenue in Chicago, when they received this anonymous letter:

> We are going to BLOW these FLATS TO HELL and if you dont want to go with them you had better move at once.[36]

The hatred that war engenders seemed to flow on of its own momentum to fill up the postwar emotional vacuum. Wartime nationalism, nativism, and xenophobia also continued, and hate found a convenient outlet in the persecution of any "outside" group, whether Jews, immigrants, or Negroes. Jews were accused alternately of being international capitalists who battened on wars that they fomented, or of being international pacifists, socialists, and Bolshevists out to destroy the capitalistic system of the United States; these undesirable people were refused at many hotels and resorts, excluded from certain residential areas, and restricted to a "quota" at most prominent universities, even in New York City with its considerable Jewish citizenry.[37] Immigrants of the "new" undesirable stocks from eastern and southern Europe were suspected of subversive designs and radical activities; many states prosecuted for "criminal syndicalism" those who expressed dissident opinions or belonged to certain disapproved organizations. A number of states banned any language but English for instructional use in their schools, believing thus to prevent the dissemination of dangerous foreign ideologies. Meanwhile, racist ideology of the most flagrant kind was carried forward by scientists like Henry Fairfield Osborn, the paleontologist whose observations convinced him that everything good was Nordic, and that men of inferior races could not by any amount of education or environmental advantage overcome the handicap of a poor heredity. Stoddard in the 1920s was in process of following up his *Rising Tide of Color* with a shower of white-supremacy books and magazine articles, very popular and generally praised by critics, although one English review called his work a "farrago of scientific half-truths and journalistic nightmare" and anthropologists Boas and Alexander A. Goldenweiser warned how sinister were Stoddard's race fantasies. Madison Grant's *The Passing of the Great Race* remained a best seller throughout the war and after.[38] Another popular writer who turned out race-hate copy was Kenneth L. Roberts, later well-known for historical novels; right after the war Roberts published an article in *The Saturday Evening Post* that declared, in line with the dog-breeding analogy of the eugenicists, that "any promiscuous crossing of breeds invariably produces mongrels" and that therefore "if a few more million members of the Alpine, Mediterranean, and Semitic races are poured among us" it is obvious that we shall no longer be able to produce "the same breed of men that founded America" but must inevitably degenerate into a race "as worthless and futile as the good-for-nothing mongrels of Central America and Southeastern Europe."[39]

An obvious response to the threat of mongrelization was to terrify, injure, or kill as many as possible of the inferior people who had gotten into America, and thus discourage any more of their kind from coming. The Ku Klux Klan, the new Klan that was organized in 1915, dedicated itself to this aim after the war; it enjoyed its greatest growth in the next few years and reached its peak membership, said to be about five million, in the mid-twenties. Always antiblack, the Klan had become increasingly anti-immigrant, anti-Catholic, and anti-Jewish as well.[40] Its handiest targets, however, were still the blacks, and its greatest popularity was in the South, which was ready to try any recipe that promised to change the "New Negroes" into "good old niggers" again. The Klan recruited many Southerners through huge newspaper ads of this sort: "If you wish to make your wives and daughters safe and happy, join the Klan to-day. . . ."[41] Klansmen paraded in many southern towns before the 1920 elections, giving blacks clear warning to stay home on election day. Besides saving the womenfolk and the vote, the Klan used its muscle to pry blacks out of any good jobs they might have gotten during the war, to persuade sharecroppers to accept whatever payment the boss offered for their cotton without demanding a written accounting, and in general to protect the tenant, croplien, sharecrop, debt-slavery system. If necessary to achieve these ends, Klansmen would throw 119 blacks into the river, as they boasted of doing in one Mississippi county.[42] Not all southern authorities suffered the Klan gladly; in 1919 the governor of North Carolina asked citizens to repudiate it, calling it "a hark back to the lawless time that followed the terrors of the Civil War. . . ."[43] But most authorities either averted their eyes from Klan doings or openly favored them, and in at least two states, Texas and Oklahoma, the Klan for a time dominated the government.[44]

The black soldier who had gone off to war with promises of full citizenship ringing in his ears came home to unprecedented abridgment of his constitutional rights. Jim Crow extended its rule to every detail of life in the South, growing so steadily more rigid through the postwar decades that Gunnar Myrdal in the 1940s said a white Southerner almost never saw a Negro except as a servant or in some other caste situation. Gone was whatever flexibility there had been in transportation, recreation, sports, and amusements, in the South and to a great extent in the North as well. Langston Hughes wrote that in postwar Cleveland, downtown restaurants and theaters turned blacks away, landlords multiplied blacks' rents by two or three, and employers fired black workers to take on white veterans.[45]

Ghetto lines were more tightly drawn than before, and maintained by illegal but effective "understandings" and "gentlemen's agreements." Upper-level interracial meetings on community affairs were things of the past. Blacks and whites shunned each other, and the less contact there was between the races, the greater grew fear and hostility. In 1919, if you were a black living in New York you had a choice of Harlem or Columbus Hill; in Washington, of the city's Northwest or Southwest quarters; in Atlanta, of Auburn Avenue or the West End; and in Chicago you had South State Street.[46] Overcrowded ghetto housing deteriorated into total slums with deplorable schools and inadequate services of every sort, but there was no escaping from them; if blacks overflowed into white neighborhoods they were likely to be told, "We are going to BLOW these FLATS TO HELL. . . ."

In 1919, seventy-six blacks were lynched, eighteen more than the previous year and the highest number in more than a decade. Some of the victims were still in uniform when they were snatched up to be hanged, mutilated, and burned. And, further distinguishing 1919 as the bloodiest peacetime year in the nation's history, there were at least twenty-five race riots, one third of which involved thousands of people.[47] Violence had to occur when the New Negro, back from fighting America's war for democracy, ran head-on into old raceways that he would no longer accept as immutable.

In the riots of summer and fall 1919, the same factors contributed as in the earlier riots in East St. Louis, Springfield, and Atlanta: the harping of the press on black crime, especially sex crimes; the headlining of violence; the corrupt politicians and police; the mutual fear and suspicion between blacks and whites "that live almost in two separate worlds";[48] the deliberate creation of labor friction; and the exacerbation of racial violence, once it was under way, by unequal law enforcement. But one striking common characteristic of the 1919 riots that had only begun to be discernible before the war was the counterattack of beleaguered black people. Older conservative Negroes like Kelly Miller expressed alarm: "The moment the Negro goes beyond the limit of self-defense, aggressive violence will mean self-destruction."[49] But the New Negro was ready to die if necessary, and there is no way of frightening a man who has made that decision. The New Negro, said the short-lived black publication called the *Veteran*, "values liberty as he does not cherish life." "New Negroes are determined to make their dying a costly investment for all concerned," said the *Messenger*; ". . . This new spirit is but a reflex of the Great War, and it is largely due to the insistent and vigorous agitation carried on by the younger men of the race." "The day of cringing is over," said another writer in the *Messenger*, "the hour of compromise is passed; and the high noon of action has come. He [the New Negro] says to the lynchers that henceforth it will be an eye for an eye, tooth for tooth, death for death, and damnation for damnation."[50]

Seligmann commented: "Never before to such an extent had the Negro fought back to repel white mobs as in Washington and Chicago"[51] in 1919, and he believed that other scheduled riots were called off because of black armed resistance.[52] If the riots resulted in "a new standing and a new recognition of the Negro," Seligmann observed, "as well as a new realization and race pride on the part of the Negroes themselves, the price of lives lost and suffering will not have been exacted altogether in vain."[53] Weighing up the gains and losses of the Red Summer, as James Weldon Johnson named it, there is no doubt but at least two of those results, self-realization and race pride, were achieved and have permanently changed black people. But the cost was terrible.

The first of the 1919 riots broke out in May in Charleston, South Carolina, between white sailors and blacks, and the second in early July in Longview, Texas, after a lynching.[54] There were deaths, injuries, and property losses from the burning of black neighborhoods in these riots, but on a scale that looked insignificant compared to the violence of the riot that began on July 19 in Washington, D.C. Rioting there followed a Negro-crime campaign in the Washington *Post*, and continued in a mounting frenzy through four days and nights until rain and federal troops ended it. On the first night, four men were killed and eleven mortally or seriously wounded; of the fifteen, only five were black. Blacks were fighting back and shooting back, even retaliating by attacks on white neighborhoods. After the riot, the black press extolled the heroic resistance of young Negroes, and demanded an end to Jim Crow and lynching. The NAACP petitioned Attorney General Palmer to proceed against the *Post* for inciting to riot, but Palmer refused. The white press recognized that Negroes were now prepared to defend themselves if the law did not, but were generally agreed that violence was the result of the impractical determination of the New Negroes to seek equality with whites, and would cease only when the black man returned to his proper place in American society.

Almost as if in direct defiance, blacks fought even more furiously in the next race riot, which broke out only a few weeks later, on July 27, in Chicago. After a week of sheer terror throughout the city, twenty-three whites and twenty-five Negroes were dead, 537 persons injured, and an estimated 1,000 homeless.[55] The violence was precipitated by a beach incident in which a black teen-age bather, alleged to have drifted past the line between black and white swimming areas, was stoned by whites; the boy drowned. On a deeper level of causation, race violence was an inevitable result of the black striving and white obdurateness that had led to the bombings of black homes, and of mounting tension on both sides because of the increase of militance among blacks. That blacks fought back is evident in the almost equal casualty figures. Chicago was paralyzed and terrified. Even the fire-eating Robert Abbott was shaken, and during the riot the *Defender* urged black people to "do your part to restore quiet and order," to forget who started the trouble and "let proper authorities finish it. . . . The police are playing no favorites,"[56] the *Defender* claimed, but that was a lie. The interracial Chicago Commission on Race Relations, quickly appointed to investigate conditions underlying the riot, found that law enforcement had been far from even-handed; police had, in fact, given the riot its incentive by refusing to arrest the white man identified by black witnesses as the one who threw the stone that pushed the black youth under water.[57]

If anything good can be said to have come of that agony in Chicago, it was the formation of the Commission on Race Relations, a group of six blacks and six whites, including such clashing personalities as Julius Rosenwald and Robert Abbott. The Commission's report was written by Charles S. Johnson, whose ability Rosenwald came to admire greatly through their association in this project,[58] and was published in 1922 under the title *The Negro in Chicago,* a sociological study of the first order of importance. The Commission made thoughtful and penetrating recommendations for social reforms that would probably have brought a profound and lasting improvement in Chicago racial relations, but, like the reports of many a subsequent commission on race, poverty, crime, health, and the like, *The Negro in Chicago* was simply bound, shelved, and occasionally dusted.

Rioting broke out soon in other places, in September in Knoxville, Tennessee, and Omaha, Nebraska, and finally, in October, in Elaine (Phillips County), Arkansas. The Elaine violence was different in that it took place in the Deep South, and was not urban in its locale or causes. Black tenant farmers had organized to force an end, by legal means, to debt slavery and peonage; a meeting of theirs was shot up by the sheriff on the charge that the black farmers were plotting to massacre all whites in the area. According to the lawyer for the farmers' organization, a former assistant United States attorney, the sheriff's attack was really designed to terrorize black tenant farmers into submission.[59] Before the terror ended, about two hundred blacks and forty whites had been killed; in subsequent court actions seventy-nine blacks were tried on charges of murder and insurrection, and twelve were sentenced to death, although, largely through the work of the NAACP, all those sentences were commuted to short prison terms.[60] The bloody story of Elaine proves that the New Negro philosophy was changing even backwoods Arkansas, with black farmers organizing to fight exploitation, and black men shooting back at white men. A letter to the Chicago *Defender* stated with cold fury the position of white Arkansas:

"You are agitating a proposition through your paper which is causing some of your good Bur heads to be

killed and the end is not in sight yet. . . . You could
be of assistance to your people if you would advise
them to be real niggers instead of fools."[61]

What the writer did not recognize was that, finally, "niggers"
were being real.

The idea of a real black man, responding in a real way to the
hate and injustice that had formed him, was to most white Americans frighteningly radical, of itself hinting sinisterly of association with Bolsheviks and the IWW. Dr. Stoddard found the
notion of black radicalization right in line with his theory of race
mongrelization and the threat of an eventual colored hegemony.
The danger was close upon us, he said in his 1920 work *The Rising Tide of Color,* because "in every quarter of the globe . . . the
Bolshevik agitators whisper in the ears of discontented colored
men their gospel of hatred and revenge."[62] Representative
James F. Byrnes of South Carolina complained during the Red
Summer that the black press was radicalizing Negroes, and urged
that "we should now prevent the I.W.W. and the Bolsheviki of
Russia from using the Negro press of America to further their
nefarious schemes"; the Negro was happy in the South, he stated,
and would remain so if the IWW and the Bolshevik propagan-
dists would only let him alone.[63]

Commentators on what Seligmann described as the "hysterical
outburst of radical baiting and hunting of 'Reds' which took place
in Northern cities late in 1919 and early in 1920"[64] often overlook
a prime cause of the hysteria: a fear that blacks would flock to
organizations that promised to treat them as real and equal men,
which the AF of L did not. As DuBois said, "Grudgingly, unwill-
ingly, almost insultingly, this federation yields to us inch by inch
the status of half a man, denying and withholding every privilege it dares at all times."[65] The IWW, on the other hand,
welcomed blacks freely, fully, and equally. The *Messenger*
pointed out the common grounds of Negroes and IWW members:
both were mostly unskilled, migratory, and without political

rights. Deprived of the franchise, the Negro had no course but to adopt industrial action, the *Messenger* pointed out; and being mostly unskilled industrial workers, blacks needed vertical, industry-based organizations that would guard equally the rights of skilled and unskilled workers in an industry, rather than the old-style horizontal, craft-based, skilled unions of the AF of L.[66]

The Department of Justice investigation of 1919 under Attorney General A. Mitchell Palmer examined among other perils to national security "Radicalism and Sedition among the Negroes as Reflected in Their Publications,"[67] and its report of findings came to some alarming conclusions about black radical thought. The race riots, said Palmer's report, had been taken up by Negro publications "as cause for the utterance of inflammatory sentiment," and "there can no longer be any question of a well-concerted movement among a certain class of Negro leaders . . . to constitute themselves a determined and persistent source of a radical opposition to the Government, and to the established rule of law and order."[68] Subjects treated in the black press that Palmer found most alarming were: "the ill-governed reaction toward race rioting" and praise of the New Negro who shot back when he was shot at; the "threat of retaliatory measures in connection with lynching"; the demand for political, social, economic, and even "sex equality"; expressions of disrespect for the Wilson administration, the South, the peace treaty, and the League of Nations; expressions of hostility toward whites and of loathing for white Southerners; and, finally, "the identification of the Negro with such radical organizations as the I.W.W. and an outspoken advocacy of the Bolsheviki or Soviet doctrines. . . ."[69]

Most black people, Palmer could have discovered, had little enthusiasm for revolutionary doctrine or theory. Where Bolshevism was embraced, it was for the pragmatic reason, as Claude McKay said, that it might make the United States safe for Negroes as it "has made Russia safe for the Jew" and "has liberated the Slav peasant from priest and bureaucrat"; it might also have shown the "Cracker slave" that his real danger was not race equality but exploitation by "the Vardamans and Cole Bleases."[70] An editorial in Briggs's *Crusader* said, "If to fight for one's rights is to be Bolshevist, then we are Bolshevists, let them make the most of it. And for further information of the asses who use the term so loosely we will make the statement that we would not for a moment hesitate to ally ourselves with any group [to achieve] the liberation of our race and the re-demption of our fatherland. A man pressed to earth by another with murderous intent is not under any obligation to choose his weapons. . . . Self-preservation is the first law of human na-ture."[71]

Except for a few philosophically convinced socialists like Chandler Owen and A. Philip Randolph, there were almost no "radical" blacks of 1919 who thought in terms more general or theoretical than making America safe for Negroes. There was little or no mention in black "radical" writings of class consciousness, the class struggle, world revolution, the proletariat, etc., but much about Negroes' wishes to live and work where they pleased, to rise according to their effort and ability, to vote, to be pro-tected in their homes and persons. Although Attorney General Palmer thought that anarchists Emma Goldman and Alexander Berkman[72] were hidden in every Harlem closet, and suspected every New Negro of anarchy, pacifism, riot, and revolution, actually the goals of political agitators were not the goals of black Americans; the "dangerous spirit of defiance and vengeance" that Palmer discerned among black leaders was not the fruit of foreign ideologies but of the 100 per cent American thesis that blacks were by nature inferior and must be kept in an inferior position. Palmer's quotations from the black press make it clear beyond question that white Americans—especially southern Americans—and not foreign agitators were the radicalizers of blacks. Roger Baldwin, himself a victim of this Red-scare period, said: "I found no trace of 'Red' propaganda [among Negroes], but I found observations and conclusions expressed in as 'Red' terms as I have ever heard them from a soap-box agitator. It is obvious that the conditions themselves produce radical think-ing."[73]

It was almost entirely a new black leadership that voiced the radical black thinking. Booker T. Washington was dead, and Robert Moton, Emmett Scott, Kelly Miller, and others of the Tuskegee-Hampton-Howard group were no longer of national importance to black people. Trotter no longer seemed militant to the new breed, and his importance as a leader had passed. Even DuBois was passé to many of the New Negroes; the Justice Department in September 1919 said there had been "nothing of a radical nature in the Crisis since July" and that it "is regarded by the *Messenger* as reactionary toward conservatism."[74] A. Philip Randolph and James Weldon Johnson retained leadership power; but Marcus Garvey and his associates William H. Domingo, Cyril V. Briggs, William Colson, and Walter White were new and increasingly powerful voices. George Haynes said in 1919 that the new goals were no different but that more and more blacks were moving away from a position of waiting, compromise, and conciliation to one of militance or actual radicalism.[75] As the New Negroes put it, they were coming out of ether.

White leaders, however, were not. They talked as if they were still addressing Booker T. Washington. President Harding said that black sacrifice in the war "has entitled them to all freedom and opportunity, all sympathy and aid,"[76] but he also said the Klan was not really hostile to blacks; he permitted even greater segregation than under Wilson in the federal Civil Service; he appointed very few blacks to federal jobs and none in the South; and at the dedication of the Lincoln Memorial in 1922, his black guests were placed in a separate section divided from the rest of the gathering by a roadway. Calvin Coolidge, as Harding's Vice President, said biological laws showed that Nordics deteriorate when mixed with other races; in 1923, having succeeded to the presidency upon Harding's death, Coolidge said in his annual message to Congress that while Negroes' rights "are just as sacred as those of any other citizen," the race problem was a southern problem and the best way to remedy difficulties was on a local basis, "by the mutual forbearance and human kindness of each community."[77] Black men had changed, no question. But had anything else?

In the early 1920s, psychologists dealt a punishing blow to blacks with the publication of studies of intelligence testing in the Army. World War I testing had been faulty in many ways, as was later revealed, but in 1920 and for years after, the results of the tests were quoted like the word of God.

The baby science of psychology enjoyed a tremendous boom during the war and because of the war. Experimental methods of testing intelligence, devised for mentally defective children by Alfred Binet and Theodore Simon around 1905, were used on more than 1,700,000 American soldiers—used and evaluated with reckless disregard for the authors' warnings about the importance of environmental factors in mental development—with the announced result that large segments of the American population were natively, irremediably stupid. The term Intelligence Quotient, or IQ, meaning the ratio of mental ability (based on test performance) to chronological age, made it easy to be glib about the extremely complex subject of intelligence. Originally intended to mean only that, for example, among children ten years old, one who scored 100 on the tests had an IQ of 100 and a mental age of ten, one who scored 120 had an IQ of 120 and a mental age of twelve, and one who scored 80 had an IQ of 80 and a mental age of eight, IQ as applied to adults yielded some dubious, but nonetheless venerated results. In 1916—significantly, the year Madison Grant's *The Passing of the Great Race* was published —psychologist Lewis Terman revealed that tests he and associates had made proved the low intelligence of Spanish-Indian, Mexican, and Negro children, and postulated: "Their dullness seems to be racial, or at least inherent in the family stocks from which they come."[78] The fact that upper-class children, almost all of whom were white, usually did better on most tests was cited as proof of the supreme importance of a good heredity. Any conflicting findings were quickly explained away. When a group of black children did better in a memory test than white children, Columbia psychologist Edward L. Thorndike said their high score proved their low intelligence, because "the apparent mental attainment of children of inferior races may be due to lack of inhibition and so witness precisely to a deficiency in mental growth."[79] It is clear that to Thorndike, and many others, the tests were useful more to document preconceptions and prejudices than to discover truths. The testing of that era was totally disqualified, in fact, by the element of expectation. Terman, for example, prophesied the results of the testing of children: "The writer predicts . . . there will be discovered enormously significant racial differences in general intelligence, differences which cannot be wiped out by any scheme of mental culture"; many, he said, would prove uneducable, and no amount of schooling would make them "intelligent voters or capable citizens in the true sense of the word"; they were the future "hewers of wood and drawers of water," Terman concluded, in advance.[80]

When the war offered an opportunity for mass testing of adults, tests were tried out in Army camps and modified until a model was devised in which 5 per cent of the subjects would get an A grade (officer potential); then the test results were interpreted to mean that only one man in twenty in the American Army possessed good intelligence. Tests were scored from A through E, and by some means these grades were transposed into IQ terms and used to establish an "average" white mental age in the Army of about thirteen.[81] Walter Lippmann pointed out the absurdity: "The average adult intelligence . . . cannot be less than the average adult intelligence . . . [any more than can] an average mile be ¾ of a mile long."[82] In vain psychologists tried to explain that this did not really mean that the average adult had the intelligence of a child a month or so over thirteen years of age, but referred only to his scores on a group of tests; the public seized on the novelties of mental age and IQ and used them loosely for any desired purpose, scientific or not. What made the concepts especially attractive to many white Americans was that the average black draftee had been found to have a mental age of just over ten; an adult mental age under twelve was considered moronic.[83]

The most damaging aspect of a low score was the claim that the tests measured inborn intelligence, which was impervious to environmental factors. Robert M. Yerkes, whose *Psychological Examining in the U. S. Army* was published in 1920, analyzed the intelligence scores of native-born, foreign-born, and black Americans; he said that the tests "were originally intended, and are now definitely known, to measure native intellectual ability," and that they "brought into clear relief . . . the intellectual inferiority of the negro. Quite apart from educational status, which is utterly unsatisfactory, the negro soldier is of relatively low intelligence." Furthermore, according to Yerkes, "education alone will not place the negro race on a par with its Caucasian competitors."[84]

A final stamp of approval of these theories came with the publication in 1923 by Carl C. Brigham, the Princeton psychologist who had directed the Army's testing program, of a definitive analysis of the Army tests: *A Study of American Intelligence.* Yerkes in a glowing Introduction to Brigham's work declared: "The author presents not theories or opinions but facts. It behooves us to consider their reliability and their meaning, for no one of us as a citizen can afford to ignore the menace of race deterioration or the evident relations of immigration to national progress and welfare." Judge how factual was Brigham's work from his own statement: "In my treatment of the race hypotheses I have relied on two books, Mr. Madison Grant's *Passing of the Great Race,* and Professor William Z. Ripley's *Races of Europe.*"[85]

Brigham's study led him to these conclusions: (1) At one extreme of American intelligence are the Nordics; at the other, the Negroes; Alpines and Mediterraneans are in between; expressed in terms of Army tests, 88.6 per cent of the native-born white draft and 70.44 per cent of the foreign-born white draft exceeded the average of the Negro draft;[86] (2) ". . . the average intelligence of succeeding waves of immigration has become progressively lower . . ." with the Russians, Italians, and other "new" immigrants less intelligent than the northern Europeans who preceded them; as for Jews, "our figures . . . would tend to disprove the popular belief that the Jew is highly intelligent . . .";[87] (3) testing revealed ". . . a very remarkable fact, viz., a steady increase in the average scores [of foreign-born whites] with increasing years of residence [in the United States] . . ."; (4) tests showed blacks as the lowest in intelligence even by comparison with whites from the same environments;[88] education cannot change this; the fact that Army tests showed that blacks from Ohio, Illinois, Indiana, and New York had test scores ranging from 45.7 to 38.6, while whites from Mississippi, Louisiana, and Arkansas had scores from 37.6 to 35.6, does not indicate that the higher-scoring blacks had benefited by a better education than the Deep South whites; but rather it indicates that migration was "selective," with the better class of blacks going North for better opportunities, and that in the North they had further benefited by more frequent intermarriage, thereby acquiring a greater admixture of "white blood";[89] (5) "according to all evidence available, then, American intelligence is declining, and the decline will proceed at an accelerating rate as the racial admixture becomes more and more extensive. . . . These are the plain, if somewhat ugly, facts that our study shows"; fortunately, a combination of a declining black birth-rate and highly selective immigration policies can prevent "continued propagation of defective strains in the present population."[90] Such were the conclusions Brigham drew from his "facts."

The postwar preoccupation with race blinded Brigham and most other psychologists to the far more operative reasons why blacks, by and large, scored low on the Army tests. The Alpha tests were admittedly dependent on learned information and language; but even the Beta tests, although designed to require no ability in reading or in understanding spoken English, were in fact culturally weighted.[91] So all tests were easier for the prosperous, educated, urban subject than for the poor, uneducated, rural subject—regardless of native intelligence, which the tests were supposed to measure. Also, despite Brigham's disclaimer, speed was essential for a high score; yet speed, as later studies by Otto Klineberg showed, was itself closely related to cultural values and did not significantly or solely relate to intelligence.[92] As for Brigham's explanation of the better showing of some northern blacks than some southern whites by the theory of "selective migration," Klineberg's studies showed that *who* migrated was far less important than *how* the migrants were changed by urban and educational advantages in the North; testing led him to the conclusion, for example, that the longer migrants and their children had lived in such cities as New York and Washington, the higher were their scores.[93]

The studies of Klineberg and his associates were still many years in the future when Brigham summed up the general conclusion, "repeatedly confirmed by experiment, that children from the professional, semi-professional and higher business classes have, on the whole, an hereditary endowment superior to that of children from the semi-skilled and unskilled laboring classes."[94] Negroes, so preponderantly semiskilled and unskilled laborers, were relegated to the bottom rung in perpetuity, however much they might improve their condition, by this theory that nature, not nurture, determined mental ability unto the children and the children's children. Racists in government, in the Army, in industry, in education, quickly recognized the value of this new weapon science had given them, and laid about with it lustily.[95]

Vast and probably irreparable damage had been suffered by blacks before Brigham in 1930 published new findings that utterly demolished the validity of prior concepts, definitions, semantics, content, method, samplings, administration, grading, and analysis of intelligence tests and their results, including the Army tests. It was misleading, Brigham declared in his new study, to say that intelligence is represented by the score of a test simply because it is called an intelligence test, whereas all the score actually represents is a certain objective test situation. In Brigham's words: "Most psychologists working in the test field have been guilty of a *naming fallacy* which easily enables them to slide mysteriously from the score in the test to the hypothetical faculty suggested by the name given to the test."[96] Brigham concluded his revolutionary article thus: "This review has summarized some of the more recent test findings which show that comparative studies of various national and racial groups may not be made with existing tests, and which show, in particular, that one of the most pretentious of these comparative racial studies—the writer's own—was without foundation."[97]

Although Brigham's *mea culpa* evidenced courage and a rare scientific spirit, the black soldier and officer had been badly hurt by the test conclusions recanted ten years later. The entire black community had been injured as practices directly or indirectly justified by the false test findings seeped down from the Army and government through every level of society, threatening to cancel out the enormous gains of blacks during the two previous decades in the white-dominated world of jobs, schools, business, professions, and politics.

Blacks had tried in the past twenty years to live like whites, fight like whites, think like whites, dress and look like whites, in the belief that this would open the gates to the happy land where whites dwelled, but it seemed that the closer they came to their goal the more strenuously they were thrust away. The psychologists' claim of genetic black inferiority gave a new, almost superfluous weapon to those who guarded the gates. A very large number of black people, both New Negroes and older, more conservative ones, both sophisticated and simple people, then turned proudly inward toward themselves, toward rediscovered value in blackness and Africanness, for an identity and a place denied them by the white American world.

CHAPTER 11

Heading Home to Blackness

> Could such a metamorphosis have
> taken place as suddenly as it has ap-
> peared to? The answer is no; not be-
> cause the New Negro is not here, but
> because the Old Negro had long be-
> come more of a myth than a man.
> . . . The day of "aunties," "uncles"
> and "mammies" is equally gone. Uncle
> Tom and Sambo have passed on, and
> even the "Colonel" and "George" play
> barnstorm roles from which they es-
> cape with relief when the public spot-
> light is off. The popular melodrama
> has about played itself out, and it is
> time to scrap the fictions, garret the
> bogeys and settle down to a realistic
> facing of facts.
>
> Alain Locke in *The New Negro*

Two roads led home: the literal, separatist way epitomized by
Marcus Garvey and his back-to-Africa movement; and the meta-
phorical way, the return through knowledge of and pride in the
African heritage, whose artistic manifestation is known as the
Black Renaissance. There were many profound differences between the two movements, to be sure. The Renaissance appealed
to and was created by intellectuals, and called for cultural au-

tonomy on the part of blacks in America; Garvey's movement
appealed to the black American masses to achieve total auton-
omy, cultural, economic, and political, and to build a new civilization along with other black people somewhere in Africa.
Nevertheless, the two movements, both children of the war, had
obvious sibling resemblances. Both adjured black people to stop
being shadows of whites, to take pride in their blackness. At a
time when black people desperately needed hope, Garvey exhorted his listeners: "Up, you mighty race, you can accomplish
what you will,"[1] and a Garveyite advised, "QUIT TRYING TO
IMITATE WHITE PEOPLE, accept segregation as a blessing
in disguise. . . ."[2] Among the intellectuals, Langston Hughes
deplored "this urge within the race toward whiteness,"[3] and
Jessie Fauset urged blacks to develop a racial pride that would
enable them "to find our own beautiful and praiseworthy, an
intense chauvinism that is content with its own types. . . ."[4]
Although both the intelligentsia and the Garveyites might regard
Booker T. Washington as a senile slave counting on his fingers,
they were both closer to the old leader's segregationist stance
than to that of the leaders who had displaced him—Trotter, Du-
Bois, Abbott, Randolph, and all the others who, in a period of
encouraging black progress, dared believe that integration was
possible and must be made to work.

Marcus Manesseh Garvey thought in large terms. The Universal Negro Improvement Association (UNIA), as he called his
organization, was to have its own press, church, businesses, industries, co-operatives, and labor unions, and would give black
people everywhere a proud sense of race solidarity, whether
they lived in the United States or the Indies or on the African
continent, so that together they could achieve their destiny as a
great people.[5] The magnitude of the concept, and Garvey's ability to project success, gave UNIA a sudden and splendid rise.
Negro World, UNIA's weekly paper edited by William Domingo,
began in 1918, and by 1920 had the largest circulation of any
black weekly in the United States, reaching a peak circulation
of 200,000, greater even than that of the *Defender*. By 1923,
Langston Hughes reported, Garvey's name was known the length

and breadth of Africa; Africans hoped he would really reunite the black world and free Africa from white oppression.[6]

As for American blacks, Garvey appeared at precisely the time they were most ready to embrace any program that would give substance to their new sense of pride, self-respect, and race consciousness, and that promised an escape from riots and lynchings. The Attorney General mistook the militance expressed in *Negro World* for political radicalism; the UNIA program, far from being revolutionary, was rather a movement of the conservative right, and was utterly opposed to socialist, communist, or violently nationalistic groups such as the African Blood Brotherhood.[7]

Jamaican-born Garvey, described by one of his sponsors in America as "a little, sawed-off hammered down black man, with determination written all over his face," descended on the United States in 1916 already experienced in black nationalist work in Jamaica and London; he had already founded UNIA in Jamaica. In the summer of 1919, just after the Washington riot, UNIA began to forge ahead. It acquired a meeting hall in Harlem, and had soon organized its own church, youth groups, women's groups, police force, Black Cross nurses, choirs, bands, and marching society. Garvey, costumed in a purple-and-gold uniform and plumed helmet, led colorful UNIA parades. The social and recreational function of UNIA filled an important need and attracted many members for its own sake. By 1920 UNIA claimed one million members and about another two million participants in its activities. UNIA was also moving ahead with its economic program. Most important, at least symbolically, was the Black Star Line, which in September 1919 bought its first ship, *Yarmouth,* intended to take immigrants to Africa as soon as a base could be established there. Soon a few other business enterprises were organized, including the Negro Factories Corporation, the Black Swan Phonograph Company, and the firm of Berry and Ross, which manufactured black dolls.[8]

The Black Star Line was financed by stock sales at $5.00 per share with a limit of 200 shares per stockholder. Sales were brisk, and the company raised nearly $750,000 in its first year. But *Yarmouth,* an old hulk built in 1887, had been overpriced at $165,000, and other purchases were similarly extravagant. There were rumors of corruption on the part of officers of the line, especially when the 1920 financial report failed to itemize expenditures of $280,000, lumped as "organizational expense." At the 1921 UNIA convention, charges of misuse of funds were openly made. By then it appeared that the Black Star ships would have nowhere to go, anyway, because in spite of much effort and negotiation, Garvey could not find a suitable base in Africa where immigrants might settle.[9]

Then Garvey committed a serious error. In 1922, he astounded the black community by meeting in Atlanta with the Imperial Giant of the Ku Klux Klan. Garvey's reasoning was that fighting the Klan could not succeed, because most white Americans shared Klan prejudices; and since the Klan wanted to get rid of blacks, why not enlist Klan support in removing blacks to Africa?[10] This approach to the Klan was a further shock to Garveyites already shaken by the Black Star scandal. Garvey's "sell-out" to the most hated of all white organizations outraged black leaders, from William Pickens to the African Blood Brotherhood. DuBois, who earlier had been interested in Garvey's movement, now wrote: "Marcus Garvey is, without doubt, the most dangerous enemy of the Negro race in America and the world. . . . He is either a lunatic or a traitor."[11] He expressed the sentiments of the entire non-Garveyite black leadership.

Garvey's star had passed its apogee, and fell fast. Dissention arose between the leader and his lieutenants. The leaders of UNIA's African Orthodox Church were accused of immoral behavior. Garvey himself was accused of mail fraud and other illegal acts, and in 1923 was found guilty of defrauding shareholders in the Black Star Line. Appeals failed. Garvey went to jail in 1925, served two years, and was deported to Jamaica. But the dream he had projected of black self-sufficiency, solidarity, pride, and independence of the oppressive white world lingered on for many years. UNIA remained the largest organization for the black masses into the 1930s, and only Garvey's death in 1940 brought it to a reluctant end.[12]

Garvey's ideas, however, never really died, because, as Charles Johnson wrote in a most illuminating commentary the year Garvey was put on trial, "The 'Garvey Movement' is just another

name for the psychology of the American Negro peasantry—for
the surge of race consciousness felt by Negroes throughout the
world. . . ."[13] Johnson quoted a Garveyite as saying, "Garvey
himself could not stop the movement."[14] But it is also impossible
that the movement could have been organized twenty years earlier even by a super Garvey—a movement involving millions of
black people, an international organization, and worldwide activities. Migration, urbanization, education, a wage-earning class,
communications, political and organizational experience, and finally the war with its broadening of horizons and heightening of
expectations, all these produced the new psychology Johnson
spoke of, and that made the Garvey movement possible. Garvey,
although early in life inspired by Booker T. Washington, in his
prime said: "We have been taught to beg rather than to make
demands. Booker T. Washington was not a leader of the Negro
race. We do not look to Tuskegee. The world has recognized
him as a leader, but we do not. We are going to make demands."[15] But Washington had been as inevitably the leader for
Negroes at the turn of the century as Garvey was for blacks, or
Afro-Americans, twenty years later.

The other path home to Africa for the New Negro with his
new psychology was the Black (or Negro, or Harlem) Renaissance, "essentially a period of self-discovery, marked by a sudden
growth of interest in things Negro," as Robert Bone has described
it.[16] The Renaissance, in its serious aspect, was indeed "not a
mere 'vogue' initiated by white 'literacy faddists,'" as Professor
Bone has amply documented in his study of that movement.
Black writers would have been writing in any case, because, as
scholar and teacher Alain Locke defined the Renaissance, it was
the culmination of "the mass movement of the urban immigration
of Negroes, projected on the plane of an increasingly articulate
elite."[17] As a result of the Great Migration, which Bone calls
"the most important event in the history of the American Negro
since his emancipation from slavery," about 90 per cent of the
parents of the Renaissance novelists were in the professional or
white-collar group, as against less than 35 per cent of the parents

of premigration writers. Writers were encouraged by much better chances of publication than they had ever had before, both because the interest and intellectual comradeship of white writers opened new publishing sources to them and because a number of black journals, nonexistent twenty years earlier, brought out new black writers.[18]

The Black Renaissance, in addition to being essentially a New Negro phenomenon, was a response by black people to the same stimuli that in the postwar years produced the Lost Generation —the Fitzgerald generation—among white people. Black writer, white writer, both were in rebellion against the middle-class values of their parents.[19] Black writer, white writer, the war had stripped them of illusions, disgusted them with idealism and pat sentimental formulas, with all falseness, as they saw it, to life in both content and style. Blacks and whites were both striving to express truth, often dismal and ugly yet joyous and beautiful by virtue of being true. The black writer had an exciting truth to tell, the truth about himself, about blackness, an added truth that gave the Black Renaissance an extra dimension of vitality and distinguished it from the effeteness, the boredom, the frenzied search for sensation and pleasure, speed and sex, that characterized white writers and writing of the period. In black "primitiveness"—ironically, a state imposed upon American blacks by white exclusion—the white Lost Generation found refreshing energy, naturalism, and freedom from inhibition. Influential white writers and critics were attracted by and inspired to write about blacks: Eugene O'Neill, Paul Green, Waldo Frank, Sherwood Anderson, DuBose Heyward, Heywood Broun, Carl Van Vechten, and many more. Through their enthusiasm, Van Vechten's in particular, white book and magazine publishers read black writing and found it publishable.[20]

White appreciation of this practical kind was helpful, but many whites became infatuated with blacks, whom they did not really understand, and that led to sillinesses and extremes such as Ethel Barrymore's playing *Scarlet Sister Mary* in blackface.[21] Van Vechten, one of the most infatuated, celebrated Harlem— *Nigger Heaven*, as he called his novel about it—in a prose as purple as Garvey's uniform: "This evening she wore a frock of ecru crepe which exactly matched the colour of her superbly formed shoulders so that, at a little distance, her back appeared to be entirely nude. A long chain of chrysoprase depended from her throat."[22] A bit of dialogue between two dancers, the man intoxicated with the exotic scent of his partner, runs like this:

"Coty?" he whispered interrogatively.
"No, body," she lisped.[23]

Loyalty, friendship, and perhaps gratitude must have at least partly motivated James Weldon Johnson to defend *Nigger Heaven* against those who found it condescending and insulting, and to call it "the most revealing, significant and powerful novel based exclusively on Negro life yet written. . . ."[24]

Simultaneously with this burst of white writing on blacks, well-intended but usually sentimental tributes to a culture not fully understood, came an outpouring of excellent black writing.[25] Jean Toomer's *Cane* was packed with sultry power, its style excitingly new; Langston Hughes's stories had a neat, sure, light touch, and some of his poetry reached deep into ancient black feelings and longings; Claude McKay, George Schuyler, Rudolph Fisher, and Wallace Thurman wrote sharply observed, sometimes very funny and sometimes corrosively bitter satire on black people's hopes and strivings. Any attempt to write off the Harlem Renaissance as a fad created by white literati runs head-on into the extraordinary work of these men and of E. Franklin Frazier, Countee Cullen, Jessie Fauset, Alain Locke, Zora Neale Hurston, Aaron Douglas, John P. Davis, Charles S. Johnson, Bruce Nugent, Gwendolyn Bennett, and others in a constellation of black writers, scientists, artists, and scholars. "New Negro" literary societies sprang up in half a dozen cities. In 1925 Alain Locke edited a black anthology called *The New Negro;* Langston Hughes and others in the mid-twenties founded the literary magazine *Fire,* whose stated purpose was "to burn up a lot of the old, dead, conventional Negro ideas of the past." The 135th Street branch of the New York Public Library, newly the repository of Arthur A. Schomburg's collection of black literature, nourished the mind

of Harlem intellectuals with lectures by Boas, Melville Hersko-
vits, DuBois, Carter Woodson, James Weldon Johnson, and
others of outstanding talent and accomplishment.[26] Blacks and
whites were beginning to meet on a hitherto unexplored plane
of race relations; as Fisher wrote, "If Nordic and Negro wish truly
to know each other, let them discuss not Negroes and Nordics;
let them discuss Greek lyric poets of the fourth century, B.C."[27]

The Renaissance ferment in writing was exceeded by the outpouring of energy in black music, dance, and entertainment,
fields in which blacks had always managed to excel but in which
they now had greatly expanded audiences and fresh appreciation from whites as well as blacks. Artists were proudly black
in these fields, too. In 1919 the National Association of Negro
Musicians was organized "to discover and foster talent, to mold
taste, to promote fellowship, and to advocate racial expression."[28] It was the Jazz Age in America, and in London and
Paris, too, thanks to their wartime exposure to black jazz music.
Seligmann wrote of the 1920 black: "He may not vote, he may
not mingle socially with white people, but the music to which
the jumbled American political scene seems to vibrate and sway
is jazz."[29] According to Van Vechten, "It is the only music produced in America today which is worth the paper it is written
on."[30] White composers and musicians, such as George Gershwin
and Benny Goodman, Tommy Dorsey and Gene Krupa, were
profoundly influenced by the great jazz that poured out of the
Black Renaissance.

Each season brought at least one black musical play to Broadway. *Shuffle Along* was a tremendous hit. Hall Johnson joined
the show's orchestra in 1921, and shortly afterward organized the
Hall Johnson singers. Florence Mills was the toast of Broadway,
and Josephine Baker the unchallenged queen of Paris entertainment. Roland Hayes was in his prime; Paul Robeson was singing
in black musicals and winning fame as an actor in O'Neill's *Emperor Jones*. Big, black Gladys Bently played and sang "St. James
Infirmary" to enthusiastic fans. W. C. Handy and Harry Pace
started a music publishing company in 1918, and blues records
were first made in 1920; Bessie Smith's blues won immediate pop-

ularity with sophisticated whites. Right after the war, Jim Europe had taken a sixty-five-man band on a world tour; when Europe died in the spring of 1919, his associate Noble Sissle teamed up with jazz pianist Eubie Blake. Will Marion Cook took his ensemble of forty-one instrumentalists and nine singers to London and Paris; Sidney Bechet won praise from King George V at a command performance. The great jazz names of the time were the great names of all jazz: "Jelly Roll" Morton, Johnny Dodds, Louis Armstrong, Duke Ellington. Bill "Bojangles" Robinson's dancing made any show a hit. Ma Rainey was captivating her listeners with "Wonder whah mah easy rider's gone," Van Vechten wrote, and Ethel Waters was on her way to Broadway fame.[31]

Those were the achievements, and those the achievers, of the Renaissance movement; and a very large part of white appreciation was not faddish, but sincere recognition of the value of black contributions in the arts. Inevitably, however, as the excitement to be found in Harlem was publicized, a faddish aspect —unsavory and sometimes vicious—emerged, a vogue of "slumming" in Harlem, until it was not easy, Langston Hughes said, for a black man to find a place to have a drink that the tourists from downtown hadn't discovered.[32] This orgiastic side of the Renaissance has led some commentators, both black and white, to label the whole movement a mere fad of white thrill-seekers who suddenly took a fancy to everything primitive and as whimsically tired of it all; and to complain that black artists were not sincere in their work but were simply trying to please their white patrons and get what they could while they were in vogue. True, it was an age of fads, for the New Negro and the New Woman, New Poetry, New Science, for styles that were the rage one year, old hat the next. Van Vechten listed in his *Firecrackers*, published in 1923, a mixed bag of fads of the previous year that he said were now passé: Freud, Einstein, Dada, glands, *vers libre*, radio, cubism, Ezra Pound, Prohibition, ectoplasm, and "Negro dancing." White tourists loved the Harlem "shouting churches"; rich white men kept black chorus girls in preference to white ones.[33] The Harlem fad led throngs of whites uptown for gin and sin, and the nightclubs, gin mills, dance halls, and brothels

did a Roaring Twenties business. Partly this resulted from a cast-
ing off of prewar Puritan attitudes, and partly from Prohibition,
then in force; but it is also reminiscent of the southern system
of concentrating every kind of vice and corruption in the Negro
quarter of a city, where white men resorted for their more dis-
reputable pleasures. It had been true of Storyville, before the
migration; it was true of Chicago and other industrial cities where
ghettos became isolated; it was especially true of the Harlem
ghetto of New York, mecca of entertainers and artists and bohemians, in the postwar years when bad whiskey was easily and
cheaply found in the nightclubs and speakeasies around Lenox
Avenue and 135th Street.

The fashionable mood of being world-weary, disillusioned, rebellious, and cynical was pleasurably enhanced by the vast
amounts of bootleg liquor consumed. Harlem was "a great play-
ground" and "white folks discovered black magic there," Claude
McKay said. The Cotton Club and Barron's were Jim Crow, Langston Hughes said, catering exclusively to gangsters and other
rich whites; at the Savoy Ballroom, black couples lindy-hopped
for the entertainment of white tourists. Rudolph Fisher said
when he and friends went to a Harlem cabaret they were often
the only black people there, and they would be stared at when
they went out on the dance floor. Whites didn't come just to
watch, either, Fisher said; they enjoyed "playing Negro games."
He wrote, "They camel and fish-tail and turkey, they geche and
black bottom and scronch, they skate and buzzard and mess-
around—and they do them all better than I!" Did it mean, Fisher
wondered, that whites have "tuned in on our wave length?"[34]

Wallace Thurman, the bitterest black critic of the period, who
in his novel *Infants of the Spring* dubbed the black intellectuals
"the niggerati" and the white do-gooders who fawned upon them
"the negrotarians," did not believe the Harlem Renaissance would
bring any permanent gain in race relations. In his opinion, what
pretended to be an approach to social equality was not that at
all, but simply drunken revelry and indiscriminate love-making;
to Thurman, black writers were simply making the most of a good
racket while it lasted.[35] Van Vechten had a character in *Nigger
Heaven* say: "Why, more of us get on through the ofays than

through the shines. . . . Who supports Roland Hayes? Who supports Florence Mills? Is it white or black audiences?"[36] Black writers, musicians, and entertainers rubbed elbows with the white literati and hangers-on at lavish parties given by Van Vechten or by the noted Harlem hostess A'lelia Walker,[37] but did it, asked Langston Hughes, betoken a solid, permanent gain in race relations to be able to refer casually in conversation to Heywood Broun and George Gershwin as Heywood and George? Many blacks, Hughes said, were joyfully convinced that "the millennium had come . . . the race problem had at last been solved . . . the New Negro would lead a new life from then on in green pastures of tolerance created by Countee Cullen, Ethel Waters, Claude McKay, Duke Ellington, Bojangles, and Alain Locke."[38] Hughes did not believe it. Fisher did not believe it. Wallace Thurman did not believe it, Hughes said, and despair of the black future led Thurman deeper and deeper into drink until his death in 1934. Fisher died within a week of Thurman. The fad for Harlem died about then, too, after the repeal of Prohibition and the settling in of the Great Depression. The millennium had not come.

The heart of the Black Renaissance, however, the New Negro, an urban man with new attitudes and goals, was by then a permanent part of American life. He was the product of a marathon struggle, a twenty-year battle in which black Americans had fought their way out of serfdom, ignorance, and political impotence into active, informed participation in modern industrial America. It is true that opportunities for change had been offered by the approach of war and the war itself, but it is not therefore less amazing how black people managed to seize these opportunities with practically no help from government or from the powers that controlled education, labor, money, and business.

Consciousness of the changes they had made through their own efforts changed black people's concept of themselves, so that although they continued objects of prejudice, privation, injustice, and brutality, they no longer accepted such treatment as inevitable; they would not any more take it passively. Awareness of the world, new perspectives and horizons opened up by migration, city life, and war service, gave the New Negro a fresh awareness of himself as a person, and an interest and pride in blackness that the mythical Old Negro, seeing himself through white eyes, could not possibly have had. The war years and postwar years were, Professor Bone has written, "essentially a period of self-discovery, marked by a sudden growth of interest in things Negro," precisely the reverse of prewar assimilationism with its "conscious imitation of white norms and its deliberate suppression of 'racial' elements."[39] The Talented Tenth, who had held themselves aloof as a special caste, finally saw that they could never truly break down Jim Crow barriers except by aligning themselves with the black masses in an assault upon, rather than a flight from, the barriers of color.[40] "Those of us who have forged forward," says a character in Jessie Fauset's novel *Plum Bun,* "are not able as yet to go our separate ways apart from the unwashed, untutored herd. We must still look back and render service to our less fortunate, weaker brethren. And the first step toward making this a workable attitude is the acquisition not so much of a racial love as a racial pride."[41]

Alain Locke wrote that the New Negro was not so much a new person as he was a *real* person—for the first time in many generations. The "old Negro" was "more of a formula than a human being" and "more of a myth than a man," Locke said, because the "good old nigger" or "mammy" had never been anything but roles created by wishful white folks and helplessly played by black folks.[42] The New Negro was the real man who had always been behind the charade, with the burnt cork washed off. In two decades of dramatic change he had become used to doing his own thinking, talking, organizing, and fighting, and would from then on defend himself personally, industrially, and politically. He was marching to meet the millennium halfway.

Notes

CHAPTER 1

1. Woodrow Wilson, "The Reconstruction of the Southern States," p. 6.
2. Jack Abramowitz, "The Negro in the Agrarian Revolt," p. 89; Anna Rochester, *The Populist Movement in the United States*, p. 12.
3. Oscar Micheaux, *The Conquest: The Story of a Negro Pioneer*, pp. 289–90.
4. See J. Rogers Hollingsworth, "Populism: The Problem of Rhetoric and Reality."
5. Abramowitz, op. cit., p. 90.
6. Herbert Shapiro says most white Populists seemed unable to free themselves of fear and dislike of blacks despite the liberal Greenback heritage, and bitterly resented the idea of federal intervention to guarantee black rights (Meier and Rudwick, eds., "The Populists and the Negro" in *The Making of Black America*, Vol. 2, p. 32.
7. Stanley P. Hirshon, *Farewell to the Bloody Shirt: Northern Republicans and the Southern Negro, 1877–1893*, pp. 185, 214–33.
8. Abramowitz, op. cit., p. 93.
9. Ibid., p. 91; John D. Hicks, *The Populist Revolt: A History of the Farmers' Alliance and the People's Party*, p. 115.
10. Abramowitz, op. cit., p. 94.
11. Anna Rochester, *The Populist Movement*, facing Contents page.
12. Ibid., p. 59.
13. Abramowitz, op. cit., p. 93.
14. Ibid., p. 94, quoting from a report in the *National Economist*.
15. Ibid. Tom Watson, the Populist leader in Georgia, was at that time extremely cordial to black Alliancemen and encouraged their advancement.
16. Ibid.; Robert H. Wiebe, *The Search for Order, 1877–1920*, p. 72.
17. Abramowitz, op. cit., p. 91.
18. U. S. Bureau of the Census, *Historical Statistics*, p. 682; John D. Hicks, *The Populist Revolt*, p. 253; see also C. Vann Woodward, "American History (White Man's Version) Needs an Infusion of Soul."
19. Shapiro, "The Populists and the Negro," p. 32; Wiebe, *The Search for Order*, p. 110.
20. Frenise A. Logan, *The Negro in North Carolina, 1876–1894*, shows the opposite side of the coin; in North Carolina elections, she says (p. 22),

"Negroes who voted with Democrats were subjected to ostracism by their own race."

21. C. Vann Woodward, "Tom Watson and the Negro in Agrarian Politics," p. 26.

22. *People's Party Handbook;* the entire complex situation is well presented by Helen G. Edmonds, *The Negro and Fusion Politics in North Carolina, 1894–1901.*

23. Woodward, op. cit., p. 18.

24. Olive Hall Shadgett, *The Republican Party in Georgia, from Reconstruction through 1900,* pp. 118–19; Woodward, op. cit., pp. 18–19, 27. Watson's dramatic turnabout in regard to blacks has led scholars to wonder if he was ever sincerely interested in justice for the Negro. An incident of later years suggests that his concern may have been sincere and lasting, although not strong enough to resist political pressure. After World War I, Watson, then in the U. S. Senate, called for an investigation of alleged illegal hangings of American soldiers in France, most of them black soldiers. The investigation was something of a farce, and may have been pure whitewash to stop the complaints, but Watson may have been really concerned.

25. Woodward, *The Strange Career of Jim Crow,* pp. 79–80.

26. Hicks, *The Populist Revolt,* p. 334.

27. Ibid., p. 253.

28. Woodward, *The Strange Career of Jim Crow,* p. 63.

29. John Hope Franklin, "History of Racial Segregation in the United States," *The Making of Black America,* Vol. 2, pp. 8–13; Charles S. Johnson, *Patterns of Negro Segregation,* pp. 159–65; Woodward, *American Counterpoint: Slavery and Racism in the North-South Dialogue,* pp. 234–60.

30. Henry Steele Commager, *Documents of American History,* p. 629.

31. Ibid.

32. Woodward, *American Counterpoint,* p. 229, quoting Robert Cushman's article on Justice Harlan in the Dictionary of American Biography. There are a number of individual instances where Southerners of the old, aristocratic, slave-owning class were more conscientious in guarding the rights of blacks than were men newly risen from the white lower classes, but as a generalization this will not stand up. For instance, Governor Oates was a conservative of Harlan's stripe, yet he did not hesitate to abridge rights that were constitutionally guaranteed to blacks. Herbert Seligmann avoided the pitfall of generalization in *The Negro Faces America,* first published in 1920; the southern aristocrat, he said (p. 76), sometimes harbored "a tolerance which came of affectionate condescension" toward blacks, reinforced by a realization of the material advantages of association with them, whereas the poor white, from his totally different point of reference, merely felt antipathy and jealousy. What is important to bear in mind is that the white leaders in the South, both high-born and low-born, rarely scrupled to use that antipathy and jealousy when it served their needs, so that there does not seem to be any class monopoly on racism.

33. Commager, *Documents of American History,* p. 630.

34. Ibid.

35. Not all scholars agree that Jim Crow did not arrive in the South until the 1890s. David Hackett Fischer in his brilliant study *Historians'*

Fallacies, has observed that, although from about 1890 onward "there were undoubtedly important changes in the quality of racial thought, and in the shape of racist institutions," nevertheless the thought and the institutions reached far back into the time of slavery; Fischer also notes that Woodward himself points out the existence of so many Jim Crow restrictions in the South before the 1890s—in churches, schools, hotels, restaurants, jails, hospitals, and many other places—that he weakens his thesis by the "fallacy of the overwhelming exception" (Fischer, op. cit., pp. 148–49). The answer perhaps lies in definition. Was this earlier racial discrimination systematic, rigid, and consistently enforced, or was it occasional, whimsical, casual, flexible, and susceptible to many exceptions in enforcement? Woodward's contention seems upheld by the unarguable fact that a deluge of Jim Crow laws descended after the mid-1890s, and what would have been the need for them if Jim Crow had already been an established mode of life? However, there had been earlier attempts to institutionalize Jim Crow, prompted, says Constance Green in her study of race relations in the national capital, by a Supreme Court decision of more than ten years before Plessy *v.* Ferguson. In this case of 1883, the Court was appealed to by a black citizen of Connecticut who had been refused service in the dining room of a Washington, D.C., restaurant. A lower court had found the restaurant owner guilty of violating the federal Civil Rights Act of 1875, and had fined him $500; but the United States Supreme Court declared the 1875 act unconstitutional in the states, although perhaps binding in the territories and the District of Columbia (Green, *The Secret City,* pp. 122–23). Many pre-1890s Jim Crow laws, state and local, must have leaned on that decision. After it, a number of northern, western, and border states protected their black citizens by passing their own civil rights statutes, although no southern state had adopted any form of civil rights statute as of 1910; on the contrary, by 1910 all southern states had discriminatory laws on their books, and the name "Jim Crow" was already so linked with such laws that in North Carolina and Maryland they were officially indexed in the annual register of statutes under the letter J (Gilbert T. Stephenson, *Race Distinctions in American Law,* pp. 121, 208).

36. August Meier and Elliott Rudwick, "A Strange Chapter in the Career of Jim Crow," *The Making of Black America,* Vol. 2, pp. 15–19; see also Meier and Rudwick, "The Boycott Movement Against Jim Crow Streetcars in the South, 1900–1906," *Journal of American History,* Vol. 55 (March 1969), pp. 756–75.

37. Woodward, *American Counterpoint,* p. 240.

38. Ray Stannard Baker, *Following the Color Line,* p. 34.

39. Ibid., p. 31.

40. John Hope Franklin, "History of Racial Segregation," p. 11; Stephenson, *Race Distinctions,* pp. 230–31.

41. Woodward, *Strange Career of Jim Crow,* pp. 97–101; Franklin, "History of Racial Segregation," p. 11; Baker, *Following the Color Line,* p. 35.

42. Green, *Secret City,* p. 126.

43. Margaret Law Callcott, *The Negro in Maryland Politics 1870–1912,* p. 137.

44. Charles S. Johnson, *Patterns of Negro Segregation,* pp. 117–55; part of the furor about President Roosevelt's having Booker T. Washington to

dinner at the White House was involuntary revulsion of southern whites at this violation of taboo.

45. Woodward, *Strange Career of Jim Crow,* p. 96.

46. V. O. Key, Jr., *Southern Politics in State and Nation,* pp. 540–45; Hicks, *The Populist Revolt,* pp. 411–12; Baker, *Following the Color Line,* p. 261; Shadgett, *Republican Party in Georgia,* p. 157; Callcott, *Negro in Maryland Politics,* pp. 102 ff.

47. William Hesseltine and David Smiley, *The South in American History,* p. 432.

48. Lewinson, *Race, Class and Party,* pp. 85–86.

49. Key, *Southern Politics,* p. 538.

50. E. Franklin Frazier, *The Negro in the United States,* pp. 156, 157; Stephenson, *Race Distinctions,* p. 296; Woodward, *Strange Career of Jim Crow,* pp. 84–85; Key, *Southern Politics,* p. 587; Hesseltine and Smiley, op. cit., p. 433.

51. Eli Ginzberg and Alfred S. Eichner, *The Troublesome Presence: American Democracy and the Negro,* pp. 227–28; Key, *Southern Politics,* pp. 538–39, 587.

52. Hesseltine and Smiley, op. cit., p. 432; Frazier, *The Negro in American History,* p. 157; Stephenson, *Race Distinctions,* p. 306. The Supreme Court found "grandfather clauses" unconstitutional in 1915.

53. Ginzberg and Eichner, *The Troublesome Presence,* pp. 227–28; Lewinson, op. cit., pp. 81, 117, 214; Hesseltine and Smiley, op. cit., p. 433; Morton Sosna, *Negroes and the Wilson Years, 1912–1916: The Politics of Race during the Progressive Era,* p. 2; Harold U. Faulkner, *The Quest for Social Justice 1898–1914,* p. 10.

54. Andrew Buni, *The Negro in Virginia Politics 1902–1965,* pp. 22–25, 31. In Virginia, as of 1900, about half the blacks of voting age were illiterate. When the new voting law became effective in 1902, these men would have to pass the understanding tests, which probably few could have done even if the tests had been fairly and seriously administered. The understanding test in Virginia consisted in answering questions posed by polling officials, and a whole new collection of racist jokes must have emerged from the answers, real or invented; it was said, for instance, that when asked to define the Virginia General Assembly, many Negroes answered that it was a place of worship, and that one Negro, when asked what was a fair punishment for a man who committed suicide, said "twelve months in jail."

55. Albert D. Kirwan, *Revolt of the Rednecks: Mississippi Politics 1876–1925,* pp. 116–18.

56. Stephenson, *Race Distinctions,* pp. 253–72; Baker, *Following the Color Line,* p. 263; Seligmann, *The Negro Faces America,* pp. 276–77.

57. Woodward, *The Strange Career of Jim Crow,* p. 86.

58. Baker, *Following the Color Line,* p. 248.

59. Idus A. Newby, *Jim Crow's Defense: Anti-Negro Thought in America 1900–1930,* p. 142; Thomas Nelson Page, *The Negro: The Southerner's Problem,* pp. 151, 159–60.

60. Lewinson, *Race, Class and Party,* pp. 84–85.

61. Newby, op. cit., p. 147.

62. Ibid., p. 141.

63. Baker, op. cit., p. 246.

64. Lewinson, op. cit., p. 84.

65. Newby, op. cit., p. 149.

66. Buni, *Negro in Virginia Politics*, p. 19.

67. Stephen R. Fox, *The Guardian of Boston: William Monroe Trotter*, p. 27; Callcott, *Negro in Maryland Politics*, pp. 122–23, 129; William Pickens, *The New Negro*, p. 184; Lewinson, op. cit., p. 127; Edward Byron Reuter, *The American Race Problem*, p. 147.

68. *America's Race Problems*, Addresses, Annual Meeting of the American Academy of Political and Social Science, p. 130.

69. Baker, *Following the Color Line*, p. 249.

70. Kirwan, *Revolt of the Rednecks*, pp. 15–17.

71. Newby, *Jim Crow's Defense*, p. 119.

72. *America's Race Problems*, Addresses, American Academy of Political and Social Science, p. 113.

73. Baker, op. cit., p. 247.

74. Woodward, *Strange Career of Jim Crow*, p. 95.

75. Baker, op. cit., p. 87; Woodward, *Strange Career of Jim Crow*, pp. 88–89; Newby, *Jim Crow's Defense*, p. 7.

76. Baker, op. cit., p. 81.

77. Benjamin Brawley, *A Social History of the American Negro*, p. 297.

78. U. S. Bureau of the Census, *Historical Statistics*, pp. 11–12, 278–79.

79. Booker T. Washington, *Story of the Negro: The Rise of the Race from Slavery*, pp. 53, 380; Baker, op. cit., p. 91; Hortense Powdermaker, *After Freedom: A Cultural Study in the Deep South*, pp. 95–108.

80. Baker, op. cit., pp. 74–77.

81. Carter G. Woodson, *The Rural Negro*, p. 48.

82. Reuter, *The American Race Problem*, p. 227.

83. Baker, op. cit., p. 76.

84. Woodson, op. cit., pp. 61–65.

85. Thomas J. Edwards, "The Tenant System and Some Changes Since Emancipation," *Making of Black America*, Vol. 2, pp. 23–24; Baker, op. cit., p. 97; Reuter, *The American Race Problem*, p. 229.

86. Woodson, op. cit., pp. 68–69, 71.

87. Baker, op. cit., pp. 81, 105; Woodson, op. cit., p. 71; Reuter, op. cit., p. 229.

88. Baker, op. cit., p. 97.

89. Ibid., p. 105.

90. Ibid.

91. George Edmund Haynes, *The Negro at Work in New York City*, p. 24; Logan, *The Negro in North Carolina*, pp. 86–87, 90–91; W. E. B. DuBois, ed., *The Negro Artisan*, p. 87.

92. Ibid., pp. 94, 165, 167, 171; Logan, op. cit., pp. 95–96.

93. DuBois, *The Negro Artisan*, p. 159.

94. Ibid., p. 176.

95. Ibid., p. 177.

96. Ibid., pp. 174–75.

97. Kelly Miller, *Race Adjustment*, pp. 120–21; Woodward, *Strange Career of Jim Crow*, p. 16.

98. Booker T. Washington, *The Future of the American Negro*, p. 75.

99. Faulkner, *Quest for Social Justice*, p. 99.

100. U. S. Bureau of the Census, *Historical Statistics*, p. 72; Washington, *Story of the Negro*, pp. 303–4.

101. Micheaux, *The Conquest*, pp. 18–19, 26–27.

102. Faulkner, op. cit., pp. 22–23.

103. *Colliers Cyclopedia and Compendium of Profitable Knowledge* (New York: P. F. Collier & Son, 1901), p. 685.

104. W. E. B. DuBois, *The Philadelphia Negro*, p. 324; Micheaux, op. cit., pp. 24–26.

105. Leslie H. Fishel and Benjamin Quarles, *The Negro American: A Documentary History*, pp. 346–50, report of "Proceedings of the National Business League, 1st Meeting, Boston, August 23–24, 1900."

106. Washington, *Story of the Negro*, pp. 37–38, 202–3, 213–33; Ray Stannard Baker, "Gathering Clouds Along the Color Line," p. 236.

107. Baker, *Following the Color Line*, p. 41.

108. Kelly Miller, *Race Adjustment*, p. 184; Washington, *Story of the Negro*, pp. 78–79, 179–80, 304.

109. Frazier, *The Negro in the United States*, pp. 205–6, 715; Frazier's description of conditions of living is of the 1930s, but there had probably not been any significant change.

110. Kelly Miller, op. cit., p. 122; Green, *Secret City*, pp. 41–43; *America's Race Problems*, pp. 122–24.

111. Woodson, *Rural Negro*, pp. 117–20; Woodward, *Strange Career of Jim Crow*, p. 101; Roi Ottley, *The Lonely Warrior: The Life and Times of Robert S. Abbott*, pp. 31–32.

112. Woodson, op. cit., pp. 7, 8, 14, 18; Reuter, *American Race Problem*, p. 181; William Miller, *Memphis During the Progressive Era, 1900–1917*, p. 116.

113. Tindall, *South Carolina Negroes*, p. 221; see below, Chapter 2, on education of children as a motive for black migration.

114. Hirshon, *Farewell to the Bloody Shirt*, p. 200.

115. Hesseltine and Smiley, *The South in American History*, pp. 447–48.

116. Washington, *Story of the Negro*, p. 144; Hesseltine and Smiley, op. cit., p. 520.

117. Baker, *Following the Color Line*, p. 306.

118. Micheaux, *The Conquest*, p. 13; Reuter, *American Race Problem*, p. 263; Howard Odum, *Social and Mental Traits of the Negro*, pp. 27–37; Tindall, *South Carolina Negro*, p. 219.

119. Baker, *Following the Color Line*, pp. 282–83.

120. Ibid., p. 52; Reuter, op. cit., pp. 263, 273–74 (his figures are as of 1920); T. J. Woofter, Jr., *Negro Problems in Cities*, pp. 208–9; Tindall, op. cit., p. 223.

121. Reuter, op. cit., pp. 257–58.

122. Baker, "Gathering Clouds Along the Color Line," p. 235.

123. Powdermaker, *After Freedom*, p. 302.

124. Baker, *Following the Color Line*, p. 247.

125. Ibid.

126. The Loyalty League during World War I revived the worst features of the black codes.

127. Reuter, op. cit., p. 230; Baker, *Following the Color Line*, p. 49; Logan, *Negro in North Carolina*, p. 211; Stephenson, *Race Distinctions*, p. 275.

128. Baker, *Following the Color Line*, p. 49.

129. Logan, op. cit., pp. 193, 211.

130. Tindall, *South Carolina Negro*, p. 261; Francis Butler Simkins and Charles P. Roland, *History of the South*, p. 513.

131. Tindall, op. cit. p. 261; DuBois, *Negro Crime*, p. 49; Baker, *Following the Color Line*, pp. 45–46; Wilbur J. Cash, *Mind of the South*, p. 120.

132. Baker, *Following the Color Line*, pp. 50, 98; Tindall, op. cit., p. 270. The death of a young black convict in 1971 on a county farm in Arkansas resulted in exposure of the intolerable conditions still prevailing in that state; New York *Times*, November 10, 1971.

133. Stephenson, *Race Distinctions*, p. 273.

134. Baker, *Following the Color Line*, p. 169; Powdermaker, *After Freedom*, pp. 181–82; William Miller, *Memphis During the Progressive Era*, pp. 90–91; Baker, op. cit., pp. 46–47; *America's Race Problems*, p. 134; DuBois, *Negro Crime*, pp. 49, 50.

135. Eileen Southern, *Music of Black Americans*, pp. 95, 99, 131, 134, 282, 312, 313, 358–59, 374–75.

136. This figure is from Gossett, *Race: The History of an Idea in America*, p. 269. It is probable that not all lynchings were reported. Tables of the numbers of lynchings each year vary slightly from source to source but show the same trends up and down. For example, cf. Kelly Miller, *The Everlasting Stain*, p. 325; Reuter, *American Race Problem*, p. 342 (based on Tuskegee figures); Grimshaw, *Racial Violence*, pp. 58–59. NAACP figures on lynching, published regularly in the *Crisis*, do not differ markedly from figures in other sources. White lynchings are also recorded in some tables; in the 1900–20 period they usually amounted to only a small percentage of black lynchings, 10 per cent or less; as Reuter pointed out (op. cit., p. 344), white lynchings were part of the frontier phenomenon and passed with it. Most black lynchings took place in Alabama, Mississippi, Arkansas, Louisiana, Georgia, Florida, Tennessee, Kentucky, and Texas (Grimshaw, op. cit., p. 57; Kelly Miller, op. cit., p. 326; Reuter, op. cit., p. 346). According to recent figures cited by Grimshaw, p. 58, the highest number of black lynchings in the first two decades of the century took place in 1900 (106) and 1901 (105), after which the number never reached 100; by 1910 the figure was 67, after which there continued a fairly steady decrease to around 50 or less until 1918, when the number bounced back to 60, and 1919, when it leaped to 76. In 1920, 1921, and 1922, black lynchings again decreased to the 50s; the number dropped significantly to 29 in 1923, and still lower in following years. Efforts to make lynching a federal crime, thus removing prosecution from the jurisdiction of prejudiced state courts, were blocked by the apathy of President Wilson and the opposition of Congress, especially southern senators; nevertheless, the NAACP lobbied vigorously over the years for an antilynch bill and produced a valuable study of lynching (see below, p. 250).

137. Frazier, *Negro in the United States*, p. 159.

138. Page, *The Negro*, pp. 99–100, 105; Reuter, op. cit., p. 60.

139. Gossett, *Race*, p. 270; between 1882 and 1951, according to Grimshaw, op. cit., p. 59, rape was the charge in 19.2 per cent of lynchings.

140. Reuter, op. cit., p. 348.

141. Pickens, *The New Negro*, p. 201.

142. Washington, *Future of the American Negro*, p. 187; Baker, *Following the Color Line*, p. 198; Seligmann, *The Negro Faces America*, p. 260.

143. Cash, *Mind of the South*, p. 116.

144. Seligmann, op. cit., p. 276; see also ibid., p. 261.

145. See especially Cash, op. cit., pp. 114–17, on the rape complex; and for a different, earlier view, Page, *The Negro*, pp. 99–119.

146. John Dollard (*Caste and Class in a Southern Town*, p. 136 and note), in a discussion of the idealization of southern women, quotes a passage from Carl Carmer's *Stars Fell on Alabama* describing a university dance ritual performed by a fraternity calling itself "The Key Ice." During a break in the dancing, a long cake of ice is solemnly wheeled in on a cart, glistening in torchlight, and is toasted (in water) as a symbol of "Woman, lovely woman of the Southland, as pure and chaste as this sparkling water, as cold as this gleaming ice"; then the icy symbol receives the pledge of the students to devote their hearts and lives "to the protection of her virtue and chastity."

147. Seligmann, op. cit., p. 272.

148. Kirwan, *Revolt of the Rednecks*, p. 152.

149. Charles Johnson, *Patterns of Negro Segregation*, p. 257.

150. Seligmann, op. cit., p. 59.

151. Pickens, *The New Negro*, pp. 191–92; Pickens was one of the new, militant, NAACP leaders.

152. Thornbrough, "Booker T. Washington," p. 162.

153. Washington, *Future of the American Negro*, p. 132.

154. Vincent, *Black Power and the Garvey Movement*, pp. 25–26.

155. Louis Filler, *Crusaders for American Liberalism*, p. 276.

156. Henry F. Pringle, *Theodore Roosevelt*, pp. 230, 248–50.

157. Ibid., p. 249.

158. Baker, *Following the Color Line*, p. 101.

CHAPTER 2

1. Carter G. Woodson, *A Century of Negro Migration*, pp. 11, 21, 40–91; Benjamin Quarles, "Evacuation with the British," *Black History: A Reappraisal*, pp. 134, 139.

2. Woodson, op. cit., pp. 104–5, 114, 117, 123, 134, 142; for details of the Exodus of 1879 see also Fishel and Quarles, op. cit., pp. 290–92; Emmett J. Scott, *Negro Migration During the War*, p. 5; George Brown Tindall, *Emergence of the New South*, pp. 173–84.

3. Lorenzo J. Greene and Carter Woodson, *The Negro Wage Earner*, p. 79 (quoting from DuBois' Farmville, Virginia, study); Woofter, *Negro Problems in Cities*, p. 26; Faulkner, *Quest for Social Justice*, p. 6; Baker, *Following the Color Line*, p. 79; Dean Dutcher, *The Negro in Modern Industrial*

Society, pp. 21, 27; Abram L. Harris, Jr., "Negro Migration to the North," p. 922; Gunnar Myrdal, *An American Dilemma: The Negro Problem and Modern Democracy,* pp. 183, 186.

4. U. S. Bureau of the Census, *Historical Statistics,* p. 56; Dutcher, op. cit., p. 22.

5. Harris, op. cit., pp. 922–23; Harris points out that a higher percentage of whites than blacks migrated from the South between 1910 and 1920.

6. U. S. Department of Labor, Division of Negro Economics, *Negro Migration in 1916–1917,* p. 156; Abraham Epstein, *The Negro Migrant in Pittsburgh,* p. 29; Baker, "The Negro Goes North," p. 319; *Crisis,* Vol. 14, p. 63.

7. Seth M. Scheiner, *Negro Mecca: A History of the Negro in New York City, 1865–1920,* p. 11 (unascribed quote).

8. U. S. Bureau of the Census, op. cit., p. 56.

9. Woodson, op. cit., pp. 159–62; Alain Locke disagreed, believing that the men at the bottom—the peasants—led the migration to the cities, and that the professional class simply followed its clientele (essay by Locke from *The New Negro: An Interpretation,* in Fishel and Quarles, *The Negro American,* pp. 437–38.

10. Baker, *Following the Color Line,* p. 113.

11. Haynes, *The Negro at Work in New York City,* p. 27.

12. Powdermaker in her 1930s study of Mississippi concluded that 70 to 75 per cent of sharecroppers got an honest settlement at year's end, but there would be trouble if any sharecropper dared demand a written accounting of purchases and earnings (Powdermaker, *After Freedom,* p. 86).

13. U. S. Department of Labor, *Negro Migration in 1916–1917;* this invaluable study of the migration was the result of investigations directed by Dr. James H. Dillard, director of the Jeanes and Slater foundations, and was published by the Department of Labor's Bureau of Negro Economics, whose newly appointed chief was the black social scientist George E. Haynes. Unfortunately, Haynes's bureau did not long survive this publication, perhaps because of its objectivity and frankness.

14. *Crisis,* Vol. 14, p. 65.

15. Harris, op. cit., p. 921.

16. Epstein, op. cit., p. 27; Gilbert Osofsky, *Harlem: The Making of a Ghetto,* p. 21; Louise Venable Kennedy, *The Negro Peasant Turns Cityward,* p. 56.

17. John Daniels, *In Freedom's Birthplace: A Study of the Boston Negroes,* p. 137.

18. Odum, *Social and Mental Traits of the Negro,* p. 39.

19. U. S. Department of Labor, op. cit., p. 9.

20. Baker, "The Negro Goes North," p. 317.

21. Scott, *Negro Migration,* pp. 16–17; Scott, "Letters of Negro Migrants of 1916–1918," p. 305; Fishel and Quarles, op. cit., "Negroes Explain the Exodus," p. 398.

22. Scott, *Negro Migration,* p. 18; Charles H. Wesley, *Negro Labor in the United States, 1850–1925,* p. 293; Baker, "The Negro Goes North," p. 315; Harris, "Negro Migration," p. 923; Haynes, *Negro at Work,* p. 27.

23. Fishel and Quarles, op. cit., "Negroes Explain the Exodus," pp. 397–99.

24. Kirwan, *Revolt of the Rednecks,* p. 162.

25. Powdermaker, *After Freedom,* pp. 310, 315.

26. Scott, "Letters of Negro Migrants," pp. 294, 298.

27. Fishel and Quarles, op. cit., "The Wartime Negro Exodus," pp. 394–96.

28. Scott, "Letters of Negro Migrants," p. 330.

29. Powdermaker, op. cit., pp. 44–46, 357.

30. Baker, *Following the Color Line,* p. 133. The withholding of polite forms of address is still practiced toward black people in the South. Robert Coles in his *Farewell to the South,* p. 375, quotes a black woman on the subject: "Here in New Orleans I hear the NAACP wants us to be called mister and missus, like they do with the whites when they go shopping. I heard a saleslady tell her friend she was never in her life going to call a nigger mister or missus; she'd quit first."

31. Scott, *Negro Migration,* p. 22; Osofsky, *Harlem,* p. 22; Charles S. Johnson, "How Much of the Migration Was a Flight from Persecution?" pp. 272–74; the Labor Department study of the migration disagreed with Johnson in this matter; it pointed out that in southwestern Georgia, where three of the worst lynchings in the state's history had taken place in 1915 and 1916, 35,000 to 40,000 black people left between May 1916 and September 1917; they had an economic motive also, however, because their section was the worst hit by the boll weevil (U. S. Department of Labor, *Negro Migration,* pp. 75–78).

32. Kennedy, *Negro Peasant Turns Cityward,* pp. 48–50; Dutcher, *Negro in Modern Industrial Society,* pp. 112–13.

33. U. S. Department of Labor, op. cit., p. 105; this assumption of their own defense perhaps contributed to the black woman's reputation for self-sufficiency and aggressiveness.

34. U. S. Department of Labor, op. cit., p. 33.

35. Fishel and Quarles, op. cit., "Negroes Explain the Exodus," p. 398.

36. The last six quotes are from Scott, "Letters of Negro Migrants," a collection of 166 letters almost all written in 1917 either to Scott or to the Chicago *Defender.*

37. Scott, *Negro Migration,* pp. 45–46; see also U. S. Department of Labor, op. cit., p. 101.

38. U. S. Department of Labor, op. cit., pp. 31, 95.

39. Kennedy, op. cit., p. 54; Scott, *Negro Migration,* p. 48.

40. Drimmer, *Black History,* p. 373.

41. Fishel and Quarles, op. cit., "Negroes Explain the Exodus," pp. 398–99.

42. Baker, "The Negro Goes North," p. 314.

43. Fishel and Quarles, op. cit., p. 398.

44. U. S. Department of Labor, op. cit., p. 28.

45. U. S. Department of Labor, op. cit., p. 64.

46. Baker, "The Negro Goes North," p. 315.

47. Ibid.

48. Ibid., pp. 317–18; Kennedy, op. cit., p. 120. By summer 1916, southern railroads were refusing to honor tickets bought in the North and presented at southern points of embarkation (U. S. Department of Labor, op. cit., p. 119).

49. U. S. Department of Labor, op. cit., p. 65.

50. Scott, "Letters of Negro Migrants," p. 330.

51. Micheaux, *The Conquest*, p. 29; Haynes, *The Negro at Work,* pp. 28–29; Mary White Ovington, *Half a Man: The Status of the Negro in New York*, p. 85.

52. Tindall, *South Carolina Negroes*, p. 180; U. S. Department of Labor, op. cit., pp. 62–63; Baker, "The Negro Goes North," p. 317; Scott, *Negro Migration*, pp. 73–85.

53. Baker, "The Negro Goes North," p. 315.

54. Scott, *Negro Migration*, p. 29; Spear, *Black Chicago*, pp. 134–35.

55. Baker, "The Negro Goes North," p. 316.

56. Ottley, *Lonely Warrior*, p. 159.

57. Spear, op. cit., p. 135; U. S. Department of Labor, op. cit., p. 103.

58. Ottley, op. cit., p. 5.

59. Ibid., p. 106.

60. U. S. Department of Labor, op. cit., p. 29.

61. Spear, op. cit., pp. 134–37; Kennedy, op. cit., pp. 52–54; Ottley, op. cit., p. 163; Scott, *Negro Migration*, p. 30.

62. U. S. Department of Labor, op. cit., p. 30.

63. Ottley, op. cit., p. 162.

64. Ottley, op. cit., p. 146.

65. Scott, *Negro Migration*, pp. 31, 37; Ottley, op. cit., pp. 136–37; Ottley says the *Defender* employed 2,359 agent-correspondents throughout the country (ibid., p. 36).

66. Ottley, op. cit., pp. 136–37.

67. Ibid., pp. 138–39.

68. Scott, "Letters of Negro Migrants," pp. 331–34. The last quote is from a letter from New Orleans; regular fare from there to Chicago would have cost $19.50, based on 930 miles at $.02097 per mile, the 1917 rate (calculated from information on distances in United States Department of War, *Official Table of Distances*, 1918 edition, and on rates in United States Bureau of Transport Economics and Statistics, *Statistics of Railways in the United States*).

69. Ottley, op. cit., p. 170.

70. U. S. Department of War, *Official Table of Distances*, pp. 173, 178, 240, 427, 450; Kennedy, *Negro Peasant Turns Cityward*, p. 30.

71. U. S. Bureau of Transport Economics and Statistics, *Statistics of Railways*, p. 151; Scott, "Letters of Negro Migrants," pp. 291, 324, 327, 333; Epstein, *The Negro Migrant*, p. 26; Osofsky, *Harlem*, p. 29 and n. 90, p. 211; also p. 58, quoting New York reformer Frances Kellor. Here are typical labor contracts signed by migrants to procure a railroad ticket from an agent:

(Male Contract) It is hereby understood that I am to work for the above-named company as _____, the rate of pay to be _____. The _____ Railroad agrees to furnish transportation and food to destination. I agree to work on any part of the _____ Railroad where I may be assigned. I further agree to reimburse the _____ Railroad for the cost of my transportation, in addition to which I agree to pay _____ to cover the cost of meals and other expenses incidental to my employment. (U. S. Department of Labor, op. cit., p. 120.)

(Female Contract) In consideration of my expenses being paid from Richmond to _____ and a situation provided for me, I agree to give _____ services after arrival as _____ to party or persons paying my expenses. And I further agree that all my personal effects may be subject to their order until I have fulfilled that contract, forfeiting all claims to said personal effects after sixty days after this date should I fail to comply with agreement. (Osofsky, *Harlem*, p. 29.)

72. Ottley, op. cit., p. 161.

73. Scott, "Letters of Negro Migrants," pp. 308, 309, 320, 321, 322, 326, 334, 335.

74. U. S. Department of Labor, *Negro Migration*, pp. 28, 110; Epstein, *The Negro Migrant*, p. 26.

75. Seth M. Scheiner, *Negro Mecca: A History of the Negro in New York City*, p. 8; Osofsky, *Harlem*, p. 30.

76. Rudolph Fisher, "The City of Refuge," p. 178.

77. Kennedy, *Negro Peasant Turns Cityward*, p. 24; Octavus Roy Cohen, *Black and Blue*, pp. 7, 37.

78. Kennedy, op. cit., pp. 24, 32; Dutcher, *The Negro in Modern Industrial Society*, p. 110; Scott Nearing, *Black America*, p. 72; Sterling D. Spero and Abram L. Harris, Jr., *The Black Worker: The Negro and the Labor Department*, pp. 150, 151; Woofter, *Negro Problems in Cities*, p. 33; Miller, *Everlasting Stain*, p. 171; most of the figures cited are from the Fourteenth Census, 1920.

79. U. S. Department of Labor, op. cit., pp. 12, 19.

80. This information about skills offered and jobs sought is compiled from Scott, "Letters of Negro Migrants," pp. 290–340.

81. Baker, "The Negro Goes North," p. 315.

82. Osofsky, *Harlem*, p. 18; Kennedy, *Negro Peasant Turns Cityward*, pp. 24, 26, 38; U. S. Bureau of the Census, *Historical Statistics*, pp. 9, 13, 46–47; Reuter, *The American Race Problem*, p. 35.

83. The New York *Times* issues of December 26, 1971, and February 4, 1973, contain illuminating information on this point. It was recently verified, for example, that 11 per cent of black males had been missed in the 1960 census.

84. Reuter, op. cit., p. 54.

85. Ibid., pp. 54–56.

86. Sosna, *Negroes and the Wilson Years*, p. 3. In 1906, Senator Tom Watson had referred to European immigrants in almost the same words; see below, p. 147.

87. Tindall, *South Carolina Negroes*, p. 148.

88. Scott, *Negro Migration*, p. 156.

89. U. S. Department of Labor, op. cit., p. 96.

90. Kirwan, *Revolt of the Rednecks*, p. 153.

91. Osofsky, *Harlem*, p. 26; Baker, *Following the Color Line*, pp. 59, 295.

92. Baker, op. cit., p. 268.

93. Page, *The Negro*, pp. 163–65.

94. Ibid., pp. 54, 77.

95. Odum, *Social and Mental Traits of the Negro*, p. 16; Osofsky, *Harlem*, p. 28.

96. Baker, "The Negro Goes North," p. 318. A number of migrants' letters in Scott's "Letters of Negro Migrants" mention the northern climate, asking how cold it was or stating that the writer owned warm clothes that he would take along. Abbott countered rumors of suffering from cold in the North with *Defender* articles about blacks in the South found frozen to death in their backwood shacks in winter weather.

97. Baker may have been guilty here of what David Fischer calls a "fallacy of semantical distortion," in this instance, the rhetorical figure of hypallage (*Historians' Fallacies*, p. 269), in which the relationship between words is distorted, generally by hooking an adjective to a word other than the one it should modify; thus, "tasks of the easy-going South" might be an acceptable proposition, especially if one were referring to the white South; but "easy-going tasks of the South," said in reference to black tasks, is not acceptable to anyone who knows how hard southern blacks had to work just to stay alive.

98. Scott, *Negro Migration*, p. 79.

99. Tindall, *Emergence of the New South*, p. 149.

100. Ottley, *Lonely Warrior*, p. 164.

101. Ibid.

102. Baker, "The Negro Goes North," p. 317.

103. U. S. Department of Labor, op. cit., p. 106.

104. Ibid., p. 31.

105. Scott, *Negro Migration*, p. 153.

106. Ibid.

107. Quoted in K. Young, *Source Book for Social Psychology* (New York: Crofts, 1933), p. 506.

108. Ottley, op. cit., p. 163.

109. Baker, "The Negro Goes North," p. 319.

110. Ibid., p. 316.

111. Washington, *Future of the American Negro*, pp. 201–3; also his *Up from Slavery*, pp. 79, 155, 174.

112. Daniels, *In Freedom's Birthplace*, p. 415.

113. Emma L. Thornbrough, "Booker T. Washington as Seen by His White Contemporaries," p. 162.

114. Ibid., p. 163.

115. Loren Miller, *The Petitioners: The Story of the Supreme Court of the United States and the Negro*, p. 20.

116. Scheiner, *Negro Mecca*, p. 55.

117. Kelly Miller, *Race Adjustment*, pp. 165–67.

118. Scott, *Negro Migration*, Chap. 7, "Efforts to Stop the Movement," pp. 73–85, devotes a lot of space to reform sentiments and promises; but neither here nor elsewhere is there convincing evidence that any of them were put into action. Carter G. Woodson, who in 1916 founded the Association for the Study of Negro Life and History, felt that southern racism was still too strong for liberals to effect their reform programs; see Woodson, *Century of Negro Migration*, p. 177.

119. Washington, *Up from Slavery*, p. 154, the famous homily "Cast down your bucket where you are."

CHAPTER 3

1. Baker, "Gathering Clouds," p. 233.
2. Ibid.
3. Baker, "The Negro Goes North," p. 319.
4. Baker, *Following the Color Line*, p. 111.
5. Myrdal, *American Dilemma*, p. 187.
6. Kennedy, *Negro Peasant Turns Cityward*, pp. 213–15, 217.
7. Otis D. and Beverly Duncan, *The Negro Population of Chicago: A Study of Residential Succession*, pp. 86–91; Spear, *Black Chicago*, pp. 11, 20; Robert R. Weaver, "The Negro Ghetto," *Making of Black America*, p. 165; Chicago Commission on Race Relations, *Negro in Chicago*, p. 79; Scheiner, *Negro Mecca*, pp. 7, 221, 223.
8. Chicago Commission on Race Relations, op. cit., pp. 113–17.
9. Seligmann, *Negro Faces America*, p. 215.
10. Ibid., pp. 215–16. Here the question arises: At what ratio of blacks to whites did a mixed neighborhood cease to be reasonably adjusted and turn into a battleground? What is the ultimate tolerable proportion of blacks to whites? What is the pressure point, or panic point, on one side of which black neighbors are accepted in a white community, although not necessarily liked, and on the other side hated? How many are too many? One to 1,000? One to 100? One to 10? There are, of course, so many variables in a mixed-race housing situation that it may never be possible to arrive at a formula. But perhaps a path to the answer is: How many persons of another group can an observer focus on *as individuals*, to be judged on individual characteristics, desirable and undesirable? Beyond that number the observer perceives only a blur, with traits all run together into a stereotype, which must be alien because, being a stereotype, it is an other-image, antipodal to the self-image by which the observer creates a perception of individuals. Where is the line between man and mass? Is it one black, two blacks, three niggers? One Jew, two Jews, three kikes? One Italian, two Italians, three wops? The answer is still being sought by interracial housing and community groups. See Bradburn, Sudman, and Cockell, *Side By Side: Integrated Neighborhoods in America*, for a recent study of the elements that make for "panic" in a mixed community; the conclusions of the authors indicate that the pressure point where the degree of black demand on a nonblack neighborhood for housing becomes intolerable is somewhere between 10 per cent and 25 per cent, depending on a number of variables.
11. Blair Justice, *Violence in the City*, p. 257.
12. Spear, op. cit., pp. 26–27, 228.
13. Ibid., pp. 7, 13–15, 24–25; Weaver, op. cit., p. 166; Chicago Commission on Race Relations, op. cit., p. 185.
14. Spear, op. cit., p. 210.
15. Ibid., pp. 11, 19, 23, 210; Duncan, op. cit., pp. 86–91; Chicago Commission on Race Relations, op. cit., pp. 106, 113–17.
16. Woofter, *Negro Problems in Cities*, pp. 18–20; Chicago Commission on Race Relations, op. cit., p. 131; Spear, op. cit., p. 25; Langston Hughes, *The Big Sea: An Autobiography*, p. 33.

17. Charles S. Johnson, *Negro Housing*, p. 36; Woofter, op. cit., pp. 69–70; Spear, op. cit., p. 23.

18. Chicago Commission on Race Relations, op. cit., p. 195.

19. Kennedy, *Negro Peasant Turns Cityward*, pp. 149–50; Chicago Commission on Race Relations, op. cit., p. 206.

20. Kennedy, op. cit., p. 148.

21. Seligmann, op. cit., pp. 39–40. Seligmann, a young journalist and one of the early white activists in the NAACP, produced in this book an illuminating study of race conditions and attitudes. Today, Seligmann's theory of southern antiblack propaganda is in eclipse; it is more fashionable to say that the North's *de facto* segregation is quite as bad as any southern *de jure* segregation. But it is an interesting question whether the absolution of the South from special guilt may not be the ultimate triumph of the propaganda Seligmann observed.

22. Spear, op. cit., p. 21, quoting from an unidentified Chicago paper.

23. Rudolph Fisher, *Walls of Jericho*, p. 41.

24. Ibid.

25. Scheiner, *Negro Mecca*, p. 19.

26. Ibid., p. 24; Osofsky, *Harlem*, pp. 9–12, 122.

27. Osofsky, op. cit., pp. 78–81.

28. Scheiner, op. cit., pp. 22, 30–31; Osofsky, op. cit., pp. 88, 106–9, 120; the term Striver's Row is found in Fisher, Hughes, and other writers of the twenties.

29. Osofsky, op. cit., p. 3; Scheiner, op. cit., p. 9; Haynes, *Negro at Work*, p. 58.

30. James Weldon Johnson, *Black Manhattan*, p. 153.

31. Fisher, "City of Refuge," pp. 181–82.

32. DuBois, *Philadelphia Negro*, pp. 7, 297–98, 309.

33. Baker, *Following the Color Line*, p. 120.

34. Daniels, *In Freedom's Birthplace*, p. 144.

35. Kennedy, op. cit., p. 217.

36. Spear, op. cit., pp. 206–7.

37. Scheiner, op. cit., p. 118.

38. Langston Hughes, *The Best of Simple*, p. 23.

CHAPTER 4

1. Woodson, *Century of Negro Migration*, p. 161.

2. Osofsky, *Harlem*, p. 20.

3. Baker, "The Negro Goes North," p. 319. Baker cites as proof that the 9,000,000 blacks who remained in the South owned property estimated at $1,000,000,000; that figure, however, would average out to holdings of $111 each, which is not by any standard solidly middle-class. Doubtless among those who stayed behind were some with very much larger estates, but also many with much smaller holdings. U. S. Department of Labor, *Negro Migration*, pp. 87–88, says that "quite a few" well-to-do landowners sold their property at a sacrifice and migrated.

4. Baker, *Following the Color Line*, p. 112.

5. Edith Abbott, *Tenements of Chicago*, p. 125.

6. Scheiner, *Negro Mecca*, p. 27.

7. Chicago Commission on Race Relations, *Negro in Chicago*, pp. 187–93.

8. Haynes, *Negro at Work*, pp. 54–55.

9. Epstein, *Negro Migrant*, pp. 18–19.

10. Kennedy, *Negro Peasant Turns Cityward*, pp. 135–36.

11. U. S. Bureau of the Census, *Historical Statistics*, p. 9; census counts since 1850 had shown an inordinate surplus of women in the black population.

12. Miller, *Race Adjustment*, pp. 171–73.

13. Osofsky, *Harlem*, p. 17; Kennedy, *Negro Peasant Turns Cityward*, p. 140; Mary Ovington, *Half a Man*, p. 87, in 1911 noted the great preponderance of women among New York black people.

14. New York *Times* (December 26, 1971); again on February 4, 1973, the *Times* discussed the significant undercount of black males.

15. Elliot Liebow, *Tally's Corner*, pp. 5–7, 20.

16. Kennedy, *Negro Peasant Turns Cityward*, p. 140.

17. Ibid., p. 142.

18. Spear, *Black Chicago*, p. 168.

19. Chicago Commission on Race Relations, *Negro in Chicago*, p. 193.

20. DuBois, *Philadelphia Negro*, p. 282.

21. Epstein, *Negro Migrant*, pp. 23–24, 50–51.

22. Odum, *Social and Mental Traits*, pp. 27–37; Kennedy, op. cit., pp. 196–98; Osofsky, op. cit., p. 148.

23. DuBois, op. cit., p. 74.

24. Daniels, *In Freedom's Birthplace*, p. 221.

25. DuBois, op. cit., p. 166.

26. Frazier, *Negro in the United States*, pp. 144–45; Osofsky, op. cit., p. 147; Ovington, *Half a Man*, p. 33; Green, *Secret City*, p. 142; DuBois, op. cit., p. 193.

27. DuBois, op. cit., pp. 194–95.

28. Osofsky, op. cit., p. 4.

29. Robert H. Bremner, *From the Depths: The Discovery of Poverty in the United States*, pp. 70, 76–77, 80, 132–36.

30. Daniels, op. cit., p. 476.

31. Both quotes are from Bremner, op. cit., p. 127.

32. Quoted by Gossett, *Race*, p. 159.

33. Ovington, op. cit., p. 28.

34. DuBois, op. cit., p. 291; other comments on the prevalence of taking lodgers are to be found in Haynes, *Negro at Work*, p. 63; Scheiner, *Negro Mecca*, p. 28; Edith Abbott, *Tenements of Chicago*, pp. 347, 362; Kennedy, op. cit., p. 165; Chicago Commission on Race Relations, op. cit., p. 158; and Spear, op. cit., p. 24.

35. Hughes, *The Best of Simple*, p. 42.

36. Chicago Commission on Race Relations, op. cit., p. 158.

37. Spear, *Black Chicago*, p. 24.

38. Baker, *Following the Color Line*, pp. 109–13.

39. Scheiner, op. cit., p. 32.

40. Abbott, op. cit., pp. 282–83; Kennedy, op. cit., pp. 162–63.

41. Abbott, op. cit., pp. 294–95; Spear, op. cit., p. 149; Woofter, *Negro*

Problems in Cities, p. 95; Kennedy, op. cit., pp. 145, 165; Chicago Commission on Race Relations, op. cit., pp. 157, 159; Scheiner, op. cit., p. 28.

42. Woofter, op. cit., p. 95.

43. Haynes, *Negro at Work,* p. 63; Scheiner, op. cit., p. 28.

44. Epstein, *Negro Migrant,* pp. 10–13.

45. Kennedy, op. cit., p. 164; Spear, op. cit., p. 149; these and other analysts of ghetto situations also make the point that blacks often shared their homes with newcomers out of kindness or as a civic duty.

46. Epstein, op. cit., pp. 15, 16.

47. Chicago Commission, op. cit., p. 93; Spear, op. cit., p. 150; U. S. Department of Labor, *Negro Migration,* p. 23; Kennedy, op. cit., pp. 154, 156–60; DuBois, *Philadelphia Negro,* p. 295.

48. Baker, "The Negro Goes North," p. 318.

49. Scheiner, op. cit., p. 35, quoting 1915 Urban League report.

50. Kennedy, op. cit., p. 33; Abbott, op. cit., pp. 294–95.

51. Abbott, op. cit., p. 330.

52. Woofter, op. cit., p. 99.

53. Epstein, op. cit., p. 13; Kennedy, op. cit., p. 156; U. S. Department of Labor, op. cit., pp. 145–47.

54. Abbott, op. cit., p. 371; Woofter, op. cit., pp. 75–76, 140, 141; Scheiner, op. cit., pp. 35–37.

55. Micheaux, *The Conquest,* p. 224.

56. Chicago Commission, op. cit., p. 215.

57. Ibid., p. 227.

58. U. S. Department of Labor, op. cit., pp. 143–44.

59. Ibid., p. 143; Kennedy, op. cit., pp. 175–76.

60. U. S. Department of Labor, op. cit., p. 153.

61. DuBois, *Mortality Among Negroes in Cities,* pp. 21–24, 28, 43.

62. DuBois, *Social and Physical Condition of Negroes,* pp. 21, 28.

63. Miller, *Memphis During the Progressive Era,* pp. 90–91.

64. Baker, *Following the Color Line,* pp. 46–47.

65. Dollard, *Caste and Class,* p. 127.

66. Fisher, "City of Refuge," p. 183.

67. Osofsky, op. cit., p. 8; Baker, *Following the Color Line,* pp. 115, 116; Reuter, *The American Race Problem,* pp. 168, 176; Epstein, op. cit., pp. 56–57; Otto Klineberg, ed. *Characteristics of the American Negro,* p. 389.

68. Baker, *Following the Color Line,* pp. 116–17; Spear, op. cit., p. 97; Chicago Commission, op. cit., pp. 150–51; Epstein, op. cit., p. 58.

69. Reuter, op. cit., p. 159; Epstein, op. cit., pp. 56–57; Kennedy, op. cit., p. 175.

70. Kennedy, op. cit., pp. 171–72; Baker, *Following the Color Line,* p. 115; Ovington, *Half a Man,* p. 29; Osofsky, op. cit., p. 8; Powdermaker, op. cit., p. 199; Reuter, op. cit., pp. 202–3.

71. Reuter, op. cit., p. 166.

72. Ovington, op. cit., p. 30.

73. Reuter, op. cit., p. 166.

74. Epstein, op. cit., pp. 61, 62–64; Reuter, op. cit., p. 167.

75. Kennedy, op. cit., pp. 208–15; Carter G. Woodson, *Negro in our History,* pp. 453–54; Osofsky, op. cit., p. 15; Washington, *Story of the Negro,* pp. 352–54; Spear, op. cit., pp. 46–47, 101.

76. Chicago Commission, op. cit., p. 341.

77. DuBois, *Philadelphia Negro,* p. 320; Kennedy, op. cit., pp. 203–4; U. S. Department of Labor, op. cit., p. 154; Odum, op. cit., pp. 57–97, describes the function of the church and its activities in the South, much of which holds for the North as well.

78. Southern, *The Music of Black Americans,* p. 403.

79. Ibid., pp. 242–97, 352, 375.

80. Fisher, *Walls of Jericho,* p. 110.

81. Vincent, *Black Power,* p. 85.

82. These lodge names are selected from a consistently magnificent list in Margaret Fisk, ed., Encyclopedia of Associations, Vol. 1.

83. Scheiner, op. cit., p. 93.

84. Ibid., p. 94; Washington, *Story of the Negro,* p. 156; Odum, op. cit., pp. 100–1; Scheiner, op. cit., p. 94; Ovington, op. cit., p. 95.

85. DuBois, *Philadelphia Negro,* p. 231; DuBois, *Some Efforts of American Negroes for Their Own Betterment,* p. 49; Abram L. Harris, *Negro as Capitalist,* p. 46.

86. Harris, op. cit., p. 63; Washington, *Story of the Negro,* pp. 165–69.

87. Harris, op. cit., p. 54; Spear, op. cit., p. 108; Scheiner, op. cit., p. 93.

88. DuBois, *Philadelphia Negro,* p. 311.

89. Reuter, op. cit., pp. 318–19; Chicago Commission, op. cit., p. 333; Kennedy, op. cit., p. 183.

90. Reuter, op. cit., pp. 319, 326–27; Kennedy, op. cit., pp. 186, 188.

91. Quoted by Reuter, op. cit., p. 317; the Chicago Commission on Race Relations, op. cit., p. 333, makes the same point.

92. Kennedy, op. cit., pp. 84, 187; DuBois, *Philadelphia Negro,* p. 283; Epstein, op. cit., p. 49; U. S. Department of Labor, op. cit., p. 139.

93. Reuter, op. cit., p. 325; Kelly Miller, *Out of the House of Bondage,* p. 98; William Miller, *Memphis During the Progressive Era,* p. 82; Epstein, op. cit., p. 52.

94. Brawley thus quotes Vardaman in *Social History of the American Negro,* pp. 325–26.

95. Chicago Commission on Race Relations, op. cit., p. 342.

96. Reuter, op. cit., p. 334.

97. Miller, *Out of the House of Bondage,* pp. 97, 99.

98. Daniels, *In Freedom's Birthplace,* p. 220.

99. Reuter, op. cit., p. 332; Epstein, op. cit., p. 47.

100. U. S. Department of Labor, op. cit., p. 138.

101. Seligmann, *Negro Faces America,* p. 117.

102. Myrdal, *American Dilemma,* p. 332.

103. U. S. Department of Labor, op. cit., p. 143.

104. Ottley, *Lonely Warrior,* p. 99.

105. Osofsky, op. cit., p. 14; Scheiner, op. cit., pp. 114–15; hence, it is said, the district's cognomen, the Tenderloin.

106. Fisher, "City of Refuge," pp. 183–86.

107. Kennedy, op. cit., p. 188; Epstein, op. cit., p. 53; Chicago Commission on Race Relations, op. cit., p. 344.

108. Kennedy, op. cit., p. 185; Chicago Commission, op. cit., p. 334; Reuter, op. cit., p. 330.

109. Scheiner, op. cit., p. 115.

110. Ibid., p. 115; Kennedy, op. cit., p. 187; the plight of young women who migrated has been discussed earlier.

111. Kennedy, op. cit., pp. 189–90; Reuter, op. cit., p. 320.

112. Ibid.

113. Baker, *Following the Color Line,* p. 138; Osofsky, op. cit., p. 61; in Cincinnati, the Schmidlapp Model Homes Company built cheap and attractive apartments to accommodate 250 families (Department of Labor, op. cit., p. 153).

114. Scheiner, op. cit., pp. 143, 149–51; Osofsky, op. cit., p. 55; DuBois, *Philadelphia Negro,* pp. 356–57.

115. Scheiner, op. cit., pp. 154, 159–69; Baker, *Following the Color Line,* p. 139.

116. Scheiner, op. cit., p. 151.

117. Ibid., pp. 150–53, 160; Osofsky, op. cit., p. 56.

118. This summary of organizations that helped the migrants is drawn from many sources, chiefly Scott, *Negro Migration,* pp. 103, 145; Scheiner, op. cit., pp. 58–59, 90, 119–20; Daniels, op. cit., p. 207; Epstein, op. cit., p. 44; Osofsky, op. cit., p. 32; Vincent, op. cit., p. 47; C. V. Roman, *American Civilization and the Negro,* p. 177; Kennedy, op. cit., p. 127; Spear, op. cit., p. 102; U. S. Department of Labor, op. cit., p. 155.

119. Tindall, *Emergence of the New South,* p. 159; Scheiner, op. cit., pp. 60–61, 153–54; Kennedy, op. cit., p. 127; Osofsky, op. cit., pp. 62ff. An impressive report by the Chicago Urban League on its activities is included in Department of Labor, op. cit., p. 23.

120. Seligmann, op. cit., pp. 133–34.

CHAPTER 5

1. George E. Mowry, *The Era of Theodore Roosevelt,* pp. 2–7.

2. U. S. Department of Labor, *Negro Migration,* p. 149.

3. Ibid., p. 127.

4. Seligmann, *Negro Faces America,* pp. 202, 204; U. S. Department of Labor, op. cit., p. 128; Kennedy, *Negro Peasant Turns Cityward,* pp. 115, 128; Baker, "The Negro Goes North," p. 317; Isabel Eaton, "Special Report on Negro Domestic Service," p. 481.

5. Chicago Commission on Race Relations, *Negro in Chicago,* pp. 374–76; U. S. Department of Labor, op. cit., p. 150.

6. Seligmann, op. cit., p. 203.

7. Greene and Woodson, *Negro Wage Earner,* p. 146.

8. Spear, *Black Chicago,* p. 156.

9. Baker, *Following the Color Line,* p. 142.

10. Scott, *Negro Migration,* p. 55; Kennedy, op. cit., p. 122; U. S. Department of Labor, op. cit., pp. 64, 119–24.

11. Ibid., pp. 126–27; Chicago Commission, op. cit., pp. 390, 397; Kennedy, op. cit., pp. 98, 128; Baker, *Following the Color Line,* p. 131.

12. Daniels, *In Freedom's Birthplace,* pp. 339–40.

13. U. S. Department of Labor, op. cit., p. 140.

14. Baker, "The Negro Goes North," p. 317; U. S. Department of Labor,

op. cit., p. 140; the census must have missed many men of this peripatetic class.

15. Liebow, *Tally's Corner*, p. 57.
16. Ibid., p. 63.
17. Ibid.
18. The entire subject is illuminatingly analyzed by Liebow, op. cit., pp. 57–64.
19. U. S. Bureau of the Census, *Historical Statistics*, pp. 128–29.
20. Osofsky, *Harlem*, p. 16; Haynes, *Negro at Work*, p. 81; U. S. Department of Labor, op. cit., p. 22; Daniels, op. cit., p. 337; Micheaux, *The Conquest*, p. 42.
21. U. S. Department of Labor, op. cit., pp. 24, 118–19; Epstein, *Negro Migrant*, p. 23; Spear, op. cit., p. 157.
22. U. S. Department of Labor, op. cit., pp. 24, 108; Spear, op. cit., p. 157.
23. Kennedy, op. cit., p. 99; Abram Harris, "Negro Migration," p. 29, gives the terms of this acceptable standard of living: (1) nourishing food; (2) houses in low-rent neighborhoods and within the smallest number of rooms consistent with decency (about four rooms and a bath); (3) the upkeep of household equipment, but no provision for the purchase of additional furniture; (4) clothing sufficient for warmth, but with no more regard for style than would permit one to appear in public without slovenliness or loss of self-respect.
24. Ibid.
25. Kennedy, op. cit., p. 96.
26. DuBois, *Philadelphia Negro*, p. 345.
27. Kennedy, op. cit., pp. 97–98.
28. This point is made in a number of studies, including Kennedy, op. cit., p. 99; Daniels, op. cit., pp. 212, 336; Scheiner, *Negro Mecca*, p. 57; Dutcher, *Negro in Modern Industrial Society*, pp. 32, 38.
29. Reuter, *The American Race Problem*, p. 219.
30. Scheiner, op. cit., p. 57.
31. Ibid., p. 58; Daniels, op. cit., pp. 212, 334, 345, 351, 358–59; Kennedy, op. cit., p. 88.
32. Kennedy, op. cit., pp. 88–92; U. S. Department of Labor, op. cit., p. 23; Dutcher, op. cit., pp. 63–68; Dutcher, p. 32, attributes the decline in the number of black women employed as domestics to the new labor-saving devices used in the home.
33. Ovington, *Half a Man*, p. 86, says a good number of normal-school graduates found teaching jobs in the New York City school system. According to Reuter, op. cit., p. 220, 25 out of every 1,000 black workingwomen throughout the country were teachers.
34. Dutcher, op. cit., pp. 63–68; Ovington, op. cit., p. 83.
35. Dutcher, op. cit., p. 64; Reuter, op. cit., p. 220; Chicago Commission, op. cit., p. 625; Spear, op. cit., p. 155; Kennedy, op. cit., p. 88.
36. M. R. Werner, *Julius Rosenwald*, pp. ix, xi, 125, 150.
37. Ibid., p. 153.
38. Ibid., p. 154.
39. Ibid.
40. Ibid.

41. Ibid., pp. 156–57, 159–60.

42. Quoted by Myrdal, *American Dilemma,* pp. 291–92.

43. U. S. Bureau of the Census, *Historical Statistics,* p. 62; the war reduced immigration from the 1914 peak of 1,218,480 to 298,826 in 1916, and of that number, 47,070 were under 16 years of age, and 30,935 were 45 years of age or over.

44. U. S. Department of Labor, op. cit., p. 97.

45. Ibid., p. 7.

46. Quoted by Gossett, p. 307.

47. Scheiner, op. cit., pp. 129, 134–35; the fact that five out of six allegedly involved in the Haymarket bombing in Chicago in 1886 were foreign-born reinforced the belief that all immigrants were socialist agitators and radicals (Gossett, op. cit., p. 295).

48. John Higham, *Strangers in the Land,* p. 169.

49. Faulkner, *Quest for Social Justice,* p. 18; Higham, op. cit., pp. 137, 159; Mowry, *Era of Theodore Roosevelt,* p. 13.

50. Quoted by Gossett, op. cit., p. 292.

51. Higham, op. cit., p. 169.

52. Newby, *Jim Crow's Defense,* p. 186.

53. Quoted by Gossett, op. cit., p. 293.

54. Ibid., p. 302; see also ibid., p. 294.

55. Ibid., p. 292.

56. Ibid., p. 293.

57. Ibid., p. 308.

58. Faulkner, op. cit., pp. 15–16. A frequently voiced justification for paying less to yellow or black workers than to white workers was that "they don't need as much to live on."

59. Higham, op. cit., p. 161; Faulkner, op. cit., pp. 13–14.

60. Higham, op. cit., p. 173.

61. Ibid., pp. 166, 170–71.

62. Dutcher, op. cit., pp. 31–32.

63. Reuter, op. cit., p. 219, and Dutcher, op. cit., p. 33, give Census Bureau tables.

64. Scheiner, op. cit., p. 224; all figures here refer to New York City.

65. Ibid., pp. 48–49; Commons, *Races and Immigrants in America,* p. 47; Ovington, op. cit., p. 47; Greene and Woodson, op. cit., p. 98. Spear, however, op. cit., p. 29, found that in Chicago 45 per cent of working black men were porters, servants, waiters, or janitors. DuBois, *Philadelphia Negro,* p. 116, made the interesting observation that the number of black barbers decreased not only because immigrants took over the trade but because many young blacks scorned to train for a traditional "Negro job."

66. U. S. Department of Labor, op. cit., p. 135. One of the few instances of skilled black workers taking the place of striking whites was among hotel waiters, the Labor Department said. The report could more accurately have used the term "Negroes in unskilled jobs" than "unskilled Negroes," because many of those in unskilled jobs were there only because their skill and craft fields were closed to them by unions. Black workers claimed the unions opposed the northward migration because they feared the labor market would be flooded with skilled southern black workers; see Epstein, op. cit., pp. 41–42, and Scheiner, op. cit., p. 68.

67. U. S. Department of Labor, op. cit., p. 135.

68. Epstein, op. cit., p. 34; Spero and Harris, *The Black Worker*, pp. 475–76.

69. Quoted by Spear, op. cit., pp. 36–37.

70. Spero and Harris, op. cit., p. 267.

71. Spear, op. cit., pp. 37–39; Spero and Harris, op. cit., p. 267.

72. Spero and Harris, op. cit., p. 129; Scheiner, op. cit., pp. 72, 75–76.

73. Spear, op. cit., p. 160.

74. Spero and Harris, op. cit., pp. 88–89.

75. Quoted by Herman D. Bloch, "Labor and the Negro," p. 177.

76. Ibid., pp. 176–79, 184; Charles H. Wesley, *Negro Labor in the United States,* p. 264.

77. Bernard Mandel, "Samuel Gompers and the Negro Workers," pp. 46–47.

78. Bloch, op. cit., p. 180; Chicago Commission, op. cit., p. 627; Baker, *Following the Color Line,* p. 135; Spero and Harris, op. cit., pp. 58–73, 208; Epstein, op. cit., p. 40.

79. Spero and Harris, op. cit., p. 199.

80. Ibid., p. 338.

81. Seligmann, op. cit., p. 210.

82. Ibid., pp. 192–93.

83. Ibid., p. 188. In addition to sources noted, information about racial policies of individual unions in this period is taken from Chicago Commission, op. cit., p. 407; Baker, *Following the Color Line,* pp. 135–36; Abram Harris, "Negro Labor's Quarrel with White Working Men," p. 905; Ovington, op. cit., p. 54; Spero and Harris, op. cit., pp. 250, 338, 475–76; Kennedy, op. cit., p. 107; Wesley, op. cit., p. 262; Bloch, op. cit., p. 180; Kelly Miller, *The Everlasting Stain,* p. 287.

84. Quoted by Mandel, op. cit., p. 60; see also ibid., p. 34.

85. The Army attitude is fully discussed in Chapter 9.

86. Spero and Harris, op. cit., p. 116.

87. U. S. Department of Justice, *Report,* p. 172; the linking of "able," "dangerous" and "educated" deserves note. At that time, Cyril Briggs and Richard Moore were associated with Owen and Randolph, but they later moved farther left and joined the American Communist Party; see Spero and Harris, op. cit., p. 389.

88. Quoted by Spero and Harris, op. cit., p. 330.

89. Wesley, op. cit., p. 327; Spero and Harris, op. cit., pp. 265, 331.

90. Spero and Harris, op. cit., p. 118.

91. Ibid., pp. 124–26, 311–13, 431.

92. Scheiner, op. cit., p. 70.

93. DuBois, ed., *The Negro in Business,* p. 6.

94. Ibid., p. 57.

95. Ibid., pp. 6, 7, 12, 16.

96. Haynes, op. cit., pp. 99, 101, 105, 108, 118; Scheiner, op. cit., p. 79; Nearing, *Black America,* pp. 245–46.

97. DuBois, *The Negro in Business,* p. 50.

98. Quoted by Scheiner, op. cit., p. 71.

99. Spear, op. cit., pp. 113–14, 184; Scheiner, op. cit., pp. 80, 81; Du-

Bois, *Philadelphia Negro*, p. 123; Haynes, op. cit., pp. 123–25; Bergman, ed., *Chronological History*, pp. 374–75. Moving and express companies were exceptional among black businesses for attracting some white customers; Haynes, op. cit., p. 125.

100. Scheiner, op. cit., p. 81; Kennedy, op. cit., pp. 85, 88; Spear, op. cit., p. 184.

101. Myrdal, op. cit., p. 316; Powdermaker, *After Freedom*, p. 121; Harris, *The Negro as Capitalist*, p. 62; Osofsky, op. cit., p. 31.

102. Osofsky, op. cit., p. 149; Harris, op. cit., p. 142.

103. Harris, op. cit., pp. 65, 165.

104. Ibid., pp. 61, 101–2, 123, 143, 158–59, 167, 176; Osofsky, op. cit., pp. 157–58.

105. Osofsky, op. cit., pp. 93–99, 117–19.

106. Hughes, *Best of Simple*, p. 196.

107. Spear, op. cit., p. 118.

108. Osofsky, op. cit., pp. 5, 33; DuBois, *Philadelphia Negro*, p. 119; Green, op. cit., p. 43.

109. Quoted by Sosna, "Negroes and the Wilson Years," pp. 6–7.

110. Ibid.

111. Described to the author many years later by residents of the town who, as children, had been given the great treat of visiting Madame Walker's mansion.

112. Hughes, *Best of Simple*, p. 107.

113. E. D. Cronon, "Marcus Garvey," p. 392; Vincent, *Black Power*, pp. 54, 122–23; Southern, *Music of Black Americans*, p. 399.

114. Reuter, op. cit., p. 241; Carter G. Woodson, *Negro Professional Man*, pp. 23–32, 331.

115. Osofsky, op. cit., p. 97; Hughes, *Big Sea*, pp. 86, 90 ff.

116. DuBois, *Philadelphia Negro*, pp. 114–15. Most of the following material on black people in the professions is extracted from Woodson's *Negro Professional Man*, which takes up each professional field in considerable detail. Woodson includes valuable information about the newly emerging professional field of social work; black social workers, according to Reuter, *American Race Problem*, were enumerated for the first time in 1920, when they were reported to number over 1,200.

117. Woodson, *Negro Professional Man*, p. 173.

118. Southern, op. cit., p. 369.

119. DuBois, *Negro in Business*, pp. 74–77; DuBois, *Philadelphia Negro*, p. 126; Baker, *Following the Color Line*, p. 136; Baker, "Gathering Clouds Along the Color Line," p. 234; Baker, "The Negro Goes North," p. 316; Spear, op. cit., p. 185; Vincent, op. cit., pp. 39, 54, 176.

120. Spear, op. cit., p. 36; Ovington, op. cit., p. 49; Green, op. cit., pp. 159–60.

121. Spear, op. cit., pp. 35–36; Scheiner, op. cit., p. 204; Dutcher, op. cit., p. 75; Green, op. cit., pp. 159–60, 187; Ovington, op. cit., p. 108; Osofsky, op. cit., p. 33.

122. Spear, op. cit., p. 35.

123. Dutcher, op. cit., p. 119; Kennedy, op. cit., pp. 72, 74, based on 1920 census figures.

124. Greene and Woodson, op. cit., pp. 225, 231, 239, 278.

125. Spear, op. cit., pp. 151, 155; Duncan, *Negro Population of Chicago*, p. 91.

126. Kennedy, op. cit., pp. 71–78.

127. Fishel and Quarles, *Negro American*, p. 406; Greene and Woodson, op. cit., pp. 250–51, 256–65; Nearing, op. cit., pp. 250–51.

128. Greene and Woodson, op. cit., p. 249.

129. Kennedy, op. cit., pp. 81–84.

130. Wesley, op. cit., pp. 267, 270–71.

131. Scott, op. cit., pp. 86–91.

132. U. S. Department of Labor, op. cit., p. 103; also, ibid., pp. 66–67, 74, 85 ff.

133. Ibid., p. 96.

134. Ibid., pp. 46, 70.

135. Ibid., p. 96.

136. Seligmann, op. cit., p. 196.

137. *Sounder* (Twentieth Century-Fox, 1972).

138. Powdermaker, *After Freedom*.

139. Seligmann, op. cit., p. 195.

140. Ibid., p. 196, quoting Mary Ovington in *Liberator* (Jan. 1920).

141. U. S. Department of Labor, op. cit., pp. 26–27.

CHAPTER 6

1. Washington's most famous speech, the Atlanta Exposition Address, in Howard Brotz, ed., *Negro Social and Political Thought*, pp. 356–59.

2. U. S. Department of Labor, *Negro Migration*, p. 106.

3. Pickens, *New Negro*, p. 165.

4. Quoted by Frazier, *Negro in the United States*, pp. 158–59.

5. Pickens, op. cit., p. 165.

6. Quoted by Frazier, op. cit., p. 158.

7. Washington, *Future of the American Negro*, pp. 110–11.

8. Ibid., p. 230.

9. Quoted by Hesseltine and Smiley, *The South in American History*, p. 446.

10. Washington, op. cit., p. 29.

11. Ibid., p. 51.

12. Kelly Miller, *Out of the House of Bondage*, p. 151.

13. Quoted by Harvey Wish, "Negro Education in the Progressive Movement," pp. 188–89.

14. Ibid., p. 189; one of the most frequently voiced excuses for restricting black opportunity was that the Negro was only a child, so that metaphors like "kindergarten of racial development" were popular.

15. Page, *The Negro*, p. 308.

16. Wish, op. cit., pp. 192–93; Kelly Miller, *Race Adjustment*, pp. 262–66.

17. J. J. Pipkin, *The Negro in Revelation*, p. 262.

18. Pickens, op. cit., p. 161.

19. Wish, op. cit., pp. 184–86, 197.

20. Reuter, *American Race Problem*, p. 272; Ovington, *Half a Man*, p. 33.

21. The table is from Reuter, op. cit., p. 263. There is also some information on teachers' pay in U. S. Department of Labor, op. cit., pp. 38–39; Kentucky, a border state rather than southern, was the exception in paying black teachers slightly more per capita than white teachers, $8.53 to $8.13. Those figures apply to public schools; black children lucky enough to go to Rosenwald schools found there standards that white schools had trouble meeting, even by the mid-1930s (Powdermaker, *After Freedom*, p. 311). Other sources of information about education of black children in the South: Woodson, *Rural Negro*, pp. 184–85, 188–89; William Miller, *Memphis During the Progressive Era*, p. 120; Kirwan, *Revolt of the Rednecks*, pp. 137–39.

22. Reuter, op. cit., p. 263; the South Carolina situation, discussed by Tindall, *South Carolina Negroes*, p. 220, dates back to 1899, but the training and pay of black teachers as compared to whites does not seem to have altered significantly in the next two decades.

23. Chicago Commission on Race Relations, *Negro in Chicago*, pp. 247, 252; Osofsky, *Harlem*, p. 36; Kennedy, *Negro Peasant Turns Cityward*, pp. 192–93, 195.

24. Kennedy, op. cit., p. 194; Scheiner, *Negro Mecca*, pp. 117–18; Spear, *Black Chicago*, p. 205; Woofter, *Negro Problems in Cities*, p. 179; Chicago Commission, op. cit., pp. 243, 614–15.

25. Stephenson, *Race Distinctions in American Law*, p. 192; Harris, *Negro Population in Minneapolis*, p. 12.

26. Reuter, op. cit., pp. 266, 275; DuBois, *College Bred Negro*, pp. 37, 55; Chicago Commission, op. cit., p. 325.

27. Kelly Miller, *Out of the House of Bondage*, pp. 165–66; Simkins and Roland, *History of the South*, p. 365; DuBois, *College Bred Negro*, pp. 16–17; black students who gained admission to northern institutions on athletic scholarships will be discussed later in this chapter.

28. Quoted by Gossett, *Race*, p. 285; see also Stephenson, op. cit., pp. 163–64.

29. Stephenson, op. cit., p. 156.

30. Ibid.

31. Ibid., p. 158.

32. Ibid., pp. 160–61.

33. Ibid., pp. 163–64.

34. Baker, *Following the Color Line*, p. 228.

35. U. S. Bureau of the Census, *Historical Statistics*, p. 214; Reuter, op. cit., pp. 268–69.

36. Epstein, *Negro Migrant*, pp. 71–72.

37. Scheiner, op. cit., pp. 87–88, 90–92; Reuter, op. cit., p. 302; Daniels, *In Freedom's Birthplace*, p. 259; Spear, op. cit., p. 97.

38. Scheiner, op. cit., p. 90; Spear, op. cit., pp. 174–75; Osofsky, op. cit., pp. 144–46.

39. William H. Thomas, *The American Negro*, esp. pp. 109–36, 254–55, 263–64.

40. Reuter, *The Mulatto in the United States*, p. 103; he cites E. V. Stonequist's characterization of the mulatto as the "marginal man," and concludes that the mulatto is therefore emotionally unstable.

41. Osofsky, op. cit., p. 43; Green, *Secret City*, pp. 140 ff.

42. Hughes, *Big Sea*, p. 206.

43. Spear, op. cit., p. 54; Osofsky, op. cit., p. 6.

44. Osofsky, op. cit., p. 43.

45. Baker, *Following the Color Line*, p. 158.

46. Reuter, *Mulatto in the United States*, pp. 192–206, has a detailed discussion of mulattoes as race leaders. Baker, *Following the Color Line*, p. 153, estimated in 1908 that one quarter to one third of American Negroes had a visible admixture of white blood, yet about 90 per cent of those named in various lists of leaders were mulattoes.

47. Ottley, *Lonely Warrior*, p. 84; ibid., p. 14. Ottley says that Abbott eventually adopted the Bahai faith because of the discrimination he had encountered in both the Episcopal and Presbyterian churches.

48. Klineberg, *Characteristics of the American Negro*, p. 313, citing an article by Charles S. Johnson, "The Vanishing Mulatto," *Opportunity* 3:291 (1925).

49. Baker, *Following the Color Line*, pp. 153, 164; Greene and Woodson, *Negro Wage Earner*, p. 287; Reuter, *Mulatto in the United States*, pp. 134–40, 155.

50. Robert A. Bone, *Negro Novel in America*, pp. 45–46; Southern, *Music of Black Americans*, pp. 19–22, 38, 49–51, 59, 294, 316; Fisher, "The Caucasians Storm Harlem," p. 349; Hughes, *Big Sea*, pp. 22–23.

51. Southern, op. cit., pp. 15–19, 56, 305–7, 418, 422.

52. Ibid., pp. 29, 51–54, 305–7, 318–23, 348–51, 379–83, 397–98, 422; the James Europe quote is ibid., pp. 348–49.

53. Edwin B. Henderson, *Negro in Sports*, p. 111.

54. Ibid., pp. 90, 92, 98; Jack Orr, *Black Athlete*, pp. 82–83, 90.

55. Orr, op. cit., pp. 103–4, 125; Henderson, op. cit., pp. 45, 65, 74–75, 81–82, 139, 231; Jesse Owens won his gold medals in 1936.

56. Bergman, *Chronological History*, pp. 426–27.

57. Orr, op. cit., pp. 87–89.

58. The breakthrough in baseball finally came in 1947 when Jackie Robinson was signed on by the Brooklyn Dodgers.

59. Quoted by Henderson, op. cit., p. 154.

60. Ibid., p. 158; Orr, op. cit., pp. 56–57.

61. Henderson, op. cit., pp. 146–48; Orr, op. cit., p. 57; Spear, op. cit., p. 183.

62. Quoted by Orr, op. cit., p. 58.

63. Spear, op. cit., p. 117; Scheiner, op. cit., p. 41; Orr, op. cit., p. 58, gives a long list of top black baseball players.

64. Orr, op. cit., p. 105, says a backlash against Johnson handicapped all black athletes until the 1930s, according to some commentators.

65. Henderson, op. cit., pp. 15–25, 30–32; Orr, op. cit., pp. 29, 36. On this original Joe Walcott, see Orr, op. cit., p. 30; the Joe Walcott who was heavyweight champion in the 1950s adopted the name of the earlier heavyweight fighter.

66. Orr, op. cit., p. 33.

67. Sosna, *Negroes and the Wilson Years*, p. 9.

68. Ibid., p. 10.

69. Bob Lucas, *Black Gladiator*, pp. 118–19.

70. Orr, op. cit., p. 33; Sosna, op. cit., p. 9; Scheiner, op. cit., p. 204.

71. Quoted by Sosna, op. cit., pp. 7–8.

72. Ottley, op. cit., p. 112.
73. Sosna, op. cit., p. 11.
74. Orr, op. cit., p. 34; Lucas, op. cit., pp. 138 ff., 158–61, 169–71, 173–78.
75. Sosna, op. cit., p. 8.
76. Klineberg, op. cit., p. 135; the study was the Lehman Play Quiz, reported by H. C. Lehman and P. A. Witty in "Some Compensatory Mechanisms of the Negro," *Journal of Abnormal and Social Psychology* 23:28–37 (1928).
77. Lucas, op. cit., p. 117.
78. Quoted by Fox, *The Guardian of Boston*, p. 187, from the Chicago *Defender* (Jan. 9, 1915).
79. DuBois, *Dusk of Dawn*, p. 72.
80. Ibid., p. 75.
81. Quoted by Daniel Walden, "The Contemporary Opposition to the Political Ideas of Booker T. Washington," *Journal of Negro History*, Vol. 45, Apr. 1960, p. 110.
82. Ibid.; August Meier, "Booker T. Washington: An Interpretation," pp. 347–52. Meier points out, ibid., p. 347, that in a posthumous publication, "My View of Segregation Laws," Washington condemned such laws as unjust.
83. Fox, op. cit., pp. 46–47, 110–12; the name of this organization went through several changes: National Independent Political League, National Independent Political Rights League, National Independent Equal Rights League, and National Equal Rights League.
84. Fox, op. cit., pp. 83–86.
85. Elliott Rudwick, "The Niagara Movement," pp. 131–48; Fox, op. cit., pp. 89–91, 101–6, 113; Brotz, op. cit., pp. 537–39; Fishel and Quarles, *Negro American*, pp. 372–73, give the text of the Niagara Movement purposes.
86. Quoted by Fox, op. cit., p. 122.
87. The text of the call to the meeting, probably written by Villard, is in Fishel and Quarles, op. cit., pp. 383–85.
88. For the formation and early history of the NAACP, see Charles Kellogg, *NAACP*, Chaps. 1 and 2 (pp. 9–45); other sources of points covered in this brief summary are Scheiner, op. cit., pp. 202–20; Fox, op. cit., pp. 126–31, 135–39, 178–79, 201–3; Osofsky, op. cit., p. 61; Tindall, *Emergence of the New South*, p. 159; Marshall Van Deusen, *J. E. Spingarn*, p. 60; Green, op. cit., p. 181; Baker, "Gathering Clouds Along the Color Line," p. 234; Sosna, op. cit., p. 112; Bergman, op. cit., pp. 357–58.
89. Quoted by Osofsky, op. cit., p. 63.
90. Ibid., pp. 63–66.
91. Ibid., p. 64.
92. Scheiner, op. cit., pp. 154–55; Fishel and Quarles, op. cit., p. 385.
93. Osofsky, op. cit., p. 66.
94. Scheiner, op. cit., p. 203.
95. Baker, *Following the Color Line*, p. 239.
96. Kelly Miller, *Out of the House of Bondage*, p. 131.
97. Pickens, op. cit., p. 223.
98. Bergman, op. cit., p. 441; Loren Miller, *The Petitioners*, pp. 219–20; Tindall, op. cit., p. 175.
99. Loren Miller, op. cit., p. 220.

100. Stephenson, op. cit., pp. 299–302, discusses literacy tests, poll taxes, and property tests in the South and elsewhere in the country.

101. Baker, *Following the Color Line*, p. 233; DuBois, *Philadelphia Negro*, pp. 376, 378, 380; Daniels, op. cit., p. 287; Scheiner, op. cit., pp. 194–96.

102. U. S. Department of Labor, op. cit., pp. 124–25; Spear, op. cit., pp. 119–22, 191–92.

103. Ovington, op. cit., p. 111.

104. Vincent, *Black Power*, p. 43, says that one out of four Harlem voters chose the Socialist ticket in 1920, but this seems too high a percentage considering that nationwide only .035 per cent of the electorate voted Socialist.

105. Osofsky, op. cit., pp. 170–71.

106. Ibid., pp. 215–16, fn. 72 in Chap. 3, says that of fifty migrants in New York questioned in a 1909 survey, all read the daily papers.

CHAPTER 7

1. Intelligence testing will be discussed at length in a later chapter.

2. Peter Finley Dunne, *Mr. Dooley in Peace and in War*, pp. 55–56.

3. Wilson, "Reconstruction of the Southern States," p. 6.

4. W. M. Bevis, "Psychological Traits of the Southern Negro," p. 69.

5. Quoted by R. W. Shufeldt, *America's Greatest Problem: The Negro*, p. 106.

6. Governor William D. Jelks, as quoted by I. A. Newby, *Jim Crow's Defense*, p. 177.

7. Newby, op. cit., p. 177.

8. Shufeldt, op. cit., p. 277.

9. Ibid., p. 146.

10. Ibid.

11. Ibid., p. 225.

12. Ibid., p. 106.

13. Ibid., p. 317.

14. Ibid., p. 139.

15. Ibid., p. 112.

16. Ibid., p. 282.

17. Frederick L. Hoffman, *Race Traits and Tendencies of the American Negro;* see also comments by Gossett, *Race*, p. 281.

18. U. S. National Archives, R. G. 165, Army War College File, Doc. 4483. It may be pure coincidence that Hoffman in his acknowledgments mentioned his debt to a Professor W. F. Willcox for "most valuable assistance in the prosecution of the investigation and final publication of the results" (Hoffman, op. cit., p. vii), and that Hoffman's book was quoted by a Major Willcox; but it is striking, and suggests the possibility of a relationship, that the professor and the major both spell their names with a double *l*, rather than the much more usual single-*l* spelling ("Wilcox" is almost five times more frequent than "Willcox" in the Manhattan, New York, telephone directory).

19. Hoffman, op. cit., pp. v–vi, 311–14.
20. Ibid., p. v.
21. Newby, op. cit., p. 69; Price in 1907 published *The Negro: Past, Present and Future.*
22. Josiah Royce, *Race Questions, Provincialism, and Other American Problems,* pp. 8–9.
23. Higham, *Strangers in the Land,* p. 148.
24. Ibid., p. 143.
25. Ibid., p. 147.
26. See Gossett, op. cit., Chap. 7, for an excellent discussion of "Race and Social Darwinism," including analyses of Spencer, Sumner, and others.
27. Ibid., pp. 146–48.
28. The concluding chapters of Richard Hofstadter, *Social Darwinism in American Thought,* cover this fully.
29. Ibid., pp. 60–61.
30. Ibid., p. 41.
31. Ibid., p. 45.
32. Odum, *Social and Mental Traits of the Negro,* Appendix, p. 299.
33. Ibid.
34. Newby, op. cit., p. 4.
35. Kelly Miller, *Race Adjustment,* p. 24.
36. Keller and Davie, eds., *Essays of William Graham Sumner,* p. 56.
37. Gossett, op. cit., pp. 154, 159.
38. Ibid., pp. 98–100.
39. Ibid., p. 100.
40. Ibid., p. 103.
41. Ibid.; Freeman was referring, presumably, to Incitatus, the horse that the Roman emperor Caligula is said to have housed in an ivory manger, fed wine from a golden pail, and made priest and consul—not a very apt metaphor, but racist rhetoric abounded in logical fallacies.
42. Michael D. Biddiss, "Houston Stewart Chamberlain," p. 17.
43. Newby, op. cit., p. 10; Gossett, op. cit., p. 347.
44. Quoted by Gossett, op. cit., p. 102.
45. Ibid., p. 122.
46. Dunne, *Mr. Dooley,* p. 56.
47. Gossett, op. cit., Chap. 3, discusses this matter fully.
48. Reuter, *American Race Problem,* pp. 63–66.
49. See Gossett, op. cit., Chap. 4, for a full discussion.
50. Gossett, op. cit., Chap. 5, covers eugenics.
51. Ibid., p. 155.
52. Ibid.
53. Ibid., p. 158.
54. Newby, op. cit., p. 33.
55. Gossett, op. cit., p. 159.
56. Newby, op. cit., p. 34.
57. Gossett, op. cit., p. 379.
58. Seligmann, *Negro Faces America,* p. 264.
59. Sosna, *Negroes and the Wilson Years,* pp. 22–23.
60. Page, *The Negro,* p. 295.
61. Gossett, op. cit., p. 174.

62. Commons, *Races and Immigrants in America*, p. 39.

63. Ibid., p. 46; lack of mechanical skill was a frequent allegation, as by Major Willcox, mentioned earlier.

64. Commons, op. cit., p. 46.

65. American Academy of Political and Social Science, *America's Race Problems*, p. 89.

66. Gossett, op. cit., p. 166.

67. Daniels, *In Freedom's Birthplace*, pp. 399–412.

68. Baker, *Following the Color Line*, p. 180.

69. Hofstadter, op. cit., p. 79; see Gossett, op. cit., Chap. 8, on Social Gospel.

70. Gossett, op. cit., p. 186.

71. Ibid., p. 187.

72. Quoted by Hofstadter, op. cit., p. 179, from Josiah Strong's *Our Country* (1885).

73. Quoted by Gossett, op. cit., p. 189.

74. Ibid., pp. 194–95.

75. Ibid., p. 195.

76. Ibid.

77. Sosna, op. cit., p. 20.

78. Daniels, op. cit., pp. 159, 198–99, 316–17.

79. Ovington, *Half a Man*, p. 39.

80. Fisher, *Walls of Jericho*, p. 29.

81. Quoted by Gossett, op. cit., p. 262.

82. Faulkner, *Quest for Social Justice*, p. 11; Baker, *Following the Color Line*, p. 267. In another book, *The Tempter of Eve* (1902), Carroll made Eve's tempter a black man instead of a snake (Newby, op. cit., pp. 94–95).

83. According to Ottley, *Lonely Warrior*, p. 132, the Chicago *Defender* was running a campaign against this disgusting practice as late as 1917.

84. Woodward, *Strange Career of Jim Crow*, p. 103, discusses the influence of learned racist thinking.

85. Wilson, op. cit., p. 11.

86. Newby, op. cit., p. 66.

87. Quoted by Newby, op. cit., pp. 76–77.

88. Ibid., pp. 64–67, 77.

89. Ibid., pp. 35, 57, 58; Gossett, op. cit., p. 353; Higham, op. cit., pp. 156–57.

90. Quoted by Thomas R. Cripps, "The Reaction of the Negro to . . . Birth of a Nation," p. 349, from a letter of Dixon's dated May 1, 1915, to President Wilson's secretary Joseph Tumulty (the emphasis is Dixon's). "Villard's Inter-Marriage Society" referred to Oswald Garrison Villard and the NAACP.

91. Woodward, *Strange Career of Jim Crow*, p. 94.

92. For more on the spectacular career of this novel, see Bloomfield, "Dixon's The Leopard's Spots."

93. Kelly Miller, *Race Adjustment*, pp. 28–29.

94. Cripps, op. cit., p. 346. Theaters on Third Avenue in New York made such a specialty of lurid and improbable melodramas that New Yorkers would comment on any far-fetched story: "Save T'oid Avenoo!"

95. Brawley, *Social History*, p. 326; Cripps, op. cit., pp. 345–46.

96. Quoted by Cripps, op. cit., pp. 346–47.

97. Ibid., p. 347, quoting NAACP's *Sixth Annual Report, 1915;* see also Kellogg, op. cit., pp. 142–45.

98. Cripps, op. cit., p. 349.

99. Ibid.

100. Ibid. The perfervid rhetoric of the remarks attributed to President Wilson and Chief Justice White suggests that they may have sprung from Dixon's imagination; but apparently the President had voiced no objections to the film, which, indeed, pared of its lurid details, presented something not too different from Wilson's own view of Reconstruction as he expressed it in his article for *Atlantic Monthly,* already cited.

101. Cripps, op. cit., p. 352; Fox, *Guardian of Boston,* p. 190.

102. DuBois, *Dusk of Dawn,* p. 240.

103. Cripps, op. cit., pp. 350–52.

104. Filler, *Crusaders for Social Justice,* p. 283.

105. Cripps, op. cit., pp. 354–58; Fox, op. cit., pp. 194–96.

106. Arthur S. Link, *Wilson and the New Freedom,* p. 253. A few years later, during the war, Wilson tried to assuage black resentment by calling the film an "unfortunate production" (ibid., p. 254). The Wilson-Trotter confrontation will be described later.

107. Cripps, op. cit., p. 359. Baker was Wilson's second Secretary of War; for a useful study of Baker's life and thought, see Daniel R. Beaver, *Newton D. Baker.*

108. Gossett, op. cit., p. 259.

109. Higham, op. cit., pp. 287–88.

110. Baker, *Following the Color Line,* pp. 81–82.

111. Gossett, op. cit., pp. 431–59; Filler, op. cit., p. 279.

112. Baker, "Gathering Clouds Along the Color Line," p. 234.

113. Seligmann, op. cit., pp. 183–84.

114. Gossett, op. cit., pp. 431–32.

115. Ibid., p. 435.

116. Ibid., p. 434.

117. Ibid., p. 437.

118. Ibid., p. 412.

119. Royce, op. cit., p. 38.

120. Ibid., p. 37.

121. Ibid., p. 44.

122. Ibid., pp. 16–17, 22–25, 48.

123. Bean's theory has been discussed earlier in this chapter.

124. Franz Boas, "The Anthropological Position of the Negro," p. 42.

125. Boas's review, which appeared first in *The Nation* (Dec. 8, 1920), is reproduced in Fishel and Quarles, *Negro American,* pp. 425–26.

126. Filler, op. cit., p. 277; "The Scientific Revolt Against Racism" is presented by Gossett, op. cit., Chap. 16.

CHAPTER 8

1. Quoted by Mowry, *Era of Theodore Roosevelt,* p. 87. For discussion of the conservativeness of the Progressive movement, see Gabriel Kolko, *Tri-*

umph of Conservatism, and Mowry, op. cit., esp. Chap. 5; Arthur Mann, *The Progressive Era,* summarizes the views of various historians about progressivism.

2. *Independent,* Boston, Vol. 70 (Feb. 1911), p. 417. The "public reform" referred to in this editorial was the election of senators by popular vote, which was threatened with defeat because southern states insisted that such elections be free of federal supervision, thus permitting the exclusion of black voters from the polls. The editor was being ironic, to be sure, but many a Progressive must have wished heartily that there were no Negroes to "bob up" and complicate national affairs.

3. See quotes from "liberal" racists in the previous chapter.

4. Quoted by Mowry, op. cit., p. 106.

5. Quoted by Lewinson, *Race, Class and Party,* p. 171.

6. Scheiner, "President Theodore Roosevelt and the Negro," p. 171.

7. Pringle, *Theodore Roosevelt,* p. 84, says that at the New York Republican convention of 1884 Roosevelt supported the unpopular nomination of a black man for temporary chairman. For the later incidents mentioned, see Kelly Miller, *Race Adjustment,* p. 285; William B. Gatewood, "Theodore Roosevelt and the Indianola Affair," pp. 55, 69–70; Mowry, op. cit., p. 166; John M. Blum, *The Republican Roosevelt,* p. 64.

8. Quotes are from William Miller, *Memphis During the Progressive Era,* p. 21; Mowry, op. cit., p. 165; Gatewood, op. cit., pp. 21, 55; Pringle, op. cit., pp. 249, 422.

9. Pringle, op. cit., p. 250.

10. Quoted by Scheiner, "President Theodore Roosevelt," p. 177; see also Pringle, op. cit., p. 250.

11. Mowry, op. cit., p. 165.

12. Buni, *Negro in Virginia Politics,* p. 56.

13. For the story of the Brownsville affair, see John D. Weaver, *The Brownsville Raid;* also Pringle, op. cit., pp. 460–64; Mowry, op. cit., pp. 213–14; Kelly Miller, *Race Adjustment,* pp. 294–302. In 1972, as a result of the efforts of Congressman Augustus F. Hawkins of California to vindicate the Brownsville 167, the Department of the Army declared the soldiers' records cleared and changed their separations "without honor" to honorable discharges. Hawkins's bill was H.R. 6866, 92nd Cong., 1st sess. (Mar. 29, 1971); see also New York *Times* (Sept. 29, 1972); in 1974 the only survivor of the Brownsville soldiers, Dorsie Willis, received token compensation of $25,000.

14. Quoted by Pringle, op. cit., p. 461.

15. Mowry, op. cit., pp. 213–14; Sosna, *Negroes and the Wilson Years,* p. 24.

16. DuBois, *Dusk of Dawn,* p. 23.

17. Scheiner, "President Theodore Roosevelt," p. 197; Buni, op. cit., p. 58.

18. Sosna, op. cit., p. 32. Considering the many and profound differences between Wilson and Taft, it is significant how close their thinking was on blacks.

19. Mowry, op. cit., p. 234.

20. Arthur S. Link, *Woodrow Wilson and the Progressive Era,* p. 7.

21. Quoted by Scheiner, *Negro Mecca,* p. 206, from the New York *Age;* ironically, Senator Champ Clark of Missouri, Wilson's rival for the Demo-

cratic nomination, distributed a campaign pamphlet titled *The Nigger and the Governor of New Jersey*, accusing Wilson of being soft on Negroes (ibid., pp. 52–53).

22. Sosna, op. cit., pp. 30, 36–37, 61.

23. Ibid., p. 50.

24. DuBois, *Dusk of Dawn*, pp. 233–34.

25. Lewinson, op. cit., p. 171; Sosna, op. cit., pp. 39–40.

26. Sosna, op. cit., p. 56.

27. Quoted ibid., p. 57.

28. DuBois, *Dusk of Dawn*, p. 235.

29. Sosna, op. cit., pp. 58–59; Henry Blumenthal, "Woodrow Wilson and the Race Question," pp. 4–5.

30. U. S. Bureau of the Census, *Historical Statistics*, pp. 682, 687.

31. Link, op. cit., p. 20.

32. Sosna, op. cit., pp. 61–62.

33. Quoted by Arthur S. Link, *Wilson and the New Freedom*, p. 244 (Washington to the New York *Times*, March 2, 1913).

34. Sosna, op. cit., p. 64.

35. Grimke to Wilson (Nov. 20, 1912), reproduced in Fishel and Quarles, *Negro American*, pp. 390–91.

36. Quoted by Sosna, pp. 64–65.

37. Ibid., p. 63.

38. Grimke to Wilson (Sept. 5, 1913), reproduced in Fishel and Quarles, op. cit., p. 391.

39. Green, *Secret City*, p. 129; Logan, *Negro in North Carolina*, pp. 45–46.

40. Green, op. cit., p. 166; Meier and Rudwick, "The Rise of Segregation in the Federal Bureaucracy," pp. 180–81; Stephenson, *Race Distinctions*, p. 227.

41. Link, *Wilson and the New Freedom*, p. 66.

42. Blum, op. cit., p. 14.

43. Tindall, *Emergence of the New South*, p. 143; Blumenthal, op. cit., p. 8. Blumenthal also points out (pp. 116–17) that Wilson never spoke out against California's anti-Japanese laws; and that he was no champion either of woman suffrage or immigrants.

44. Fox, *Guardian of Boston*, p. 116; see also Sosna, op. cit., p. 66.

45. Wilson taught at Bryn Mawr, Wesleyan, and Princeton; then became president of Princeton, then governor of New Jersey.

46. The other Cabinet members were Secretary of State William Jennings Bryan of Nebraska; Secretary of War Lindley Garrison of New Jersey; Secretary of Interior Franklin Lane of California; Secretary of Commerce William Redfield of New York; and Secretary of Labor William Wilson of Pennsylvania.

47. Link, *Wilson and the New Freedom*, p. 93; Tindall, op. cit., p. 3.

48. Woodward, *Strange Career of Jim Crow*, pp. 90–92; also Kirwan, *Revolt of the Rednecks*, p. 218.

49. Gossett, op. cit., p. 271.

50. Kirwan, op. cit., p. 218.

51. Quoted by Gossett, op. cit., p. 271.

52. Hesseltine and Smiley, *The South in American History*, p. 486.

53. William Miller, op. cit., p. 13.

54. See Dewey W. Grantham, Jr., "The Progressive Movement and the Negro."

55. Kirwan, op. cit., p. 265; William Miller, op. cit., p. 190.

56. Sosna, op. cit., pp. 120–29.

57. Green, op. cit., p. 172.

58. Tindall, op. cit., pp. 143–44; Sosna, op. cit., pp. 71–72; Fox, op. cit., p. 170.

59. Sosna, op. cit., pp. 75, 78; Link, *Woodrow Wilson and the Progressive Era*, p. 65.

60. Sosna, op. cit., pp. 70, 72–73; Link, *Wilson and the New Freedom*, p. 246, quotes an obscene broadside put out by the National Fair Play Association concerning the humiliation suffered by white girls who were forced to work with black men and women.

61. Baker, *Woodrow Wilson*, p. 220; Link, *Woodrow Wilson and the Progressive Era*, p. 66.

62. Ibid., p. 65; Greene and Woodson, *Negro Wage Earner*, p. 122, n. 103.

63. Quoted by Sosna, op. cit., p. 74.

64. Ibid.; also Fox, op. cit., p. 171.

65. Sosna, op. cit., p. 89. Some of the militants believed Bishop Walters had approved segregation, but certainly most blacks protested it; a study shows that at least 95 per cent of letters to Wilson from Negroes objected to segregation, according to George C. Osborn, "The Problem of the Negro in Government," p. 344.

66. Sosna, op. cit., p. 91.

67. Osborn, op. cit., p. 344; Sosna, op. cit., p. 94, quotes protests from the black press and from letters to the President.

68. Quoted by Sosna, op. cit., pp. 91–92.

69. Baker, *Woodrow Wilson*, pp. 223–24.

70. Ibid., p. 222.

71. Quoted by Sosna, op. cit., p. 107.

72. Fox, op. cit., pp. 169–72.

73. Sosna, op. cit., p. 99; see also Fox, op. cit., pp. 179–83.

74. Sosna, op. cit., pp. 102–3, reveals that Wilson later told his secretary, Joe Tumulty, that it was he, not Trotter, who had lost his temper; and on another occasion Wilson said, "I lost my temper and played the fool." The Trotter visit is related in a number of sources: Fox, op. cit., pp. 180–83; Link, *Wilson and the New Freedom*, p. 252; Sosna, op. cit., pp. 99–100; Fishel and Quarles, op. cit., pp. 392–93, reproduces the text of a Chicago *Defender* report of the incident.

75. Sosna, op. cit., pp. 101–3; Fox, op. cit., p. 183; Link, *Wilson and the New Freedom*, p. 250.

76. Quotes by Link, *Wilson and the New Freedom*, p. 251, from the New York *World* (Nov. 13, 1914).

77. Quoted by Link, ibid., p. 252.

78. Sosna, op. cit., p. 79; Green, op. cit., pp. 171–72.

79. Letter to Williams (Apr. 2, 1914), quoted by Baker, *Woodrow Wilson*, p. 224.

80. Sosna, op. cit., pp. 81–82.

81. Ibid., p. 78.

82. Ibid., pp. 109–10; the bills, neither of which was reported favorably

out of committee, were introduced by Representative James Aswell of Louisiana and Representative Charles Edwards of Georgia.

83. Ibid., pp. 116–20.

84. Ibid., pp. 130–41.

85. Ibid., pp. 111–12.

86. Ibid., p. 88.

87. Ibid., p. 82.

88. Quoted by Drimmer, *Black History*, p. 365, from *Crisis* (Oct. 1916).

89. Barbara W. Tuchman, *The Zimmerman Telegram*, p. 146.

90. Eli Ginzberg and Alfred S. Eichner, *The Troublesome Presence*, p. 265, quoting a report in the New York *Times*.

91. Green, op. cit., p. 173.

92. Kelly Miller, *Everlasting Stain*, p. 10.

93. Fox, op. cit., p. 167, quoting a letter from Villard to Francis G. Garrison (Aug. 14, 1912).

94. Baker, "Gathering Clouds Along the Color Line," p. 233.

95. Pickens, op. cit., p. 190.

96. Newton D. Baker Papers, Library of Congress, Manuscript Division; Baker to Wilson (Jul. 1, 1918), Item 54. It will be recalled that Baker as mayor of Cleveland had prohibited the showing of *Birth of a Nation* in that city.

97. Quoted by Fox, op. cit., p. 221.

98. Remarks of Representative Dyer, Congressional Record, 67th Cong., 2nd sess. (Jan. 4, 1922), reproduced in Fishel and Quarles, op. cit., pp. 427–32; also ibid., p. 405, and Tindall, op. cit., pp. 173–74. The early version (1918) of the Dyer bill was unacceptable to the NAACP (Kellogg, *NAACP*, p. 231); for the story of the NAACP's continuing fight against lynching, see Kellogg's Chap. 10, *NAACP*, pp. 209–46.

99. Fishel and Quarles, op. cit., p. 427; Tindall, op. cit., p. 173; Bergman, *Chronological History*, p. 387.

100. Seligmann, *Negro Faces America*, p. 39.

101. Charles S. Johnson, *Patterns of Negro Segregation*, p. 313; Baker, "Gathering Clouds Along the Color Line," pp. 232, 234; Gossett, op. cit., p. 452; Walter White, *Rope and Faggot*, p. 21.

102. Seligmann, op. cit., p. 39.

103. Osofsky, op. cit., pp. 46–52; Baker, *Following the Color Line*, pp. 126–28; George C. Haynes, "Race Riots in Relation to Democracy," p. 698.

104. Ibid.

105. Baker, *Following the Color Line*, pp. 3–4, 14–17; Brownsville, Georgia, not to be confused with Brownsville, Texas, where the soldiers' "mutiny" had taken place a month earlier.

106. James L. Crouthamel, "The Springfield Race Riot," p. 178. Springfield, Ohio, had also had its share of race riots in 1904 and 1906, although not of the magnitude of this 1908 riot in Springfield, Illinois; both Springfields were notorious for lawlessness, vice, and political corruption. Baker, *Following the Color Line*, pp. 201–10, describes the Ohio riots.

107. Allen D. Grimshaw, *Racial Violence in the United States*, reprinting an anonymous article, "The So-Called Race Riot at Springfield, Illinois," from *Charities and the Commons* (called *Survey* after 1909) (Sept. 19, 1908).

108. Grimshaw, op. cit., p. 55 says there were 4,500 blacks in Springfield out of a total population of 60,000; Crouthamel, op. cit., p. 177, arrives at about the same figure, estimating that Negroes formed one tenth of a population of 50,000. The woman who had charged the Negro with rape later admitted that her assailant had been a white man (Crouthamel, op. cit., p. 177).

109. Quoted by Grimshaw, op. cit., p. 47.

110. Ibid., p. 48; Crouthamel, op. cit., p. 177.

111. Crouthamel, op. cit., p. 178.

112. Vardaman's remarks, Congressional Record, 63rd Cong., 2nd sess. (Feb. 6, 1914), reproduced in Fishel and Quarles, op. cit., p. 378.

113. Quoted by Grimshaw, op. cit., p. 47.

114. The Niagara Movement and the emergence of the NAACP have been more fully described earlier. Kellogg, op. cit., Chap. 9, pp. 155–82, "The NAACP and the Wilson Administration," is very helpful.

115. Elliott M. Rudwick, *Race Riot at East St. Louis,* provides most of the information here summarized; also, *Crisis,* Vol. 14 (May–Oct. 1917) and Vol. 15 (Nov. 1917–Apr. 1918).

116. Quoted by Rudwick, op. cit., p. 5; ibid., pp. 89, 165, 174; *Crisis,* Vol. 14, p. 220, and Vol. 15, p. 117; Scott, *Negro Migration,* pp. 100–1.

117. Kennedy, *Negro Peasant Turns Cityward,* p. 104.

118. Johnson, *Patterns of Negro Segregation,* p. 312.

119. Rudwick, op. cit., pp. 142, 172–73.

120. U. S. Department of Labor, op. cit., p. 135.

121. *Crisis,* Vol. 15, p. 118.

122. Rudwick, op. cit., p. 165.

123. Ibid., pp. 11–15. The same kind of political maneuvering seems to have been at least a partial cause of the "Exodus" of 1879, when Republican politicians sought to swing over the Democratic state of Indiana by bringing in Negroes (Hirshon, *Farewell to the Bloody Shirt,* p. 73).

124. *Crisis,* Vol. 15, p. 121.

125. U. S. Department of Labor, op. cit., pp. 129–30, 132.

126. Ibid., p. 132.

127. Ibid.

128. Quotes all from Kelly Miller, *Everlasting Stain,* in the following order: pp. 139, 148, 145, 139, 144, 153, 155.

CHAPTER 9

1. Arthur Barbeau and Florette Henri, *The Unknown Soldiers,* p. 7.

2. Ibid., p. 15; David G. Mandelbaum, *Soldier Groups and Negro Soldiers,* pp. 90, 91; Irvin H. Lee, *Negro Medal of Honor Men,* pp. x, 40; William R. Mueller, "The Negro in the Navy," pp. 110–15.

3. Lee, op. cit., pp. 58–59, 85; Barbeau and Henri, op. cit., p. 15.

4. Lee, op. cit., p. xi.

5. Emmett J. Scott, *Scott's Official History of the American Negro in the World War,* p. 18.

6. When the United States entered the war, a quick decision was made

not to send the black Regulars to France but to station them where they could be useful and yet not "cause trouble"—as, presumably, they might do in Europe. The 9th Cavalry was posted in the Philippines, the 10th on the Mexican border, the 25th Infantry in Hawaii, and the 24th split up among several posts in New Mexico and Texas (Barbeau and Henri, op. cit., p. 27).

7. Ibid., pp. 28–30; Library of Congress, Manuscript Division, *Newton D. Baker Papers* (hereafter cited as *Baker Papers*, L.C.), Baker to Wilson, Aug. 22, 1918.

8. Barbeau and Henri, op. cit., p. 31.

9. *Baker Papers*, L.C., Baker to Wilson, Aug. 22, 1918.

10. Ibid.

11. Ibid.

12. Ibid.; also, Barbeau and Henri, op. cit., p. 30.

13. The McLemore Resolution, H. Res. 131, 65th Cong., 1st sess., Aug. 30, 1917, declared that "the policy of sending negro soldiers to the South is detrimental to the best interests of the country and should be abandoned."

14. *National Archives*, Record Group (hereafter cited as *N.A.*, R.G.) 94, Document 15779, Feb. 26, 1895.

15. *N.A.*, R.G. 165, Army War College File, Document 4483, 1907 (n.d.).

16. Ibid.

17. *N.A.*, R.G. 94, Document 2024576W/, May 1913.

18. Shufeldt, *America's Greatest Problem*, p. 18; the race theories of Hoffman and Shufeldt have been discussed earlier, in Chap. 7.

19. *N.A.*, R.G. 94, Document 2356535, Dec. 10, 1915; this bill, H.R. 17183, failed to pass.

20. Richard M. Dalfiume, *Desegration of the U. S. Armed Forces*, p. 8.

21. *N.A.*, R.G. 94, Document 2583754, Apr. 25, 1917.

22. *N.A.* files contain dozens of such letters, from both blacks and whites, such as *N.A.*, R.G. 94, Document 2639352, May 10, 1917, letter from Senator William Calder of New York supporting a request for a black OTC.

23. *N.A.*, R.G. 94, Document 2392349, letter from Oswald Garrison Villard.

24. Ibid., letter from Richard P. Roots.

25. *N.A.*, R.G. 94, Document 2566564, letter from G. H. Edmonds.

26. U. S. Department of Justice, *Report*, p. 183.

27. Vincent, *Black Power*, pp. 34, 41; Ottley, *Lonely Warrior*, p. 154.

28. Fox, *Guardian of Boston*, p. 217; Barbeau and Henri, p. 6. The Kaiser commissioned a painting from a design of his own; called "The Yellow Peril!" it showed Buddha riding a dragon across Europe, leaving cities in burned ruins behind him; Germania, foremost of the nations of Europe, was represented by a blond lady with breastplates and drawn sword (Tuchman, *The Zimmerman Telegram*, pp. 25–26).

29. Quoted by Fox, op. cit., p. 220.

30. Ibid., p. 220–21. Not all blacks went along on integration; the Afro-American Republican League of Michigan wanted a separate black regiment raised there, explaining that "the colored race of Michigan do not feel that they will be satisfied by being mixed with white troops" (*N.A.*, R.G. 94, Document 2566564).

31. Drimmer, *Black History*, p. 387; Ginzberg and Eichner, *The Troublesome Presence*, pp. 280–81.

32. Ottley, *Lonely Warrior*, p. 157.

33. *Crisis*, Vol. 16, No. 3 (July 1918).

34. *Crisis*, Vol. 16, No. 1 (May 1918).

35. Fox, op. cit., p. 219.

36. Tuchman, op. cit., p. 89; Woodson, *Century of Negro Migration*, p. 151.

37. *N.A.*, R.G. 94, Document 1714937, letter from Major General Duvall to the Adjutant General, Oct. 7, 1910.

38. This was a kind of ecumenical convention at a time when Trotter was trying to attract to the NIPL leaders of various philosophies, such as DuBois, Walters, and Waldron.

39. Tuchman, op. cit., pp. 30, 35, 37, 58.

40. *N.A.*, R.G. 94, Document 2377632, letter from the Secretary of War to the Adjutant General June 16, 1916.

41. In 1919 the Department of Justice cited *Challenge*, edited by William Bridges, and *Messenger*, edited by Randolph, Owen, and others, for showing pro-Mexican sympathies (U. S. Department of Justice, *Report*, pp. 168, 175).

42. Ottley, op. cit., p. 129; George W. Cullum, *Biographical Register of the Officers and Graduates of the U. S. Military Academy*, p. 2.

43. The first graduate, Henry Flipper, has been discussed. The second was John H. Alexander of Ohio (the same state as Charles Young), who graduated in 1887 and died suddenly a few years later. For more information on Flipper and Young, see Wesley A. Brown, "Eleven Men of West Point."

44. The story of Young's appointment, protest, and transfer is documented in *N.A.*, R.G. 94, Documents 5345ACP1889, 5867ACP1889, and 6250ACP-1889.

45. *N.A.*, R.G. 94, Document 5345ACP1889, letter from Maj. Guy V. Henry to the Adjutant General, Jan. 3, 1890.

46. *N.A.*, R.G. 94, Document 192ACP1890 (also called 229AGO1890), memo from the Adjutant General's office, "to the Maj. Genl. Comdg.," Jan. 17, 1890; Document 192 90, the Adjutant General to Henry, Jan. 22, 1890.

47. *N.A.*, R.G. 94, Document 4869, Efficiency Report on Lieut. Charles Young by Colonel Tilford, May 1, 1890.

48. *N.A.*, R.G. 94, Document 10704, Efficiency Report on Lieut. Charles Young by Colonel Biddle, Dec. 15, 1891.

49. *N.A.*, R.G. 94, Document 692649, memo for the chief of staff, Feb. 1916 (no day).

50. *N.A.*, R.G. 165, *Scott Papers*, "Concerning Colored Troops," (hereafter cited as *Scott Papers*) Ass't Sec'y War to Chief of Staff, and Chief of Staff to Ass't Sec'y War, Dec. 28, 1915.

51. Ulysses G. Lee, *Employment of Negro Troops*, p. 9.

52. *Baker Papers*, L.C., Item 216, letter from Wilson to Baker, June 25, 1917.

53. Ibid., Item 7-E, longhand memo from Baker to Bliss. Baker was genuinely concerned about race matters; it was he who, in the 1930s, suggested to the Carnegie Corporation the study that was done by Gunnar Myrdal (Coffman, op. cit., pp. 69–70).

54. *Baker Papers*, L.C., Item 7-E, longhand memo, illegible signature (giving General McCain's answer to questions raised in Baker's memo to Bliss, see n. 53).

55. Ibid., Item 219, carbon (unsigned) of letter from Baker to Wilson, June 26, 1917. The reference is to the black OTC established at Fort Des Moines in July 1917, but Young was not assigned there.

56. Ibid.

57. In spite of, or perhaps because of, Dockery's race feelings, he apparently won a promotion at this time. He is designated "Albert B. Dockery, First Lieutenant" in Wilson's letter to Baker of June 25, and is called a lieutenant in Baker's reply of the next day; but in correspondence of June 29 and subsequently he is referred to as "Captain Dockery."

58. *Baker Papers*, L.C., Item 7-2.

59. Ibid., Item 7-1, letter from John Sharp Williams to Wilson, June 30, 1917.

60. Ibid., Item 18, carbon (unsigned) of letter from Baker to Wilson, July 7, 1917. Bright's disease is characterized by high blood pressure, among other pathological conditions.

61. Ibid. Baker was being either obstinate or obtuse, because that did not settle the matter, of course. At Williams's repeated demand, Wilson had to appeal yet again to Baker to have Dockery transferred because "it has got on his [Dockery's] nerves that he himself remains an officer in a negro regiment. . . ." (ibid., Item 21, letter from Wilson to Baker, July 9, 1917). It may well be imagined that the Secretary of War, at a time when the country had been plunged unprepared into war, had small patience with Lieutenant (or Captain) Dockery's racial problem. Baker showed the same irascibility toward another white officer, a Lieutenant Sperry, who asked to be relieved of duty on a board to examine Negro applicants for an officer reserve corps because, Sperry explained, his personal loathing and contempt for Negroes was so strong that he could not conceal it, which would be an embarrassment to the Army; Baker not only disapproved this request but asked that disciplinary measures be taken against Sperry. Despite Baker's annoyance, however, Sperry was relieved of the loathsome duty, and was merely "admonished" by his new commander when he was reassigned (*N.A.*, R.G. 94, Document 2614009, the case of Lieutenant Sperry). It is worth noting that in another case in which the powerful Senator Williams intervened, this one having nothing to do with race, Baker stood firm and his decision was final. This was the case of a young captain, a Mississippian, found guilty of selling passes to soldiers in a detention camp; in response to Williams's request for clemency, on grounds that the captain was nervous because his wife was ill, Baker reviewed the case and found that she had not become ill until two months after the captain began his little racket; Baker firmly advised the President that nothing could be done for Sperry (*Baker Papers*, L.C., letter from Baker to Wilson, Oct. 30, 1918).

62. Roscoe E. Lewis, "Role of Pressure Groups," p. 466; Barbeau and Henri, op. cit., p. 67.

63. Letter by Colonel Young, reprinted from the Pittsburgh *Courier*, in *Crisis*, Vol. 15, p. 33.

64. Ibid.

65. *N.A.*, R.G. 165, *Scott Papers*, letters from William H. Davis to Emmett Scott, Nov. 8, 1917, and July 25 (no year—probably 1918).

66. This was true; some retired white officers who applied for reactivation were denied, including a seventy-year-old general. The President at his dis-

cretion could give commands in the field to retired officers, but rarely did (*N.A.*, R.G. 165, Document 1005–5, letter from Baker to W. S. Scarborough, president of Wilberforce University, Nov. 27, 1917; op. cit., Document 1005–3, denying reactivation of Maj. Gen. William P. Duvall, USA [Ret.] Nov. 22, 1917).

67. Op. cit., Document 1005–6, Apr. 30, 1918, memo for chief of staff from Brig. Gen. William S. Graves.

68. Brown, op. cit., p. 151. Prof. Rayford Logan in a conversation with the author (Dec. 8, 1967) expressed the opinion that to send Young back to Liberia, where water and food pollution was so prevalent, was criminal.

69. Barbeau and Henri, op. cit., p. 56; DuBois, *Dusk of Dawn*, pp. 256–57.

70. *N.A.*, R.G. 94, Document 2588821, letter from Joel Spingarn to Sec'y War, Apr. 19, 1917; Richard M. Dalfiume, *Desegregation of the U. S. Armed Forces*, pp. 8–9; Walter Dyson, *Howard University*, pp. 70–73.

71. In the older group there were fewer who had benefited by the increased educational and other opportunities that resulted from the northward migration; many of the older men had had only the poor secondary education offered by inferior southern schools, or at best some further schooling at a southern Negro college where, according to a 1900 Atlanta University study of thirty-four such colleges, most students were doing only secondary-school work (DuBois, *College Bred Negro*, pp. 16–17).

72. Barbeau and Henri, op. cit., p. 59.

73. Ibid., p. 57.

74. Ibid., p. 58.

75. Ibid., pp. 42–43, 59, 64.

76. *N.A.*, R.G. 165, Document 8142–20.

77. Ibid.; putting them in ORC was the suggestion of the War College Division to the chief of staff (Aug. 31, 1917). Blacks, however, would tend to be overage in grade, since the minimum age for black officer candidates was 25.

78. Ibid.

79. Ibid. Reports of the number of Des Moines officer graduates differ slightly from one source to another; Charles Houston said that 106 captains, 329 first lieutenants, and 204 second lieutenants were commissioned (Pittsburgh *Courier*, Mar. 19, 1960, quoting Charles Houston), which adds up to 639, not 622.

80. *N.A.*, R.G. 94, Document 2615816.

81. *N.A.*, R.G. 165, Documents 8142–28, 8142–181, 8142–178, 8142–172.

82. Barbeau and Henri, op. cit., pp. 62–63.

83. Ibid., pp. 64–65.

84. Ibid., p. 64.

85. Ibid., p. 84.

86. Coffman, op. cit., pp. 318–19, discusses the broad range of age, education, and background among black officers.

87. Barbeau and Henri, op. cit., p. 60.

88. W. N. Colson and A. B. Nutt, "The Failure of the Ninety-Second Division," p. 22; *N.A.*, R.G. 165, *Scott Papers*, letter from Moton to Scott, Nov. 21, 1917.

89. *N.A.*, R.G. 165, *Scott Papers*, a circular letter sent to Sec'y War by Congressman Ragsdale of South Carolina; see also, same file, a report on the bitter race feeling at Camp Grant, Illinois, where, the report said, men were called niggers, were cursed and pushed, latrines were marked "White" and "Colored," and the treatment was so bad every black man wanted to get out.

90. Barbeau and Henri, op. cit., p. 56; Eugene Varlin, *The Negro and the Army*, p. 14.

91. Pittsburgh *Courier* (Mar. 19, 1960), quoting Charles Houston. Houston, an officer in the 368th Infantry Regiment in World War I, later became a noted constitutional lawyer.

92. Conversation with Professor Logan (Dec. 8, 1967).

93. *N.A.*, R.G. 165, "Concerning Colored Troops," memo from General Staff Statistics Branch to chief, War Plans Division, Aug. 2, 1918.

94. Barbeau and Henri, op. cit., p. 43. In December 1917, Secretary Baker assured DuBois that 30,000 black men would be trained for combat; he was less accurate (or frank) in adding that blacks would get the same training and employment as whites, and that 50,000 blacks in depot brigades might serve as either labor or combat troops, whereas in fact they were simply laborers in uniform.

95. Barbeau and Henri, op. cit., p. 81.

96. The number of men in the National Guard is frequently stated to have been between 10,000 and 14,000, which is about double their actual strength (Barbeau and Henri, op. cit., p. 70).

97. *Baker Papers*, L.C., telegram from A. F. Lever, Aug. 20–21, 1917; and attached longhand note to Baker from Wilson, initialed.

98. Ibid. Splitting up the black divisions for training among a number of northern and border state camps, which put them under a severe handicap, was specifically done to avoid concentrating black troops at Camp Jackson, South Carolina (*N.A.*, R.G. 165, Document 8142–34, Oct. 1917).

99. Barbeau and Henri, op. cit., pp. 71–77, 79–81; soon after arriving in France, Dennison was relieved on grounds of ill health; Maj. James E. Walker, a battalion commander in the 372d, was also replaced for alleged ill health. Young, Dennison, Walker—highest-ranking black officers, all too ill to serve—rather too much of a coincidence?

100. Barbeau and Henri, op. cit., p. 81.

101. Capt. Napoleon Marshall of the 369th, Harvard alumnus and member of the New York Bar, in Spartanburg was insulted and thrown off a streetcar (Barbeau and Henri, op. cit., p. 73).

102. Ibid., p. 70.

103. Ibid., p. 82. "Knowing the Negro" was generally regarded as the prime qualification for white officers placed with black troops (Colson and Nutt, "Failure of the Ninety-Second," p. 23). Seligmann held that "the white man who 'knows the nigger' is almost entirely ignorant," because he does not know the black person in his home, his meetings, his church, and seldom does he know what the black man is thinking (Seligmann, op. cit., p. 91). Seligmann quoted the Harvard historian Albert Bushnell Hart as saying: "'The Southern whites, with few exceptions, teach no Negroes, attend no Negro church services, penetrate into no Negro society, and they see the Negro near at hand chiefly as unsatisfactory domestic servants, as

field hands of doubtful profit, as neglected and terrified patients, as clients in criminal suits or neighborhood squabbles, as prisoners in the dock, as convicted criminals, as wretched objects for the vengeance of a mob'" (Seligmann, op. cit., p. 277).

104. N.A., R.G. 165, *Scott Papers*, General Ballou's Bulletin No. 35, Mar. 28, 1918, "By command of Major General Ballou, [signed] Allen J. Greer, Lieutenant Colonel, General Staff, Chief of Staff."

105. Barbeau and Henri, op. cit., p. 86. Italics are Ballou's.

106. N.A., R.G. 165, *Scott Papers*, letter from Maj. Gen. C. C. Ballou to Emmett J. Scott, Apr. 22, 1918. Italics are Ballou's.

107. N.A., R.G. 165, Document 8142–150, memo from Col. E. D. Anderson, "Disposal of Colored Drafted Men." The complete text is printed in Barbeau and Henri, op. cit., pp. 191–201.

108. Emmett Scott's office noted that at Camp Lee, Virginia, colored draftees due to go overseas in one week were dressed in "blue overalls and brogans" (N.A., R.G. 165, *Scott Papers*, letter from William H. Davis, Nov. 8, 1917); there are other references to blue-overalled soldiers here and there in the literature of the war, and occasionally the black draftees are described as being outfitted with surplus Union blues from the Civil War.

109. Barbeau and Henri, op. cit., p. 39.

110. N.A., R.G. 165, Document 8142–150, memo from Colonel Anderson.

111. Barbeau and Henri, op. cit., p. 43.

112. Ibid., pp. 36, 49–50; studies of Negro intelligence had been made by psychologist George O. Ferguson (ibid., pp. 44–48); a wartime study by Carl C. Brigham was published in 1923, and will be discussed as a postwar event. For the way the Army exploited these findings, see James G. Harbord (commanding general of the SOS), *The American Army in France*, p. 27.

113. Ibid., pp. 91–92. This proportion of labor troops to combat troops already exceeded Baker's promise of 65 to 35, made to DuBois, and it was going to increase; yet Baker in December 1917 rather testily deplored "what seems to be a certain amount of overworked hysteria on the part of some of the complainants, who seem to think that only colored draftees are being assigned to duty in the labor battalions" (ibid., p. 91). It is true that there were white SOS troops. By the Armistice, the SOS numbered 644,540 men, or about *one third* of all American soldiers in Europe; however, *four fifths* of black soldiers were in the SOS. So the fear of blacks being assigned only to labor battalions seems well founded, and not "overworked hysteria." Military authorities were constantly trying to transfer combat troops to pioneer infantry or service battalions, in circumvention of what seems an honest effort on Baker's part to be fair (insofar as his own biases would allow) to black troops and officers.

114. Barbeau and Henri, op. cit., p. 94. Lieut. Col. U. S. Grant was a descendant of the commander in chief of the Union Army in the Civil War.

115. Ibid., p. 95.

116. For these and other details concerning the life and work of the labor troops, see ibid., Chap. 6, "Laborers in Uniform," pp. 89–110.

117. This was true for all black troops. In an extraordinary document called "Secret Instructions Concerning Black American Troops," the French authorities were appealed to by Colonel Linard of the U. S. Army not to permit familiar relations with Negroes, which would offend the American view that they were inferior and must be kept in their place. The French Assembly, outraged by this document, declared that anyone on French soil would be obliged to respect French law, which proclaimed equality of all men without distinction of origin or color (France, Assemblée Nationale, *Annales*, N.S. 1919, Session Extraordinaire; Chambre Débats, 2 Séance du 25 Juillet 1919, pp. 3,365 and 3,366.

118. Barbeau and Henri, op. cit., pp. 40, 41; about 14,000 American war dead were buried at Romagne (U. S. Congress, House of Representatives, Committee on Foreign Affairs, July 4–5, 1926); bill proposed by Hamilton Fish, New York, formerly colonel, 371st Regiment, 93d Division, for *A Monument in France to Certain American Infantry Regiments Attached to the French Army.*

119. Frederick Palmer, *America in France*, p. 60.

120. Barbeau and Henri, op. cit., p. 105.

121. The 369th sailed in December 1917, and the other three regiments of the 93d Division in February, March, and April 1918; the 92d Division did not sail until June 1918.

122. Little, *From Harlem to the Rhine*, p. 146.

123. Barbeau and Henri, op. cit., pp. 113–14.

124. Little, op. cit., pp. 192–201; Barbeau and Henri, op. cit., pp. 121, 126–27.

125. Little, op. cit., pp. xi, 126–41. Other famous bands in the black regiments were led by such outstanding musical figures as Norman Scott, Dorsey Rhodes, Egbert Thompson, Jack Thomas, George Duff, Tim Brymn, and Will Vodery. After the war, Vodery was given an award by Robert Casadesus (Southern, *Music of Black Americans*, pp. 361–64).

126. Even Captain Europe was transferred at one point, but was later restored to the regiment to maintain the fame of its band, of which the American Army was very proud (Barbeau and Henri, op. cit., pp. 121–22).

127. Barbeau and Henri, op. cit., pp. 124–28. Ironically, Maj. L. R. Fredenhall, who inspected the battleground to judge the performance of the regiment, admitted that he himself had almost gotten lost traversing the very difficult terrain (ibid., pp. 126–27).

128. Ibid., pp. 129–30.

129. *Baker Papers*, L.C., Item 192–1 (Oct. 20, 1918). The commander of the 371st, Col. Hamilton Fish, seems to have been proud of his men and probably set an example in praising them.

130. Barbeau and Henri, op. cit., p. 133.

131. Ibid.

132. Ibid., pp. 86–90; see Coffman, op. cit., pp. 317–20, for the contempt and distrust with which white officers regarded black officers.

133. Barbeau and Henri, op. cit., p. 138.

134. Ibid.

135. Ibid., p. 137.

136. Coffman, op. cit., p. 319. Secretary Baker objected to the restraint on promotions, and insisted that existing captains be utilized in jobs of that

grade. When Scott protested the barrier to black promotions, he was assured by the military that there were no grounds for complaint "that the colored soldier is not given opportunity for advancement in the ranks of our Army" (Barbeau and Henri, op. cit., p. 147). But this was a lie. General Ballou tried to get a promotion to captain for Lieut. T. T. Thompson, who was his acting personnel officer, so that Thompson would have the requisite rank for permanency in his job. Evidently Thompson was good at his work or Ballou would not have put in for the promotion; but his request was denied by the War Department "on the ground that the personnel officer should be white," as specified in the table of organization (ibid., pp. 146–47).

137. Conversation with Professor Rayford Logan (Dec. 8, 1967).

138. Barbeau and Henri, op. cit., p. 144.

139. Ibid., pp. 143–45.

140. Full text of this leaflet given ibid., pp. 148–49, from *N.A.*, R.G. 165, German Propaganda Leaflet, "To the Colored Soldiers of the U. S. Army." Other leaflets are quoted by Chester D. Heywood, *Negro Combat Troops in the World War*, pp. 211, 212; these were entitled "Never Say Die" and "How to Stop the War," and were directed at all American soldiers without regard to color, urging them to desert or simply stop fighting "and slip across 'No-Man's Land' and join the bunch that's taking it easy there waiting to be exchanged and taken home. . . . All the fine words about glory are tommyrot. . . . You would better be fighting the money trust at home instead of fighting your fellow soldiers in gray over here. . . ."

141. For this same situation in the 371st Regiment of the 93d, see Barbeau and Henri, op. cit., p. 135.

142. For day-by-day accounts of the action, see *N.A.*, R.G. 120, Organization Records, 92d Division, Summaries of Intelligence, 368th Infantry; Barbeau and Henri, op. cit., pp. 150–52, give a narrative summary based on the intelligence reports. Coffman, op. cit., pp. 314–20, gives an excellent, clear account of the whole confused engagement.

143. Barbeau and Henri, op. cit., p. 163.

144. Lee, *Employment of Negro Troops*, pp. 15–20, noted that after World War I practically all commanders agreed that blacks had done badly, and that with few exceptions the black officers had failed. Army planners, on the basis of these opinions, decided that in future blacks should be utilized as far as possible in service units; or, if black combat units were to be formed, all officers and noncoms should be white. As explained by E. W. Kenworthy, "The Case Against Army Segregation," this policy governed decisions about the use of black personnel in World War II, despite the injustices, inefficiency, and waste of manpower that resulted. It was not until after World War II that the policy was officially re-examined, under order of President Truman, by the U. S. President's Committee on Equality and Opportunity in the Armed Forces, whose findings and conclusions were published in 1950 as *Freedom to Serve*. The committee set out to determine whether blacks should be trained for the full range of Army jobs, as was by that time being done in the Navy and Air Force, and whether or not they should serve only in segregated units. The question of black military performance in World War I was exhumed, and testimony was given that, although some black units fought well enough to be decorated, performance

was not consistent. Clichés, inaccuracies, and lies about the inefficiency of black officers were reviewed. On the question of integrating the armed forces, there was a quoteworthy exchange between two witnesses: Lieutenant General Gillem, supporting the position that the military must follow the racial pattern prevailing in civilian life rather than attempt to set precedents, spun an elaborate football metaphor, the gist of which was that the backfield should not jump ahead of the front line; to which Dwight Palmer retorted that there were two kinds of football, the more modern version featuring the forward pass. The final pronouncement of the committee was that, contrary to Army belief, unequal treatment had made for inefficiency; and, furthermore, that "The integrity of the individual, his equal worth in the sight of God, his equal protection under law, his equal rights and obligations of citizenship and his equal opportunity to make just and constructive use of his endowment—these are the very foundation of the American system of values." Still, Kenworthy wrote in 1951, during the Korean conflict, not so much noble thoughts as desperation finally brought about integration in the Army, "when field commanders have desperately needed bodies for replacement . . . white or black" (Kenworthy, op. cit., p. 27).

145. Barbeau and Henri, op. cit., p. 160. Yet, concerning the 7th Division, General Bullard's comment was simply that it had had "hard fighting but advanced some, perhaps half a kilometer . . ." (ibid.). Elements of the 368th had advanced six miles (ibid., pp. 151–52).

146. Ibid., pp. 152–57. Elser said he broke down under the strain of trying to reform his men and push them forward, but he did not explain why a satisfactory officer should break down in performance of his proper duties.

147. Ibid., pp. 160, 162, 163; Major Ross of the 365th Regiment complained bitterly that his recommendations for awards were not approved (ibid., p. 161).

148. N.A., R.G. 165, Colored Troops, Official Release, Casualties as of May 10, 1919. What the typed record actually says about 93d Division casualties is "Killed 57"; but alongside that figure is penciled "? Ayres gives 574 PBS." By all reliable accounts, including the War Department's, 574 is the correct number, but the 57 figure, apparently a typographical error, crops up here and there in other reports, and may be one reason for complaints that black casualties were too low.

149. Representative Hamilton Fish of New York, in support of his bill proposing a monument in France to the black regiments, said that the 369th, 371st, and 372d regiments had 300 killed and 2,100 wounded out of 7,500 (total casualties of 32 per cent) who were in a ten-day drive; Fish pointed out that the 42d Division was granted a special monument for losing 257 (or 267) killed and 800 wounded out of 2,700 men (total casualties of 39 per cent) in a one-day drive (U. S. Congress, House of Representatives, Committee on Foreign Affairs, Mar. 4–5, 1926).

150. Barbeau and Henri, op. cit., pp. 166–67; Brawley, *Social History*, p. 354; Robert A. Moton, *Finding a Way Out*, pp. 262–64 (Moton told the troops: "I hope no one will do anything in peace to spoil the magnificent record you have made in war"); Little, op. cit., pp. 357–62; N.A., R.G. 165, Document 7853–83, Aug. 8, 1919.

151. Barbeau and Henri, op. cit., p. 175.

CHAPTER 10

1. Ottley, *Lonely Warrior*, p. 151; Claude A. Barnett, "Role of the Press . . . and Negro Morale," p. 478; U. S. Department of Justice, *Report*, p. 162 (hereafter cited as USDJ *Report*).

2. Seligmann, *Negro Faces America*, p. 307.

3. *Negro Migration in 1916–1917*, the Labor Department study here referred to and frequently cited in this book, was the report of investigations directed by Dr. James H. Dillard, director of the Jeanes and Slater foundations, and was published by the Department of Labor in 1919. Scott's philosophy is apparent in his advice to Tyler, whom he asked to tone down dispatches from France on subjects like YMCA discrimination and the friendliness of French women toward black soldiers, saying: "I very much hope that you will preserve as much equanimity of spirit as possible . . . [and not] permit yourself to be overcome by the injustices which surround us" (see Barbeau and Henri, *The Unknown Soldiers*, p. 179).

4. Kelly Miller, *Everlasting Stain*, p. 32.

5. Barbeau and Henri, *The Unknown Soldiers*, pp. 171, 176.

6. Pittsburgh *Courier* (Mar. 19, 1960).

7. Dalfiume, *Desegregation of the U. S. Armed Forces*, p. 21.

8. Seligmann, op. cit., p. 58.

9. Ulysses G. Lee, *Employment of Negro Troops*, pp. 15, 21–27; Barbeau and Henri, op. cit., pp. 172–73.

10. Ibid., pp. 173–74; see also Charles Bolte, "He Fought for Freedom."

11. USDJ *Report*, pp. 136, 178; Colson and Nutt, "The Failure of the Ninety-Second Division."

12. USDJ, op. cit., pp. 177–78.

13. Ibid., p. 179.

14. Barbeau and Henri, op. cit., p. 17.

15. Vincent, *Black Power*, p. 45; Fox, *Guardian of Boston*, pp. 225–30; Trotter's full name was William Monroe Trotter, although he rarely used the "William."

16. Fox, op. cit., pp. 226–29; conversation with Professor Rayford Logan (Dec. 8, 1967); Hughes, *Big Sea*, pp. 144–57.

17. USDJ, op. cit., p. 166, quoting *Crusader*, a black-nationalistic, radical magazine, the organ of the African Blood Brotherhood, edited by Cyril V. Briggs.

18. USDJ, op. cit., p. 187.

19. Ibid., p. 179.

20. Ibid.

21. Ibid., p. 177.

22. Ibid., pp. 163, 167, 170, 173. Of the author of the quoted quatrain, the jingoistic Attorney General Palmer commented: ". . . Razafkeriefo (if that is a name) . . ." (ibid., p. 166).

23. Ibid., pp. 169, 171.

24. Ibid., p. 186.

25. Ibid., pp. 166, 167.

26. Ibid., p. 186; Washington died in 1915.

27. Ibid., p. 180.

28. Tindall, *South Carolina Negroes,* p. 62; U. S. Bureau of the Census, *Historical Statistics,* p. 278. In 1920 there were, in addition to 703,555 black tenant farmers, 333,713 black sharecroppers, a class not counted in the 1910 census; the 1 per cent increase in tenants may have been sharecroppers who had worked their way up to tenant status by 1920. Or, some migrants may have returned to become tenant farmers after the war.

29. Scheiner, *Negro Mecca,* p. 53; Woodward, *Strange Career of Jim Crow,* p. 115; Kennedy, *Negro Peasant Turns Cityward,* pp. 130–32; U. S. Bureau of the Census, *Statistical Abstract of the United States,* p. 356.

30. *Opportunity,* Vol. 1 (Jun. 1923), pp. 12–19, quoted in Fishel and Quarles, *Negro American,* pp. 418–19.

31. Harris, "Negro Labor's Quarrel," p. 905; Harris, "Negro and Economic Radicalism," pp. 199–203; according to Greene and Woodson, *Negro Wage Earner,* p. 352, fewer blacks became union members in the thirty years after 1900 (28,263) than in the ten years preceding 1900 (29,246).

32. Vincent, op. cit., p. 53.

33. Fisher, *Walls of Jericho,* p. 282; Fisher was a doctor of medicine as well as a writer.

34. Abbott, *Tenements of Chicago,* p. 125; Spear, *Black Chicago,* pp. 211–12; Chicago Commission, *Negro in Chicago,* pp. 122–23.

35. Gossett, *Race,* p. 386.

36. Spear, op. cit., p. 213.

37. Gossett, op. cit., p. 372. In 1920, Henry Ford's house organ, the Dearborn *Independent,* which had a large readership, carried what purported to be an exposé of Jewish perfidy in documents called "Protocols of the Learned Elders of Zion," later shown to be forgeries.

38. Gossett, op. cit., pp. 370–71. Osborn went so far as to insist that the Nordic influx into Italy had produced all the great artists of the Renaissance, and that Dante's surname, Alighieri, was German (ibid., pp. 387–89); Stoddard published twenty-two books and many magazine articles presenting his race fantasies (ibid., pp. 395–96).

39. Ibid., p. 402.

40. Woodward, *Strange Career of Jim Crow,* p. 115; Higham, *Strangers in the Land,* pp. 288–89; the Klan was in the forefront of the battle for immigration restriction, which was finally won by passage of the drastic Johnson-Reed Act of 1924.

41. Seligmann, op. cit., p. 257.

42. Higham, op. cit., pp. 290–91; this incident is cited for its incredible viciousness by Professor Albert B. Hart in remarks of his quoted by Seligmann, op. cit., p. 256.

43. Seligmann, op. cit., pp. 257–58.

44. Woodward, *Strange Career of Jim Crow,* p. 115.

45. Ibid., p. 116; Hughes, *Big Sea,* p. 51.

46. Haynes, "Race Riots," p. 697; Hughes, *Big Sea,* p. 33.

47. Bergman, *Chronological History,* p. 387; Hesseltine and Smiley, *South in American History,* p. 510; Arthur J. Waskow, *From Race Riot to Sit-In,* p. 12. The 1919 lynchings apparently set new records for sadism; USDJ *Report,* pp. 173–74, quotes an unbearably gruesome poem, *The Mob Victim,* which appeared in the July 1919 *Messenger,* describing a death-by-inches

lynching and the souvenir-hunting members of the murder mob who took home bits of the victim.

48. Haynes, "Race Riots," p. 697.
49. Kelly Miller, *Everlasting Stain*, p. 39.
50. USDJ *Report*, pp. 165, 179, 181.
51. Seligmann, op. cit., pp. 141–42.
52. Ibid., pp. 148–49.
53. Ibid., p. 63.
54. Much of the following summary of the riots is drawn from Waskow, *From Race Riot to Sit-In*.
55. Gossett, op. cit., p. 371.
56. Ottley, op. cit., p. 183.
57. Chicago Commission, op. cit., pp. 595–601.
58. Werner, *Julius Rosenwald*, p. 273.
59. Seligmann, op. cit., pp. 51–52. Accounts of the Elaine riot differ somewhat on casualties and details; cf. Lerone Bennett, Jr., *Confrontation: Black and White*, p. 142; Bergman, op. cit., p. 190.
60. Seligmann, op. cit., pp. 225–48; Woodson, *Rural Negro*, p. 86.
61. Ottley, op. cit., p. 142.
62. Gossett, op. cit., p. 394.
63. Fox, op. cit., p. 233.
64. Seligmann, op. cit., p. 68.
65. Harris, "Negro Labor's Quarrel," p. 907.
66. USDJ *Report*, p. 137.
67. Ibid., p. 161.
68. Ibid., p. 162.
69. Ibid., pp. 161–62.
70. Ibid., p. 164.
71. Ibid., p. 167.
72. Editors of the anarchist publication *Mother Earth*, both deported to Russia as a result of the Palmer investigation and raids.
73. Seligmann, op. cit., p. 194. A. Philip Randolph was arrested in 1918 during a speech in Cleveland in which he discussed racism in relation to America's war involvement (Vincent, op. cit., p. 44).
74. USDJ, op. cit., p. 185.
75. Haynes, op. cit., p. 698.
76. Green, *Secret City*, p. 199.
77. Fox, op. cit., pp. 249–50; Gossett, op. cit., p. 405.
78. Gossett, op. cit., p. 366.
79. Ibid., p. 364.
80. Ibid., p. 366.
81. Carl C. Brigham, *A Study of American Intelligence*, pp. 54–56. Brigham, who was chiefly responsible for the Army testing program, here devotes considerable effort to unsnarling what he calls this "ridiculous" statement. The Army Alpha and Beta tests are discussed in Barbeau and Henri, op. cit., pp. 45–48.
82. Gossett, op. cit., p. 368.
83. Harbord, *American Army in France*, p. 27.
84. Gossett, op. cit., p. 368.
85. Brigham, op. cit., p. xvii; Brigham was not, however, in agreement in all details with Grant's hypotheses; Professor Ripley was not quite as destructively racist as Grant.

86. Ibid., pp. 85, 86, 197.
87. Ibid., p. 190.
88. Ibid., pp. 209–10.
89. Ibid., p. 192.
90. Ibid., p. 210.
91. Alpha and Beta tests used by the Army are reproduced in full in Brigham, op. cit., pp. 3–51.
92. Klineberg, *Characteristics of the American Negro*, p. 122; in any case, both Alpha and Beta required responses to intellectual stimuli; later testing showed Indians and blacks quicker than whites in responses to auditory, visual, and electrical stimulation, according to Klineberg, op. cit., p. 121.
93. Ibid., pp. 44–45.
94. Brigham, op. cit., p. 188. Certain scientists today, notably psychologists H. J. Eysenck and Richard Herrnstein, and physicist Arthur R. Jensen who turned his attention from transistors to race, have put forward theories more or less reminiscent of Brigham's early work. See Herrnstein, "I.Q.," and Jensen, "How Much Can We Boost IQ and Scholastic Achievement?" and an illuminating discussion of all three men by Sandra Scarr-Salapatek, "Unknowns in the IQ Equation."
95. Newby, op. cit., pp. 40–41.
96. Brigham, "Intelligence Tests of Immigrant Groups," p. 159; italics are his.
97. Ibid., p. 165.

CHAPTER 11

1. Charles S. Johnson, "After Garvey—What?" *Opportunity*, Vol. 1 (Aug. 1923), reprinted in Fishel and Quarles, *Negro American*, p. 434.
2. Fox, *Guardian of Boston*, p. 251.
3. Ibid., p. 250.
4. Bone, *Negro Novel in America*, p. 63.
5. Edmund D. Cronon, *Black Moses*, pp. 185–87. Garvey was by no means the inventor of Back-to-Africa; its long history is told by Robert G. Weisbord, "The Back-to-Africa Idea."
6. Vincent, *Black Power*, pp. 39, 127; Hughes, *Big Sea*, p. 102.
7. USDJ *Report*, pp. 163–65; Vincent, op. cit., pp. 74–84. Cronon, in his biography of Garvey, points out a degree of racism in the movement; not only was black more beautiful than white, but black blacks were preferred by Garvey to those of paler shades of coloring; this preference is thought to have alienated some lighter-complexioned blacks, such as DuBois and Cyril Briggs (Cronon, op. cit., pp. 78, 199).
8. Vincent, op. cit., pp. 13, 18–19, 54, 92–99, 102; Cronon, op. cit., p. 175.
9. Vincent, op. cit., pp. 102, 122–23, 177–85.
10. Ibid., p. 190.
11. Cronon, op. cit., p. 198.
12. Vincent, op. cit., pp. 91, 189–214.
13. Charles Johnson, "After Garvey—What?" in Fishel and Quarles, op. cit., p. 433. The father of Malcolm X, himself a devout Garveyite, brought

up his son to believe in Garvey's thesis that "freedom, independence, and self-respect could never be achieved by the Negro in America. . . ." (quoted from Malcolm X's *Autobiography* in Drimmer, *Black History*, p. 388).

14. Charles Johnson, op. cit., p. 435.

15. Vincent, op. cit., pp. 25–26.

16. Bone, op. cit., p. 62; Professor Bone's chapter "The Background of the Negro Renaissance" is full of illuminating insights. Langston Hughes said ordinary blacks didn't even know about the Renaissance (*Big Sea*, p. 228), but in fact the name was popular in nonliterary as well as literary circles. There was, for example, the Renaissance Big Five, a great basketball team organized in 1923, which in sixteen years of competition won 1,588 games and lost only 239; in 1928 the Renaissance Big Five defeated the champion Celtics team, which included the basketball great Nat Holman (Henderson, *Negro in Sports*, pp. 133–35; Orr, *Black Athlete*, p. 126).

17. Bone, op. cit., p. 53.

18. Ibid., pp. 56, 58.

19. A number of Black Renaissance people took potshots at "Strivers' Row," symbol of all despised black middle-class aspirations—the beautiful Harlem street of tree-flanked brick houses designed in the early 1900s by Stanford White and in the Renaissance era occupied by rich Negroes whom the bohemians scorned: Fletcher Henderson, the "society" band leader; prizefighter Harry Wills; and assorted well-to-do lawyers, doctors, real estate operators, beauticians, and cosmeticians. Carl Van Vechten, *Nigger Heaven*, p. 77, describes Strivers' Row.

20. Bone, op. cit., p. 60. For example, Van Vechten called the attention of Alfred Knopf to a prize-winning group of poems by Langston Hughes, which Knopf published as *Weary Blues*, Hughes's first book (Hughes, *Big Sea*, pp. 215–16).

21. Hughes, *Big Sea*, p. 228.

22. Carl Van Vechten, *Nigger Heaven*, pp. 95–96.

23. Ibid., p. 246. This quote and the preceding are admittedly among the worst bits of writing in the book, but there are many close runners-up; *Nigger Heaven* was a best seller because of what passed at the time for sensational and erotic content and not because of literary value.

24. Edward Lueders, *Carl Van Vechten*, p. 104. The title *Nigger Heaven*, although used sympathetically by Van Vechten to compare the Harlem ghetto with the top balcony of a theater, to which blacks were customarily relegated, incensed many black people (Hughes, *Big Sea*, p. 269; Lueders, op. cit., p. 102). Van Vechten founded the James Weldon Johnson Memorial Collection of Negro Arts and Letters at Yale University (Lueders, op. cit., p. 96), among other important benefactions to black people, whom he sincerely admired.

25. For an over-all view of this writing and those who did it, see Bone, op. cit., Chap. 4, "The Harlem School."

26. Ibid., pp. 56–58; Hughes, *Big Sea*, p. 235; Osofsky, *Harlem*, p. 181.

27. Fisher, *Walls of Jericho*, p. 133. Fisher was B.A. and M.A., Brown University; M.D., Howard University; and practiced as a roentgenologist; the Arno edition of his *Walls of Jericho* has an excellent biographical introduction by Professor William H. Robinson, Jr.

28. Southern, *Music of Black Americans,* p. 414.

29. Seligmann, op. cit., p. 280.

30. Lueders, op. cit., p. 44.

31. Hughes, *Big Sea,* pp. 223–28, 257; Southern, op. cit., pp. 339, 367–68, 431; Fisher, "Caucasians Storm Harlem," pp. 396–97; Van Vechten, *Nigger Heaven,* p. 13. The Garveyite Black Swan Phonograph Company was a Harry Pace enterprise.

32. Hughes, *Big Sea,* p. 228.

33. Osofsky, *Harlem,* p. 183; Lueders, op. cit., p. 115; Hughes, *Big Sea,* p. 227. On the popularity of Harlem with whites, see Hugh Gloster, "The Van Vechten Vogue," and Fisher, "Caucasians Storm Harlem."

34. Osofsky, op. cit., p. 184; Hughes, *Big Sea,* pp. 225–26; Fisher, "Caucasians Storm Harlem," pp. 395–98.

35. Wallace Thurman, *Infants of the Spring;* Hughes, *Big Sea,* pp. 233–38, gives some interesting biographical information about Thurman.

36. Van Vechten, op. cit., p. 120. "Ofay" and "shine" were generally used Negro slang expressions for white man and black man, respectively. Black Renaissance authors made a point of introducing slang into their writing. Especially interesting for students of sociolinguistics is Rudolph Fisher's exposition of Harlem slang in the twenties, in his *Walls of Jericho,* p. 297. Many of the slang words he defined are still current in the meanings he assigned, as, "freeby," a free ticket; "jive," flattery, deceit, a passing fancy; "the man," authority, and by extension, the white man. Fisher listed a number of slang terms for Negro, many of them still used; but, oddly, the list included "hunky," which seems to have reversed its meaning, if it is the same word as today's "honky." "Ofay," according to Fisher, was a contraction of a much older slang term for white person: "old fay." Van Vechten, in a "Glossary of Negro Words and Phrases," which he appended to *Nigger Heaven,* listed "ofay" for white man, but ventured no guess at its derivation. However, there may be etymological suggestions in two other slang terms in Van Vechten's glossary, which he claims are "theatrical hog Latin": "fagingy-fagade" for white man, and "spagingy-spagade" for black man. Perhaps the "fay" of "ofay" was a variant of "fagingy-fagade"; or "ofay" itself may have been ordinary hog Latin for "foe" (hog Latin puts the last sound first and adds "ay" at the end)—and, by extension, white man.

37. A'lelia (or sometimes Ledia) Walker, referred to by Hughes as "the joy goddess of Harlem in the 1920s," was the daughter of Madame C. J. Walker, the Louisiana migrant who made a fortune in the hair-straightening business. A'lelia, besides spending lavishly on pleasure and luxuries, was a generous contributor to Garvey projects. Garvey, consistently with "black is beautiful," would permit no advertising of skin lighteners or hair straighteners in his *Negro World,* but apparently made an exception for the Walker products (Hughes, *Big Sea,* pp. 227, 244; Vincent, op. cit., p. 133).

38. Hughes, *Big Sea,* pp. 227–28.

39. Bone, op. cit., p. 62.

40. Ibid., p. 63.

41. Ibid.

42. Alain Locke, *The New Negro,* excerpt in Fishel and Quarles, op. cit., p. 437.

Bibliography

The interest of scholars and publishers during the past ten or fifteen years in revealing the black American role in the early twentieth century has produced a large legacy for today's student of the subject. First, we are enriched by the many dissertations and books resulting from that interest, which brought into the light materials until then buried in private collections and state and national archives. Another valuable part of the bequest consists of reprints of illuminating works of the century's first two decades or so, works that until recently survived precariously in rare copies but that today the student can own or can borrow from almost any library: the groundbreaking study made by the Chicago Commission on Race Relations; the brilliant, often astonishing publications of Ray Stannard Baker, Charles S. Johnson, Kelly Miller, Seligmann, Woodson, Ovington, Stephenson, Daniels; and socially revealing fiction by Fisher, Micheaux, and James Weldon Johnson—to count only a small part of the wealth available in recent reprints. Other publications that ease our access to the knowledge of fifty to seventy-five years ago are several anthologies of magazine articles, essays, and historical documents, collections well chosen and edited by scholars like Fishel and Quarles, Meier and Rudwick, Brotz, and Drimmer.

It is earnestly to be hoped that this interest will continue, increasing the availability of other important investigations such as the Atlanta University series guided by DuBois, the socioeconomic studies of Haynes and Harris, and two extremely valuable government publications, the report of the Department of Labor on black northward migration in 1916–17, and the 1919 report of the Department of Justice detailing the witch-hunts of

Attorney General A. Mitchell Palmer; assuring continued printings of major historical studies of recent years, for instance, those of Woodward, Hirshon, Dalfiume, Spear, Green, and Osofsky, to name only a few out of many; and promising that the social sciences will further gift our understanding of the black experience through the works of sound and exciting scholars like Gossett and Newby on prejudice, Loren Miller on law and justice, Bremner on poverty, Cole and Liebow on social patterns.

Sources consulted in the preparation of this book are organized below into a single alphabetical list, without the conventional (and, in the author's opinion, often dysfunctional) separate groupings into books, articles, government publications, pamphlets, manuscript materials, etc.

Abbott, Edith. *The Tenements of Chicago 1908–1935.* Chicago: University of Chicago Press, 1936.

Abramowitz, Jack. "The Negro in the Agrarian Revolt," *Agricultural History,* Vol. 24, No. 2, Apr. 1950.

American Academy of Political and Social Science. *America's Race Problems.* New York: Negro University Press, 1969 (first publ. 1901).

Baker, Ray Stannard. *Following the Color Line.* New York: Harper & Row, 1964 (first publ. 1908).

——. "Gathering Clouds along the Color Line," *World's Work,* Vol. 32, June 1916.

——. "The Negro Goes North," *World's Work,* Vol. 34, July 1917.

——. *Woodrow Wilson: Life and Letters,* Vol. II. Garden City, N.Y.: Doubleday, 1931.

Barbeau, Arthur E., and Henri, Florette. *The Unknown Soldiers: Black American Troops in World War I.* Philadelphia: Temple University Press, 1974.

Barnett, Claude A. "The Role of the Press, Radio and Motion Pictures, and Negro Morale," *Journal of Negro Education,* Vol. 12, Summer 1943.

Beale, Howard. *Theodore Roosevelt and the Rise of America to World Power.* Baltimore: The Johns Hopkins University Press, 1956.

Beaver, Daniel R. *Newton D. Baker.* Lincoln, Neb.: University of Nebraska Press, 1966.

Benedict, Ruth, and Weltfish, Gene. *Race: Science and Politics.* New York: Viking, 1962 (first publ. 1940).

Bennett, Lerone, Jr. *Confrontation: Black and White*. Chicago: Johnson, 1965.

Bergman, Peter M. and Mort N., eds. *The Chronological History of the Negro in America*. New York: New American Library, 1969.

Bevis, W. M. "Psychological Traits of the Southern Negro with Observations as to Some of His Psychoses," *American Journal of Psychiatry*, Vol. 1, July 1921.

Biddiss, Michael D. "Houston Stewart Chamberlain: Prophet of Teutonism," *History Today*, Vol. 19, No. 1, 1969.

Blair, Lewis Harvie. *A Southern Prophesy: The Prosperity of the South Dependent upon the Elevation of the Negro* (ed. C. Vann Woodward). Boston: Little, Brown, 1964 (first publ. 1889).

Bloch, Herman D. "Labor and the Negro, 1866–1910," *Journal of Negro History*, Vol. 50, July 1965.

Bloomfield, Maxwell. "Dixon's *The Leopard's Spots*: A Study in Popular Racism," *American Quarterly*, Vol. 16, Fall 1964.

Blum, John Morton. *The Republican Roosevelt*. Cambridge: Harvard University Press, 1954.

——. *Woodrow Wilson and the Politics of Morality*. Boston: Little, Brown, 1956.

Blumenthal, Henry. "Woodrow Wilson and the Race Question," *Journal of Negro History*, Vol. 48, Jan. 1963.

Boas, Franz. "The Anthropological Position of the Negro," *Van Norden: The World's Mirror*, Apr. 1907.

——. Book Review (of *The Rising Tide of Color* by Stoddard), *Nation*, Dec. 8, 1920 (repr. in Fishel and Quarles, *The Negro American*, q.v.).

Bolte, Charles G. "He Fought for Freedom," *Survey Graphic*, Vol. 36, No. 1, Jan. 1947.

Bone, Robert A. *The Negro Novel in America*, rev. ed. New Haven: Yale University Press, 1965.

Bradburn, Norman M.; Sudman, Seymour; and Gockell, Galen. *Side by Side: Integrated Neighborhoods in America*. Chicago: Quadrangle, 1971.

Brawley, Benjamin. *A Social History of the American Negro*. New York: Collier, 1970 (first publ. 1921).

Bremner, Robert H. *From the Depths: The Discovery of Poverty in the United States*. New York: New York University Press, 1956.

Brigham, Carl C. "Intelligence Tests of Immigrant Groups," *Psychological Review*, Vol. 37, Mar. 1930.

——. *A Study of American Intelligence*. Princeton, N.J.: Princeton University Press, 1923.

Brotz, Howard, ed. *Negro Social and Political Thought 1850–1920*. New York: Basic Books, 1966.

Brown, Wesley A. "Eleven Men of West Point," *Negro History Bulletin*, Apr. 1956.

Buni, Andrew. *The Negro in Virginia Politics 1902–1965*. Charlottesville, Va.: University Press of Virginia, 1967.

Callcott, Margaret Law. *The Negro in Maryland Politics 1870–1912*. Baltimore: The Johns Hopkins University Press, 1969.

Cash, Wilbur J. *The Mind of the South*. New York: Knopf, 1941.

Chicago Commission on Race Relations. *The Negro in Chicago: A Study of Race Relations and a Race Riot* (prepared by Charles S. Johnson). New York: Arno and New York *Times*, 1968 (first publ. 1922).

Coffman, Edward M. *The War to End All Wars*. New York: Oxford University Press, 1968.

Cohen, Octavus Roy. *Black & Blue*. Freeport, N.Y.: Books for Libraries Press, 1970 (first publ. 1926).

———. *Florian Slappey Goes Abroad*. Freeport, N.Y.: Books for Libraries Press, 1970 (first publ. 1928).

Coles, Robert. *Farewell to the South*. Boston: Little, Brown, 1972.

Colson, W. N., and Nutt, A. B. "The Failure of the Ninety-Second Division," *Messenger*, Vol. 2, No. 9, July 1919.

Commager, Henry Steele. *Documents of American History* (8th ed.). New York: Appleton-Century-Crofts, 1968.

Commons, John R. *Races and Immigrants in America*. New York: Macmillan, 1920 (first publ. 1907).

Cripps, Thomas R. "The Reaction of the Negro to the Motion Picture Birth of a Nation," *Historian*, Vol. 25, No. 3, 1962–63.

Crisis. NAACP, New York, Vol. 14, May–Oct. 1917.

———. NAACP, New York, Vol. 15, Nov. 1917–Apr. 1918.

———. NAACP, New York, Vol. 16, May–Oct. 1918.

Cronon, Edmund Davis. *Black Moses*. Madison, Wis.: University of Wisconsin Press, 1955.

———. "Marcus Garvey," in Drimmer, ed., *Black History*, q.v.

Crouthamel, James L. "The Springfield Race Riot of 1908," *Journal of Negro History*, Vol. 45, July 1960.

Crowe, Charles. "Racial Violence and Social Reform—Origins of the Atlanta Race Riot of 1906," *Journal of Negro History*, Vol. 53, July 1968.

Cullum, George Washington. *Biographical Register of the Officers and Graduates of the U. S. Military Academy . . .* (3rd ed.), Vol. 4, Supplement for 1910. Boston: Houghton Mifflin, 1910.

Cunningham, Raymond J. *The Populists in Historical Perspective*. Boston: D. C. Heath, 1968.

Dalfiume, Richard M. *Desegregation of the U. S. Armed Forces: Fighting on Two Fronts, 1939–1953*. Columbia, Mo.: University of Missouri Press, 1969.

Daniels, John. *In Freedom's Birthplace: A Study of the Boston Ne-groes.* New York: Johnson Reprint, 1969 (first publ. 1914).

Destler, Chester A. *Henry Demarest Lloyd.* Philadelphia: University of Pennsylvania Press, 1963.

Dollard, John. *Caste and Class in a Southern Town.* Garden City, N.Y.: Anchor Books, 1957 (first publ. 1937).

Drimmer, Melvin, ed. *Black History: A Reappraisal.* Garden City, N.Y.: Anchor Books, 1969.

DuBois, W. E. B. *The Dusk of Dawn: An Essay Toward an Auto-biography of a Race Concept.* New York: Harcourt, Brace, 1940.

——, ed. *The College Bred Negro* (Atlanta Study No. 5). Atlanta, Ga.: Atlanta University Press, 1900.

——, ed. *The Health and Physique of the Negro American* (Atlanta Study No. 11). Atlanta, Ga.: Atlanta University Press, 1900.

——, ed. *Mortality Among Negroes in Cities* (Atlanta Study No. 1). Atlanta, Ga.: Atlanta University Press, 1896.

——, ed. *The Negro Artisan* (Atlanta Study No. 7). Atlanta, Ga.: Atlanta University Press, 1902.

——, ed. *The Negro in Business* (Atlanta Study No. 4). Atlanta, Ga.: Atlanta University Press, 1899.

——, ed. *The Negro Church* (Atlanta Study No. 8). Atlanta, Ga.: Atlanta University Press, 1903.

——, ed. *The Negro Common School* (Atlanta Study No. 6). Atlanta, Ga.: Atlanta University Press, 1901.

——, ed. *Negro Crime* (Atlanta Study No. 9). Atlanta, Ga.: Atlanta University Press, 1904.

——, ed. *The Philadelphia Negro.* New York: Blom, 1967 (first publ. 1899).

——, ed. *A Select Bibliography of the Negro American* (Atlanta Study No. 10). Atlanta, Ga.: Atlanta University Press, 1905.

——, ed. *Social and Physical Condition of Negroes in Cities* (Atlanta Study No. 2). Atlanta, Ga.: Atlanta University Press, 1897.

——, ed. *Some Efforts of American Negroes for Their Own Better-ment* (Atlanta Study No. 3). Atlanta, Ga.: Atlanta University Press, 1898.

Duncan, Otis D. and Beverly. *The Negro Population of Chicago: A Study of Residential Succession.* Chicago: University of Chicago Press, 1957.

Dunne, Finley Peter. *Mr. Dooley in Peace and in War.* Boston: Small, Maynard, 1905.

Dutcher, Dean. *The Negro in Modern Industrial Society: An Analysis of Changes in the Occupations of Negro Workers, 1910–1920.* Lancaster, Pa.: Science Press, 1930.

Dyson, Walter. *Howard University: The Capstone of Negro Educa-tion.* Washington, D.C.: Howard University Press, 1941.

Eaton, Isabel. "Special Report on Negro Domestic Service in the Seventh Ward of Philadelphia," in DuBois, W. E. B., ed., *The Philadelphia Negro*, q.v.

Edmonds, Helen G. *The Negro and Fusion Politics in North Carolina, 1894–1901.* Chapel Hill: University of North Carolina Press, 1951.

Ellis, Elmer, "Populist Party," *Dictionary of American History* (2nd ed., rev.), Vol. 4. New York: Scribner's, 1940.

Epstein, Abraham. *The Negro Migrant in Pittsburgh.* New York: Arno and New York *Times*, 1969 (first publ. 1918).

"The Everlasting Negro," *Independent*, editorial, Vol. 70, Feb. 1911.

Faulkner, Harold Underwood. *Politics, Reform and Expansion, 1890–1900.* New York: Harper & Row, 1959.

——. *The Quest for Social Justice, 1898–1914.* New York: Macmillan, 1931.

Filler, Louis. *Crusaders for American Liberalism.* New York: Harcourt, 1939.

Fischer, David Hackett. *Historians' Fallacies.* New York: Harper & Row, 1970.

Fishel, Leslie H., Jr., and Quarles, Benjamin. *The Negro American: A Documentary History.* Glenview, Ill.: Scott, Foresman and William Morrow, 1967.

Fisher, Rudolph. "The Caucasians Storm Harlem," *American Mercury*, Vol. 11, Aug. 1927.

——. "The City of Refuge," *Atlantic Monthly*, Vol. 135, Feb. 1925.

——. *The Walls of Jericho.* New York: Arno and New York *Times*, 1969 (first publ. 1928).

Fox, Stephen R. *The Guardian of Boston: William Monroe Trotter.* New York: Atheneum, 1970.

Franklin, John Hope. *From Slavery to Freedom* (3rd ed., rev.). New York: Knopf, 1967 (first publ. 1947).

——. "History of Racial Segregation," in Meier and Rudwick, eds., *The Making of Black America*, q.v.

——. "Jim Crow Goes to School," *South Atlantic Quarterly*, Vol. 58, Spring 1959.

Frazier, E. Franklin. *The Negro in the United States* (rev. ed.). New York: Macmillan, 1957.

Gatewood, William B. "Theodore Roosevelt and the Indianola Affair," *Journal of Negro History*, Vol. 53, Jan. 1968.

Ginzberg, Eli, and Eichner, Alfred S. *The Troublesome Presence: American Democracy and the Negro.* Glencoe, Ill.: Free Press, 1964.

Gloster, Hugh. "The Van Vechten Vogue," in *Negro Voices in American Fiction.* Chapel Hill, N.C.: University of North Carolina Press, 1948.

Gossett, Thomas F. *Race: The History of an Idea in America*. Dallas, Tex.: Southern Methodist University Press, 1963.

Grantham, Dewey W., Jr. "The Progressive Movement and the Negro," *South Atlantic Quarterly*, Vol. 54, Oct. 1955.

Green, Constance McLaughlin. *The Secret City: A History of Race Relations in the Nation's Capital*. Princeton, N.J.: Princeton University Press, 1967.

Greene, Lorenzo J., and Woodson, Carter G. *The Negro Wage Earner*. Washington, D.C.: Association for the Study of Negro Life, 1930.

Grimshaw, Allen D., ed. *Racial Violence in the United States*. Chicago: Aldine, 1969.

Handlin, Oscar. "Reconsidering the Populists," *Agricultural History*, Vol. 39–40, 1965–66.

Harbord, James G. *The American Army in France*. Boston: Little, Brown, 1936.

Harlan, Louis R. "The Southern Education Board and the Race Issue in Public Education," *Journal of Southern History*, Vol. 23, May 1957.

Harris, Abram L., Jr. *The Negro as Capitalist*. Philadelphia: American Academy of Political and Social Science, 1936.

———. "The Negro and Economic Radicalism," *Modern Quarterly*, Vol. 2, Feb. 1925.

———. "Negro Labor's Quarrel with White Working Men," *Current History*, Vol. 24, Sept. 1926.

———. "Negro Migration to the North," *Current History*, Vol. 20, Sept. 1924.

———. *The Negro Population in Minneapolis*. Minneapolis: Minneapolis Urban League and Phyllis Wheatley Settlement House, 1926.

Haynes, George Edmund. *The Negro at Work in New York City*. New York: Arno and New York *Times*, 1968 (first publ. 1912).

———. "Race Riots in Relation to Democracy," *Survey*, Vol. 42, Aug. 9, 1919.

Henderson, Edwin Bancroft. *The Negro in Sports*. Washington, D.C.: The Associated Publishers, 1939.

Herrnstein, Richard. "I.Q., *Atlantic*, Vol. 228, No. 3, Sept. 1971.

Hesseltine, William, and Smiley, David. *The South in American History* (2nd ed.). Englewood Cliffs, N.J.: Prentice-Hall, 1960.

Heywood, Chester D., *Negro Combat Troops in the World War*. New York: n.p., 1921.

Hicks, John D. *The Populist Revolt: A History of the Farmers' Alliance and the People's Party*. Lincoln, Neb.: University of Nebraska Press, 1961 (first publ. 1955).

Higham, John. *Strangers in the Land: Patterns of American Nativism 1860–1925*. New Brunswick, N.J.: Rutgers University Press, 1955.

Hirshon, Stanley P. *Farewell to the Bloody Shirt: Northern Republicans and the Southern Negro, 1877–1893.* Bloomington, Ind.: Indiana University Press, 1962.

Hoffman, Frederick L. *Race Traits and Tendencies of the American Negro.* New York: Macmillan, 1896.

Hofstadter, Richard. *Social Darwinism in American Thought* (rev. ed.). Boston: Beacon, 1955.

Hollingsworth, J. Rogers. "Populism: The Problem of Rhetoric and Reality," *Agricultural History,* Vol. 39–40, 1965–66.

Hughes, Langston. *The Best of Simple.* New York: Hill & Wang, 1961.

——. *The Big Sea: An Autobiography.* New York: Hill & Wang, 1940.

Hughes, Langston, and Meltzer, Milton. *Black Magic: A Pictorial History of the Negro in American Entertainment.* Englewood Cliffs, N.J.: Prentice-Hall, 1967.

The Independent, Boston, Vol. 70, Feb. 1911.

Jensen, Arthur R. "How Much Can We Boost IQ and Scholastic Achievement?" in *Environment, Heredity, and Intelligence.* Cambridge, Mass.: Harvard Educational Review, 1969.

Johnson, Charles S. "After Garvey—What?", *Opportunity,* Vol. 1, Aug. 1923; repr. in Fishel and Quarles, *The Negro American,* q.v.

——. "How Much of the Migration Was a Flight from Persecution?", *Opportunity,* Sept. 1923.

——. *Patterns of Negro Segregation.* New York: Harper & Row, 1970 (first publ. 1943).

——. *See* U. S. President's Conference on Home Building . . . ; *also see* Chicago Commission on Race Relations.

Johnson, Guion G. "Southern Paternalism Toward Negroes after Emancipation," *Journal of Southern History,* Vol. 23, Nov. 1957.

Johnson, James Weldon. *Black Manhattan.* New York: Arno and New York *Times,* 1968 (first publ. 1930).

Jordan, Winthrop D. *White over Black: American Attitudes Toward the Negro, 1550–1812.* Chapel Hill, N.C.: University of North Carolina Press, 1968.

Justice, Blair. *Violence in the City.* Fort Worth, Tex.: Texas Christian University Press, 1969.

Kaplan, Sidney. *The Black Presence in the Era of the American Revolution, 1778–1800.* New York: New York Graphic, 1973.

Keller, Albert G., and Davie, Maurice R., eds. *Essays of William Graham Sumner,* Vol. 2. New Haven: Yale University Press, 1934.

Kellogg, Charles Flint. *NAACP,* Vol. I, 1909–20. Baltimore: The Johns Hopkins University Press, 1967.

Kennedy, Louise Venable. *The Negro Peasant Turns Cityward: Effects of Recent Migrations to Northern Centers.* New York: Columbia University Press, 1930.

Kenworthy, E. W. "The Case Against Army Segregation," *Annals of the American Academy of Political and Social Science*, Vol. 275, 1951.

Key, V. O., Jr. *Southern Politics in State and Nation*. New York: Knopf, 1949.

Kirwan, Albert D. *Revolt of the Rednecks: Mississippi Politics, 1876–1925*. Magnolia, Mass.: P. Smith, 1964.

Klineberg, Otto, ed. *Characteristics of the American Negro*. New York: Harper, 1944.

———. "Negro-White Differences in Intelligence Test Performance: A New Look at an Old Problem," *American Psychologist*, Vol. 18, Apr. 1963.

Kolko, Gabriel. *The Triumph of Conservatism*. Chicago: Quadrangle, 1967.

Lee, Irwin H. *Negro Medal of Honor Men*. New York: Dodd, Mead, 1967.

Lee, Ulysses G. *The Employment of Negro Troops*. Washington, D.C.: U. S. Army, 1966.

Lewinson, Paul. *Race, Class and Party*. New York: Russell & Russell, 1963 (first publ. 1932).

Lewis, Elsie M. "The Political Mind of the Negro, 1865–1900," *Journal of Southern History*, Vol. 21, May 1955.

Lewis, Roscoe E. "Role of Pressure Groups in Maintaining Morale Among Negroes," *Journal of Negro Education*, Vol. 12, Summer 1943.

Library of Congress, Manuscript Division. *Newton D. Baker Papers*.

Liebow, Elliot. *Tally's Corner*. Boston: Little, Brown, 1967.

Link, Arthur S. *Wilson and the New Freedom* (Vol. 2 of *Wilson*). Princeton, N.J.: Princeton University Press, 1956.

———. *Woodrow Wilson and the Progressive Era, 1910–1917*. New York: Harper, 1954.

Little, Arthur W. *From Harlem to the Rhine: The Story of New York's Colored Volunteers*. New York: Covici Friede, 1936.

Locke, Alain, ed. *The New Negro: An Interpretation*. New York: Boni, 1925; repr. in Fishel and Quarles, *The Negro American*, q.v.

Logan, Frenise A. *The Negro in North Carolina, 1876–1894*. Chapel Hill, N.C.: University of North Carolina Press, 1964.

Lucas, Bob. *Black Gladiator: A Biography of Jack Johnson*. New York: Dell, 1970.

Lueders, Edward. *Carl Van Vechten*. New York: Twayne, 1965.

———. *Carl Van Vechten and the Twenties*. Albuquerque, N.M.: University of New Mexico Press, 1955.

Mandel, Bernard. "Samuel Gompers and the Negro Workers, 1866–1914," *Journal of Negro History*, Vol. 40, Jan. 1955.

Mandelbaum, David G. *Soldier Groups and Negro Soldiers*. Berkeley, Calif.: University of California Press, 1952.

Mangum, Charles S., Jr. *Legal Status of the Negro.* Chapel Hill, N.C.: University of North Carolina Press, 1940.

Mann, Arthur. *The Progressive Era: Liberal Renaissance or Liberal Failure.* New York: Holt, Rinehart & Winston, 1963.

Meier, August. "Booker T. Washington: An Interpretation"; repr. in Drimmer, *Black History*, q.v.

Meier, August, and Rudwick, Elliott, eds. *The Making of Black America: Essays in Negro Life and History.* New York: Atheneum, 1969.

——. "The Rise of Segregation in the Federal Bureaucracy, 1900–1930," *Phylon*, Vol. 28, Summer 1967.

——. "A Strange Chapter in the Career of Jim Crow," repr. in Meier and Rudwick, *The Making of Black America*, q.v.

Mertins, Gustav Frederick. *The Storm Signal.* New York: Bobbs-Merrill, 1905.

Micheaux, Oscar. *The Conquest: The Story of a Negro Pioneer. By the Pioneer.* Miami, Fla.: Mnemosyne, 1969 (first publ. 1913).

Miller, Kelly. *The Everlasting Stain.* New York: Arno and New York Times, 1968 (first publ. 1924).

——. *Out of the House of Bondage.* New York: Arno and New York Times, 1969 (first publ. 1914).

——. *Race Adjustment.* New York: Arno and New York Times, 1968 (first publ. 1908).

Miller, Loren. *The Petitioners: The Story of the Supreme Court of the United States and the Negro.* New York: Pantheon, 1966.

Miller, William D. *Memphis During the Progressive Era, 1900–1917.* Memphis, Tenn.: Memphis State University Press, 1957.

Moton, Robert R. *Finding a Way Out.* Garden City, N.Y.: Doubleday, Page, 1928.

Mowry, George E. *The Era of Theodore Roosevelt, 1900–1912.* New York: Harper, 1958.

Mueller, William R. "The Negro in the Navy," *Social Forces*, Vol. 24, 1945.

Myrdal, Gunnar. *An American Dilemma: The Negro Problem and Modern Democracy.* New York: Harper, 1963 (first publ. 1944).

National Archives. *Record Groups 94, 120, and 165.*

Nearing, Scott. *Black America.* New York: Vanguard, 1929.

Newby, Idus A. *Jim Crow's Defense: Anti-Negro Thought in America, 1900–1930.* Baton Rouge, La.: Louisiana State University Press, 1965.

Odum, Howard W. *Social and Mental Traits of the Negro.* New York: Columbia University Press, 1910.

Orr, Jack. *The Black Athlete: His Story in American History.* New York: Lion, 1969.

Osborn, George C. "The Problem of the Negro in Government," *Historian*, Vol. 23, May 1961.

Osofsky, Gilbert. *Harlem: The Making of a Ghetto, Negro New York, 1890–1930.* New York: Harper & Row, 1966.

Ottley, Roi. *The Lonely Warrior: The Life and Times of Robert S. Abbott.* Chicago: Henry Regnery, 1955.

Ovington, Mary White. *Half a Man: The Status of the Negro in New York.* New York: Hill & Wang, 1969 (first publ. 1911).

Page, Thomas Nelson. *The Negro: The Southerner's Problem.* New York: Scribner's, 1904.

Palmer, Frederick. *America in France.* New York: Dodd, Mead, 1918.

People's Party Handbook (pamphlet). [North Carolina]: 1898.

Pickens, William. *The New Negro.* New York: Negro University Press, 1969 (first publ. 1916).

Pipkin, J. J. *The Negro in Revelation, in History, and in Citizenship: What the Race Has Done and Is Doing.* St. Louis, Mo.: Thompson, 1902.

Powdermaker, Hortense. *After Freedom: A Cultural Study in the Deep South.* New York: Atheneum, 1968 (first publ. 1939).

Pringle, Henry F. *Theodore Roosevelt: A Biography.* New York: Harcourt, Brace, 1931.

Quarles, Benjamin. "Evacuation with the British"; repr. in Drimmer, *Black History,* q.v.

Redkey, Edwin S. *Black Exodus: Black Nationalist and Back-to-Africa Movements, 1890–1910.* New Haven, Conn.: Yale University Press, 1969.

Reuter, Edward Byron. *The American Race Problem* (rev. ed.). New York: Thomas Y. Crowell, 1970 (first publ. 1927).

———. *The Mulatto in the United States.* New York: Negro University Press, 1969 (written as doctoral dissertation, 1918).

Rochester, Anna. *The Populist Movement in the United States.* New York: International, 1943.

Rogers, William W. "The Negro Alliance in Alabama," *Journal of Negro History,* Vol. 45, Jan. 1960.

Roman, C. V. *American Civilization and the Negro.* Philadelphia: Davis, 1916.

Royce, Josiah. *Race Questions, Provincialism, and Other American Problems.* Freeport, N.Y.: Books for Libraries Press, 1967 (first publ. 1908).

Rudwick, Elliott M., "The Niagara Movement," repr. in Meier and Rudwick, *The Making of Black America,* q.v.

———. *Race Riot at East St. Louis, July 2, 1917.* Carbondale, Ill.: Southern Illinois University Press, 1964.

Scarr-Salapatek, Sandra. "Unknowns in the IQ Equation," book review, *Science,* Vol. 174, Dec. 17, 1971.

Scheiner, Seth M. *Negro Mecca: A History of the Negro in New York City, 1865–1920.* New York: New York University Press, 1965.

——. "President Theodore Roosevelt and the Negro, 1901–1908," *Journal of Negro History*, Vol. 47, July 1962.

Scott, Emmett J., ed. "Letters of Negro Migrants of 1916–1918," *Journal of Negro History*, Vol. 4, July 1919.

——. *Negro Migration During the War*. New York: Arno and New York *Times*, 1969 (first publ. 1920).

——. *Scott's Official History of the American Negro in the World War*. New York: n.p., 1919.

Seligmann, Herbert J. *The Negro Faces America*. New York: Harper & Row, 1969 (first publ. 1920).

Shadgett, Olive Hall. *The Republican Party in Georgia, from Reconstruction through 1900*. Athens, Ga.: University of Georgia Press, 1964.

Shapiro, Herbert. "The Populists and the Negro: A Reconsideration," repr. in Meier and Rudwick, *The Making of Black America*, q.v.

Shufeldt, R. W. *America's Greatest Problem: The Negro*. Philadelphia: Davis, 1915.

Simkins, Francis Butler, and Roland, Charles P. *A History of the South* (3rd ed.). New York: Random House, 1965.

Smith, Samuel Denny. *The Negro in Congress, 1870–1901*. Port Washington, N.Y.: Kennikat, 1966.

Sosna, Morton. "Negroes and the Wilson Years, 1912–1916: The Politics of Race During the Progressive Era." Unpublished master's thesis, University of Wisconsin, 1969.

Southern, Eileen. *The Music of Black Americans: A History*. New York: Norton, 1971.

Spear, Allan H. *Black Chicago: The Making of a Negro Ghetto, 1890–1920*. Chicago: University of Chicago Press, 1967.

Spero, Sterling D., and Harris, Abram L., Jr. *The Black Worker: The Negro and the Labor Movement*. Port Washington, N.Y.: Kennikat, 1931 (reissued 1966).

Stephenson, Gilbert T. *Race Distinctions in American Law*. New York: AMS, 1969 (first publ. 1910).

Thomas, William Hannibal. *The American Negro: What He Is, What He Was, What He May Become*. New York: Macmillan, 1910.

Thornbrough, Emma L. "Booker T. Washington as Seen by His White Contemporaries," *Journal of Negro History*, Vol. 53, Apr. 1968.

Thurman, Wallace. *Infants of the Spring*. New York: Macaulay, 1932.

Tindall, George Brown. *Emergence of the New South, 1913–1945*. Baton Rouge, La.: Louisiana State University Press, 1967.

——. *South Carolina Negroes 1877–1900*. Baton Rouge, La.: Louisiana State University Press, 1966 (first publ. 1952).

Tuchman, Barbara W. *The Zimmerman Telegram*. New York: Macmillan, 1967.

Union League Club. *The Presentation of Colors to the 367th Regiment of Infantry.* [New York]: Parsons, [1918].

United States Army. *See* Lee, Ulysses G.

United States Bureau of the Census. *Historical Statistics of the United States, Colonial Times to 1957.* Washington, D.C.: U. S. Government Printing Office, 1960.

——. *Statistical Abstract of the United States.* Washington, D.C.: U. S. Government Printing Office, 1964.

United States Bureau of Transport Economics and Statistics, Interstate Commerce Commission. *Statistics of Railways in the United States for the Year Ended Dec. 31, 1946.* Washington, D.C.: U. S. Government Printing Office, 1948.

United States Department of Justice. *Report* (transmitted by A. Mitchell Palmer, Attorney General), Vol. 12, Senate Documents, No. 153, 66th Cong., 1st sess., 1919. Washington, D.C.: U. S. Government Printing Office, 1919.

United States Department of Labor, Division of Negro Economics. *Negro Migration in 1916–1917.* Washington, D.C.: U. S. Government Printing Office, 1919.

United States Department of War. *Official Table of Distances.* Washington, D.C.: U. S. Government Printing Office, 1918.

U. S. President's Committee on Equality of Treatment and Opportunity in the Armed Forces. *Freedom to Serve.* Washington, D.C.: U. S. Government Printing Office, 1950.

U. S. President's Conference on Home Building and Home Ownership. *Negro Housing* (prepared by Charles S. Johnson). Washington, D.C.: U. S. Government Printing Office, 1932.

Van Deusen, Marshall, *J. E. Spingarn.* New York: Twayne, 1971.

Van Vechten, Carl. *Nigger Heaven.* New York: Knopf, 1926.

Varlin, Eugene. *The Negro and the U. S. Army* (pamphlet). New York: Pioneer, n.d.

Vincent, Theodore G. *Black Power and the Garvey Movement.* Berkeley, Calif.: Ramparts, 1971.

Walden, Daniel. "The Contemporary Opposition to the Political Ideas of Booker T. Washington," *Journal of Negro History,* Vol. 45, Apr. 1960.

Washington, Booker T. *The Future of the American Negro.* New York: Haskell House, 1969 (first publ. 1899).

——. *The Story of the Negro: The Rise of the Race from Slavery.* Garden City, N.Y.: Doubleday, Page, 1909.

——. *Up from Slavery: An Autobiography.* New York: Bantam Books, 1967 (first publ. 1901).

Waskow, Arthur J. *From Race Riot to Sit-In.* Garden City, N.Y.: Doubleday, 1966.

Weaver, John D. *The Brownsville Raid: The Story of America's Black Dreyfus Affair.* New York: Norton, 1970.

Weaver, Robert C. "The Negro Ghetto", repr. in Meier and Rudwick, *The Making of Black America,* q.v.

Weisbord, Robert G. "The Back-to-Africa Idea," *History Today,* Feb. 1968.

Werner, M. R. *Julius Rosenwald.* New York: Harper, 1939.

Wesley, Charles H. *Negro Labor in the United States, 1850–1925.* New York: Vanguard, 1927.

White, Morton Gabriel. *Social Thought in America: The Revolt Against Formalism* (rev. ed.). Boston: Beacon, 1957.

White, Walter. *Rope and Faggot.* New York: Arno and New York Times, 1969 (first publ. 1929).

Wiebe, Robert H. *The Search for Order, 1877–1920.* New York: Hill & Wang, 1967.

Williams, William Appleman. *The Tragedy of American Diplomacy.* New York: Dell, 1962.

Wilson, Woodrow. "The Reconstruction of the Southern States," *Atlantic Monthly,* Vol. 87, No. 119, Jan. 1901.

Wish, Harvey. "Negro Education in the Progressive Movement," *Journal of Negro History,* Vol. 49, July 1964.

Woodson, Carter G. *A Century of Negro Migration.* New York: Russell & Russell, 1969 (first publ. 1918).

———. *The Negro in Our History.* Washington, D.C.: Associated Publications, 1947.

———. *The Negro Professional Man and the Community.* New York: Russell & Russell, 1969 (first publ. 1934).

———. *The Rural Negro.* New York: Russell & Russell, 1969 (first publ. 1930).

Woodward, C. Vann. *American Counterpoint: Slavery and Racism in the North-South Dialogue.* Boston: Little, Brown, 1971.

———. "American History (White Man's Version) Needs an Infusion of Soul," *New York Times Magazine,* Apr. 20, 1969.

———. *Reunion and Reaction.* Boston: Little, Brown, 1966.

———. *The Strange Career of Jim Crow* (rev. ed.). New York: Oxford University Press, 1966.

———. "Tom Watson and the Negro in Agrarian Politics," *Journal of Southern History,* Vol. 4, Feb. 1938.

Woofter, T. J., Jr. (dir. of study). *Negro Problems in Cities.* New York: Negro University Press, 1969 (first publ. 1928).

Wynes, Charles E. "Lewis Harvie Blair, Virginia Reformer: The Uplift of the Negro and Southern Prosperity," *Virginia Magazine of History,* Vol. 72, Jan. 1964.

Index

Abbott, R. S., 35, 47, 48, 277, 320, 321, 333;
  migration and, 59, 62–66, 77–78, 79, 189;
  quoted, 275
Abramowitz, Jack, cited, 7
Adams, Henry, 50
Addams, Jane, 245
Africa, 49, 50, 167, 223, 257; identification
  with, 163, 275, 309, 310, 331, 332–36, 337;
  Western science and, 218, 219, 221, 236
African Blood Brotherhood, 334, 335
Afro-American Liberty League, 275
Afro-American Realty Co., 89, 107, 161, 164
Afro-American Steam and Gas Engineers
  and Skilled Laborers, 156
Aged, 58, 94, 185; homes for, 17, 118, 186
Agriculture, 1–6, 8, 9, 26–27, 32, 50, 312–13;
  education for, 38, 251; migration and, 51–
  52, 53–54, 70, 72–76, 139, 168, 171; worker
  exploitation in, 27–29, 39, 53, 170–71, 200,
  246, 317
Alabama, 25, 169, 170, 171, 178–79, 185,
  211, 257, 259; convict labor in, 40, 62; dis-
  franchisement in, 10, 18, 19, 20, 21, 22;
  High Court, 41; migration from, 57, 66,
  70, 130, 145; mining in, 169, 171
Alcorn College, 38, 70
Alderman, Edward, quoted, 177
Allen, William Francis, quoted, 218
Amalgamated Meat Cutters, 151–52
American (periodical), 233
American Civil Liberties Union, 154
American Colonization Society, 50
American Federation of Labor, 153, 156,
  157, 170, 313–14, 322, 323
American Legion, 308
American Medical Association, 128
American Missionary Society, 183
Amherst College, 193
Anderson, E. D., 293–94, 295
Anderson, Marian, 192
Anthropology, 210, 218–19, 220
Arkansas, 17, 22, 50, 57, 179, 328–29; poll
  tax, 20; riot (1919) in, 321–22
Arlington National Cemetery, 284
Armour Co., 152
Armstrong, Louis, 116, 192, 340
Arthur, Chester Alan, 247
Artisans, 30, 69, 93, 94, 141
Associated Colored Employees of America,
  127
Association of Train Porters, Brakemen and
  Switchmen, 157
Athletics, 191, 192, 193–98, 230
Atlanta, Ga., 16, 34, 39, 51, 86, 110; arrest
  rates in, 40, 41; riots in, 52, 262, 318
Atlanta Constitution (newspaper), 23, 54,
  62, 75, 79
Atlanta Exposition (1895), 1, 79, 174, 200
Atlanta Independent (newspaper), 78
Atlanta Journal (newspaper), 22
Atlanta University Studies, 100, 109–10, 176,
  182; Fourth, 158, 159
Augusta, Ga., 170
Automobile industry, 134, 142, 169, 170,
  313–14
Aycock, Charles B., 250

Back-to-Africa Movement, 163, 332–36
Bailey, Thomas P., quoted, 215–16
Baker, Josephine, 192, 339
Baker, Newton D., 155, 231, 259, 284, 287,
  290, 294–95; quoted, 272, 281–82, 283

Baker, Ray Stannard, 124, 125, 239; on
  crime, 29, 93, 110, 222; on disfranchisement, 22, 204; on education, 37, 38, 39,
  132, 184, 189; on ghettoization, 91, 102;
  on labor, 25, 27, 40, 73, 74–75, 132, 135,
  136; on lynching, 44, 259, 260; on medical
  care, 34, 111–12; on migration, 52, 57, 60–
  61, 62, 70, 71, 81, 82; on the press, 167,
  233; on segregation, 16, 37, 91; on Wilson,
  252, 256
Baldwin, Roger, quoted, 154–55, 324
Baldwin, Ruth Standish, 203–4
Ballou, Charles C., 284, 285, 289, 299;
  quoted, 287, 292, 300, 302
Baltimore, Md., 17, 68, 86
Banking, 34, 118, 130, 158, 160–61, 190;
  mortgages and, 107–8
Barrymore, Ethel, 337
Baseball, 194–95
Basketball, 194
Bean, Dr. R. B., 218
Beard, Charles A., 218
Bechet, Sidney, 340
Belgium, 275
Bellows, George, 234
Benedict, Ruth, 236; quoted, 1
Bentley, C. E., 201
Bently, Gladys, 339
Berea College, 183–84
Berry and Ross (firm), 163, 334
Bessemer, Ala., 60, 61
Bevis, Dr. W. M., quoted, 211
Biddle, James, quoted, 279
Bilbo, Theodore, 77, 177, 250, 312
Biloxi Herald (newspaper), 73
Binet, Alfred, 326
Binga, Jesse, 130, 161
Birmingham, Ala., 31, 35, 51, 61, 86; wages
  in, 55
Birth of a Nation, The (film), 227–31, 232,
  233, 258
Birth rates, 112–13, 147, 213, 227; birth con-
  trol issues, 214, 216, 219–20, 329; mulatto,
  190
Black Codes, 12, 39, 171, 233
Black nationalism, 207; Garvey and, 163,
  167, 332–36. See also Identity; Resistance
Black Star Line, 163, 334–35
Blair Education Bill (1890), 36, 37
Blake, Eubie, 42, 192, 340
Blease, Coleman, 18, 177, 250, 290, 312, 323
Blum, John Norton, quoted, 249
Boas, Franz, 220, 316, 339; quoted, 235–36
Bogalusa, La., 172
Bombings, 87, 314, 315, 320
Bone, Robert A., quoted, 336, 343
Boston, Mass., 23, 50, 101, 125, 127, 162, 222,
  230–31; churches, 186; ghettoization in,
  90, 91; labor in, 54, 141; lodges, 117
Boston Guardian (newspaper), 200, 201, 244
Boston Symphony Hall, 192
Bowen, Andy, 196
Boxing, 195–98, 230, 233, 234
Brawley, Benjamin G., quoted, 25
Briggs, Cyril, 167, 206, 323, 325
Brigham, Carl C., 328, 329–30
Brooklyn, N.Y., 88
Brotherhood of Sleeping Car Porters, 157
Broun, Heywood, 337, 342
Brown, L., quoted, 289, 295–96
Brownsville, Tex., 52, 241–42, 243, 244, 247,
  271, 273

Bruce, Blanche K., 17
Bryan, William Jennings, 243, 244
Bulkley, William L., 130, 164, 181, 203;
    quoted, 204
Bullard, Robert, 299–300, 301
Bull Moose party, 243–44, 245
Burleigh, Harry T., 42, 116, 192
Burleson, Albert S., 249, 251–52
Burnett, John, 257
Burns, Tommy, 196
Business, 238, 342; black ownership, 30, 33–
    34, 59, 69–70, 93, 94, 118, 130, 158–64,
    190, 314, 333, 334–35; corruption and, 265;
    liquor and, 127; postwar decline, 313–14;
    profit sharing, 144; Social Darwinism and,
    215, 221; Social Gospel, 151, 154–55, 266–
    67; Wilson and, 246, 250
Busing, for segregation, 180, 181
Butler, Nicholas Murray, quoted, 218
Butler, Sol, 194
Byrnes, James F., quoted, 322

Cable, George Washington, 233
California, 35, 147–48
California, University of, 194
Camp, Walter, 193
Camp Stuart, Va., 290–91
Camp Wadsworth, Spartanburg, 290
Canada, 49, 50
Carey, Joseph M., 273
Carnegie, A., 46, 200; quoted, 79
Carnegie Steel, 169
Carpenters and Joiners Union, 203
Carranza, Venustiano, 276
Carroll, Charles, 225
Cash, W. J., 45; quoted, 44
Catholics, 230, 232, 317
Cemeteries, 117–18, 162, 296
Challenge, The (periodical), 237
Chamberlain, H. S., quoted, 217–18
Charleston, S.C., 240; riot (1919), 319
Charlotte, N.C., 32, 51
Chemical Wonder Co., 163
Chesnutt, Charles W., quoted, 18
Chester, Pa.: riots, 267
Chicago, Ill., 58, 66, 67, 69, 77, 112, 116,
    125, 195, 201, 231, 305; black businesses
    in, 159; churches, 115, 186–87, 189; ghet-
    toization in, 83–84, 85–87, 89, 90, 102, 103,
    105, 106, 115, 121, 130, 318, 341; home
    ownership in, 107, 108, 314–15; labor in,
    32, 33, 61, 64, 99, 134, 135, 138, 139, 142,
    143, 144–45, 153, 167, 168, 169, 313; riots
    (1919) in, 83, 319, 320–21; schools of,
    179–80, 181; voting in, 206
Chicago Commission on Race Relations, 83,
    320–21; *Report* (1922), cited, 81, 86–87,
    94, 102, 108, 120, 122, 140, 179–80, 181
Chicago Crime Commission, 115
Chicago *Daily News,* 63
Chicago *Defender* (newspaper), 35, 97, 167,
    198, 199, 245, 307, 333; Flipper and, 277,
    278; migration and, 49, 59, 62–66, 67, 77,
    79, 96, 130, 192; riots and, 320, 321
Chicago *Herald-Examiner,* 84
Chicago Real Estate Board, 85
Chicago *Tribune* (newspaper), 84
Chicago Urban League, 96–97
Chicago Vice Commission, 143
Child labor, 38, 149, 250
Chinese, 217; Exclusion Act, 147
Church of Christ, New York, 187
Churches, 27, 160, 182, 183, 186–87, 230,
    231; Garvey and, 333, 334, 335; real es-
    tate and, 89, 107, 127, 161–62; recreation
    and, 42, 114, 115–16, 340; segregation and,
    17, 90, 91, 92

Cincinnati, Ohio, 50, 66, 69, 112, 134, 142,
    168, 305
Civil rights, 81, 128, 201, 255, 324; the Army
    and, 268–69, 272, 275, 276, 305, 306, 307–
    11, 312, 317; NAACP and, 202, 245, 256,
    264; racist doctrines and, 211, 212, 215,
    216, 221, 226, 316. *See also specific rights*
Civil service, 167–68, 207, 248–49, 251–52,
    253, 255, 256; Harding administration
    and, 325
Civil War, 2, 12, 50, 53, 125, 183; black
    veterans, 20, 187, 270; Griffith on, 227–32
Claflin Institute, 38
Class structure, 118, 157, 314, 324; education
    and, 175, 176, 177, 183, 207; ghettoization
    and, 93–94, 102; identity and, 336–37, 343;
    IQ tests and, 326, 329, 330; Northern mi-
    gration and, 52, 187–91, 207; Progressiv-
    ism and, 238; racism and, 25, 35, 146, 260;
    voting and, 204, 207
Clerical work, 141, 142, 143, 168
Cleveland, Grover, 7, 247, 248, 254, 256–57
Cleveland, Ohio, 60, 66, 69, 76, 231, 259,
    305, 311, 317; health in, 109; labor in, 54–
    55, 134, 142, 318; population densities, 105
Cleveland *Gazette,* 167, 247
Cobb, Frank, quoted, 256
Cohen, Octavus R., 117; quoted, 68
Cole, Bob, 116, 191
Collins, Carita Owens, 311
Colored American Review, The, 189
Colored Farmers' Alliance, 4–5, 6, 7, 11, 14,
    26
Colored Women's Conference, Chicago, 128
Colson, William N., 309, 311, 325
Columbia, S.C., 32, 35, 60, 75
Columbus (Ga.) *Enquirer Sun,* 72
Committee for Improving the Industrial
    Condition of Negroes (CIICN), 127, 203,
    204
Commons, John P., quoted, 221
Congo, 275
Connecticut, 70, 134, 203, 290
Consolidated Coal, 114–15
Cook, Will Marion, 116, 191, 340
Coolidge, Calvin, quoted, 325
Cosmopolitan (periodical), 233
Cotton, 2, 4, 27, 51–52, 313
Courts, 21–22, 124; black recourse in, 9–10,
    40, 43–44, 57, 75, 76, 128, 129, 216; farm
    labor and, 28–29, 39, 321; military, 52,
    242, 271–72, 277, 301; sentencing, 118–19,
    121, 197, 212, 271–72
Cox, Minnie, 240, 248
Creamer, Henry, 191
Crime, 101, 127, 145; convict labor and, 9,
    28–29, 39–40; education and, 175, 177,
    211; ghettoization and, 41, 92, 93–94, 96,
    103, 118–24, 261, 268; juvenile, 41, 89, 99,
    109–10, 121, 123–24, 178; migration efforts
    treated as, 62, 64, 67–68; official corrup-
    tion and, 261, 262–63, 265, 267, 318; press
    and, 121, 262, 318, 319, 320; segregation
    laws and, 17, 39, 40–41, 43, 197–98. *See
    also* Courts; Law; Lynching; Rape
Cripps, Thomas R., quoted, 229
Crisis, The (periodical), 53, 167, 202, 233,
    255, 266, 283, 325; on voting, 245, 246; in
    World War I, 276, 306, 307
Crum, William, 240
Crusader, 167, 311, 323
Cuba, 89, 239, 270, 271
Cullen, Countee, 328, 342
Cummings, Albert, quoted, 221
Curley, Jack, 198
Curley, James, 230
Curtis, James L., 257

Custom, 11–12, 13, 17–18, 35, 74, 180; imitative, 163, 331, 333; industrialization and, 135, 142; military, 288, 297; poverty and, 82, 96–97; sexual, 40–41; titles and, 18, 56–57, 60, 130, 239

Dallas, Tex., 51, 86
Dance, 42, 339, 340, 341
Daniels, John, 124; on ghettos, 91; on labor, 136–37, 141–42; on migration, 54; on morality, 98, 101, 120, 162, 222; on Washington (Booker), 79
Daniels, Josephus, 241, 249, 250, 251
Darwin, Charles, 214, 215, 219
Davenport, Charles B., 220
Dayton, Ohio, 180
Death rates, 108, 109, 110, 111, 112–13, 160; infant, 113–14
Democratic party, 36, 227–28; black voters and, 6, 7, 10, 18, 205, 206–7, 243, 244, 245–46, 253, 255, 256, 257, 258, 267; Southern dominance of, 1, 4, 8–9, 15, 18–19, 247, 249–50, 251, 261
Dennison, Franklin A., 290, 298
Depression (1930s), 101–2, 172, 342
De Priest, Oscar, 204, 206
Des Moines, Iowa, 305; camp at, 281, 282, 284–86, 290, 291
Detroit, Mich., 66, 67, 69, 90, 112, 115, 127; labor in, 134, 140, 142, 168, 169, 170, 313
Dillard, James H., 56; quoted, 54
District of Columbia. *See* Washington, D.C.
Dixon, George, 196
Dixon, Thomas, Jr., 231, 234, 254, 262; quoted, 227–28, 229
Dockery, Albert B., 281, 282, 283
Doctors, 165, 166, 182; shortage of, 33, 34, 35–36, 109, 129, 162, 164
Dollard, John, quoted, 110–11
Domingo, William H., 325, 333
Dorsey, Tom, 116
Douglass, F., 17, 145, 248
Douglass, Lewis H., 248
Drew, Howard P., 194
Drinking, 97–98, 99, 100, 109–10, 111, 127, 162, 261, 267, 268; Prohibition, 97, 340–41, 342
Druggists, 34, 36, 100, 111, 162–63; education of, 165, 166
Drugs, 29, 41, 100, 110–11, 122, 162
DuBois, W. E. B., 77, 125, 128, 158, 162, 198, 233, 325, 339; on "Birth of a Nation," 230; on class structure, 52, 93, 118, 189; on drink, 97, 109; on education, 47, 175–77; on Garvey, 335; on ghettos, 35, 90, 102, 105, 109, 115; on labor, 30, 33, 132, 140, 203, 314, 322; on lynching, 257; on marriage, 98–99, 100; on migration, 79, 92, 93; Pan-Africanism of, 310; on the press, 167; on Taft, 243; Trotter and, 198, 200, 201, 202, 255, 333; on voting, 24, 205–6, 244–45, 246; on Washington (Booker), 199; on World War I, 269, 275–76, 287, 291, 295, 306; on youth crime, 41
Duluth, Minn., 139
Dunbar, Paul Laurence, 116, 191
Dunbar National Bank, N.Y., 161
Dunne, Peter Finley, quoted, 210
Dunning, W. A., 228, 234; quoted, 226
Dutcher, Dean, quoted, 57
Dyer, Leonidas, 259

East St. Louis, Ill., 259; riot (1917), 150, 261, 264–67, 268, 271, 273, 285, 318
Edwards, Harry, 194
Elaine, Ark., 321–22
Eliot, C. W., 230; quoted, 182–83, 184

Elites, 52, 93, 118, 343; Northern, 187–91, 207; Renaissance and, 332–33, 336–43
Ellington, Duke, 340, 342
Elser, Max, 302, 303
England, 49, 217, 219, 235, 275; emigrants from, 101
Entertainers, 42–43, 310–11, 339
Epstein, Abraham: cited, 51, 54, 71, 97, 125, 139; quoted, 104
Eugenics, 219–21, 222, 234, 316
Europe, J. R., 298, 340; quoted, 192–93
Evolution theory, 210, 214–15, 218–19

Fairchild, Henry Pratt, quoted, 315
Family structure, 98–100, 102, 103, 139–40, 149; birth rates and, 113; juvenile delinquency and, 123–24. *See also* Marriage; Women
Farmer's Improvement Society, 26–27
Fauset, Jessie, 338; quoted, 333, 343
Federation of Churches, 102, 231
Fire (periodical), 338
Fish, Hamilton, cited, 304
Fisher, Rudolph, 68, 162, 338, 342; quoted, 81, 88, 90, 111, 116–17, 122, 224–25, 314, 339, 341
Fisk University, 110, 183, 191, 192
Flemming, Walter L., 228; quoted, 226
Flipper, Henry O., 277–78
Florida, 16, 21, 22, 56, 66, 68, 130, 178, 181; poll tax, 20
Football, 192, 193–94
Foraker, Joseph R., 242, 243
Forbes, George, 200
Force Bill (1890), 4, 7, 12, 220, 223
Fort Huachuca, Ariz., 280
Fortune, T. Thomas, 127, 130, 244
Fort Worth, Tex., 51
Foster, Rube, 195
Foster, Stephen C., 42
France, 49, 68, 176, 203; U. S. Army in, 275, 280, 288, 290, 291, 293, 296–304, 306, 308–9, 310–11, 312, 339
France, Army, 297, 298, 304
Frazier, E. Franklin, 338; quoted, 43
Freeman, Edward A., quoted, 217
Frissell, A. S., 77; quoted, 78

Galton, Francis, quoted, 219, 220
Gans, Joe, 196
Garfield, James A., 247
Garrison, William Lloyd, 264
Garvey, Marcus Manesseh, 47, 163–64, 167, 207, 275, 325, 332–36
Gary, Ind., 116, 180
Genetics, 210, 218, 219–20
Georgia, 2, 6, 40, 49, 57, 185, 249; disfranchisement in, 9, 10, 19, 21, 22, 23; income averages (1920) in, 55, 171; land ownership (1906) in, 26; legalized segregation in, 15, 16, 181, 197; migration from, 63, 66, 70, 75–76, 78, 92, 116, 126, 145, 171, 232; teacher salaries in, 178–79
Germany, 203, 214, 217, 258, 275, 277; emigrants from, 88, 89, 101, 147, 150, 213; Royce on, 235
Germany, Army, 275, 297, 302, 309; propaganda of, 301
Ghettoization, 35, 80, 81–92, 165; business in, 93, 94, 159; elites and, 189; of Jews, 315; life-styles and, 41, 93–131, 135, 166, 187, 261, 340–41; riots and, 265, 268, 318; schools and, 179, 180, 181, 318
Giddings, Franklin, quoted, 216
Gladden, Washington, 223
Glass, Carter, 250; quoted, 19
Godfrey, George, 196

Goldenweiser, Alexander A., 316
Gompers, S., 30–31, 153, 155
Gourdin, Ned, 194
"Grandfather clauses," 20, 205, 257
Grange, The, 3, 4–5
Grant, Charlie, 195
Grant, M., 226, 227, 234, 316, 326, 328
Grant, U. S., quoted, 295
Great Northern Drive of May 15 (1917), 63, 65–68
Great Southern Lumber Co., 172
Greenback Labor party, 3–4
Greensburg, Ind., 261
Greer, Allen J., 299–300, 301
Griffith, D. W., 228, 230, 231, 234
Grimké, Archibald, 200, 201, 232, 257, 275; quoted, 274
Grimké, Francis, quoted, 247, 269

Hadley, Charles, 196
Haiti, 256, 257, 281
Hall, G. Stanley, 216
Hampton Institute, 38, 48, 77, 134, 183, 287
Handy, W. C., 41–42, 130, 191, 339
Hanna, Mark, 240, 241
Harding, Warren G., quoted, 325
Harlan, J. M., 14, 183–84
Harlem, N.Y., 54, 68, 81, 87–90, 106, 130, 187, 318; business in, 159, 161–62; crime in, 111, 122, 123; Garvey and, 334; lodges, 117; the Renaissance in, 116, 166, 340–42; schools, 98, 99
Harris, Abram, quoted, 53–54, 160
Harris, Eugene, quoted, 110
Harris, Lillian, 130, 162
Harrison, Benjamin, 7, 247
Harrison, Hubert, 167, 206, 275
Harvard University, 175, 182–83, 193, 216
Hayes, Roland, 192, 339, 342
Hayes, Rutherford B., 239
Haynes, George Edmund, 125, 128, 204, 207, 307; cited, 53, 55, 90, 138, 325; quoted, 261, 262
Haynes, H. C., 130
Hayward, William, 297
Haywood, Bill, quoted, 156
Hazelhurst (Miss.) *Courier*, 73
Health, 108–14, 128, 213; doctor availability and, 33, 34, 35–36, 109, 129, 162, 164; military, 280, 281–82, 283, 284, 293, 295, 296, 303; poverty and, 82, 85, 90, 100, 101, 104, 105, 111, 114, 172–73
Helper, Hinton Rowan, quoted, 225
Henderson, Edwin B., quoted, 193
Henry, Guy V., quoted, 279
Herron, George T., 223
Higham, John, quoted, 148
Hitler, Adolf, 217
Hoffman, Frederick L., 212–13, 273
Hollingsworth, J. Rogers, cited, 3
Holmes, Oliver W., quoted, 205
Homer, Winslow, 234
Homestead, Pa., 154–55, 267–68
Hooton, Edward A., quoted, 220
Hope, John, 202; quoted, 158, 200
Hope Day Nursery for Colored Children, 126
Hospitals, 16, 36, 109, 112, 118, 166, 186; military, 281–82, 283
House, Edward M., 250
Housing, 125, 135, 268; crowding, 102–6, 111, 114, 122, 123–24, 265; home ownership, 107–8, 140, 314; in labor camps, 106–7; migration and, 55, 61, 74, 82, 83–84, 85, 94, 96, 97–98; military shelters, 286, 288, 294, 296; property values and, 85–87, 88–89, 106, 318; rent levels in, 100,

102–3, 105, 107, 144, 318; segregation and, 16, 17, 35, 148, 161, 260, 314–15, 318
Houston, Charles, quoted, 307
Houston, David F., 250
Howard, Dr. W. L., 211, 212
Howard University, 34, 165, 176, 284
Howard University Law School, 70
Houston, Tex., 4, 35, 51; riot (1917) in, 271–73, 274, 285, 290
Hubbard, DeHart, 194
Hughes, Langston, 86, 163, 310, 317, 338; quoted, 92, 102, 162, 188, 333, 340, 342
Humphrey, Andrew B., cited, 244
Hurston, Zora Neale, 236, 338

Identity, 128; counterattack tactic and, 260–61, 318–22; DuBois on, 199; education and, 177, 184; elitism and, 187–91; Garvey and, 163–64, 332–36; migration and, 55, 56–57, 58–59, 60, 92, 180; military service and, 309, 310–11; "New Negro" and, 311–12, 331, 336–43; religion and, 187; sexual, 100. *See also* Resistance
Illinois, 35, 50, 66, 81, 178, 231, 267, 328; Congressmen from, 204, 206; wages in, 55, 143, 170, 171
Illinois National Guard, 289, 290, 291
Illiteracy rates, 36, 38, 39, 174, 185. *See also* Literacy tests
Immigration (European), 32, 98, 101, 151, 185; crime and, 99, 145; employment level (1910), 149, 150; home ownership and, 107; immigration volume, 51, 52, 81–82, 133, 145, 146; intelligence testing of, 328, 329; nativist harassment of, 145–48, 209, 213–14, 217, 220, 221, 227, 232, 315–16, 317; neighborhoods of, 84, 85, 88, 89, 102; riots and, 262, 263, 265, 266; in Southern labor force, 31, 73–74, 145, 146; working women, 141
Income: annual averages, 55, 108; family structure and, 97, 99, 100, 102, 103, 139–40, 141, 149; inflation and, 138, 313; legal defense and, 119; of professionals, 166. *See also* Wages
Independent, 233, 238–39, 263
Indianapolis, Ind., 69, 102–3, 107, 112, 180, 181
Indianapolis *Freeman* (newspaper), 200
Indianola, Miss., 240, 248
Indians, 148, 190, 194, 195, 326; public office and, 254, 256
Industrialization, 25, 81, 133, 138, 313–14. *See also* Business; Labor; Wages
Industrial Workers of the World, 156, 322–23
Institutional Church and Social Settlement, Chicago, 186–87
Insurance, 33, 34, 60, 100, 117–18, 160
Integration, 83–84, 292, 333; in organizations (19th century), 3–4, 5, 6–7, 9, 11, 30–31; in schools, 60, 179–80, 181–83. *See also* Segregation
Intelligence tests, 146, 210, 295, 325–31
International Association of Machinists, 153
International Ladies' Garment Workers Union, 154
International League of Darker Peoples, 310
Irish immigrants, 88, 101, 217
Iron and Steel Workers Union, 31
Italian immigrants, 73–74, 85, 146, 147, 150, 210, 217, 263, 328; in New York City, 88, 223

Jackson, Miss., 34, 51
Jacksonville, Fla., 62, 66

Japan, 258, 276, 277; emigrants, 147–48, 277, 278
Jasper County, Ga., 57
Jefferson County, Ala., 57
Jeffries, Jim, 196
Jennings, Mrs. Walter, 125
Jews, 89, 91, 148, 323, 328; racist harassment of, 146, 147, 210, 217–18, 227, 232, 315, 316, 317
Johnson, Charles S., 46, 57, 87, 321, 338; quoted, 63, 265–66, 335–36
Johnson, Earl, 194
Johnson, Edward Austin, 207
Johnson, Hall, 192, 339
Johnson, Henry, 297
Johnson, J. Rosamond, 116, 130, 191
Johnson, Jack, 130, 195–98
Johnson, James Weldon, 77, 116, 130, 186, 191, 233, 284, 325, 339; quoted, 83, 90, 319, 338
Joliet, Ill., 32
Jones, Sissieretta, 65, 192
Jordan, David Starr, quoted, 101
Justice, Blair, quoted, 84

Kansas, 2, 35, 50, 292
Kansas *Advocate* (newspaper), 5
Kellor, Frances A., 124, 126
Kennedy, L. V., 54, 57, 96, 105
Kentucky, 22, 39, 181, 250; schools of, 183–84, 185
Kenwood and Hyde Park Property Owners' Association, 84, 85
Kirwan, Albert D., cited, 21
Klineberg, Otto, 236, 329
Knoxville, Tenn., riot, 321
Kropotkin, Peter, 92; quoted, 48
Ku Klux Klan, 9, 12, 13, 78, 130, 226, 316–17; *Birth of a Nation* and, 229, 230, 231–32; Garvey and, 335; Harding on, 325

Labor, 29–34, 45, 125, 129, 132–73, 221, 310–11, 342; black business enterprise and, 13, 158, 314; contract, 27–29, 36, 60–62, 67, 174; convict, 9, 28, 39–40, 78; educational goals and, 175–77, 185, 188; employment levels (1910), 148–49; farm worker organizational efforts, 4–5, 11, 30–31, 321 (*see also* Labor unions); government workers, 167–68, 207, 248, 251, 252, 255, 256, 260, 325; health and, 108, 109, 111, 113, 114, 135; Ku Klux Klan and, 317; military, 273–74, 285, 289, 293–97, 308; Northern migration and, 25–26, 52, 53, 54–55, 57, 58, 59, 60–63, 64, 66–67, 68, 69–70, 72–76, 77, 79, 81, 93, 94, 95, 96, 126, 133, 135–36, 145, 168–70, 269; occupational range of migrants, 69–70, 93, 137–38, 141–42, 149–50, 168; Oriental, 147–48; postwar economy and, 312–14, 318; Progressivism and, 221–22, 238, 246, 250; race riots and, 262, 265, 266, 321–22, 323
Labor agents, 60–62, 67, 75, 79, 95, 109, 135–36; Europeans and, 73; prostitution and, 123
Labor camps, 106–7, 137
Labor unions, 30–31, 133, 150–58, 203, 266, 313–14, 333; Orientals and, 147; Red Scare and, 322–23; Southern, 170, 172. *See also specific unions*
Ladies Home Journal, 211, 212
Laissez-faire doctrine, 209–10, 214–15, 219, 221, 222
Land, 2, 5, 26–27, 38, 148, 313. *See also* Agriculture; Real estate
Land Grant Act (1862), 38

Langford, Sam, 196
Langford, William C., quoted, 23
Law, 11–12, 13–26, 39, 75, 120, 191, 204, 318, 320; "anti-subversive," 316; Ballou on, 292; conscription, 272–73, 285, 293–95, 306; education and, 36, 124, 178, 179, 181, 183–84, 251; farm worker exploitation and, 27, 28–29, 39, 53, 246, 321; housing and, 86, 105; labor agents and, 62, 136; lynching and, 9–10, 258–60, 268, 275, 276; marriage and, 17, 190, 197, 220, 249, 257; NAACP approach through, 128–29, 202, 204, 205, 216; Progressive causes and, 238, 250; woman suffrage, 257. *See also* Courts; Prison *and see specific laws*
Lawson, M. R. C., 187
Lawyers, 164, 165, 166, 182
Layton, Turner, 191
League of Nations, 310, 323
Lewis, William H., 193, 230, 256
Liberia, 50, 257, 280, 281, 284
Liebow, Elliott, 96; quoted, 137
Lincoln, Abraham, 264
Lindsay, Vachel, 233; quoted, 229
Link, A. S., 248–49, 252, 256
Lippmann, Walter, quoted, 327
Literacy tests, 36, 37; voting rights and, 20–21, 24, 205
Little Rock, Ark., 197
Locke, Alain L., 312, 338, 342; quoted, 332, 336, 343
Lodge, Henry C., 4, 7, 220, 241
Lodges, 17, 100, 116–18, 160, 162, 166
Lodging houses, 102–4, 108, 141, 142
Logan, Frenise, on labor, 30, 39–40
Logan, Rayford W., 310–11; cited, 247, 288, 300–1, 304
Longview, Tex., riot, 319
Louisiana, 6, 13–14, 16, 50, 61, 64, 66, 70, 73–74, 229; disfranchisement in, 19, 20, 21; education in 37, 178, 179, 185, 328–29; labor movement resistance in, 171, 172
Louisville, Ky., 86
Lowie, Robert, 220, 236
Lukens Steel Co., 106
Lynching, 9–10, 43–46, 172, 212, 225, 233, 234, 237, 246; counterattack by riot, 319, 320, 323; disfranchisement and, 22, 23; DuBois on, 257, 276; migration and, 57–58, 59, 62, 63–64, 75, 78, 130, 232; the "New Negro" on, 311, 312, 323; postwar resurgence of, 316–17, 318; Watson on, 250; Wilson administration and, 258–61, 268, 275

McAdoo, William Gibbs, 249, 253
McDougall, William, 216, 225
McGraw, John, 195
McKay, Claude, 311, 338, 342; quoted, 323, 341
McKellar, Kenneth, 299
McKinley, William, 23, 239, 247
Macon, Ga., 62
Macon *Telegraph*, 72, 75–76
McReynolds, James C., 250
McVey, Sam, 196
Mall, Dr., 219
Manufacturing, 30–31, 32, 33, 130, 142, 149, 168; concentration, 133
Marriage, 94, 97, 98–99, 214, 215, 308; crowding and, 102, 103, 104; segregationist laws and, 17, 190, 197, 220, 249, 257
Marx, Karl, 223
Maryland, 15–16, 17, 151, 290; disfranchisement and, 19, 22, 23–24
Massachusetts, 4, 22, 50, 120, 230, 231, 256, 290

Massachusetts Anti-Roosevelt Committee, 244
Matthews, Victoria E., 126, 127
Mays, Robert L., 157
Mead, Margaret, 236
Meat packing, 133, 135, 138, 142, 153, 169; strike (1904), 151–52
Meharry Medical College, 165
Meier, August, cited, 15, 204
Memphis, Tenn., 41, 110–11, 119–20, 251; schools, 178, 215
Memphis *Commercial Appeal* (newspaper), 79, 110, 240–41
Mertins, Gustav, 24
Messenger (periodical), 156, 167, 311, 319, 322–23, 325
Meuse-Argonne, battles (1918) of, 298–99, 302–3
Mexico, 223, 258, 270–71, 276, 277–78, 280; emigrants, 326
Micheaux, Oscar, 32, 33, 48, 61, 107–8; quoted, 2–3; films, 159
Michigan, 35, 50, 66
Milholland, J. E., 201, 202, 310
Military service, 260, 269–305; Brownsville affair, 52, 241–42, 243, 244, 247, 271. *See also specific wars*
Mill, John Stuart, quoted, 234
Miller, Kelly, 77, 189, 200, 201, 202, 232, 257, 324; on black resistance, 307, 318–19; on crime, 120; on education, 174, 176, 177; on ghettoization, 35; on occupations, 34, 79, 95, 240; on voting, 204; on white supremacy, 216, 228, 268; on Wilson, 258
Miller, William D., quoted, 250
Mills, Florence, 192, 339, 342
Mining, 30, 51, 154, 313; Northern, 32, 60, 61, 114–15, 133, 169, 171; strikes, 151
Ministers, 33, 34, 164, 165, 186–87; migration and, 59, 61, 62
Minnesota, 181–82
Mississippi, 16, 26, 29, 66, 117, 139; disfranchisement in, 18, 19, 20–21, 22, 23; education in, 37, 38, 56, 175, 179, 185, 216, 251, 328–29; lynching in, 46, 130–31; population loss (1910–20), 70, 73, 77, 145
Missouri, 39, 257
Mitchel, John P., 230
Mitchell, John, 151
Mobile, Ala., 16, 55, 66, 67
Molyneux, Tom, 196
Montgomery, Ala., 16, 40, 62; business ownership in, 33–34
Montgomery Ward Co., 143
Morton, Ferdinand Q., 130, 168, 191
Morton, Jelly Roll, 192, 340
Moskowitz, Henry, 202, 245
Motion pictures, 159, 172, 197; racism and, 227–32, 233, 234, 258, 260
Moton, R. R., 200, 275, 287, 304, 324
Mounds, Ill., 197
Mulattoes, 16, 71–72, 212, 220–21, 329; migration of, 31, 187–88, 189, 190
Music, 41–42, 115–16, 163, 164, 191–93, 224, 298, 339
Myrdal, G., 46, 117, 121, 160, 317

Nail, John E., 161, 191
Nashville *Banner* (newspaper), 76
Natchez *Democrat* (newspaper), 73
Nation (periodical), 256
National Association for the Advancement of Colored People (NAACP), 167, 191, 200, 201–2, 203, 204, 216, 233, 256, 258, 310; anti-lynch bills and, 258, 259–60; *Birth of a Nation* and, 229–30, 231; Elaine riot trials and, 321; labor unions and, 152;

migration and, 77, 128–29; military service and, 274, 284, 292, 307–8; Race Commission proposal of, 253–54; Smith Lever Act and, 251; Springfield riot (1908) and, 264; voting and, 205, 245
National Association of Negro Musicians, 155, 339
National Board of Censorship, 229
National Brotherhood of Workers of America, 157
National Equal Rights League, 202, 310
National Fair Play Association, 252
National Farmers' Alliance (Southern Alliance), 4–5, 6–7, 11, 14
National Guard, 263, 274; in World War I, 289–90, 291, 297, 298
National Independent Political League, 244, 255, 276
National League for the Protection of Colored Women, 127, 129, 203, 204
National Medical Association, 34, 128
National Negro Business League, 33, 127, 152, 158
National Urban League, 53, 85, 114, 128, 130, 167, 202–3, 204, 307; labor and, 129, 142, 313–14. *See also specific city branches*
Nativism, 145–48, 209, 213–14, 220, 221, 227, 315–16; Ku Klux Klan, 232; race riots and, 263
Nearing, Scott, cited, 140
Nebraska, 2, 50, 70
Negro Advisory Committee, 128
Negro Political League, 244, 255
Negro Suffrage League, 23–24
Negro Voice (periodical), 167
Negro Welfare Committee, 105
Negro World, 167, 333, 334
Newark, N.J., 55, 66, 105–6
Newby, Idus A., cited, 25
New Jersey, 31, 35, 180, 244
"New Negro, The," 311–12, 317, 318–19, 320, 331; leadership of, 324–25; Locke on, 332, 336, 343; Palmer on, 323, 324; Renaissance and, 336–43; rural areas and, 321
New Orleans, La., 17, 21, 66, 67, 305; Storyville, 42, 116, 341
New Orleans *Picayune*, 72
New Republic (periodical), 230, 233
New York *Age* (newspaper), 79, 92, 123, 127, 145, 167, 189, 200, 244
New York, N.Y., 50, 66, 67, 68, 69, 112, 195, 197; *Birth of a Nation* in, 229–30, 231; business firms in, 158–59, 160, 161–62, 163; elites in, 188, 189; ghettoization in, 83, 86, 87–90, 95, 96, 103, 114, 122, 125, 315, 318 (*see also* Harlem); home ownership in, 107; labor movement in, 151, 154, 203; migrant social services in, 125–27, 129, 186, 203–4; occupational fields in, 142, 149, 167, 168; protest march (1917), 268; riot of 1900 in, 261; schools, 180, 181, 185, 203; veterans' march (1919), 304–5; voting in, 206, 207; wages in, 53, 55, 138
New York City, Department of Health, 114, 168
New York Colored Mission, 125–26
New York *News* (newspaper), 167
New York *Post* (newspaper), 233, 256
New York Public Library, 194, 338–39
New York State, 31, 50, 66, 112–13, 178, 240, 328
New York State National Guard, 289, 290, 291
New York *Sun* (newspaper), 276
New York *Times*, 90, 94, 96, 258
New York *Tribune* (newspaper), 88

New York Urban League, 103, 140
New York *World* (newspaper), 256
Niagara Movement, 201, 202, 264
Norfolk, Va., 35, 66, 68, 86, 126
North, the, 2, 12; birth rates, 113; black press of, 167; education in, 24, 37, 38–39, 174–75, 178, 179–86, 328–29; employment in, 32, 51, 123, 132–45, 168–70; ghettos of, 35, 81–92, 93–131, 179–80, 265; postwar segregationism increase, 317–18; Red scare, 322–23; voting in, 204–7. *See also* South, the, black exodus from; *and see specific place names*
North Carolina, 16, 17, 25, 179, 204, 207, 241, 249, 250; disfranchisement in, 8, 19–20, 22; Ku Klux Klan in, 317; labor (1890–1900) in, 30, 39–40, 171
Nurses, 142, 164, 165, 334

Oates, William C., 10
Oberlin College, 182, 193
Odum, H., cited, 54, 74, 211, 215
O'Hara Committee, 143–44
Ohio, 32, 50, 170, 171, 178, 231, 290, 328; Young (C.) in, 282, 283
Ohio River, 59
Oklahoma, 16, 50, 57, 86, 181, 317; disfranchisement in, 19, 22, 205
Oliver, King, 116, 192
Olympic Games, 194
Omaha, Nebr., riot of 1919, 321
O'Neill, Eugene, 337, 339
Opportunity (periodical), 167
Orientals, 146, 147–48, 184, 277
Osborn, Henry Fairfield, 316
Osofsky, Gilbert, cited, 54, 100
Ottley, Roi: cited, 189; quoted, 63, 66, 121–22, 197
Ovington, Mary White, 124, 125, 201, 202, 239; cited, 99, 178; quoted, 93, 113, 172, 206, 224, 233
Owen, Chandler, 153, 156, 157, 167, 206, 324
Oxford University, 217

Pace Phonograph Co., 163, 339
Page, Thomas N., 232; cited, 177; quoted, 22, 74, 221
Paige, Satchel, 195
Painting, 234
Palmer, A. M., 311, 312, 323, 324
Palmer, Frederick, quoted, 296
Pan-Africanism, 310
Paris, France, 304, 310–11, 339, 340
Parker, H. C., 130, 161
Parks, 16, 41, 114
Patterson, A. E., 253, 254
Payton, P., Jr., 89, 107, 161, 164–65
Pennsylvania, 50, 61, 66, 140, 169
Pennsylvania Railroad, 61, 107, 135
Peonage, 28–29, 39, 233, 321
Pershing, J. J., 280, 293, 295, 296, 297; quoted, 301
Personal service jobs, 30, 32, 62, 99, 134, 136–37, 141–42; declining levels of, 149, 168, 169; postwar, 313; wages, 54, 138, 139
Philadelphia, Pa., 69, 97, 126, 188, 228; ghettoization in, 90–91, 92, 102, 105, 115; health in, 108, 109, 112; labor in, 33, 57, 60, 125, 142, 162, 168; riots in, 267; voting in, 205–6
Philippine Islands, 243, 251, 270
Phillips, U. B., 226
Phillips High School, Chicago, 179
Pickens, William, 335; quoted, 46, 175, 177, 204, 208, 259
Pipkin, J. J., quoted, 177

Pittsburgh, Pa., 49, 66, 69, 90, 97, 115, 185, 197, 206; crime in, 119, 120, 121, 122; health in, 104, 109, 111–12, 113; labor in, 31, 55, 60, 94, 134, 135–36, 139, 155, 168, 169; riots, 267
Pittsburgh *Courier*, 167, 283
Pittsburgh Urban League, 134
Plessy v. *Ferguson* (case, 1896), 1, 11, 13, 183, 184
Pneumonia, 108, 111, 112, 113, 172
Poag, G. C., 194
Police, 41, 86, 119, 129, 167, 334; drugs and, 110; ghettoization and, 85, 88, 121, 124; lynching and, 46, 197; migration efforts and, 68, 75, 76, 136; riots and, 261, 265, 267–68, 271, 272, 318, 320
Polish immigrants, 107, 146, 147, 217, 263
Polk, L. L., 4–5
Pollard, F. D., 193
Poll taxes, 19, 20, 21, 205
Population: age distribution (1920), 94; agricultural (southern, 1900), 26; crime rates and, 118–19, 120, 124; disfranchisement and, 18, 21, 22; ghetto densities, 105, 265; school funds and, 36–37, 182; sex distribution (1900–20), 95–96; south-north shift (1900–20), 51–52, 68–69, 70–72, 89–90, 265, 266; urban-rural distribution, 29–30, 31, 50–51, 168; Western increase in, 57
Populist party, 1–2, 4, 5–11, 13, 14, 18, 238
Poverty, 100–4. *See also* Income
Powderly, Terence V., 5
Powdermaker, H., 38, 56, 113, 172
Powell, A. C., Sr., 159, 165
Pree, T. J., 157
Press: black, 5, 34, 59, 60, 92, 145, 156, 158, 166–67, 197, 198–99, 275, 306–7, 308, 322, 323, 324, 333, 337; racist agitation in, 22, 23, 121, 145, 196, 214, 233, 240–41, 255, 262, 316, 317, 318, 319–20. *See also* specific journals
Price, John Ambrose, quoted, 213
Prisons, 16, 20, 76, 335; convict leasing, 9, 28, 39–40, 78, 120; population, 118–19, 123
Privus, Dr. C. B., quoted, 247
Professions, 32, 33, 34, 35–36, 70, 141, 149, 164–67, 168, 314; education for, 30, 37, 42, 177, 182; ghettoization and, 93, 94, 165
Progressivism, 177–78, 221–24, 243–44, 245; objectives of, 25, 100, 124, 125, 133, 238–39, 246, 249, 250–51, 261
Prohibition, 97, 340, 341, 342
Prostitution, 29, 62, 98, 103, 121, 261, 340–41; jazz and, 42, 116; police and, 41, 86, 265; wages and, 143–45; white women and, 17, 45, 123
Protective Circle, Chicago, 85
Provident Hospital, Chicago, 112
Psychology, 210, 216, 295, 325–31
Public facilities, 16–17, 20, 41, 76, 83, 248, 251–52, 260; ghettoization and, 85, 91, 114–15, 124
Public office, 8, 205, 206, 207, 217, 307, 325; Roosevelt on, 239, 240; Taft on, 243; Wilson on, 253, 254, 256–57
Pullman Co., 138–39, 143, 157

Quakers, 49, 125
Queens Borough, New York City, 107

Racist ideology, 208–36. *See also* specific doctrines, i.e., Nativism; Teutonism; White supremacy doctrine
Railroads, 59, 60–61, 64–68, 79, 157, 238; porters, 138–39, 143, 313; segregation and, 11, 13–16, 17, 200, 248, 249, 251; worker health, 109; worker housing, 106, 107, 135

Railwaymen's International Benevolent and Industrial Association, 157
Rainey, Ma, 116, 192, 340
Raker, quoted, 267
Raleigh, N.C., 35, 39
Randolph, A. P., 153, 156, 157, 167, 206, 324; "New Negro" and, 325, 333
Ransom, Reverdy C., 186
Rape, 43–46, 63, 119, 212, 222, 262, 308; Brownsville affair, 242; military reports of, 301
Rauschenbusch, W., 100, 101, 223–24
"Razafkeriefo," quoted, 312
Real estate, 33, 130, 161–62, 186, 190; property values, 85–87, 88–89, 106, 107–8, 117–18; terrorism and, 87, 314, 315, 318, 320
Reconstruction, 2, 3, 11, 15, 19, 50, 94, 204, 211; historians of, 225–26, 227–28; Klan in, 231–32
Recreation, 114–18, 124, 260, 334; postwar segregation of, 317, 320, 341; soldiers and, 292, 296, 304
Red scare (1919–20), 322–24
Red Shirts, 8, 11
Reed, James, 257
Renaissance, 116, 166, 332–33, 336–43
Republican party, 6, 8–9, 36, 50, 52, 226, 239, 240, 241, 267; disfranchisement and, 4, 18–19, 205, 206–7; schism of 1910–12, 243–44; Versailles and, 310
Resistance, 25–26, 342–43; to conscription, 274–75; demonstration tactic, 227, 230, 268; to disfranchisement, 22, 23–24, 206–7, 276; elitism and, 188–89, 190–91, 343; labor and, 170, 171, 172; to legalized segregation, 14–15, 33, 63, 184, 252, 253–56, 271–72; to lynching, 257, 258–61, 276, 311, 312, 319, 320, 323; to military inequities, 285, 286, 287, 289, 296, 298; organizations for, 201–3, 264, 310, 333–34, 336; press expressions of, 232–33, 244, 245, 255–56, 308–9, 311–12, 320, 323–24; to racist custom, 11–12, 56–57, 60, 292; riot as counterattack, 318–22, 323; Washington (Booker T.) and, 48, 199, 200, 333, 336
Restaurants, 160, 162, 166
Restrictive covenants, 86, 148
Reuter, E. B., 120; quoted, 208–9
Revolutionary War, 49, 270
Rhodes, James Ford, 226, 241
Richmond, Va., 17, 51, 86, 118
Richmond *Reformer* (newspaper), 63
Richmond *Times* (newspaper), 23
Riis, Jacob, 101, 103, 125, 233
Riots (1919), 318–22, 323, 334. *See also specific cities*
Roberts, Charles H., 207
Roberts, Kenneth L., quoted, 316
Roberts, Needham, 297
Robeson, Paul, 192, 193–94, 339
Robinson, Bill, 340, 342
Rockefeller, J. D., 38, 115, 215
Rockefeller, J. D., Jr., 161
Romagne, France, 296
Roosevelt, Franklin Delano, 284
Roosevelt, Theodore, 48, 52, 214, 221, 238, 246, 247; quoted, 79, 239, 240, 241, 242, 271; Bull Moose party of, 243–44, 245; Cuban expedition, 239, 270, 271
Rosenwald, Julius, 63, 143–44, 200, 255, 321; philanthropy of, 24, 38, 48, 115, 143
Ross, E. A., quoted, 146–47, 221–22
Royce, J., quoted, 208, 213, 234–35
Rudwick, Elliott, cited, 15
Rural areas, 35, 50, 53–54, 60, 69, 70, 78, 135; education in, 36–38, 174–75, 328–29; Elaine riot, 321
Russia, 48, 322, 323; emigrants, 99, 147, 210, 328

Sage (Russell) Foundation, 93, 101
St. Louis, Mo., 6, 86, 112, 265
St. Louis *Globe-Democrat*, 195
St. Philips Protestant Episcopal Church, N.Y., 107, 161, 186
Salvation Army, 115
Sandburg, Carl, 233; quoted, 63, 64
San Francisco, Calif., 83, 147–48, 184, 229, 231, 281, 282
Sanitation: ghettoization and, 82, 85, 90, 104, 105, 106, 107, 109, 110, 111
San Juan Hill, New York City, 88, 125
San Juan Hill, battle of, 239, 270
Sapir, Edward, 236
Saturday Evening Post, 316
Savannah, Ga., 15, 35, 36, 66, 75
Schomburg, Arthur A., 194, 338–39
Schools, 16, 20, 24–25, 27, 96, 99, 129, 211, 342; integrated, 60, 179–80, 181–83, 201; intelligence tests in, 327–28, 329, 330; kindergarten and day care, 125, 126, 128, 186; professional, 165, 166, 177, 182; racist doctrines in, 73, 215–16, 221, 223, 226, 316; sports and, 193; standards in, 7, 36–39, 53, 55–56, 57, 59, 98, 174–75, 177–78, 179, 182, 207; truancy laws and, 124; vocational training in, 30, 38, 48, 175–76, 177, 185, 188, 251
Schurz, Carl, 200, 233
Science: racist doctrine and, 210, 211–24, 234–36, 248, 260, 273–74, 295, 316, 325–31
Scott, Emmett J., 77, 79, 200, 202, 207, 324; cited, 55, 59, 62, 69, 127, 170, 172; military service and, 273, 283, 287, 307
Sears Roebuck, 143, 144–45
Segregation: business fields and, 159–60; cemetery, 117; civil service, 167, 168, 207, 248–49, 251–52, 253, 256, 325; hospital, 166; of Italians, 73; of Jews, 315; kindergarten, 126; labor union, 30–31, 150–52, 153–54, 155, 156, 157, 170, 172, 314; legal institution of, 11–12, 13–26, 33, 35, 37, 39, 52, 86, 179, 181, 183–84, 232, 247–58, 260; migration and, 60, 63, 68, 91, 130, 136; military, 155, 270–71, 272, 273–74, 284, 285–86, 287, 288–89, 294, 296, 299, 300–1, 308–9; of mulattoes, 71–72, 187–90; neighborhood, 35–36, 41, 42, 83–84, 86, 91, 161 (*see also* Ghettoization); Niagara Movement against, 201; Northern schools and, 179–86; of Orientals, 147–48; postwar intensification of, 317–18, 325; recreation facilities, 16, 41, 114–15, 292, 317, 320, 341; separatist view of, 333; sexual conduct and, 17, 40–41, 43–46, 190, 220; Social Darwinism and, 216; in sports, 193, 194–95, 196, 197; of veteran groups, 308
Seligmann, H. J., 125; on labor, 123, 154, 172, 307; on music, 339; on red-baiting, 322; on resistance, 261, 319; on sex and racism, 44, 46; on Southern influence, 22, 87, 121, 233, 260, 308
"Separate-but-equal" doctrine, 14, 37, 184. *See also* Segregation
Separatism, 332–36
Settlement houses, 125
Sexual codes, 121–22, 323; intermarriage and, 17, 190, 197, 220, 249, 308; lynch law and, 43–46, 259, 317; racist focus on, 40–41, 211–12, 230, 301, 308, 318; working women and, 141, 252

Sharecropping, 5, 26, 27–28, 52, 54, 70, 317
Shaw University, 165
Shufeldt, Robert W., 213, 224, 273–74; quoted, 211–12
Sierra Leone Co., 49
Simkins, Francis B., cited, 40
Simkovitch, Mary Kingsley, 125
Simmons, Furnifold, 25
Simmons, William J., 232
Simms, R. T., 157
Simon, Theodore, 326
Singleton, Moses, 50
Sissle, Noble, 192, 340
Slater, John F., Fund, 39
Slavery, 2, 12, 35, 42, 49–50, 94, 126, 176, 333; Washington (George) and, 270; white supremacy doctrine and, 210, 211, 212, 213, 224, 233
Smallwood, J. Franklin, 130
Smith, Bessie, 192, 339
Smith, Bob, 196
Smith, Hoke, 18, 25, 239, 250, 256, 262, 312; quoted, 22, 24
Smith-Lever Act, 251
Sobel, Jacob, 114
Social Gospellers, 222–23
Social Darwinism, 209–10, 214–17, 218–21, 222, 227; Boas on, 235–36
Socialism, 153, 156, 157, 207, 275; "Christian," 222–24; Garvey and, 334; red-baiting, 145, 315, 322–24
Sounder (film), 172
South, the, 3, 47, 87, 227–28, 246, 323; birth rates in, 113; black exodus from, 49–80, 81–82, 92, 93, 94, 96, 100, 102, 123, 126–27, 128–30, 140, 148, 168–73, 174–75, 180, 187–90, 209, 232, 329, 336; black-owned banks in, 34, 160–61; black press in, 167; black soldiers and, 272–73, 288–89, 290–91, 294, 305, 307–8; disfranchisement and, 18–24, 130, 204–7, 243, 245, 250; drug traffic in, 110–11; education standards in, 36–39, 174–75, 177–78, 182, 185; housing in, 35; industrialization of, 25, 29–30, 31–32, 139, 221; Ku Klux Klan power in, 317; lynching practice and, 43–46, 232, 234, 260; northern race riots and, 263–64, 322; Populism and, 1–2, 8–9, 10; rural-urban percentages (1900), 26, 29–30, 50–51; segregation laws of, 11–12, 13–16, 130, 317; Wilson and, 244, 246, 249, 252, 253, 254, 256–57, 258, 261, 312. *See also specific place names*
South Carolina, 9–10, 49, 187, 203, 241, 288, 290; convict labor in, 40; disfranchisement in, 19, 22; education in, 16, 37, 38, 179, 185; labor agents and, 62; professionals in, 34, 130; red-baiting in, 322
Southern Negro Anti-Exodus Association, 74
Southern Sociological Congress, 38
Spanish-American War, 133, 146; service in, 239, 270–71
Spartanburg, S.C., 290
Spear, Allan H., cited, 84, 86, 94
Spencer, Herbert, 214, 215, 225
Spight, Thomas, quoted, 23
Spingarn, Joel, 202, 245, 310; quoted, 281–85
Springfield, Ill., riot (1908) in, 262–64, 318
Springfield, Ohio, riot, 201
Stallings, Lawrence, quoted, 291
Standard Oil Co., 243
Steamboats, 16, 17, 68
Steel industry, 31, 32, 51, 133, 134, 139, 169; strikebreaking, 154–55; worker housing, 106, 135
Stoddard, T. L., 226–27, 236, 316, 322

Stokes, quoted, 220
Story, Sidney, 42
Streetcars, 15, 16, 20, 60, 249, 257
Strikes, 4–5, 61, 213; black labor and, 31, 145, 150, 151–52, 154–55, 266–67
Strong, Josiah, quoted, 223
Stubbs, William, quoted, 217
Sullivan, John L., 196
Sumner, W. G., 214–15, 216, 225, 234

Taft, William Howard, 52, 193, 242, 244, 246, 247; quoted, 243
Taxation, 36–37, 175, 177, 178–79, 181–82, 185, 250
Taylor, John B., 194
Teachers, 32, 34, 42, 70, 98, 130, 164, 203; education of, 165, 166, 179, 216; Northern, 142, 179–80, 181; salaries of, 37, 178–79
Tenant farmers, 5, 26, 27, 28, 200, 313; migration, 52, 53, 55, 70, 172; riot, 321
Tennessee, 16, 20, 22, 50, 66, 170, 290, 299; schools, 181
Terman, Lewis, quoted, 326, 327
Terrell, Mary Church, 17
Terrell, Robert H., 248, 256–57, 275
Teutonism (Nordicism), 217–18, 219, 221, 222, 226–27, 234, 316, 339; of Coolidge, 325; intelligence testing and, 328; Royce on, 235
Texas, 20, 22, 34, 50, 57, 86, 130, 181, 249, 250; Greenback party in, 3–4; Klan and, 317; land ownership (1908) in, 26–27
Theater, 42–43, 166, 191–93, 339–40
Thomas, James C., 130, 164
Thomas, William Hannibal, 187–88
Thorndike, Edward L., quoted, 326
Thorpe, Jim, 194
Thurman, Allen G., quoted, 299
Thurman, Wallace, 338, 341, 342
Tillman, Ben, 9–10, 241, 250, 312; quoted, 19, 152
Timmonsville *Watchman* (newspaper), 63
Toomer, Jean, 338
Track stars, 194
Trade, 163, 314; consumer exploitation by, 29, 53, 91, 171, 174; employment in, 30, 143–45, 149, 159, 168; segregation and, 17, 33, 91, 159–60
Travers, Bob, 196
Tripp, S. O., 267
Trotter, W. M., 77, 233, 244, 325; quoted, 247, 255, 275, 276; *Birth of a Nation* and, 230, 231; DuBois and, 198, 200, 201, 202, 276, 333; at Versailles, 310; Wilson confrontation of, 254–55
True Reformer (periodical), 118
True Reformers Bank, 160, 161
Truly, Jeff, quoted, 73–74
Tuberculosis, 108, 109, 111, 113, 172, 293
Turner, F. J., 147, 218
Tuskegee Institute, 38, 48, 143, 174, 176, 200, 244
Twain, Mark, quoted, 234
Twentieth Century Club, 183, 184
Tyler, Ralph W., 306
Tylor, Edward Burnett, 235

Unemployed, 95–96, 99, 101, 102
United Mine Workers, 151, 154, 274
United States, Army, 20, 169, 176, 211, 212, 277; Brownsville Affair, 52, 241–42, 243, 244, 247, 271, 273; conscription and, 272–73, 285, 293–95, 306; intelligence testing in, 325–26, 327–28, 329, 330; segregation in, 155, 270–71, 272, 273–74, 284, 285–89, 292, 294, 296, 299, 300–1, 308–9; officer training in, 281, 282, 284–89, 290, 291,

298, 299, 300, 309; war honors and, 302–4; Young (Charles) case, 278–84
United States, Army Bulletin No. 35, 292, 293, 299–300
United States, Army General Staff, 280, 281, 282, 286, 289, 295–96; Anderson memo, 293–94
United States, Army Officers' Reserve Corps, 286
United States, Army Services of Supply (SOS), 296, 297, 300
United States, Army War College, 299, 300
United States, Bureau of the Census, 71, 95, 119, 248
United States, Bureau of Indian Affairs, 148
United States, Bureau of Labor Statistics, 139
United States, Bureau of Printing and Engraving, 248, 252
United States, Civil Service Commission, 252
United States, Congress, 9, 36, 204, 205, 206, 229, 231; lynching and, 259; riots and, 267, 268; seats, 22; Southern bloc, 247, 250, 252, 253, 257, 258, 261; veterans and, 308
United States, Constitution, 14, 44, 128, 197; disfranchisement and, 19, 20, 21, 23; Fifteenth Amendment, 12, 23, 205, 257; First Amendment, 231; Fourteenth Amendment, 12
United States, Department of Justice, 277, 278, 325; Attorney General's office, 256, 311, 323, 334
United States, Department of Labor, 31, 51, 53, 63, 134, 168, 207; on crime, 121; on disease, 108–9; on education, 175; on Homestead riot (1917), 267–68; on housing, 135; on labor conditions, 58, 107, 133, 137; Negro Economics Division in, 125, 134, 307; on poverty, 101; on unionization, 150–51, 266; on voting, 206; on wages, 138, 139, 145, 170–71
United States, Department of the Interior, 248
United States, Department of the Navy, 241, 249, 252, 284
United States, Department of the Post Office, 167, 240, 248, 249, 251–52
United States, Department of State, 279–80
United States, Department of the Treasury, 248, 249, 252, 253, 254, 256
United States, Department of War, 155, 231, 242, 248, 259, 307; on casualties, 304; recruitment and, 272–73, 274, 285–86, 287, 290, 291, 293–97; on re-enlistment, 308; Young (Charles) and, 279, 281–82, 283
United States, Industrial Commission, 101, 151
United States, Internal Revenue Service, 252
United States, Navy, 270
United States, Presidency, 48, 237–68; election (1892), 5, 7; election (1904), 9, 240, 241; election (1912), 243–47. *See also individual Presidents*
United States, Senate, 4, 17, 19, 36, 238, 241, 242, 243, 259, 310; Southern bloc in, 250, 253, 254, 257
United States, Supreme Court, 28, 39, 205, 229; segregation and, 1, 13–14, 17, 86, 183–84
United States Steel, 139
Universal Negro Improvement Association, 333–35
Urban areas, 35–36, 50–51, 69, 70; age distribution (1920), 94; birth and death rates in, 112–13; education in, 37–38, 174–75,

328–29; ghettoization process in, 81–92, 93–131; labor in, 29–34, 54–55, 81, 168; sex distribution (1910–20), 95–96, 123
Urban League. *See* National Urban League
Uvalde, Tex., 197

Van Vechten, Carl, quoted, 337–38, 339, 340, 341–42
Vardaman, J. K., 18, 38, 73, 74, 131, 239, 257, 308, 312, 323; quoted, 22, 23, 24, 39, 46, 55, 120, 175, 177, 240, 241, 250, 254, 263–64
Venereal disease, 36, 108–9, 112, 293
Versailles Treaty, 310, 323
Veteran (periodical), 319
Vicksburg *Herald* (newspaper), 76–77
Villa, Pancho, 271, 276, 277, 280
Villard, Oswald Garrison, 200, 201, 202, 228, 233, 274; Wilson and, 245–46, 249, 253–54, 256, 258–59
Violence. *See* Lynching; Rape; Riots
Virginia, 6, 16, 17, 68, 221, 241, 275; banking in, 160; disfranchisement in, 19, 21, 22, 23; education in, 37, 38, 179, 185; labor in, 31, 74, 151
Voting, 6, 7, 17, 60, 239, 240, 244, 267; disfranchisement, 9, 10, 11, 18–24, 36, 37, 44, 52, 55–56, 130, 204–7, 221, 233, 243, 250, 262, 276; election (1912), 244–45, 246, 247; election (1920), 317; Niagara Movement on, 201; women and, 257

Wages, 101, 105, 137, 213, 248; averages (1900–20), 138–39; farm, 28, 54, 55, 139, 170–71, 317; migration and, 54–55, 57, 59, 60, 75, 76, 123, 169–70, 171; teacher salaries, 37, 178–79; unequal scales, 30, 32–33, 53, 54, 140–41, 143–45, 147
Wagner, Richard, 217
Wald, Lillian, 125
Waldron, J. Milton, 245–46
Walker, A'lelia, 342
Walker, Madame C. J., 130, 163
Walker, Francis, 147, 213, 214
Walker, Nash, 191
Walling, W. E., 201, 263, 264
Walsh, David I., 230
Walters, Bishop Alexander, 200, 246, 251, 255
Walton Free Kindergarten, N.Y., 125
Ward, Lester F., 223; quoted, 222
War of 1812, 270
Warwick, William, 6
Washington, Booker T., 1, 22, 26, 27, 128, 137, 156, 198–200, 257, 325; *Birth of a Nation* and, 230; business ownership and, 33–34, 127, 158, 159, 314; CIICN and, 203; Committee of Twelve and, 201; death of, 77, 312, 324; education and, 24–25, 36–37, 38, 143, 174, 175–77; Garvey and, 47, 333, 336; immigrants and, 31, 145; on labor unions, 152; on lynching, 44, 57, 78; music and, 41, 42; Northern migration and, 77, 78–79, 92, 190; Republican influence of, 243, 244, 247, 248; Roosevelt and, 48, 239–41, 244, 271; Young and, 280
Washington, George, 47, 270
Washington, D.C., 17, 50, 162, 182, 188, 189, 197, 202, 283, 289; employment in, 167, 248, 252, 254, 255, 256, 307; housing in, 103, 318; Lincoln Memorial in, 325; public facilities in, 115, 248, 249, 251–52, 257; riots, 52–53, 319–20, 334
Washington *Colored American*, 200
Washington *Post*, 319, 320
Waters, Ethel, 192, 340, 342

Watson, Tom, 177; quoted, 8, 9, 10, 147, 250
Weaver, James B., 7
Weehawken, N.J., riots, 267
West, 1, 2–3, 4, 12, 38, 50, 57, 83; Orientals in, 146, 147–48
West Indies, 49, 310; Garvey and, 333, 334, 335; New York immigration from, 89–90, 158
Westinghouse Corp., 169
West Point, 270, 277, 278, 285
West Virginia, 154, 246
White, Edward, 231; quoted, 229
White, George, 204
White, Walter F., 260, 325
White, William Allen, quoted, 238
White Rose Industrial Association, 126, 203
White supremacy doctrine, 8–10, 187–88, 252, 269, 305; disfranchisement and, 18, 23; films and, 227–32, 233, 234, 258, 260; lynching and, 43, 44, 260–61, 268, 317; the military and, 300–4, 308–9; nativism and, 147–48, 210, 213–14, 227, 263; "New Negro" and, 311–12, 324; reformers and, 221–24, 250–51; riots and, 263–64, 268, 292; "science" and, 210, 211–22, 224, 235–36, 248, 272–73, 295, 316, 325–31
Wilberforce University, 283
Willard, Jess, 198, 230, 233
Willcox, Major, 212; quoted, 273
Williams, Bert, 191
Williams, John S., 25, 256, 257, 282, 283; quoted, 24, 258, 274, 281
Williams, W. T. B., quoted, 56
Wills, Harry, 196, 198
Wilson, Ellen, 252, 255
Wilson, William B., quoted, 145
Wilson, Woodrow, 19, 229, 238, 323; antilynching laws and, 258–61, 268; on emancipation, 1, 211, 226; on Europeans,

146, 214; Mexico and, 276; race riots and, 264, 272, 290; segregation and, 167, 247–58, 312, 325; Trotter and, 231, 244, 245–46, 247; Young and, 281–82, 283
Winston, George T., quoted, 24
Wister, Owen, 240, 241
Women, 40–41, 43–46, 58, 103, 126–27, 129, 154, 203, 212; child care and, 99, 113, 114, 121, 125, 128, 139–40; education of, 176, 182; labor agents and, 62, 67; migration numbers, 95, 96; occupations of, 32, 34, 69, 134, 136, 141–43, 168, 313; prison and, 123; public office and, 240; voting rights of, 257; wages of, 54, 100, 138, 139, 142, 143–45, 171
Woodson, Carter G., 339; cited, 36, 52, 85–86, 93, 165; quoted, 27
Woodward, C. Vann, cited, 12, 14–15
Woofter, T. J., Jr., 103, 106, 107
Wooley, Celia Parker, 125
World War I, 37, 47, 146, 217, 258, 342, 343; labor and, 52, 68, 81, 125, 133, 142, 157, 168–69, 170, 171–72, 207, 266, 269; military service in, 48, 68, 97, 155, 170, 176, 212, 268, 269–305, 306–11, 312, 318, 319, 339
World War II, 302–3

Yerkes, Robert M., 327, 328
Young, Charles, 278–84, 289
Young, Glendie B., 290–91
YMCA, 41, 114–15, 126, 296
Young Negroes' Progressive Association, Detroit, 127
Youth, 16, 41, 74, 123, 206, 318–20; ghettoization and, 94, 96, 104; migration and, 58, 64, 98–99

Zion African Methodist Church, Boston, 186